T0131163

Get the eBook FREE!
(PDF, ePub, Kindle, and liveBook all included)

We believe that once you buy a book from us, you should be able to read it in any format we have available. To get electronic versions of this book at no additional cost to you, purchase and then register this book at the Manning website.

Go to https://www.manning.com/freebook and follow the instructions to complete your pBook registration.

That's it!
Thanks from Manning!

Deep Learning Patterns and Practices

Deep Learning
Patterns and Practices

ANDREW FERLITSCH

MANNING
SHELTER ISLAND

For online information and ordering of this and other Manning books, please visit
www.manning.com. The publisher offers discounts on this book when ordered in quantity.
For more information, please contact

> Special Sales Department
> Manning Publications Co.
> 20 Baldwin Road
> PO Box 761
> Shelter Island, NY 11964
> Email: orders@manning.com

Manning Publications Co.
20 Baldwin Road
PO Box 761
Shelter Island, NY 11964

Development editor:	Frances Lefkowitz
Technical development editor:	Al Krinker
Review editor:	Aleksandar Dragosavljević
Production editor:	Deirdre S. Hiam
Copy editor:	Sharon Wilkey
Proofreader:	Keri Hales
Technical proofreader:	Karsten Strobaek
Typesetter:	Gordan Salinovic
Cover designer:	Marija Tudor

ISBN 9781617298264

Printed in the United States of America

brief contents

v

contents

CONTENTS ix

preface

As a Googler, one of my duties is to educate software engineers on how to use machine learning. I already had experience creating online tutorials, meetups, conference presentations, training workshops, and coursework for private coding schools and university graduate studies, but I am always looking for new ways to effectively teach.

Prior to Google, I worked in Japanese IT as a principal research scientist for 20 years—all without deep learning. Almost everything I see today, we were doing in innovation labs 15 years ago; the difference is we needed a room full of scientists and a vast budget. It's incredible how things have so rapidly changed as a result of deep learning.

Back in the late 2000s, I was working with small structured datasets with geospatial data from national and international sources all over the world. Coworkers called me a data scientist, but nobody knew what a data scientist really was. Then came big data, and I didn't know the big data tools and frameworks, and suddenly I wasn't a data scientist. What? I had to scramble and learn the tools and concepts behind big data and once again I was a data scientist.

Then emerged machine learning on big datasets, like linear/logistic regression and CART analysis, and I hadn't used statistics since graduate school decades ago, and once again I was not a data scientist. What? I had to scramble to learn statistics all over again, and once again I was a data scientist. Then came deep learning, and I didn't know the theory and frameworks for neural networks and suddenly I wasn't a data scientist. What? I scrambled again and learned deep learning theory and other deep learning frameworks. And once again, I am a data scientist.

acknowledgments

I would like to thank all those at Manning who helped throughout this process: Frances Lefkowitz, my development editor; Deirdre Hiam, my project editor; Sharon Wilkey, my copyeditor; Keri Hales, my proofreader; and Aleksandar Dragosavljević, my reviewing editor.

To all the reviewers: Ariel Gamino, Arne Peter Raulf, Barry Siegel, Brian R. Gaines, Christopher Marshall, Curtis Bates, Eros Pedrini, Hilde Van Gysel, Ishan Khurana, Jen Lee, Karthikeyarajan Rajendran, Michael Kareev, Muhammad Sohaib Arif, Nick Vazquez, Ninoslav Cerkez, Oliver Korten, Piyush Mehta, Richard Tobias, Romit Singhai, Sayak Paul, Sergio Govoni, Simone Sguazza, Udendran Mudaliyar, Vishwesh Ravi Shrimali, and Viton Vitanis, your suggestions helped make this a better book.

To all Google Cloud AI staff who have shared their personal and customer insights, your insights helped the book cover a broader audience.

about this book

Who should read this book

Welcome to my latest endeavor, *Deep Learning Patterns and Practices*. This book is for software engineers; machine learning engineers; and junior, mid-level, and senior data scientists. Although you might assume that the initial chapters would be redundant for the latter group, my unique approach will likely leave you with additional insight and a welcomed refresher. The book is structured so that every reader reaches the point of "ignition" and is able to self-propel forward into deep learning.

I teach the design patterns and practices mostly in the context of computer vision, as this is where design patterns for deep learning first evolved. Developments in natural-language understanding and structured data models lagged behind and continued to be focused on classical approaches. But as they caught up, these fields developed their own deep learning design patterns, and I discuss those patterns and practices throughout the book.

Though I provide code for the computer vision models, my emphasis is on the concepts underlying the approaches and innovations: how they are set up and why they are set up that way. These underlying concepts are applicable to natural-language processing, structured data, signal processing, and other domains, and by generalizing, you should be able to adapt the concepts, methods, and techniques to the problems in your field. Many of the models and techniques I discuss are domain-agnostic, and throughout the book I also discuss key innovations in natural-language processing, natural-language understanding, and structured data domains where appropriate.

As for general background, you should know at least the basics of Python. It's OK if you still struggle with what a comprehension is or what a generator is, or if you still have some confusion about the weird multidimensional array slicing, and this thing about which objects are mutable and nonmutable on the heap. For this book, that's OK.

For those software engineers wanting to become machine learning engineers—what does that mean? A machine learning engineer (MLE) is an applied engineer. You don't need to know statistics (really, you don't!), and you don't need to know computational theory. If you fell asleep in your college calculus class on what a derivative is, that's OK, and if somebody asks you to do a matrix multiplication, feel free to ask, "Why?"

Your job is to learn the knobs and levers of a framework, and apply your skills and experience to produce solutions for real-world problems. That's what I am going to help you with, and that's what the design patterns using TF.Keras are about.

This book is designed for machine learning engineers and data scientists at comparable levels. For those pursuing the data scientist route, I encourage you to study supplemental statistics-related material.

Before we get started, I want to explain how you will learn, so this first section explains more about my philosophy and approach to teaching. Then we'll review some foundational material, including terminology, the progression from classical or semantic AI to narrow or statistical AI, and an overview of the basic steps in machine learning. Finally, we'll take a high-level look at what this book is all about: the modern model amalgamation approach to machine learning.

I don't use the traditional Western approach of rote memorization, iterate, iterate, test for correct answers, and then vertically advance. Beyond my view that it is less effective, I believe it is unintentionally discriminatory.

Instead, I have had the benefit of teaching engineering and science across diverse cultures and teaching methods, and have developed a unique teaching style that uses what I call a *lateral approach*: I start with core concepts, and then spiral out using what I call *abstraction*. When questions are asked, I will gradually start to point to other students on their thoughts to the answer, before I reflect on their thoughts. I don't do quizzes, where students try to get a 100%. Instead, I give assignments that each student will fail. I let the students pound away at the problem, struggling, and in doing so they will start to discover the underlying principles of what they need to learn. For example, I might give an assignment to train a CIFAR-10 dataset using a stock ResNet50 model, noting that the authors of the corresponding ResNet papers achieved 97% accuracy on CIFAR-10. Every student will fail, the model won't converge, they won't get over 70%, and so forth.

I then assemble the students into teams to tackle the problems together. By conferring with each other, they learn to generalize together. And before they can get it, I do the leap where I present the students with another challenge that will be difficult to solve—and the process starts again. I never give the students a chance to rote memorize.

Using my example, I might put on the whiteboard four possible solutions, like 1) image augmentation, 2) more regularization, 3) more hyperparameter search, 4) defer downsampling deep into the neural network (that's the right answer). Then in the middle, I will stop the students and have each team state which solution they tried and what they learned so far. I then explain the why/why not of each solution, and then change the problem again.

As the students progress to more advanced levels, I switch from the teacher role to what I call the master-student role and participate in the learning. The students are teaching me and each other as I am teaching them. I observe every student and look for what I call *ignition*—where the student will self-propel as a learner, and that is when the student is continuously learning. I find in my teaching method that the entire classroom comes up together, and no student is left behind.

From time to time, a school administrator would sit in on one of my sessions to observe. They would hear chatter trickling up from students and want to observe how it works. Of course, administrators need to give a name to everything. At one private coding school, the administrator described it as "everyone is a learner." The students learn from the teacher, the teacher learns from the students, and the students learn from the students. The administrator called it "Let's Learn Together."

I have my own name for my teaching methodology, which I call "I believe in myself." I tell my students, how can you believe in me ("the teacher"), if you don't first believe in yourself?

How this book is organized: A roadmap

This book is organized into three parts: fundamentals, design patterns, and design patterns for training and deployment for production.

Part 1, "Deep learning fundamentals," provides readers with a refresher on deep learning that includes an introduction to convolutional neural networks, as well as a discussion of the concepts and terminology that are mainstream today for all domains—computer vision, natural language processing, and structured data.

The design patterns for models are presented in Part 2, "Basic design patterns." In chapters 5 through 7, I introduce modern design patterns, and how they are applied to many current and former state-of-the-art deep learning models. I cover the procedural reuse design pattern, which has been the prevailing approach for hand-engineered models. I teach the design approaches, refinements, and pros/cons for large models discovered by researchers for going deeper in layers (chapter 5), wider in layers (chapter 6), and using alternative or out-of-the-box connectivity patterns (chapter 7).

Chapter 5 looks at a procedural design pattern for convolutional neural networks, as well as the development of residual blocks with identity links to attention in transformers for natural language understanding.

Chapter 6 expands on the procedural design pattern for convolutional neural networks and how researchers explored going wide in layers as an alternative to going deep. I show how this approach, such as ResNeXt, resulted in achieving comparing accuracy when compared to deep layers with less exposure to memorization and vanishing gradients. I also explore how wide convolutional neural networks are relevant to developments in wide and deep and TabNet models for structured data.

Chapter 7 covers model design patterns that explored other alternative layer connections to going deeper or wider in layers to increase accuracy, reduce the number of parameters, and increase information gain at intermediate latent space within the model.

Chapter 8 examines the unique design considerations and special constraints for mobile convolutional neural networks. Because of the memory constraints of these devices, tradeoffs between and size and accuracy had to be considered. I will teach the progression in these tradeoffs, the pros/cons, and how the designs of mobile networks differ from their large model counterparts to accommodate the tradeoffs.

Chapter 9 introduces autoencoders for unsupervised learning. As standalone models, the practical application of autoencoders is very narrow. But the discoveries from autoencoders have contributed to advancements in pretraining models. These models better generalize to out-of-distribution serving—that is, prediction requests in a production-deployed model that have a different distribution then the data the model was trained on. I also explore how autoencoders are comparable to embeddings in natural language understanding.

All the models in the second part of this book made seminal advancements to the research and development of deep learning, and continue to either be in use today, or their contributions have been incorporated in today's models.

Part 3, "Working with the pipelines," looks at design patterns and practices for production pipelines. In chapter 10, we look at hyperparameter tuning, both manual and automatic. I teach the design decisions, pros/cons, and best practices for specifying the search space, and the patterns for searching it.

Chapter 11 discusses transfer learning and introduces the concepts and methods of handling weight transfers and tuning for similar and distant tasks. I also look at the application to domain transfer for weight reuse during pretraining for models that are fully trained from scratch.

Chapters 12 through 14 take a high-level look at production pipelines. We dive deep into the data side in chapters 12 and 13. Chapter 12, which introduces data distributions, is the only chapter that goes into some detail about statistics. A lot has changed since 2017, when one was expected to have PhD-level knowledge of statistics. Today, much of that is hidden or otherwise automated in deep learning frameworks like TensorFlow. Understanding data distributions and search spaces remains one of the prevailing areas of expected knowledge in statistics, and can substantially influence the cost of training and the ability of the model to generalize when deployed into production.

Finally, chapters 13 and 14 turn from the data side to the deployment side. I cover the concepts and best practices for constructing the data side and then training side of a production pipeline.

About the code

This book contains many examples of source code both in numbered listings and in line with normal text. In both cases, source code is formatted in a `fixed-width font` `like this` to separate it from ordinary text. Sometimes code is also **in bold** to highlight code that has changed from previous steps in the chapter, such as when a new feature adds to an existing line of code.

In many cases, the original source code has been reformatted; we've added line breaks and reworked indentation to accommodate the available page space in the book. Additionally, comments in the source code have often been removed from the listings when the code is described in the text. Code annotations accompany many of the listings, highlighting important concepts.

All the code samples in the book are written in Python and are working code; albeit they may be absent of import statements. In many cases, the code samples are part of a larger code component, such as a model. In these cases, the entire code is available in my Google Cloud AI Developer Relations public GitHub repo (https://github.com/GoogleCloudPlatform/keras-idiomatic-programmer/tree/master/zoo).

liveBook discussion forum

Purchase of *Deep Learning Patterns and Practices* includes free access to a private web forum run by Manning Publications where you can make comments about the book, ask technical questions, and receive help from the author and from other users. To access the forum, go to https://livebook.manning.com/#!/book/deep-learning-patterns-and-practices/discussion. You can also learn more about Manning's forums and the rules of conduct at https://livebook.manning.com/#!/discussion.

Manning's commitment to our readers is to provide a venue where a meaningful dialogue between individual readers and between readers and the author can take place. It is not a commitment to any specific amount of participation on the part of the author, whose contribution to the forum remains voluntary (and unpaid). We suggest you try asking the author some challenging questions lest his interest stray! The forum and the archives of previous discussions will be accessible from the publisher's website as long as the book is in print.

Other online resources

For a framework, I use TensorFlow 2.x, which has incorporated the Keras model API. I think that the combination of the two is a fantastic vehicle for education beyond its production value.

The material is multimodal. In addition to the book and full code samples in repo, there are presentation slides, workshops, labs, and prerecorded lectures for each chapter on my Google Cloud AI Developer Relations YouTube account (www.youtube.com/channel/UC8OV0VkzHTp8_PUwEdzlBJg).

about the author

I strongly believe that my lifelong experience makes me one of the most ideal individuals to teach concepts of deep learning. When this book is first printed, I will be nearly 60 years old. I have a wealth of knowledge and experience that translates to expectations today in the workforce. In 1987, I got my advanced degree in artificial intelligence. I specialized in natural language processing. When I got out of college, I thought I would be writing talking books. Well, it was the AI winter.

I took other directions in my early career. First, I became an expert in government security for mainframe computers. As I became more proficient designing and coding in operating system kernels, I became a kernel developer for UNIX, being one of the contributors to today's heavyweight UNIX kernel. In those same years, I participated in shareware (before open source) and was the founder of WINNIX, a shareware program that competed with the commercial MKS Toolkit for running the UNIX shell and commands in a DOS environment.

Subsequently, I developed low-level object code tooling. I became an expert at both secured-level computing and compiler/assemblers for massively parallel computers in the early 1990s. I developed MetaC, which provided instrumentation into the operating system kernels of both conventional operating systems and highly secured and massively parallel computers.

In the late 1990s, I made a career change and became a research scientist for Sharp Corporation of Japan. Within a couple of years, I became the company's principal research scientist in North America. Over a 20-year period, Sharp filed over 200 US patent applications on my research, with 115 granted. My patents covered areas for solar energy, teleconferencing, imaging, digital interactive signage, and autonomous vehicles. Additionally, in 2014–2015 I was recognized as a leading world expert on open data and data ontologies, and founded the organization opengeocode.

In March of 2017, at a nudging of a friend of mine, I looked into "what's this thing called deep learning?" It was natural for me. I had a big data background, had worked as an imaging scientist and research scientist, had an AI graduate degree, worked on autonomous vehicles—it all seemed to align. So, I made the leap.

In the summer of 2018, Google approached me about being a staff member in Google Cloud AI. I accepted a position that October. It's been a great experience at Google. Today, I work with vast numbers of AI experts within both Google and Google's enterprise clients, teaching, mentoring, advising, and solving challenges to make deep learning operational on a large production scale.

about the cover illustration

The figure on the cover of *Deep Learning Patterns and Practices* is captioned "Indien," or a man from India. The illustration is taken from a collection of dress costumes from various countries by Jacques Grasset de Saint-Sauveur (1757–1810), titled *Costumes de Différents Pays*, published in France in 1784. Each illustration is finely drawn and colored by hand. The rich variety of Grasset de Saint-Sauveur's collection reminds us vividly of how culturally apart the world's towns and regions were just 200 years ago. Isolated from each other, people spoke different dialects and languages. In the streets or in the countryside, it was easy to identify where they lived and what their trade or station in life was just by their dress.

The way we dress has changed since then and the diversity by region, so rich at the time, has faded away. It is now hard to tell apart the inhabitants of different continents, let alone different towns, regions, or countries. Perhaps we have traded cultural diversity for a more varied personal life—certainly for a more varied and fast-paced technological life.

At a time when it is hard to tell one computer book from another, Manning celebrates the inventiveness and initiative of the computer business with book covers based on the rich diversity of regional life of two centuries ago, brought back to life by Grasset de Saint-Sauveur's pictures.

Part 1

Deep learning fundamentals

In this first part, you'll learn the fundamentals to get started building deep learning models. We start with the basic principles and steps of deep neural networks (DNN), with lots of diagrams illustrating these steps along with code snippets to implement the steps. I'll describe each step and then walk you through the code. Next, we cover the principles and steps of convolutional neural networks (CNN). I'll walk you through the seminal design patterns behind early state-of-the-art ConvNets, VGGs, and ResNets. You'll learn how to code each one of these model architectures, with complete code accessible from our public GitHub repository.

Once you are coding CNNs, what's next? You train them. We wrap up this part by learning fundamentals of training CNN models.

Designing modern machine learning

This chapter covers

- Evolving from classical AI to cutting-edge approaches
- Applying design patterns to deep learning
- Introducing the procedural reuse design pattern for modeling neural networks

The latest revolution in deep learning is at the macro level rather than the micro level, with the introduction of an approach that I coined while working at Google Cloud AI as *model amalgamation*. In this approach, models are broken into composable units that share and adapt components to achieve different objectives with the same initial data. The components are interconnected in a variety of connectivity patterns, in which each component *learns* communication interfaces between the models through design, without the necessity of a backend application.

In addition, model amalgamation can be used to train Internet of Things (IoT) devices for data enrichment, turning IoT sensors from static to dynamically learning devices—a technique called *model fusion*. Amalgamation is providing the means for putting AI into production at a scale and operational complexity not conceivable in 2017, when the push into production first started to emerge.

Think, for example, of the operational complexity of visual real estate data on a variety of aspects of the rental market, such as pricing, property condition, and amenities. Using the model amalgamation approach, you could create a vision analysis pipeline that connects individual models' components, each working on one of those aspects. In the end, you'd have a system in place to automatically *learn* to determine the condition, amenities, and general market appeal with the corresponding appropriate rental pricing.

The model amalgamation approach encourages engineers to view models as design patterns or templates that can be adapted to create individual components. So if you hope to use this approach, you'll need to understand the designs of the key models and systems that other engineers have developed to solve problems similar to the ones you will encounter.

The goal of this book is to aid you in that deep understanding by introducing you to the design patterns of seminal deep learning models, as well as the design or system architecture that puts those components together to develop, train, deploy, and serve larger deep learning systems. Even if you never work with huge enterprise amalgamations, becoming fluent in the underlying designs of these models and architectures will improve the engineering of any deep learning system you create.

1.1 A focus on adaptability

Because this book is aimed at less-experienced deep learning engineers and data scientists, part 1 starts with the designs of the basic deep neural networks (DNNs), convolutional neural networks (CNNs), and residual neural networks (ResNets). Part 1 also looks at the architecture of simple training pipelines. Whole books are written about just these networks and architectures, so here you'll get more of a reminder of how they work, with an emphasis on design patterns and principles. The point here is to lay out the design of basic deep learning components that all of the models you'll see in part 2 will fit into.

That said, if you are well versed in the fundamentals, you can go directly to part 2, which looks at the seminal models in the development of deep learning. My approach is to provide enough information about each model design so that you can play around with them and come up with solutions to the AI challenges you may encounter. The models are introduced more or less chronologically, so part 2 also serves as a kind of history of deep learning, with an emphasis on the evolution from one model to the next.

Now, if enterprise production is moving toward automatic learning for model development, you may wonder about the value of examining these manually designed, formerly state-of-the-art (SOTA) models. Many of these models, however, continue to be used as stock models, particularly for transfer learning. Some of the others never made it into production at all, but were responsible for discoveries that continue to be used today.

Model development for production continues to be a combination of automatic and hand-designed learning—which is often crucial for proprietary needs or advantages. But designing by hand does not mean starting from scratch; typically, you would start with a stock model and make tweaks and adjustments. To do this effectively, you need to know *how* the model works and *why* it works that way, the concepts that underlie its design, and the pros and cons of alternative building blocks you will learn from other SOTA models.

The final part of the book takes a deep dive into the design patterns for training and deployment for production. While not all readers will be deploying the kinds of enterprise systems that are my focus, I feel this information is relevant to all. Becoming familiar with many types—and sizes—of systems addressing a variety of problems can help you when you need to think outside the box to solve a problem. The more you know about the underlying concepts and designs, the more able and adaptable you become.

This adaptability is probably the most valuable takeaway from this book. Production involves a vast number of moving parts, and an endless flow of "monkey wrenches" being tossed into the mix. If engineers or data scientists simply rote-memorize sets of reproducible steps in a framework, how will they handle the diversity of tasks they'll encounter and resolve the monkey wrenches thrown at them? Employers look for more than just skill and experience; they want to know how technically adaptive you are.

Imagine yourself in an interview: you score high on skill and work experience and nail the stock machine learning (ML) coding challenge. Then the interviewers throw you a monkey wrench, an unexpected or unusual problem. They do this to observe how you think through a challenge, which concepts you apply and the reasoning behind them, how you evaluate the pros and cons of the various solutions, and your ability to debug. That's adaptability. And that's what I hope deep learning developers and data scientists will get from this book.

1.1.1 Computer vision leading the way

I teach all of these concepts primarily in the context of computer vision, because design patterns evolved first in computer vision. But they are applicable to natural-language processing (NLP), structured data, signal processing, and other fields. If we roll the clock back to prior to 2012, ML in all fields was mostly using classical statistics-based methods.

Various academic researchers, such as Fei-Fei Liu at Stanford University and Geoffrey Hinton of the University of Toronto, began to pioneer applying neural networks to computer vision. Liu, along with her students, compiled a computer vision dataset, now known as ImageNet, to advance the research into computer vision. ImageNet, along with the PASCAL dataset, became the basis for the annual ImageNet Large Scale Vision Recognition Challenge (ILSVRC) competition in 2010. Early entries used traditional image recognition/signal processing methods.

Then, in 2012, Alex Krizhevsky, also of the University of Toronto, entered a deep learning model, AlexNet, using convolution layers. This model won the ILSVRC contest and by a sizable margin. The AlexNet model, jointly designed with Hinton and Ilya Sutskever, kicked off deep learning. In their corresponding paper, "ImageNet Classification with Deep Convolutional Neural Networks" (http://mng.bz/1ApV), they showed how neural networks can be designed.

In 2013, Matthew Zeiler and Rob Fergus of New York University won the competition by fine-tuning AlexNet into what they called ZFNet. This pattern of building on each other's success continued. The Visual Geometry Group at Oxford expanded on the AlexNet design principles and won the 2014 contest. In 2015, Kaiming He and others at Microsoft Research further expanded on the AlexNet/VGG design principles and introduced new design patterns, winning the competition. Their model, ResNet, and their "Deep Residual Learning for Image Recognition" paper (https://arxiv.org/abs/1512.03385), set off a surge in discovering and exploring the design space of CNNs.

1.1.2   *Beyond computer vision: NLP, NLU, structured data*

In these early years of developing design principles and design patterns using deep learning for computer vision, developments in natural-language understanding (NLU) and structured data models lagged behind and continued to focus on classical approaches. They used classical ML frameworks, like the Natural Language Toolkit (NLTK) for text input, and classical algorithms based on decision trees, like random forest, for structured data input.

In the NLU field, progress was made with the introduction of RNNs and long-short-term-memory (LSTM) and gated recurrent unit (GRU) layers. That progress took a leap in 2017 with the introduction of the Transformer design pattern for natural language, and the corresponding paper "Attention Is All You Need" by Ashish Vaswani et. al (https://arxiv.org/abs/1706.03762). Google Brain, a deep learning research organization within Google AI, adopted early a comparable attention mechanism in ResNet. Likewise, advancements in design patterns for structured data evolved with the introduction of the wide-and-deep model pattern, outlined in "Wide & Deep Learning for Recommender Systems" (https://arxiv.org/abs/1606.07792) by Heng-Tze Cheng et. al, at the technology-agnostic research group Google Research, in 2016.

While I focus on computer vision to teach both the evolution and current state of the art in design patterns, I refer to corresponding progress in NLU and structured data where appropriate. Many of the concepts in this book are applicable across fields and data types. For instance, chapters 2 through 4 cover universal fundamentals, and all but one chapter in part 3 cover concepts that are agnostic of the model and data type.

In chapters where it makes sense, mostly in part 2, I introduce an example from beyond computer vision. For example, in chapter 5, I compare the development of residual blocks with identity links to attention in transformers for NLU. In chapter 6, we'll explore how wide CNNs are relevant to developments in wide-and-deep and Tab-Net models for structured data. Chapter 9 explains how autoencoders are comparable to embeddings in NLU, and chapter 11 discusses how the steps for transfer learning are comparable to both NLU and structured data.

By generalizing from the examples I share from computer vision, NLP, and structural data, you should be able to adapt the concepts, methods, and techniques to problems in your domain.

1.2 The evolution in machine learning approaches

To understand the modern approach, we first have to understand where we are with AI and ML, and how we got here. This section presents several top-level approaches and design patterns for working in today's production environment, including intelligent automation, machine design, model fusion, and model amalgamation.

1.2.1 Classical AI vs. narrow AI

Let's briefly cover the difference between classical AI and today's modern narrow AI. In *classical AI* (also known as *semantic AI*), models were designed as rule-based systems. These systems were used to solve problems that could not be solved by a mathematical equation. Instead, the system was set up to mimic a subject matter or domain expert. Figure 1.1 offers a visual of this approach.

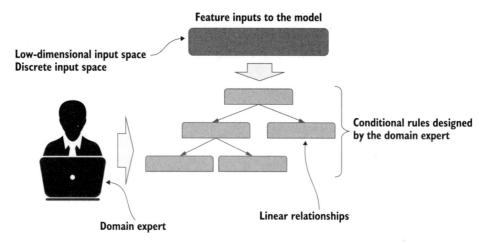

Figure 1.1   In a classical AI approach, the domain expert designs rules to mimic their knowledge.

Classical AI worked well in input spaces that were low-dimensionality (as in, had a low number of distinct inputs); had an input space that could be broken into discrete segments, such as categories or bins; and maintained a strong linear relationship between the discrete space and the output. The domain expert designed a set of rules, based on inputs and state transformations, that mimicked their expertise. A programmer then converted these rules into a rule-based system, typically of the form "If A and B are true, then C is true."

Systems like this were well suited for problems like predicting the quality and appropriateness of a wine, which required only a small set of rules. For example, for the wine selector, the inputs might have been whether the meal was lunch or dinner, the entree, the occasion, and whether dessert would be included. But classical AI failed to scale to larger problems; accuracy would drop dramatically, and rules required continuous refinement to try to stave off the drop. Inconsistencies among domain experts designing the rules was another problem contributing to inaccuracies.

In *narrow AI* (also known as *statistical AI*), a model gets trained on a large amount of data, alleviating the need for domain experts. Instead, the model uses principles of statistics to learn patterns in the distribution of the input data, also referred to as a *sampling distribution.* These patterns can then be applied with high accuracy to samples not seen in training. When trained with a sampling distribution made up of large amounts of data that is representative of the larger population, or *population distribution*, we can model problems without the constraints that come with classical AI. In other words, narrow AI can work very well with substantially higher dimensionality in the input space (meaning a large number of distinct inputs), and with inputs that can be a mix of discrete and continuous.

Let's contrast rule-based with narrow AI by applying both to predicting the sale price of a house. A rule-based system could generally consider only a small number of inputs; for instance, lot size, square footage, number of bedrooms, number of bathrooms, and property tax. A system like this could predict a median price for comparable homes, but not for any one home, because of nonlinearity in the relationships of the property to the price.

Let's take a step back and discuss the difference between a linear and nonlinear relationship. In a *linear relationship,* the value of one variable predicts the value of another. For example, say we have the function $y = f(x)$, which we define as $2 \times x$. The value of y can be predicted with 100% confidence for any value x. In a *nonlinear relationship*, the value of y can be predicted only with a probability distribution on any value x.

Using our housing example, we could try to say $y = f(x)$ as the *selling price = sqft × price_per_sq_ft.* The reality is that a lot of other variables affect *price_per_sq_ft*, and there is some uncertainty in how those affect the price. In other words, the square footage of the house has a nonlinear relationship to the selling price, which, by itself, could predict only a probability distribution of the selling price.

In narrow AI, we substantially increase the number of inputs to learn the nonlinearity, such as adding the year the house was built, when permits for upgrades were granted, the type of architecture, materials used for roofing and siding, school district information, employment opportunities, average income, the neighborhood, as well as crime, and vicinity to parks, public transportation, and highways. These additional variables help the model learn the probability distribution with high confidence. Inputs whose value is from a fixed set, such as building architecture, are *discrete*, while inputs that are from an unbounded range, like average income, are *continuous.*

Narrow AI models work well with inputs that have a high level of nonlinearity to the outputs (predictions), by learning the boundaries to segment the inputs—again, if those segments have a strongly linear relationship to the output. These types of models are based on statistics, requiring large amounts of data, and are called *narrow AI* because they are good at solving narrow problems consisting of a limited range of tasks within one field. Narrow models are not so good at generalizing to problems of a wide scope. Figure 1.2 illustrates the narrow AI approach.

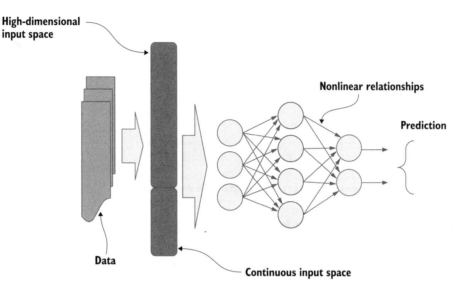

Figure 1.2   In narrow AI, the model learns to be the domain expert by training on a large dataset that is representative of the larger population.

Another way to see the difference between classical AI and narrow AI is by looking at the error-rate reduction in both kinds of models, as deep learning is continuously pushing to the Bayes theoretical error limit. Bayes described this theoretical error limit as a progression, as shown in figure 1.3.

First, what would be the error rate of an average non-expert solving a task? Then, what would be the error rate of an expert solving the task (this is analogous to semantic AI)? What would be the error rate with a roomful of experts solving the task? And finally, the theoretical limit: what would be the error rate of an infinite number of experts solving the task?

Deep learning in vast numbers of computer vision and NLP tasks has achieved the error rate of a roomful of experts, vastly outperforming both conventional software applications and expert systems. In 2020, researchers and enterprise ML engineers began pursuing production systems that are in the realm of the Bayes theoretical error limit.

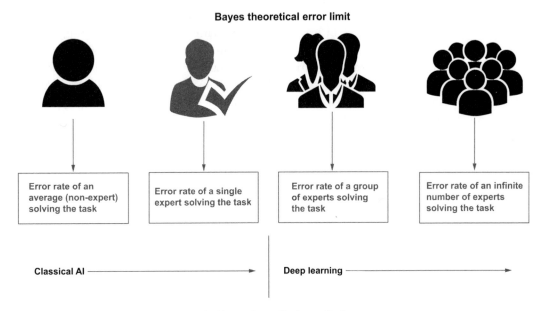

Figure 1.3   **ML has progressed toward the Bayes theoretical error limit.**

1.2.2   *Next steps in computer learning*

Now that we understand how we got here, where, exactly, are we? As computer learning has changed, we first moved from artificial intelligence to intelligent automation. And then we've moved into machine design, model fusion, and model amalgamation. Let's define these modern advances.

INTELLIGENT AUTOMATION

As we've just seen, early artificial intelligence meant classical AI, which was mostly rule-based and required domain experts. This allowed us to essentially write software programs to start automating tasks that were typically done manually. Then, in narrow AI, we applied statistics to learning, eliminating the need for a domain expert.

The next major advance was *intelligent automation* (IA). In this approach, the models learn a (near) optimal way to automate the process, exceeding the performance and accuracy when compared to the manual or computer-automated counterpart.

Typically, the IA system works as a pipeline process. Cumulative information, transformations, and state transitions are the inputs to a model at various points in the pipeline. The output, or prediction, of each model is used to perform the next information transformation and/or decide the next state transition. Typically, each model is trained and deployed independently, usually as a microservice, with a backend application driving the whole pipeline process.

An example of IA is automating the extraction of patient information from patient medical records from diverse sources and formats, including sources the model was never trained on. I worked on architecting such systems in the healthcare field in

2018. Today, numerous turnkey providers make these kinds of systems available; Google Cloud Healthcare API (https://cloud.google.com/healthcare) is one.

In 2019, AI was moving into full production in a vast number of enterprise-size companies. Throughout the year, I would be in a growing number of meetings with Google's largest clients. We now talk about AI in business terms. These technology concepts have evolved into business concepts.

In these meetings, we have moved away from saying *AI* and replaced it with *IA* to demystify the process. We have the client describe each step (manual and computer assisted) in the process that they want to apply AI to. Let's say that one step costs $100,000. In the past, our tendency would be to jump to that step and apply AI—the "big reward." But let's say another step costs just a penny, but occurs a million times a day—that's $10,000 a day, or $3.65 million a year. And let's say we could replace this low-hanging fruit with a model that learns the optimal way to automate this step and that operationally costs $40,000 a year. No one leaves $3.61 million dollars on the table.

That's intelligent automation. Instead of programmers coding a predesigned algorithm to automate, the programmers guide the model to intelligently learn the optimal algorithm. Figure 1.4 maps out how we would apply IA to a single step in a claim-processing pipeline.

Let's do a high-level review of what is happening in this pipeline. At step 1, documents relating to a claim are scanned and ingested into the IA pipeline. At step 2, the prior practice of a document operator subsequently viewing each scanned document and tagging it is replaced with a natural-language classification model that has been trained for this claims-processing task.

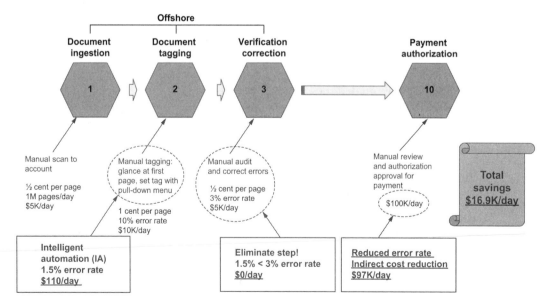

Figure 1.4 Intelligent automation applied to claims processing

This replacement has several advantages. First, the cost of manual labor is eliminated. In addition to the speed improvement of a computer versus a human, the process can be distributed so that a mass number of documents can be processed in parallel.

Second, the error rate on correctly tagging the document's classes is substantially reduced from the human error rate. Let's consider why. Each human operator may have different levels of training and experience and wide variance in accuracy. Additionally, human fatigue contributes to the error rate. But let's say we had one thousand trained human operators viewing the same document(s) and we use a majority voting method on how to tag the document. We would expect the error rate to be substantially reduced, approaching near zero.

That's what the model does: it has been trained on vast numbers of documents that have been tagged by vast numbers of trained human operators. In that way, once trained, the model's performance is equal to that of a collective of trained human operators.

At step 3 in the manual version, an expert human operator would inspect the tagging to further reduce errors. This step is not eliminated in the IA process—but with the substantial reduction in errors from step 2, the workload on the human operator is significantly further reduced.

The IA processes downstream continue to reduce/eliminate human operator costs and further reduce error rates. Once we get to the final step, a trained subject-matter expert (SME) makes the final review for authorization (or nonauthorization) of payment. Now that the information that the SME reviews is of higher accuracy, the human subjective decision is more reliable, further reducing costs of making the wrong subjective decision.

We in the industry have stopped using the term *machine learning* and replaced it with *machine design*, to make the analogy to computer-aided design (CAD). We applied CAD to problems that were too complex to engineer even a suboptimal solution. These systems had building components, mathematical knowledge, and expert system rules, and the SMEs guided the CAD systems to find a good suboptimal solution.

In machine design, the system instead learns the building components, the mathematical knowledge, and the rules, and the ML engineer guides the machine design to find the optimal solution. By moving to machine design, we free up the high-value people assets to work on the next level of challenging problems, accelerating their technical progression and bringing a higher return on investment (ROI) per staffer for the business.

MACHINE DESIGN

Before deep learning, SMEs designed software programs to search for good solutions in parts of the software and hardware that had high complexity. Typically, these programs were a combination of search optimization and rule-based techniques.

In the next advancement, *machine design*, the models learn a (near) optimal way to design and integrate the software and hardware components. These systems exceed in performance, accuracy, and complexity, even when compared to models designed by an SME with the assistance of a CAD program. The human designer uses their real-world expertise to guide the model's search space for solutions.

Consider a hospital with two X-ray departments; one department has an expensive X-ray machine, and the other a low-cost one. An examining physician chooses which department to send a patient to for confirmation of a pneumonia diagnosis *depending on the likelihood of the patient having pneumonia.* If the likelihood is low, or unlikely, for pneumonia, the doctor sends the patient to the low-cost X-ray machine, following hospital policy and the desire to lower costs for the insurance provider. If the determination is high, or likely, the patient merits the high-cost X-ray. This is an example of machine design informing the hyperparameter and architecture search space and guiding the pipeline in a system for automatic learning of medical images from different distributions (medical devices, in this case, X-ray machines).

Keep in mind that if the accumulative X-rays and diagnostic determinations from the two X-ray devices are used to train a model, we have bias in the data. Instead of learning from the data, the model may inadvertently learn the unique characteristics of the two medical devices—a bias of the *view perspective.* The classic example of a view-perspective problem in a model is the case of determining dogs versus wolves, in which the model inadvertently learned snow for wolves, since all the training pictures of the wolves were taken during winter.

In machine design, in addition to training a model, the system learns the optimal training pipeline for an adversarial model, known as the *surrogate.* If you want to delve into this more, "An Adversarial Approach for the Robust Classification of Pneumonia from Chest Radiographs" (https://arxiv.org/pdf/2001.04051.pdf) is a foundational machine-design paper related to this very problem.

MODEL FUSION

Model fusion is the next advancement in developing more-accurate, lower-cost systems for predictive maintenance and fault detection, such as those used in IoT sensor systems. Traditionally, very expensive equipment and infrastructure, such as factory machines, airplanes, and regional power infrastructures, have had built-in IoT sensors. This continuous sensory data would be fed to rule-based algorithms designed by an expert.

The problem with these traditional systems has been that they are subject to high environmental variance that affects their reliability. For example, in the electrical power industry, transmission lines have sensors at each tower that monitor for anomalies in the line impedance between the towers. The impedance can fluctuate as a result of stress on the line connection due to wind, changes in temperature affecting conductivity, and secondary factors such as moisture buildup.

Model fusion improves the reliability of IoT systems by using a machine-learned model with higher operational cost to generate label data to convert the expert-designed system. Continuing with our example, the power industry today uses drones and deep learning models trained in computer vision to periodically inspect power-transmission lines. This process is highly accurate and more operationally expensive.

Therefore, it is used to generate label data for the impedance sensor data created by the lower-cost sensor system. The labeled data generated at high operational cost is then used to train another model, which impedance sensors (the low-cost system) then use to achieve comparable reliability.

MODEL AMALGAMATION

Before deep learning, applications were constructed as either a monolithic application running on a backend server or a core backbone on a server that used distributed microservices. In *model amalgamation*, the model(s) essentially become the entire application, which directly shares model components and outputs and learns a communication interface between the models. All this happens without the need for a bulky backend application or microservices.

Imagine a model pipeline for the real estate industry that uses vision analysis on photographs of houses and apartment buildings to determine rental pricing. Models within a set are chained together, with each model trained on a particular feature; together, they automatically determine rental condition, rental amenities, and market appeal, and come up with the corresponding pricing.

Let's compare this to more traditional IA, where each step in the process pipeline is a separate deployed model instance, taking as input either the original image, or a transformation and state, all of which is controlled by a backend rule-based application designed by expert(s). In contrast, in an amalgamation, the model instances communicate directly with each other. Each model has learned the optimal method for performing its specialized task (e.g., determine condition); learned the optimal communication path and representation between the models (models for home, room, and amenities); and learned the optimal method for determining state changes (condition of the property).

In 2021, I anticipate that at the enterprise level, production will move to model amalgamation. We are still trying to figure out how to make that work. Prior to amalgamation, a plurality of models would be deployed performing different tasks, and developers would construct a backend application that made representational state transfer (REST) or microservice calls. We still coded the logic of the application, and the interface and data communication between the application and the models. Figure 1.5 is an example of a model amalgamation I designed in late 2019 for sports broadcasting.

Let's walk through this process. First, the amalgamation ingests live video; that is, the amalgamation is continuously processing the video in real time. The video is parsed in real time as a time-sequence set of frames. Each frame is an image of the game, such as a baseball player ready to bat. Each frame is first processed by a shared set of convolutional layers (*shared convolutional layers*) that generates a common internal encoding across downstream tasks. In other words, instead of each downstream task (model) starting with the same input image and processing it into an internal encoding, the input image is encoded once and the encoding is reused downstream. This speeds up the model's response and shrinks its size in memory.

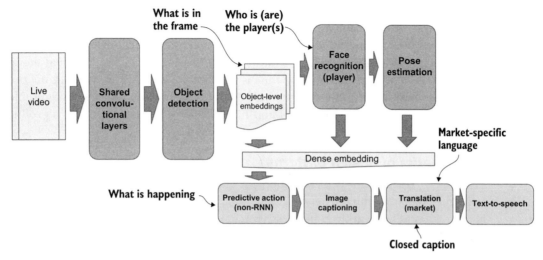

Figure 1.5   Model amalgamation applied to sports broadcasting

Next, the generated common encoding goes through an object-detection model, which has been trained on the common encoding as input instead of the input image, reducing the size and increasing the speed of the object detection. Let's say the object detection is trained to recognize objects including people, player equipment, stadium, and field. For each object it recognizes in the frame, it will output an object-level embedding, which is a lower-dimensional representation (for example, reduced-size encoding) along with the spatial coordinates within the upstream input frame.

These object-level embeddings now become inputs to another set of downstream tasks. Next, you see that embeddings classified as people are passed to a facial-recognition model that has been trained on the embeddings versus the original image. The model may be trained, for example, to recognize players, officials, referees, coaches, and security, and correspondingly tags the embedding. The player-specific object embeddings are then passed on to a pose-estimation model that finds human key points and classifies the identified person's pose in the frame, such as player *A* is in a batting position.

Next, the object-level embeddings (players, gears, stadium, and so forth) combine with the player-specific pose into an information-enriched dense embedding. And all this rich information is passed to another model to predict the player's action, such as player *A* is at the mound, ready to bat. This predictive action is then passed to another model that converts the action into closed-captioned text that is overlaid on the live broadcast.

Let's assume the sports event is being broadcasted across the world and watched by viewers in a wide variety of languages. The output from the image-captioning model (for example, English) is passed to another model that performs language translation specific to each market. In each market, the translated text is converted to speech for real-time commentary.

As you can see, models have evolved from single-task predictions and standalone deployments, to models that perform multiple tasks, share model components, and are integrated to form a solution, such as in the healthcare document-handling and the sports broadcasting examples. Another way of describing these integrated model solutions is as a *serving pipeline*. A pipeline is made of connected components; the output of one component is the input to another, and each component is configurable, replaceable, and has version control and history. Using pipelines in today's production ML extends across the entire end-to-end pipeline.

1.3   *The benefits of design patterns*

Prior to 2017, the majority of renditions of neural network models in all fields were coded in a batch scripting style. As AI researchers and experienced software engineers became increasingly involved in research and design, we started to see a shift in the coding of models that reflected software engineering principles for reuse and design patterns.

A *design pattern* implies that a best practice exists for constructing and coding a model that can be reapplied across a wide range of cases, such as image classification, object detection and tracking, facial recognition, image segmentation, super-resolution, and style transfer for image data; document classification, sentiment analysis, entity extraction, and summarization for text data; and classification, regression, and forecasting for unstructured data.

The development of design patterns for deep learning is what led to model amalgamation, model fusion, and machine design—in which model components can be reused and adapted. These design patterns for model components allowed researchers and other deep learning practitioners to incrementally develop both model components and best practices for applications, across all models and data types. This knowledge sharing accelerated the development of design patterns and the reuse of model components that makes it possible to deploy deep learning into widespread production applications.

Many of the historical SOTA models I cover in this book revealed knowledge and concepts that have been incorporated into today's modern production. Even though many of these models eventually stop being used, an understanding of the knowledge, concepts, and building-block components behind them is essential to understanding and practicing deep learning at today's large scale.

One of the earliest design patterns for neural network models was *procedural reuse*, which was simultaneously adopted across computer vision, NLU, and structured data. As with a software application, we design a procedural reuse model as components that reflect the data flow and decompose components into reusable functions.

There were—and still are—many benefits to using a procedural reuse design pattern. First, it simplifies the task of representing models in architectural diagrams. Prior to the use of a formal design pattern, each team of researchers invented its own way of representing its model architecture in the papers it published. A design pattern also defines how a model structure and flow are represented. Having a consistent and refined method simplified the representation of architectural diagrams. Second, the model architectures are more understandable by other researchers and ML engineers. Furthermore, working from a standard pattern exposes the inner workings of the design, which, in turn, makes the models easier to modify and easier to troubleshoot and debug.

In 2016, research papers began presenting component flow—typically referred to as the *stem*, (representational) *learner*, and (transformational) *task*. Prior to 2016, research papers presented their models as a monolithic architecture. These monolithic architectures made it challenging for researchers to prove that a new concept improved any individual part of a model. Because these components contain repeated flow patterns, eventually the concept of configurable components emerged. These repeated flow patterns were subsequently reused and refined by other researchers in the design of their model architectures. While the application of model components lagged behind in NLU and structured data, by 2017 we started to see their appearance in research papers. Today, regardless of the model type and field, you see the model design comprising the same comparable three primary model components.

An earlier version of a design pattern that decomposed a model into components was SqueezeNet (https://arxiv.org/pdf/1602.07360.pdf), which used configurable components based on metaparameters. The introduction of metaparameters, which describe how to configure model components, helped formalize how to represent, design, and implement configurable components. Designing models based on configurable components provided the means for researchers to measure performance improvements on a per-component basis, while trying various component configurations. This design approach is standard practice when developing application software; among its many of the benefits is that it promotes code reuse.

Procedural patterns for reuse were the first, and remain the most fundamental, reusable designs, so they are the focus of this book. Later, what we call factory and abstract factory patterns would be introduced to do machine design. A *factory design pattern* uses SOTA building blocks as a factory and an objective to search for the best design that matches the requirements. An *abstract factory pattern* abstracts down another level and searches for the best factory, which is then used to search for the best model.

But in this book, you will learn the cornerstone designs, starting with the architectures of the basic DNNs and CNNs in part 1, moving to the seminal models coded for procedural reuse in part 2, and finishing up with a tour of the modern production pipeline in part 3.

Summary

- Deep learning evolved from classical AI to narrow AI, which led to using AI to solve problems with high-dimensionality inputs.

- Deep learning has evolved from experimenting with models to a reusable and reconfigurable pipeline approach for data, training, deployment, and serving.
- At the leading edge at the enterprise scale, ML practitioners are using model amalgamation, model fusion, and machine design.
- The procedural reuse design pattern is the building block and segue into today's leading edge at the enterprise scale.

Deep neural networks

2

This chapter covers

- Breaking down the structure of neural networks and deep neural networks
- Using feed-forward and backward propagation during training to learn model weights
- Coding neural network models in both TF.Keras sequential and functional APIs
- Understanding the various types of model tasks
- Using strategies to prevent overfitting

This chapter starts with some basics on neural networks. Once you've gotten the basics down, I'll introduce you to how deep neural networks (DNNs) can be easily coded using TF.Keras, which has two styles for coding neural networks: a sequential API and functional API. We will code examples using both styles.

This chapter also covers the fundamental types of models. Each model type, such as regression and classification, learns different types of tasks. The task you want to learn determines the model type you will design. You'll also learn the fundamentals of weights, biases, activations, and optimizers, and how they contribute to the accuracy of the model.

To wrap up this chapter, we'll code an image classifier. And finally, I'll introduce the problem of overfitting when training along with an early approach to solving overfitting with dropout.

2.1 Neural network basics

Let's start with some basics on neural networks. First, this section covers the input layer to a neural network, then how this is connected to an output layer, and then how hidden layers are added in between to become a deep neural network. From there, we cover how the layers are made of nodes, what nodes do, and how layers are connected to each other to form fully connected neural networks.

2.1.1 Input layer

The *input layer* to a neural network takes numbers! All the input data is converted to numbers. Everything is a number. The text becomes numbers, speech becomes numbers, pictures become numbers, and things that are already numbers are just numbers.

Neural networks take numbers as vectors, matrices, or tensors. These are simply names for the number of dimensions in an array. A *vector* is a one-dimensional array, such as a list of numbers. A *matrix* is a two-dimensional array, like the pixels in a black-and-white image. And a *tensor* is any array of three or more dimensions—for example, a stack of matrices in which each matrix is the same dimension. That's it. Figure 2.1 illustrates these concepts.

Speaking of numbers, you might have heard terms like *normalization* or *standardization*. In standardization, numbers are converted to be centered around a mean of zero, with one standard deviation on each side of the mean. If you're saying,

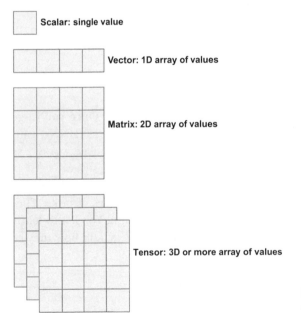

Scalar: single value

Vector: 1D array of values

Matrix: 2D array of values

Tensor: 3D or more array of values

Figure 2.1   Types of arrays in deep learning

"I don't do statistics" right about now, I know how you feel. But don't worry. Packages such as scikit-learn (https://scikit-learn.org) and NumPy (https://numpy.org) have library calls that do this for you. Standardization is basically a button to push, and it doesn't even need a lever, so there are no parameters to set.

Speaking of packages, you're going to be using NumPy a lot. What is NumPy, and why is it so popular? Given the interpretive nature of Python, the language handles large arrays poorly—like really big, super-big arrays of numbers—thousands, tens of thousands, millions of numbers. Think of Carl Sagan's infamous quote on the size of the universe: billions and billions of stars. That's a tensor!

One day a C programmer got the idea to write, in low-level C, a high-performance implementation for handling super-big arrays, and then added an external Python wrapper. NumPy was born. Today NumPy is a library with lots of useful methods and properties, like the property `shape`, which tells you the shape (or dimensions) of the array, and the `where()` method, which allows you to do SQL-like queries on your super-big array.

All Python ML frameworks, such as TensorFlow and PyTorch, will take as input on the input layer a NumPy multidimensional array. And speaking of C, or Java, or C+, . . . , the input layer in a neural network is just like the parameters passed to a function in a programming language. That's it.

Let's get started by installing Python packages you will need. I assume you have version 3.x of Python installed (www.python.org/downloads/). Whether you directly installed it or had it installed as part of a larger package such as Anaconda (www.anaconda.com/products/enterprise), you got with it a nifty command-line tool called `pip`. This tool is used to install any Python package you will ever need again, from a single command invocation. You use `pip install` and then the name of the package. It goes to the Python Package Index (PyPI), the global repository of Python packages, and downloads and installs the package for you. It's quite easy.

We want to start off by downloading and installing the TensorFlow framework and the NumPy package. Guess what? Their names are in the registry, *tensorflow* and *numpy*—thankfully, very obvious. Let's do it together. Go to the command line and issue the following:

```
pip install tensorflow
pip install numpy
```

With TensorFlow 2.0, Keras is built in and the recommended model API, referred to now as *TF.Keras*. TF.Keras is based on object-oriented programming with a collection of classes and associated methods and properties.

Let's start simply. Say we have a dataset of housing data. Each row has 14 columns of data. One column indicates the sale price of a home. We are going to call that the *label*. The other 13 columns have information about the house, such as the square footage and property tax. It's all numbers. We are going to call those the *features*. What we want to do is learn to predict (or estimate) the label from the features.

Now, before we had all this computing power and these awesome ML frameworks, data analysts did this stuff by hand or by using formulas in a Microsoft Excel spreadsheet with a certain amount of data and lots and lots of linear algebra. We, however, will use Keras and TensorFlow.

We will start by first importing the Keras module from TensorFlow, and then instantiate an `Input` class object. For this class object, we define the shape or dimensions of the input. In our example, the input is a one-dimensional array (a vector) of 13 elements, one for each feature:

```
from tensorflow.keras import Input

Input(shape=(13,))
```

When you run these two lines in a notebook, you will see this output:

```
<tf.Tensor 'input_1:0' shape=(?, 13) dtype=float32>
```

This output shows you what `Input(shape=(13,))` evaluates to. It produces a tensor object named `input_1:0`. This name will be useful later in assisting you in debugging your models. The `?` in `shape` shows that the input object takes an unbounded number of entries (examples or rows) of 13 elements each. That is, at runtime it will bind the number of one-dimensional vectors of 13 elements to the actual number of examples (rows) you pass in, referred to as the (mini) *batch size*. The `dtype` shows the default data type of the elements, which in this case is a 32-bit float (single precision).

2.1.2 *Deep neural networks*

DeepMind, deep learning, deep, deep, deep. Oh my, what's all this? *Deep* in this context just means that the neural network has one or more layers between the input layer and the output layer. As you will read later, by going deeper into hidden layers, researchers have been able to get higher accuracy.

Visualize a directed graph in layers of depth. The root nodes are the input layer, and the terminal nodes are the output layer. The layers between are known as the *hidden*, or *deep*, layers. So a four-layer DNN architecture would look like this:

- Input layer
- Hidden layer
- Hidden layer
- Output layer

To get started, we'll assume that every neural network node in every layer, except the output layer, is the same type of neural network node. We'll also assume that every node on each layer is connected to every other node on the next layer. This is known as a *fully connected neural network* (FCNN), depicted in figure 2.2. For example, if the input layer has three nodes, and the next (hidden) layer has four nodes, then each

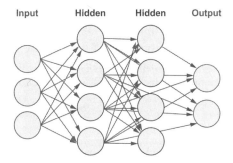

Figure 2.2   **Deep neural networks have one or more hidden layers between the input and output layers. This is a fully connected network, so the nodes at each level are all connected to one another.**

node on the first layer is connected to all four nodes on the next layer—for a total of 12 connections (3 × 4).

2.1.3   Feed-forward networks

The DNN and CNN (you'll learn more about the CNN in chapter 3) are known as *feed-forward neural networks*. *Feed-forward* means that data moves through the network sequentially, in one direction, from the input layer to the output layer. This is analogous to a function in procedural programming. The inputs are passed as parameters in the input layer, and the function performs a sequenced set of actions based on the inputs (in the hidden layers) and then outputs a result (the output layer).

When coding a feed-forward network in TF.Keras, you will see two distinctive styles in blogs and other tutorials. I will briefly touch on both so when you see a code snippet in one style, you can translate it to the other.

2.1.4   Sequential API method

The *sequential API method* is easier to read and follow for beginners, but the tradeoff is that it is less flexible. Essentially, you create an empty feed-forward neural network with the Sequential class object, and then "add" one layer at a time, until the output layer. In the following examples, the ellipses represent pseudocode:

```
from tensorflow.keras import Sequential

model = Sequential()                         ◁──── Creates an empty model
model.add( ...the first layer... )
model.add( ...the next layer... )            Placeholders for adding
model.add( ...the output layer... )          layers in sequential order
```

Alternatively, the layers can be specified in sequential order as a list passed as a parameter when instantiating the Sequential class object:

```
model = Sequential([ ...the first layer...,
                     ...the next layer...,
                     ...the output layer...
               ])
```

So, you might ask, when would you use the add() method versus specifying as a list in the instantiation of the Sequential object? Well, both methods generate the same model and behavior, so it's a matter of personal preference. I tend to use the more verbose add() method in instructional and demonstration material for clarity. But if I am writing code for production, I use the sparser list method, where I can visualize and edit the code more easily.

2.1.5   *Functional API method*

The *functional API method* is more advanced, allowing you to construct models that are nonsequential in flow—such as branches, skip links, and multiple inputs and outputs (you'll see how multiple inputs and outputs work in section 2.4). You build the layers separately and then tie them together. This latter step gives you the freedom to connect layers in creative ways. Essentially, for a feed-forward neural network, you create the layers, bind them to another layer or layers, and then pull all the layers together in a final instantiation of a Model class object:

Constructs the input layer

Constructs the hidden layer and binds it to the input layer

```
input = layers.(...the first layer...)
hidden = layers.(...the next layer...)( ...the layer to bind to... )
output = layers.(...the output layer...)( /the layer to bind to... )
model = Model(input, output)
```

Constructs the output layer and binds it to the hidden layer

Assembles the model by following the bindings from the input to output layers

2.1.6   *Input shape vs. input layer*

The input *shape* and input *layer* can be confusing at first. They are not the same thing. More specifically, the number of nodes in the input layer does not need to match the shape of the input vector. That's because every element in the input vector will be passed to every node in the input layer, as shown in figure 2.3.

For example, if our input layer is 10 nodes, and we use our earlier example of a 13-element input vector, we will have 130 connections (10 × 13) between the input vector and the input layer.

Each connection between an element in the input vector and a node in the input layer has a *weight*, and each node in

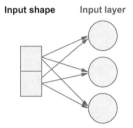

Input shape   Input layer

Figure 2.3   The input (shape) and input layer differ. Every element in the input is connected to every node in the input layer.

the input layer has a *bias*. Think of each connection between the input vector and input layer, as well as connections between layers, as sending a signal forward indicating how strongly it believes the input value will contribute to the model's predictions. We need to have a measurement of the strength of this signal, and that is what the weight does. It is a coefficient that is multiplied against the input value for the input layer, and previous value for subsequent layers.

Now, each one of these connections is like a vector on an x-y plane. Ideally, we want each of these vectors to cross the y-axis at the same central point (for example, the 0 origin). But they don't. To make the vectors relative to one another, the bias is the offset of each vector from the central point on the y-axis.

The weights and biases are what the neural network will "learn" during training. The weights and biases are also referred to as *parameters*. These values stay with the model after it is trained. This operation will otherwise be invisible to you.

2.1.7 *Dense layer*

In TF.Keras, layers in an FCNN are called *dense layers*. A dense layer has *n* number of nodes and is fully connected to the previous layer.

Let's continue by defining in TF.Keras a three-layer neural network, using the sequential API method, for our example. Our input layer has 10 nodes and takes as input a 13-element vector (the 13 features), which is connected to a second (hidden) layer of 10 nodes, which is then connected to a third (output) layer of one node. Our output layer needs to be only one node since it will be outputting a single real value (for example, the predicted price of the house). In this example, we are going to use a neural network as a *regressor*, which means the neural network will output a single real number:

Input layer = 10 nodes
Hidden layer = 10 nodes
Output layer = 1 node

For input and hidden layers, we can pick any number of nodes. The more nodes we have, the better the neural network can learn. But more nodes means more complexity, and more time in training and predicting.

In the following code example, we have three `add()` calls to the class object `Dense`. The `add()` method adds the layers in the same sequential order that we specified them. The first (positional) parameter is the number of nodes, 10 in the first and second layer, and 1 in the third layer. Notice that in the first `Dense` layer, we add the (keyword) parameter `input_shape`. This is where we will define the input vector and connect it to the first (input) layer in a single instantiation of the `Dense` layer:

```
from tensorflow.keras import Sequential
from tensorflow.keras.layers import Dense

model = Sequential()
model.add(Dense(10, input_shape=(13,)))
model.add(Dense(10))
model.add(Dense(1))
```

The first layer requires the input_shape parameter in a sequential model.

Constructs the hidden layer

Constructs the output layer as a regressor—single node

Alternatively, we can define the sequential sequence of the layers as a list parameter when instantiating the Sequential class object:

```
from tensorflow.keras import Sequential
from tensorflow.keras.layers import Dense

model = Sequential([
                Dense(10, input_shape=(13,)),
                Dense(10),
                Dense(1)
                ])
```

The layers are specified in sequential order as a list.

Let's now do the same but use the functional API method. First, we create an input vector by instantiating an Input class object. The (positional) parameter to the Input object is the shape of the input, which can be a vector, matrix, or tensor. In our example, we have a vector that is 13 elements long. So our shape is (13,). I am sure you noticed the trailing comma. That's to overcome a quirk in Python. Without the comma, (13) would be evaluated as an expression: the integer value 13 surrounded by parentheses. Adding a comma tells the interpreter this is a *tuple* (an ordered set of values).

Next, we create the input layer by instantiating a Dense class object. The positional parameter to the Dense object is the number of nodes, which in our example is 10. Note the peculiar syntax that follows: (inputs). The Dense object is a callable; the object returned by instantiating Dense can be callable as a function. So we call it as a function, and in this case, the function takes as a (positional) parameter the input vector (or layer output) to connect it to; hence we pass it inputs so the input vector is bound to the 10-node input layer.

Next, we create the hidden layer by instantiating another Dense object with 10 nodes. Using it as a callable, we (fully) connect it to the input layer.

Then we create the output layer by instantiating another Dense object with one node. Using it as a callable, we (fully) connect it to the hidden layer.

Finally, we put it all together by instantiating a Model class object, passing it the (positional) parameters for the input vector and output layer. Remember, all the other layers between are already connected, so we don't need to specify them when instantiating the Model() object:

Constructs the input vector (13 elements)

```
from tensorflow.keras import Input, Model
from tensorflow.keras.layers import Dense

inputs = Input((13,))
input = Dense(10)(inputs)
hidden = Dense(10)(input)
output = Dense(1)(hidden)
model = Model(inputs, output)
```

Constructs the first (input) layer (10 nodes) and connects it to the input vector

Constructs the next (hidden) layer (10 nodes) and connects it to the input layer

Constructs the neural network, specifying the input and output layers

Constructs the output layer (1 node) and connects it to the previous (hidden) layer

2.1.8 *Activation functions*

When training or predicting (via inference), each node in a layer will output a value to the nodes in the next layer. We don't want to pass the value as-is, but instead sometimes want to change the value in a particular manner. This process is called an *activation function*.

Think of a function that returns a result, like return result. In the case of an activation function, instead of returning result, we would return the result of passing the result value to another (activation) function, like return A(result), where A() is the activation function. Conceptually, you can think of this as follows:

```
def layer(params):
    """ inside are the nodes """
    result = some_calculations
    return A(result)

def A(result):
    """ modifies the result """
    return some_modified_value_of_result
```

Activation functions assist neural networks in learning faster and better. By default, when no activation function is specified, the values from one layer are passed as-is (unchanged) to the next layer. The most basic activation function is a *step function*. If the value is greater than 0, a 1 is outputted; otherwise, a 0 is outputted. The step function hasn't been used in a long, long time.

Let's pause for a moment and discuss the purpose of an activation function. You likely have heard the term *nonlinearity*. What is this? To me, more importantly, what is it not?

In traditional statistics, we worked in low-dimensional space with a strong linear correlation between the input and output. This correlation could be computed as a polynomial transformation of the input that, when transformed, had a linear correlation to the output. The most fundamental example is the slope of a line, which is represented as $y = mx + b$. In this case, x and y are coordinates of the line, and we want to fit the value of m, the slope, and b, where the line intercepts the y-axis.

In deep learning, we work in high-dimensional space with substantial nonlinearity between the input and output. This nonlinearity means that an input is not uniformly related to (not near) an output based on a polynomial transformation of the input. For example, let's say property tax is a fixed percentage rate (r) of the house value. The property tax can be represented by a function that multiplies the rate by the house value. Thus we have a linear (straight-line) relationship between the value (input) and property tax (output):

$$\text{tax} = f(value) = r \times value$$

Let's look at the logarithmic scale for measuring earthquakes, in which an increase of 1 means the power released is 10 times greater. For example, an earthquake of 4 is 10 times stronger than a 3. By applying a logarithmic transform to the input power, we have a linear relationship between power and scale:

$$\text{scale} = f(power) = \log(power)$$

In a nonlinear relationship, sequences within the input have different linear relationships to the output, and in deep learning we want to learn the separation points as well as the linear functions for each input sequence. For example, consider age versus income to demonstrate a nonlinear relationship. In general, toddlers have no income, elementary-school children have an allowance, early teens earn an allowance plus money for chores, later teens earn money from jobs, and then when they go to college, their income drops to zero! After college, their income gradually increases until retirement, when it becomes fixed. We could model this nonlinearity as sequences across age and learn a linear function for each sequence, as depicted here:

income = F1(age) = 0   for age [0..5]
income = F2(age) = c1   for age [6..9]
income = F3(age) = c1 + (w1 × age)   for age [10..15]
income = F4(age) = (w2 × age)   for age [16..18]
income = F5(age) = 0   for age [19..22]
income = F6(age) = (w3 × age)   for age [23..64]
income = F7(age) = c2   for age [65+]

Activation functions assist in finding the nonlinear separations and corresponding clustering of nodes within input sequences, which then learn the (near) linear relationship to the output. Most of the time, you will use three activation functions: the rectified linear unit (ReLU), sigmoid, and softmax.

We will start with the ReLU, since it is the one that is most used in all but the output layer of a model. The sigmoid and softmax activations are covered in sections 2.2 and 2.3. The ReLU, depicted in figure 2.4, passes values greater than zero as-is (unchanged); otherwise, it passes zero (no signal).

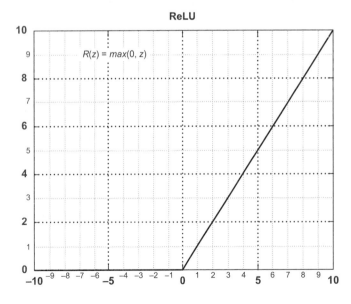

Figure 2.4 **The function for a rectified linear unit clips all negative values to zero. In essence, any negative value is the same as no signal, or ~ zero.**

The ReLU is generally used between layers. While early researchers used different activation functions (such as a hyperbolic tangent) between layers, researchers found that the ReLU produced the best result in training a model. In our example, we will add a ReLU between each layer:

```
from tensorflow.keras import Sequential
from tensorflow.keras.layers import Dense, ReLU

model = Sequential()
model.add(Dense(10, input_shape=(13,)))
model.add(ReLU())          ◁───┐  Convention is to add ReLU activation
model.add(Dense(10))           │  to each non-output layer
model.add(ReLU())          ◁───┘
model.add(Dense(1))
```

Let's take a look inside our model object to see if we constructed what we think we did. You can do this by using the `summary()` method. This method is useful for visualizing the layers you constructed and verifying that what you intended to build is what you actually built. It will show in sequential order a summary of each layer:

```
model.summary()
Layer (type)                 Output Shape              Param #
=================================================================
dense_56 (Dense)             (None, 10)                140

re_lu_18 (ReLU)              (None, 10)                0

dense_57 (Dense)             (None, 10)                110

re_lu_19 (ReLU)              (None, 10)                0

dense_58 (Dense)             (None, 1)                 11
=================================================================
Total params: 261
Trainable params: 261
Non-trainable params: 0
```

For this code example, you see that the summary starts with a dense layer of 10 nodes (input layer), followed by a ReLU activation function, followed by a second dense layer (hidden) of 10 nodes, followed by a ReLU activation function, and finally followed by a dense layer (output) of 1 node. So, yes, we got what we expected.

Next, let's look at the parameter field in the summary. The input layer shows 140 parameters. How is that calculated? We have 13 inputs and 10 nodes, so 13×10 is 130. Where does 140 come from? Each connection between the inputs and each node has a weight, which adds up to 130. But each node has an additional bias. That's 10 nodes, so $130 + 10 = 140$. As I've said, it's the weights and biases that the neural network will "learn" during training. A *bias* is a learned offset, conceptually equivalent to the y-intercept (b) in the slope of a line, which is where the line intercepts the y-axis:

$y = b + mx$

At the next (hidden) layer, you see 110 parameters. That's 10 outputs from the input layer connected to each of the 10 nodes from the hidden layer (10 × 10) plus the 10 biases for the nodes in the hidden layers, for a total of 110 parameters to learn.

2.1.9   *Shorthand syntax*

TF.Keras provides a shorthand syntax when specifying layers. You don't actually need to separately specify activation functions between layers, as we did in the previous example. Instead, you can specify the activation function as a (keyword) parameter when instantiating a Dense layer.

You might ask, why not always use the shorthand syntax? As you will see in chapter 3, in today's model architecture, the activation function is preceded by another intermediate layer (batch normalization) or precedes the layer altogether (pre-activation batch normalization). The following code example does exactly the same thing as the previous one:

```
from tensorflow.keras import Sequential
from tensorflow.keras.layers import Dense

model = Sequential()
model.add(Dense(10, input_shape=(13,), activation='relu'))
model.add(Dense(10, activation='relu'))
model.add(Dense(1))
```

> The activation function is specified as a keyword parameter in the layer.

Let's call the summary() method on this model:

```
model.summary()
Layer (type)                    Output Shape                    Param #
=================================================================
dense_1 (Dense)                 (None, 10)                      140
_____
dense_2 (Dense)                 (None, 10)                      110
_____
dense_3 (Dense)                 (None, 1)                       11
=================================================================
Total params: 261
Trainable params: 261
Non-trainable params: 0
_____
```

Hmm, you don't see the activations between the layers as you did in the earlier example. Why not? It's a quirk in the way the summary() method displays output. They are still there.

2.1.10   *Improving accuracy with an optimizer*

Once you've completed building the feed-forward portion of your neural network, as we have for our simple example, you need to add a few things for training the model. This is done with the compile() method. This step adds the *backward propagation* during training. Let's define and explore this concept.

Each time we send data (or a batch of data) forward through the neural network, it calculates the errors in the predicted results (known as the *loss*) from the actual values (called *labels*) and uses that information to incrementally adjust the weights and biases of the nodes. This, for a model, is the process of learning.

The calculation of the error, as I've said, is called a *loss*. It can be calculated in many ways. Since we designed our example neural network to be a *regressor* (meaning that the output, house price, is a real value), we want to use a loss function that is best suited for a regressor. Generally, for this type of neural network, we use the *mean square error* method of calculating a loss. In Keras, the `compile()` method takes a (keyword) parameter `loss` used to specify how we want to calculate the loss. We are going to pass it the value `mse` (for *mean square error*).

The next step in the process is minimizing the loss with an optimizer that occurs during backward propagation. The optimizer is based on *gradient descent*; different variations of the *gradient descent algorithm* can be selected. These terms can be hard to understand at first. Essentially, each time we pass data through the neural network, we use the calculated loss to decide how much to change the weights and biases in the layers. The goal is to gradually get closer and closer to the correct values for the weights and biases, to accurately predict or estimate the label for each example. This process of progressively getting closer and closer to the accurate values is called *convergence*. The job of the optimizer is to calculate the updates to the weights to progressively get closer to the accurate values to reach convergence.

As the loss gradually decreases, we are *converging*. After the loss plateaus out, we have *convergence*. The result is the accuracy of the neural network. Before using gradient descent, the methods used by early AI researchers could take years on a supercomputer to find convergence on a nontrivial problem. After the discovery of using the gradient descent algorithm, this time was reduced to days, hours, and even just minutes on ordinary computing power. Let's skip the math and just say that gradient descent is the data scientist's pixie dust that makes converging on a good local optimum possible.

For our regressor neural network, we will use the `rmsprop` method (*root mean square property*):

```
model.compile(loss='mse', optimizer='rmsprop')
```

Now we have completed building your first trainable neural network. Before embarking on preparing data and training the model, we will cover several more neural network designs. These designs use the two other activation functions I mentioned earlier: sigmoid and softmax.

2.2 DNN binary classifier

Another form of a DNN is a *binary classifier*, also known as a *logistic classifier*. When we use a binary classifier, we want the neural network to predict whether the input is or is not something. The output can have two states or classes: yes/no, true/false, 0/1, and so forth.

For example, let's say we have a dataset of credit card transactions, and each transaction is labeled as fraudulent or not fraudulent. Remember, the label is what we want to predict.

Overall, the design approach we've learned so far doesn't change, with the exception of the activation function of the single-node output layer and the loss/optimizer method. Instead of using a *linear* activation function, as for a regressor, we will use a *sigmoid* activation function on the output node. The sigmoid squashes all values so they are between 0 and 1, as shown in figure 2.5. As values move away from the center, they quickly move to the extremes of 0 and 1 (the asymptotes).

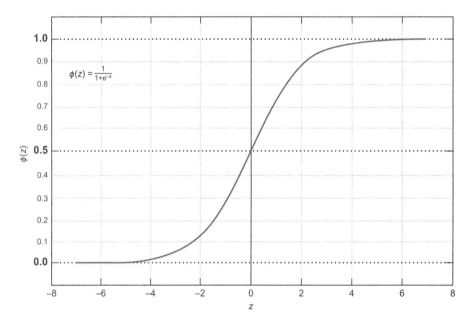

Figure 2.5   The function for a sigmoid

We will now code this in the two styles we've discussed. Let's start with our previous code example, in which we specify the activation function as a (keyword) parameter. In this example, we add to the output `Dense` layer the parameter `activation='sigmoid'` to pass the output result from the final node through a sigmoid function.

Next, we change our loss parameter to `binary_crossentropy`. This is the loss function that is generally used in a binary classifier:

```
from tensorflow.keras import Sequential
from tensorflow.keras.layers import Dense

model = Sequential()
model.add(Dense(10, input_shape=(13,), activation='relu'))
model.add(Dense(10, activation='relu'))
model.add(Dense(1, activation='sigmoid'))
```

A sigmoid is used for a binary classification.

```
model.compile(loss='binary_crossentropy',
              optimizer='rmsprop',                    Common convention for loss and
              metrics=['accuracy'])                   optimizer for binary classifier
```

Not all activation functions have their own class, like `ReLU`. This is another quirk in the TF.Keras framework. Instead, a class called `Activation` creates any of the supported activations. The parameter is the predefined name of the activation function. In our example, `relu` is for the rectified linear unit, and `sigmoid` is for the sigmoid. The following code does the same as the preceding code:

```
from tensorflow.keras import Sequential
from tensorflow.keras.layers import Dense, Activation

model = Sequential()
model.add(Dense(10, input_shape=(13,)))
model.add(Activation('relu'))
model.add(Dense(10))                        Activations can be
model.add(Activation('relu'))               specified using the
model.add(Dense(1))                         Activation() method.
model.add(Activation('sigmoid'))

model.compile(loss='binary_crossentropy',
              optimizer='rmsprop',
              metrics=['accuracy'])
```

Now we will rewrite the same code using the functional API approach. Notice that we repeatedly used the variable x. This is a common practice. We want to avoid creating lots of one-time-use variables. Since we know that in this type of neural network, the output of every layer is the input to the next layer (or activation), except for the input and output, we continuously use x as the connecting variable.

By now, you should start becoming familiar with the two approaches:

```
from tensorflow.keras import Model, Input
from tensorflow.keras.layers import Dense, ReLU, Activation

inputs = Input((13,))
x = Dense(10)(inputs)
x = Activation('relu')(x)
x = Dense(10)(x)
x = Activation('relu')(x)                    Activations specified
x = Dense(1)(x)                              using functional API
output = Activation('sigmoid')(x)
model = Model(inputs, output)

model.compile(loss='binary_crossentropy',
              optimizer='rmsprop',
              metrics=['accuracy'])
```

2.3 *DNN multiclass classifier*

Let's say we have a set of body measurements (height and weight, for instance) and the gender associated with each set of measurements, and we want to predict whether someone is a baby, toddler, preteen, teenager, or adult. We want our model to classify, or predict, from more than one class or label—in this example, we have a total of five classes of age categories. To do this, we can use another form of a DNN, called a *multiclass classifier*.

We can already see we will have some complications. For example, men on average as adults are taller than women. But during the preteen years, girls tend to be taller than boys. We know on average that men get heavier early in their adult years in comparison to their teenage years, but women on average are less likely to become heavier. So we should anticipate problems in predicting around the preteen years for girls, teenage years for boys, and adult years for women.

These problems are examples of *nonlinearity*; the relationship between a feature and a prediction is not linear. Instead, the relationship can be broken into segments of disjointed linearity. This is the type of problem neural networks are good at.

Let's add a fourth measurement, the nose surface area. Studies such as one from the *Annals of Plastic Surgery* (https://pubmed.ncbi.nlm.nih.gov/3579170/) have shown that for both girls and boys, the surface area of the nose continues to grow from ages 6 to 18 and essentially stops at 18.

So now we have four features, and a label that consists of five classes. We will change our input vector in the next example to 4, to match the number of features, and change our output layer to 5 nodes, to match the number of classes. In this case, each output node corresponds to one unique class (baby, toddler, and so forth). We want to train the neural network so each output node outputs a value between 0 and 1 as a prediction. For example, 0.75 would mean that the node is 75% confident that the prediction is the corresponding class.

Each output node will independently learn and predict its confidence on whether the input is the corresponding class. This process leads to a problem, however: because the values are independent, they won't add up to 1 (100%). This is where the *softmax* function is useful. This mathematical function will take a set of values (the outputs from the output layer) and squash them into a range from 0 to 1 while also ensuring that all the values add up to 1. Perfect. This way, we can take the output node with the highest value and say what is predicted as well as the confidence level in that prediction. So if the highest value is 0.97, we can say we estimated the confidence at 97% in our prediction.

Figure 2.6 is a diagram of a multiclass model. In this example, the output layer has two nodes, each corresponding to predicting a different class. Each node makes an independent prediction of how strongly it believes that the input is the corresponding class. The two independent predictions are then passed through a softmax activation, which squashes the values to add up to 1 (100%). In this example, one class is predicted at 97%, and the other at 3% confidence level.

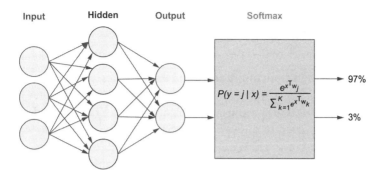

Figure 2.6 Adding softmax activation to the output layer for a multiclass classifier helps improve the confidence level in the model's prediction.

The following code shows an example of constructing a multiclass classifier DNN. We start by setting up our input and output layers with the multiple features and multiple classes, respectively. Then we change the activation function from `sigmoid` to `softmax`. Next we set our loss function to `categorical_crossentropy`. This is generally the most recommended for a multiclass classification. We won't go deep into the statistics behind cross-entropy, other than cross-entropy computes a loss from multiple probability distributions. In a binary classifier, we have two probability distributions and use the `binary_crossentropy` calculation; and in a multiclass classifier, we use `categorical_crossentropy` for calculating the loss from multiple (more than two) probability distributions.

Finally, we will use a popular and widely used variant of gradient descent called the *Adam optimizer* (adam). *Adam* incorporates several aspects of other methods, such as rmsprop (*root mean square*) and `adagrad` (*adaptive gradient*), along with an adaptive learning rate. It's generally considered the best-in-class optimizer for a wide variety of neural networks:

```
from tensorflow.keras import Sequential
from tensorflow.keras.layers import Dense

model = Sequential()
model.add(Dense(10, input_shape=(4,), activation='relu'))
model.add(Dense(10, activation='relu'))
model.add(Dense(5, activation='softmax'))

model.compile(loss='categorical_crossentropy',
        optimizer='adam',
        metrics=['accuracy'])
```

The input layer for an input shape of 1D vector of four features

In the output layer, a softmax activation is used for a multiclass classifier.

Common conventions for the loss function and optimizer for a multiclass classifier

2.4 *DNN multilabel multiclass classifier*

Now let's look at predicting two or more classes (labels) per input. Let's use our previous example of predicting whether someone is a baby, toddler, preteen, teenager, or adult. This time, we will remove gender from one of the features and instead make it one of the labels to predict. Our input will be the height, weight, and nose surface area, and our outputs will be two classes: age category (baby, toddler, etc.) and gender (male or female). An example prediction might look like this:

[height, weight, nose surface area] -> neural network -> [preteen, female]

To predict two or more labels from multiple inputs, as we do here, we use—you guessed it—a *multilabel multiclass classifier.* To do this, we need to make a few changes from our previous multiclass classifier. On our output layer, our number of output classes is the sum of all the output categories. In this case, we previously had five and now we add two more for gender, for a total of seven. We also want to treat each output class as a binary classifier, meaning we want a yes/no type of answer, so we change the activation function to `sigmoid`. For our compile statement, we mimic what we've done with simpler DNNs in this chapter, and set the loss function to `binary_crossentropy`, and the optimizer to `rmsprop`. You can see the implementation of each step here:

```
from tensorflow.keras import Sequential
from tensorflow.keras.layers import Dense

model = Sequential()
model.add(Dense(10, input_shape=(3,), activation='relu'))
model.add(Dense(10, activation='relu'))
model.add(Dense(7, activation='sigmoid'))

model.compile(loss='binary_crossentropy',
        optimizer='rmsprop',
        metrics=['accuracy'])
```

Input vector is just the height, weight, and nose surface area

Both age demographic and gender categories combined into one classifier output

Uses a sigmoid activation with binary_crossentropy loss function to independently predict each class as either, or close to, 0 or 1.

Do you see a potential problem with this design? Let's assume we output the two classes (labels) with the highest values (from 0 to 1); that is, the most confident predictions. What if, on a prediction, the neural network predicts both preteen and teenager with high confidence, and both male and female with lower confidence? Well, we could fix this with some post-logic by selecting the highest confidence from the first five output classes (age demographic), and selecting the highest confidence from the last two classes (gender). In other words, we separate the seven output classes into the two corresponding categories, and from each category we select the output with the highest confidence level.

The functional API gives us the ability to fix this without adding any post-logic. In this case, we want to replace the output layer, which combines the two sets of classes, with *two parallel output layers*, one for the first set of classes (age categories) and one for the second set of classes (gender). You can see this setup in figure 2.7.

In the following code example, only the final output layer differs from the previous code listing. Here, instead of a single output layer, we have the two parallel layers.

Then when we put it all together with the `Model` class, instead of passing in a single output layer, we pass in a list of output layers: [output1, output2]. Finally, since each

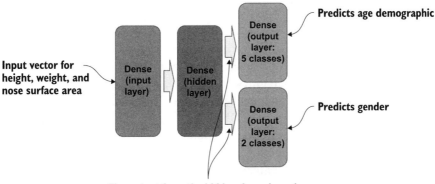

The output from the hidden dense layer is copied to both parallel output layers (reused).

Figure 2.7 Output layers of a multilabel multiclassifier with two parallel output layers

output layer makes independent predictions, we can return to treating them as a *multiclass classifier*—meaning we return to using `categorical_crossentropy` as the loss function and `adam` as the optimizer.

This design of a multilabel multiclassifier can also be referred to as a *neural network with multiple outputs*, in which each output learns a different task. Since we will be training this model to do multiple independent predictions, this is also known as a *multitask* model:

```
from tensorflow.keras import Input, Model
from tensorflow.keras.layers import Dense

inputs = Input((3,))
x = Dense(10, activation='relu')(inputs)
x = Dense(10, activation='relu')(x)
output1 = Dense(5, activation='softmax')(x)
output2 = Dense(2, activation='softmax')(x)
model = Model(inputs, [output1, output2])

model.compile(loss='categorical_crossentropy',
        optimizer='adam',
        metrics=['accuracy'])
```

> Each of the two categories has a separate output layer and gets a copy of the same input.

So which design is correct (or better) for a multilabel multiclass classifier? It depends on the application. If all the classes are from a single category—such as age demographic—use the first pattern, the single task. If the classes come from different categories—such as age demographic and gender—use the second pattern, the multitask. In this example, we use the multitask pattern, because we want to learn two categories as output.

2.5   *Simple image classifier*

You've now seen the basic types of DNNs and how to code them with TF.Keras. So now let's build our first simple model for image classification.

Neural networks are used for image classification throughout computer vision. Let's start with the basics. For small grayscale images, as depicted in figure 2.8, we can use a DNN similar to that we have already described for the multiclass classifier for predicting the age demographic. This type of DNN has been widely published using the Modified National Institute of Standards and Technology (MNIST) dataset, which is a dataset for recognizing handwritten digits. The dataset consists of grayscale images of size 28 × 28 pixels. Each pixel is represented by an integer value from 0 to 255 (0 is black, 255 is white, and values between are shades of gray).

We need to make one change, though. A grayscale image is a *matrix* (2D array). Think of a matrix as a grid, of size height × width, where the width represents the columns and the height represents the rows. A DNN, though, takes as input a *vector*, which is a 1D array. So what can we do? We can *flatten* the two-dimensional matrix into a one-dimensional vector.

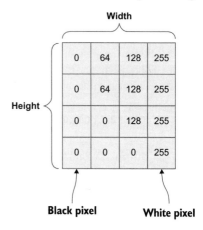

Figure 2.8   Matrix representation of a grayscale image

2.5.1   *Flattening*

We are going to do classification by treating each pixel as a feature. Using the example of the MNIST dataset, the 28 × 28 images will have 784 pixels, and thus 784 features. We convert the matrix (2D) into a vector (1D) by flattening it.

Flattening is the process of placing each row in sequential order into a vector. So the vector starts with the first row of pixels, followed by the second row of pixels, and continues by ending with the last row of pixels. Figure 2.9 depicts flattening a matrix into a vector.

Figure 2.9   A matrix flattened into a vector

You might be asking at this point, why do we need to flatten the 2D matrix into a 1D vector? It's because in a DNN, the input to a dense layer must be a 1D vector. In the next chapter, when we introduce CNNs, you will see examples of convolutional layers that take 2D input.

In the next example, we add a layer at the beginning of our neural network to flatten the input, using the class `Flatten`. The remaining layers and activations are typical for the MNIST dataset. Note that the input shape to the `Flatten` object is the 2D shape (28, 28). The output from this object will be a 1D shape of (784,):

The 2D grayscale image is flattened into a 1D vector for input to the DNN.

```
from tensorflow.keras import Sequential
from tensorflow.keras.layers import Dense, Flatten, ReLU, Activation

model = Sequential()
model.add(Flatten(input_shape=(28,28)))
model.add(Dense(512, activation='relu'))
model.add(Dense(512, activation='relu'))
model.add(Dense(10, activation='softmax'))

model.compile(loss='categorical_crossentropy',
              optimizer='adam',
              metrics=['accuracy'])
```

MNIST is typically done as an input and one hidden dense layer between 128, 256, and 512 nodes.

Let's now look at the layers by using the `summary()` method. As you can see, the first layer in the summary is the flattened layer and shows that the output from the layer is 784 nodes. That's what we want. Also notice how many parameters the network will need to learn during training, nearly 700,000:

```
model.summary()
Layer (type)                 Output Shape              Param #
=================================================================
flatten_1 (Flatten)          (None, 784)               0

dense_69 (Dense)             (None, 512)               401920

re_lu_20 (ReLU)              (None, 512)               0

dense_70 (Dense)             (None, 512)               262656

re_lu_21 (ReLU)              (None, 512)               0

dense_71 (Dense)             (None, 10)                5130

activation_10 (Activation)   (None, 10)                0
=================================================================
Total params: 669,706
Trainable params: 669,706
Non-trainable params: 0
```

2.5.2 Overfitting and dropout

During training, a dataset is split into training data and test data (also known as *hold-out data*). Only the training data is used during the training of the neural network. Once the neural network has reached convergence, which we discuss in detail in chapter 4, training stops, as shown in figure 2.10.

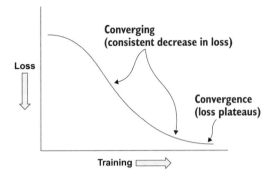

Figure 2.10   Convergence happens when the slope of the loss plateaus.

Afterward, to obtain the accuracy of the model on the training data, the training data is forward-fed again without backward propagation enabled, so there is no learning. This is also known as running the trained neural network in *inference* or *prediction mode*. In a train/test split, the test data, which has been set aside and not used as part of training, is forward-fed again without backward propagation enabled to obtain an accuracy.

Why do we split and hold out the test data from training? Ideally, the accuracy on the training data and the test data will be nearly identical. In reality, the test data will always be a little less. There is a reason for this.

Once you reach convergence, continually passing the training data through the neural network will cause the neurons to more and more memorize the training samples versus generalizing to samples that are never seen during training. This is known as *overfitting*. When the neural network is overfitted to the training data, you will get high training accuracy, but substantially lower accuracy on the test/evaluation data.

Even without training past the convergence, you will have some overfitting. The dataset/problem is likely to have nonlinearity (hence why you're using a neural network). As such, the individual neurons will converge at an unequal rate. When measuring convergence, you're looking at the overall system. Prior to that, some neurons have already converged, and the continued training will cause them to overfit. This is why the test/evaluation accuracy will always be at least a bit less than the accuracy of the training data.

To address overfitting when training neural networks, we can use *regularization*. This adds small amounts of random noise during training to prevent the model from memorizing samples and better generalize to unseen samples after the model is trained.

The most basic type of regularization is called *dropout*. Dropout is like forgetting. When we teach young children, we use rote memorization, as when we ask them to memorize the multiplication table of numbers 1 through 12. We have them iterate, iterate, iterate, until they can recite in any order the correct answer 100% of the time. But if we ask them "What is 13 times 13?" they will likely give us a blank look. At this point, the times table is overfitted in their memory. The answer to each multiplication pair, the samples, is hardwired in the brain's memory cells, and they don't have a way to transfer that knowledge beyond 1 through 12.

As children get older, we switch to abstraction. Instead of teaching a child to memorize the answers, we teach them how to compute the answer—albeit they may make computation mistakes. During this second teaching phase, some neurons related to the rote memorization will die. The combination of the death of those neurons (which means forgetting) and abstraction allows the child's brain to generalize and now solve arbitrary multiplication problems, though at times they will make a mistake, even at times in the 12×12 times table, with some probabilistic distribution.

The dropout technique in neural networks mimics this process of moving to abstraction, and learning, with probabilistic distribution of uncertainty. Between any layer, you can add a dropout layer, where you specify a percentage (between 0 and 1) to forget. The nodes themselves won't be dropped, but instead a random selection on each forward feed during training will not pass a signal forward. The signal from the randomly selected node will be forgotten. So, for example, if you specify a dropout of 50% (0.5), on each forward feed of data, a random selection of half of the nodes will not send a signal.

The advantage here is that we minimize the effect of localized overfitting while continuously training the neural network for overall convergence. A common practice for dropout is setting values between 20% and 50%.

In the following code example, we've added a 50% dropout to the input and hidden layers. Notice that we placed it before the activation (ReLU) function. Since dropout will cause the signal from the node, when dropped out, to be zero, it doesn't matter whether you add the Dropout layer before or after the activation function:

```
from tensorflow.keras import Sequential
from tensorflow.keras.layers import Dense, Flatten, ReLU, Activation, Dropout

model = Sequential()
model.add(Flatten(input_shape=(28,28)))
model.add(Dense(512))
model.add(Dropout(0.5))      ◁─┐
model.add(ReLU())               │   Dropout is added to
                                │   prevent overfitting.
model.add(Dense(512))           │
model.add(Dropout(0.5))      ◁─┘
model.add(ReLU())

model.add(Dense(10))
model.add(Activation('softmax'))

model.compile(loss='categorical_crossentropy',
              optimizer='adam',
              metrics=['accuracy'])
```

Summary

- The neural network's input and input layer are not the same thing and do not need to be the same size. The input is the features of the samples, while the input layer is the first layer of weights and biases to learn to predict the corresponding label.
- A deep neural network has one or more layers between the input and output layers, which are called hidden layers. Using a programming function as an analogy, the input layer is the parameters to the function, the output layer is the return value from the function, and the hidden layers are the code within the function that transform the input parameters to an output return value.
- Neural networks are directed acyclic graphs, in that data is fed forward from the input layer to the output layer.
- Activations, like ReLU and softmax, squash the output signals of layers, which researchers found help models learn better.
- The role of the optimizer is to update weights from the current batch loss so that the loss on subsequent batches gets smaller.
- A regressor uses a linear activation to predict a continuous real value, like predicting the sale price of a house.
- A binary classifier uses a sigmoid activation to predict a binary state: true/false, 1/0, yes/no.
- A multiclass classifier uses a softmax activation to predict a class from a set of classes, like predicting the age demographic of a person.
- The sequential API is easy to get started but limited in that it does not support branching in the model.
- The functional API is preferred over the sequential API for production models.
- Overfitting occurs when the model memorizes training samples during training, which prevents the model from generalizing to samples it was not trained on. Regularization methods inject small amounts of random noise during training, which has shown to be effective in preventing memorization.

Convolutional and residual neural networks

3

This chapter covers

- Understanding the structure of convolutional neural networks
- Constructing a ConvNet model
- Designing and constructing a VGG model
- Designing and constructing a residual network model

Chapter 2 introduced the fundamentals behind deep neural networks (DNNs), a network architecture based on dense layers. We also demonstrated how to make a simple image classifier using dense layers, and discussed the limitations when attempting to scale a DNN to larger sizes of images. The introduction of neural networks using convolutional layers for feature extraction and learning, known as *convolutional neural networks* (CNNs), made it possible to scale image classifiers for practical applications.

This chapter covers the design patterns, and evolution in the design patterns, for early SOTA convolutional neural networks. We cover three design patterns in this chapter, in sequence of their evolution:

- ConvNet
- VGG
- Residual networks

Each of these design patterns made contributions toward today's modern CNN designs. ConvNet, with AlexNet as an early example, introduced a pattern of alternating feature extraction and dimensionality reduction through pooling, and sequentially increasing the number of filters as we went deeper in layers. VGG introduced grouping convolutions into blocks of one or more convolutions and delaying dimensionality reduction with pooling until the end of the block. Residual networks introduced further grouping blocks into groups, delaying dimensionality reduction to the end of the group, and using feature pooling as well as pooling for the reduction, as well as the concept of branched paths—the identity link—for feature reuse between blocks.

3.1   *Convolutional neural networks*

Early convolutional neural networks are a type of neural network that can be viewed as consisting of two parts, a frontend and a backend. The backend is a DNN, which we have already covered. The name *convolutional neural network* comes from the frontend, referred to as a *convolutional layer*. The frontend acts as a preprocessor. The DNN backend does the *classification learning*. The CNN frontend preprocesses the image data into a form that is computationally practical for the DNN to learn from. The CNN frontend does the *feature learning*.

Figure 3.1 depicts a CNN in which the convolutional layers act as a frontend for learning features from the image, which is then passed to a backend DNN for classification from the features.

This section covers the basic steps and components in assembling these earlier CNNs. While we do not specifically cover AlexNet, its success as the 2012 ILSVCR winner for

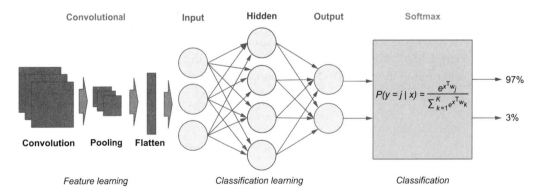

Figure 3.1   A convolution acts as a frontend to a deep neural network to learn features instead of pixels.

image classification can be considered the catalyst for researchers to explore and develop convolutional designs. The assembly and design principles of the frontend of AlexNet were incorporated into the earliest design pattern, ConvNet, for practical application.

3.1.1 *Why we use a CNN over a DNN for image models*

Once we get to larger image sizes, the number of pixels for a DNN becomes computationally too expensive to be feasible. Presume you have a 1 MB image, in which each pixel is represented by a single byte (0..255 value). At 1 MB, you have 1 million pixels. That would require an input vector of 1 million elements. And let's assume that the input layer has 1024 nodes. The number of weights to *update and learn* would be over a billion (1 million × 1024) at just the input layer! Yikes. Back to a supercomputer and a lifetime of computing power.

Let's contrast this to our Chapter 2 MNIST example of 784 pixels × 512 nodes on our input layer. That's 400,000 weights to learn, which is considerably smaller than 1 billion. You can do the former on your laptop, but don't dare try the latter.

In the following subsections, we will look at how the components of CNNs networks solve the problem of what would otherwise have been a computational impractical number of weights, also referred to as *parameters*, for image classification.

3.1.2 *Downsampling (resizing)*

To solve the problem of having too many parameters, one approach is to reduce the resolution of the image through a process called *downsampling*. But if we reduce the image resolution too far, at some point we may lose the ability to clearly distinguish what's in the image; it becomes fuzzy and/or has artifacts. So, the first step is to reduce the resolution down to a level that we still have enough details.

A common convention for everyday computer vision is around 224 × 224 pixels. We do this by resizing. Even at this lower resolution and three channels for color images, and an input layer of 1024 nodes, we still have 154 million weights to update and learn (224 × 224 × 3 × 1024); see figure 3.2.

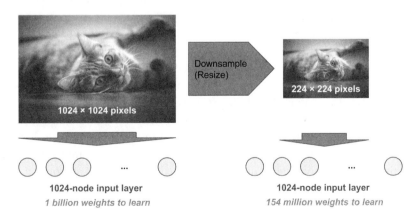

Figure 3.2 Number of parameters at the input layer before and after resizing (image source: Pixabay, Stockvault)

So training on real-world images was out of reach with neural networks until the introduction of using convolutional layers. To begin with, a convolutional layer is a frontend to a neural network, which transforms the images from a high-dimensional pixel-based image to a substantially lower-dimensionality feature-based image. The substantially lower-dimensionality features can then be the input vector to a DNN. Thus, a convolutional frontend is a frontend between the image data and the DNN.

But let's say we have enough computational power to use just a DNN and learn 154 million weights at the input layer, as in our preceding example. Well, the pixels are very position-dependent on the input layer. So we learn to recognize a cat on the left side of the picture. But then we shift the cat to the middle of the picture. Now we have to learn to recognize a cat from a new set of pixel positions—wah! Now move it to the right, add the cat lying down, jumping in the air, and so forth.

Learning to recognize an image from various perspectives is referred to as *translational invariance*. For basic 2D renderings like digits and letters, this works (brute-force), but for everything else, it's not going to work. Early research showed that when you flattened the initial image into a 1D vector, you lost the spatial relationship of the features that make up the object being classified, like a cat. Even if you successfully trained a DNN to, say, recognize a cat, based on pixels, in the middle of the picture, that DNN is unlikely to recognize the object if it is shifted in the image.

Next, we will discuss how convolutions learn features instead of pixels, along with retaining the 2D shape for spatial relationships, which solved this problem.

3.1.3   *Feature detection*

For these higher-resolution and more-complex images, we perform recognition by detecting and classifying *features* instead of classifying pixel positions. Visualize an image, and ask yourself what makes you recognize what's there? Go beyond the high level of asking, "Is that a person, a cat, or a building?" to ask why you can distinguish a person from the building they're standing in front of, or separate a person from the cat they're holding. Your eyes are recognizing low-level features, such as edges, blurs, and contrast.

As depicted in figure 3.3, these low-level features are built up into contours and then spatial relationships. Suddenly, the eye/brain has the ability to recognize nose, ears, eyes—and perceive that's a cat face, or that's a human face.

In a computer, a *convolutional layer* performs the task of feature detection within an image. Each convolution consists of a set of filters. These filters are $N \times M$ matrices of values that are used to detect the likely presence of a feature. Think of them as little windows. They are slid across the image, and at each location, a comparison is made between the filter and the pixel values at that location. That comparison is done with a matrix dot product, but we will skip the statistics here. What's important is that the result of this operation will generate a value that indicates how strongly the feature was detected at that location in the image. For example, a value of 4 would indicate a stronger presence of the feature than the value of 1.

Prior to neural networks, imaging scientists hand-designed these filters. Today, the filters, along with the weights in the neural network, are *learned*. In a convolutional

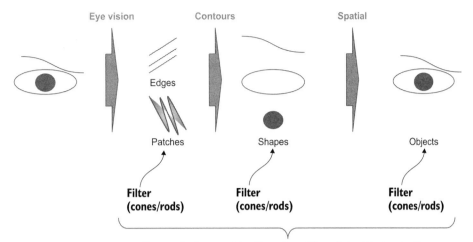

Progressively assembles items from filters into objects, starting with primitives such as edges and patches, then assembles into shapes using contours, and then assembles shapes into objects

Figure 3.3 Flow of the human eye's recognition of low-level features to high-level features

layer, we specify the size of the filter and the number of filters. Typical filter sizes are 3 × 3 and 5 × 5, with 3 × 3 the most common. The number of filters varies more, but they are typically multiples of 16, such as 16, 32, or 64 for shallow CNNs, and 256, 512, and 1024 in deep CNNs.

Additionally, we specify a *stride*, which is the rate that the filter is slid across the image. For example, if the stride is 1, the filter advances 1 pixel at a time; thus the filter would partially overlap with the previous step in a 3 × 3 filter (and consequently so would a stride of 2). A stride of 3 has no overlap. The most common practice is to use strides of 1 and 2. Each filter that is *learned* produces a feature map, which is a mapping that indicates how strongly the feature is detected at a particular location in the image, as depicted in figure 3.4.

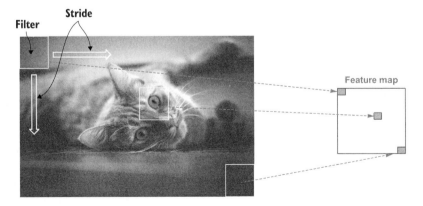

Figure 3.4 A filter is slid across an image to produce a feature map of detected features.

The filter can either stop when it gets to the edge of the image, or continue until the last column is covered, as shown in figure 3.5. The former case is called *no padding*. The latter case is called *padding*. When the filter goes partially over the edge, we want to give a value for these imaginary pixels. Typical values are zero or same—the same as the last column.

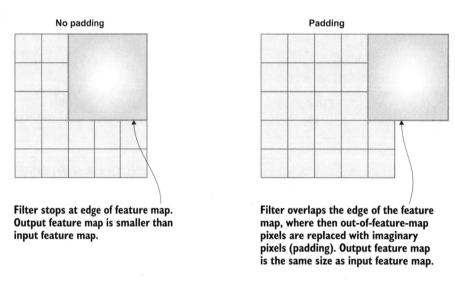

No padding

Padding

Filter stops at edge of feature map. Output feature map is smaller than input feature map.

Filter overlaps the edge of the feature map, where then out-of-feature-map pixels are replaced with imaginary pixels (padding). Output feature map is the same size as input feature map.

Figure 3.5   Where the filter stops depends on padding.

When you have multiple convolutional layers, a common practice is to either keep the same number or increase the number of filters on deeper layers, and to use a stride of 1 on the first layer and 2 on deeper layers. The increase in filters provides the means to go from coarse detection of features to more detailed detection within coarse features. The increase in stride offsets the increase in the size of retained data; this process is referred to as *feature pooling,* where the feature maps are downsampled.

CNNs use two types of downsampling: pooling and feature pooling. In *pooling*, a fixed algorithm is used to downsample the size of the image data. In *feature pooling*, the best downsampling algorithm for the specific dataset is learned:

More filters   => More data
Bigger strides => Less data

We'll look at pooling in more detail next. We'll delve into feature pooling in section 3.2.

3.1.4   *Pooling*

Even though each feature map that's generated is typically equal in size to or smaller than the image, the total amount of data increases because we generate multiple feature maps (for example, 16). Yikes! The next step is to reduce the total amount of data, while retaining the features detected and corresponding spatial relationships among the detected features.

As I've said, this step is referred to as *pooling*, which is the same as *downsampling* (or *subsampling*). In this process, the feature maps are resized to a smaller dimension using either the max (downsampling) or mean pixel average (subsampling) within the feature map. In pooling, as depicted in figure 3.6, we set the size of the area to pool as an $N \times M$ matrix as well as a stride. The common practice is a 2×2 pool size with a stride of 2. This will result in a 75% reduction in pixel data, while still preserving enough resolution that the detected features are not lost.

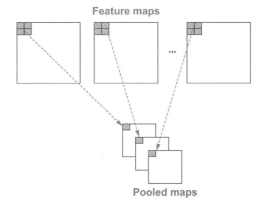

Figure 3.6   Pooling resizes feature maps to a smaller dimension.

Another way to look at pooling is in the context of information gain. By reducing unwanted or less-informative pixels (for example, from the background) we are reducing entropy and making the remaining pixels more informative.

3.1.5   *Flattening*

Recall that deep neural networks take vectors as input—one-dimensional arrays of numbers. In the case of the pooled maps, we have a list (plurality) of 2D matrices, so we need to transform them into a single 1D vector, which then becomes the input vector to the DNN. This process is called *flattening*: we flatten the list of 2D matrices into a single 1D vector.

It's pretty straightforward. We start with the first row of the first pooled map as the beginning of the 1D vector. We then take the second row and append it to the end, and then the third row, and so forth. We then proceed to the second pooled map and do the same, continuously appending each row until we've completed the last pooled map. As long as we follow the same sequencing through pooled maps, the spatial relationships among detected features will be maintained across images for training and inference (prediction), as depicted in figure 3.7.

For example, if we have 16 pooled maps of size 20×20 and three channels per pooled map (for example, RGB channels in a color image), our 1D vector size will be $16 \times 20 \times 20 \times 3 = 19,200$ elements.

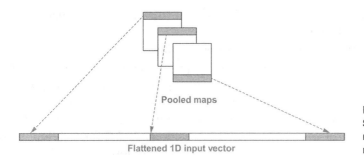

Pooled maps

Flattened 1D input vector

**Figure 3.7
Spatial relationships are
maintained when pooled
maps are flattened.**

3.2   *The ConvNet design for a CNN*

Let's get started now with TF.Keras. Let's assume a situation that's hypothetical but resembles the real world today. Your company's application supports human interfaces and currently can be accessed through voice activation. You've been tasked with developing a proof of concept to demonstrate expanding the human interface to include sign language in order to comply with federal accessibility laws. The relevant law, Section 503 of the Rehabilitation Act of 1973, "prohibits federal contractors and subcontractors from discriminating in employment against individuals with disabilities and requires employers take affirmative action to recruit, hire, promote, and retain these individuals" (https://www.dol.gov/agencies/ofccp/section-503).

What you should not do is assume that you can train the model by using arbitrary labeled sign-language images and image augmentation. The data, its preparation, and the design of the model must match the actual "in the wild" deployment. Otherwise, beyond resulting in disappointing accuracy, the model might learn noise, exposing it to false positives that could lead to unexpected consequences, and be vulnerable to hacking. Chapter 12 covers this in more detail.

For our proof of concept, we are going to show only recognizing hand signs for the letters of the English alphabet (A to Z). Additionally, we assume that the individual will be signing directly in front of the camera from a dead-on perspective. We don't want the model to learn, for example, the ethnicity of the hand signer. So for this and other reasons, color is not important.

To make our model not learn color (the noise), we will train it in grayscale mode. We will design the model to learn and predict, a process also referred to as *inference*, in grayscale. What we do want the model to learn are contours of the hand. We will design the model in two parts, the convolutional frontend and the DNN backend, as shown in figure 3.8.

The following code sample is written in the sequential API method and in long form; activation functions are specified using the corresponding method (instead of specifying them as a parameter when adding the corresponding layer).

We start by adding a convolutional layer of 16 filters as the first layer by using the Conv2D class object. Recall that the number of filters equals the number of feature maps that will be generated (in this case, 16). The size of each filter will be 3×3,

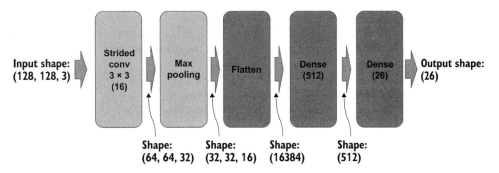

Figure 3.8 A ConvNet with a convolutional frontend and DNN backend

which is specified by the parameter `kernel_size`, and a stride of 2 by the parameter `strides`.

Note that for `strides`, a tuple of (2, 2) is specified instead of a single value 2. The first digit is the horizontal stride (across), and the second digit is the vertical stride (down). It's a common convention for these horizontal and vertical values to be the same; therefore, we commonly say a "stride of 2" instead of "a 2 × 2 stride."

You may ask, what's with the 2D part of the name `Conv2D`? The 2D means that input to the convolutional layer will be a stack of matrices (two-dimensional array). For this chapter, we will stick with 2D convolutionals, which are a common practice for computer vision.

Let's calculate what the output size will be from this layer. As you recall, at a stride of 1, each output feature map will be the same size as the image. With 16 filters, that would be 16 times the input. But since we used a stride of 2 (feature pooling), each feature map will be reduced by 75%, so the total output size will be 4 times the input.

The output from the convolutional layer is then passed through a ReLU activation function, which is then passed to the max pooling layer, using the `MaxPool2D` class object. The size of the pooling region will be 2 × 2, specified by the parameter `pool_size`, with a stride of 2 by the parameter `strides`. The pooling layer will reduce the feature maps by 75% into pooled feature maps.

Let's calculate the output size after the pooling layer. We know that the size coming in is 4 times the input. With an additional 75% reduction, the output size is the same as the input. So what have we gained here? First, we have trained a set of filters to learn a first set of coarse features (resulting in information gain), eliminated nonessential pixel information (reducing entropy), and learned the best method to downsample the feature maps. Hmm, seems we gained a lot.

The pooled feature maps are then flattened, using the `Flatten` class object, into a 1D vector for input into the DNN. We will glance over the parameter `padding`. It is sufficient for our purposes to say that in almost all cases, you will use the value `same`; it's just that the default is `valid`, and therefore you need to explicitly add it.

Finally, we pick an input size for our images. We like to reduce the size to as small as possible without losing detection of the features needed for recognizing the contours of the hand. In this case, we choose 128×128. The Conv2D class has a quirk: it always requires specifying the number of channels, instead of defaulting to 1 for grayscale; thus we specified it as (128, 128, 1) instead of (128, 128).

Here's the code:

Image data is inputted to a convolutional layer.

```
from tensorflow.keras.models import Sequential
from tensorflow.keras.layers import Dense, ReLU, Activation
from tensorflow.keras.layers import Conv2D, MaxPooling2D, Flatten

model = Sequential()
model.add(Conv2D(16, kernel_size=(3, 3), strides=(2, 2), padding="same",
                 input_shape=(128, 128, 1)))
model.add(ReLU())
model.add(MaxPooling2D(pool_size=(2, 2), strides=(2, 2)))
model.add(Flatten())

model.add(Dense(512))
model.add(ReLU())
model.add(Dense(26))
model.add(Activation('softmax'))
model.compile(loss='categorical_crossentropy',
              optimizer='adam',
              metrics=['accuracy'])
```

The 2D feature maps are flattened into a 1D vector before the output layer.

The size the feature maps is reduced by pooling.

Let's look at the details of the layers in our model by using the summary() method:

The output from the convolutional layer is 16 feature maps of 2D size 64 × 64.

The output from the pooling layer reduces the feature map sizes to 32 × 32.

```
model.summary()
Layer (type)                   Output Shape            Param #
=================================================================
conv2d_1 (Conv2D)              (None, 64, 64, 16)      160

re_lu_1 (ReLU)                 (None, 64, 64, 16)      0

max_pooling2d_1 (MaxPooling2    (None, 32, 32, 16)      0

flatten_1 (Flatten)            (None, 16384)           0

dense_1 (Dense)                (None, 512)             8389120

re_lu_2 (ReLU)                 (None, 512)             0

dense_2 (Dense)                (None, 26)              13338

activation_1 (Activation)      (None, 26)              0
=================================================================
Total params: 8,402,618
Trainable params: 8,402,618
Non-trainable params: 0
```

The number of parameters for the 512-node dense layer is over 8 million; every node in the flatten layer is connected to every node in the dense layer.

The final dense layer has 26 nodes, one for each letter in the English alphabet.

Here's how to read the Output Shape column. For the `Conv2D` input layer, the output shape shows (None, 64, 64, 16). The first value in the tuple is the number of examples (batch size) that will be passed through on a single forward feed. Since this is determined at training time, it is set to `None` to indicate it will be bound when the model is being fed data. The last number is the number of filters, which we set to 16. The two numbers in the middle (64, 64) are the output size of the feature maps—in this case, 64 × 64 pixels each (for a total of 16). The output size is determined by the filter size (3 × 3), the stride (2 × 2) and the padding (same). The combination that we specified will result in the height and width being halved, for a total reduction of 75% in size.

For the `MaxPooling2D` layer, the output size of the pooled feature maps will be 32 × 32. By specifying a pooling region of 2 × 2 and stride of 2, the height and width of the pooled feature maps will be halved, for a total reduction of 75% in size.

The flattened output from the pooled feature maps is a 1D vector of size 16,384, calculated as 16 × (32 × 32). Let's see if this adds up to what we calculated earlier, that the output size of the feature maps should be the same as the input size. Our input is 128 × 128, which is 16,384 which matches the output size from the `Flatten` layer.

Each element (pixel) in the flattened pooled feature maps is then inputted to each node in the input layer of the DNN, which has 512 nodes. The number of connections between the flattened layer and the input layer is therefore 16,384 × 512 = ~8.4 million. That's the number of weights to learn at that layer, and where most of the computation will (overwhelmingly) occur.

Let's now show the same code example in a variation of the sequential method style. Here, the activation methods are specified using the parameter `activation` in each instantiation of a layer (such as `Conv2D()`, `Dense()`):

```
from tensorflow.keras.models import Sequential
from tensorflow.keras.layers import Dense

from tensorflow.keras.layers import Conv2D, MaxPooling2D, Flatten

model = Sequential()

model.add(Conv2D(16, kernel_size=(3, 3), strides=(2, 2), padding="same",
                 activation='relu', input_shape=(128,128, 1)))
model.add(MaxPooling2D(pool_size=(2, 2), strides=(2, 2)))
model.add(Flatten())

model.add(Dense(512, activation='relu'))
model.add(Dense(26, activation='softmax'))

model.compile(loss='categorical_crossentropy',
              optimizer='adam',
              metrics=['accuracy'])
```

Let's now show the same code example in a third way, using the functional API method. In this approach, we separately define each layer, starting with the input vector and proceeding to the output layer. At each layer, we use polymorphism to invoke the instantiated class (layer) object as a callable and pass in the object of the previous layer to connect it to.

For example, for the first `Dense` layer, when invoked as a callable, we pass as the parameter the layer object for the `Flatten` layer. As a callable, this will cause the `Flatten` layer and the first `Dense` layer to be fully connected (each node in the `Flatten` layer will be connected to every node in the `Dense` layer):

```
from tensorflow.keras import Input, Model
from tensorflow.keras.layers import Dense
from tensorflow.keras.layers import Conv2D, MaxPooling2D, Flatten

inputs  = Input(shape=(128, 128, 1))
layer   = Conv2D(16, kernel_size=(3, 3), strides=(2, 2), padding="same",
                 activation='relu')(inputs)
layer   = MaxPooling2D(pool_size=(2, 2), strides=(2, 2))(layer)
layer   = Flatten()(layer)
layer   = Dense(512, activation='relu')(layer)
outputs = Dense(26, activation='softmax')(layer)

model = Model(inputs, outputs)
```

The input vector for a convolutional layer requires specifying the number of channels.

Constructs the convolutional layer

Reduces the size of feature maps by pooling

3.3   VGG networks

The *VGG* type of CNN was designed by the Visual Geometry Group at Oxford. It was designed to compete in the international ILSVRC competition for image recognition for 1000 classes of images. The VGGNet in the 2014 contest took first place on the image location task and second place on the image classification task.

While AlexNet (and its corresponding ConvNet design pattern) is considered the granddaddy of convolutional networks, the VGGNet (and its corresponding VGG design pattern) is considered the father of formalizing a design pattern based on groups of convolutions. Like its AlexNet predecessors, it continued to view the convolutional layers as a frontend, and to retain a large DNN backend for the classification task. The fundamental principles behind the VGG design pattern are as follows:

- Grouping multiple convolutions into blocks, with the same number of filters
- Progressively doubling the number of filters across blocks
- Delaying pooling to the end of a block

When discussing a VGG design pattern in today's context, initial confusion may arise over the terms *group* and *block*. In their research for VGGNet, the authors used the term *convolutional group*. Subsequently, researchers refined the grouping patterns into convolutional groups, consisting of convolutional blocks. In today's nomenclature, the VGG group would be called a *block*.

It is designed using a handful of principles that are easy to learn. The convolutional frontend consists of a sequence of pairs (and later triples) of convolutions of the same size, followed by a max pooling. The max pooling layer downsamples the generated feature maps by 75%, and the next pair (or triple) of convolutional layers then doubles the number of learned filters. The principle behind the convolution design was that the early layers learn coarse features, and subsequent layers, by increasing the filters, learn finer and finer features, and the max pooling is used between the layers to minimize growth in size (and subsequently parameters to learn) of the feature maps. Finally, the DNN backend consists of two identically-sized dense hidden layers of 4096 nodes each, and a final dense output layer of 1000 nodes for classification. Figure 3.9 depicts the first convolutional groups in a VGG architecture.

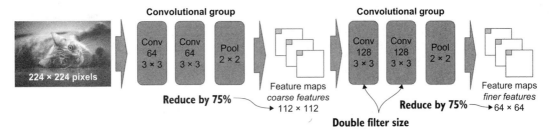

Figure 3.9   In the VGG architecture, convolutions are grouped, and pooling is delayed to the end of the group.

The best-known versions are the VGG16 and VGG19. The VGG16 and VGG19 that were used in the competition, along with their trained weights from the competition, were made publicly available. As they have been frequently used in transfer learning, others have kept the convolutional frontend of an ImageNet pretrained VGG16 or VGG19, and corresponding weights, and attached a new DNN backend for retraining for new classes of images. Figure 3.10 is an architectural depiction of a VGG16.

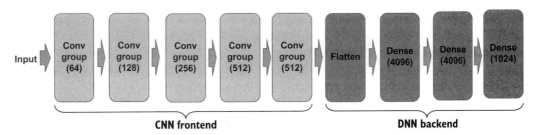

Figure 3.10   A VGG16 architecture consists of a convolutional frontend of VGG groups, followed by a DNN backend.

So, let's go ahead and code a VGG16 in two coding styles: the first in a sequential flow, and the second procedurally using *reuse* functions for duplicating the common blocks of layers, and parameters for their specific settings. We will also change specifying `kernel_size` and `pool_size` as keyword parameters and instead specify them as positional parameters:

```
from tensorflow.keras import Sequential
from tensorflow.keras.layers import Conv2D, MaxPooling2D, Flatten, Dense

model = Sequential()

model.add(Conv2D(64, (3, 3), strides=(1, 1), padding="same",
          activation="relu", input_shape=(224, 224, 3)))
model.add(Conv2D(64, (3, 3), strides=(1, 1), padding="same",
          activation="relu"))
model.add(MaxPooling2D((2, 2), strides=(2, 2)))

model.add(Conv2D(128, (3, 3), strides=(1, 1), padding="same",
          activation="relu"))
model.add(Conv2D(128, (3, 3), strides=(1, 1), padding="same",
          activation="relu"))
model.add(MaxPooling2D((2, 2), strides=(2, 2)))

model.add(Conv2D(256, (3, 3), strides=(1, 1), padding="same",
          activation="relu"))
model.add(Conv2D(256, (3, 3), strides=(1, 1), padding="same",
          activation="relu"))
model.add(Conv2D(256, (3, 3), strides=(1, 1), padding="same",
          activation="relu"))
model.add(MaxPooling2D((2, 2), strides=(2, 2)))

model.add(Conv2D(512, (3, 3), strides=(1, 1), padding="same",
          activation="relu"))
model.add(Conv2D(512, (3, 3), strides=(1, 1), padding="same",
          activation="relu"))
model.add(Conv2D(512, (3, 3), strides=(1, 1), padding="same",
          activation="relu"))
model.add(MaxPooling2D((2, 2), strides=(2, 2)))

model.add(Conv2D(512, (3, 3), strides=(1, 1), padding="same",
          activation="relu"))
model.add(Conv2D(512, (3, 3), strides=(1, 1), padding="same",
          activation="relu"))
model.add(Conv2D(512, (3, 3), strides=(1, 1), padding="same",
          activation="relu"))
model.add(MaxPooling2D((2, 2), strides=(2, 2)))

model.add(Flatten())
model.add(Dense(4096, activation='relu'))
model.add(Dense(4096, activation='relu'))

model.add(Dense(1000, activation='softmax'))

model.compile(loss='categorical_crossentropy',
              optimizer='adam',
              metrics=['accuracy'])
```

First convolutional block ←

Second convolutional block—double the number of filters ←

Third convolutional block—double the number of filters ←

Fourth convolutional block—double the number of filters ←

Fifth (final) convolutional block ←

← **DNN backend**

← **Output layer for classification (1000 classes)**

You just coded a VGG16—nice. Let's now code the same using a procedural reuse style. In this example, we create a procedure (function) conv_block(), which builds the convolutional blocks and takes as parameters the number of layers in the block (2 or 3), and number of filters (64, 128, 256, or 512). Note that we keep the first convolutional layer outside `conv_block`. The first layer needs the `input_shape` parameter. We could have coded this as a flag to `conv_block`, but since it would occur only one time, that's not reuse. So we inline it instead:

```
from tensorflow.keras import Sequential
from tensorflow.keras.layers import Conv2D, MaxPooling2D, Flatten, Dense

def conv_block(n_layers, n_filters):                      ◁————————  Convolutional block
    """                                                              implemented as a procedure
        n_layers : number of convolutional layers
        n_filters: number of filters
    """
    for n in range(n_layers):
        model.add(Conv2D(n_filters, (3, 3), strides=(1, 1), padding="same",
                         activation="relu"))
    model.add(MaxPooling2D(2, strides=2))

model = Sequential()
model.add(Conv2D(64, (3, 3), strides=(1, 1), padding="same",
                 activation="relu",
                 input_shape=(224, 224, 3)))    ◁———  First convolutional specified
conv_block(1, 64)         ◁—————————————              separately since it requires
conv_block(2, 128)                                    the input_shape parameter
conv_block(3, 256)   Second through
conv_block(3, 512)   fifth convolutional
conv_block(3, 512)   blocks          Remainder of first convolutional block

model.add(Flatten())
model.add(Dense(4096, activation='relu'))
model.add(Dense(4096, activation='relu'))

model.add(Dense(1000, activation='softmax'))

model.compile(loss='categorical_crossentropy',
              optimizer='adam',
              metrics=['accuracy'])
```

Try running `model.summary()` on both examples, and you will see that the output is identical.

3.4   ResNet networks

The *ResNet* type of CNN was designed by Microsoft Research to compete in the international ILSVRC competition. The ResNet in the 2015 contest took first place in all categories for the ImageNet and Common Objects in Context (COCO) competition.

The VGGNet design pattern covered in the previous section had limitations in how deep the model architecture could go in layers, before suffering from vanishing and exploding gradients. In addition, different layers converging at different rates could lead to divergence during training.

The researchers for the residual block design pattern component of the residual network proposed a new novel layer connection they called an *identity link*. The identity link introduced the earliest concept of feature reuse. Prior to the identity link, each convolutional block did feature extraction on the previous convolutional output, without retaining any knowledge from prior outputs. The identity link can be seen as a coupling between the current and prior convolutional outputs to reuse feature information gained from earlier extraction. Concurrently along with ResNet, other researchers—such as at Google, with Inception v1 (GoogLeNet)—further refined convolutional design patterns into groups and blocks. In parallel to these design improvements was the introduction of batch normalization.

Using identity links along with batch normalization provided more stability across layers, reducing both vanishing and exploding gradients and divergence between layers, allowing model architectures to go deeper in layers to increase accuracy in prediction.

3.4.1   *Architecture*

ResNet, and other architectures within this class, use different layer-to-layer connection patterns. The patterns we've discussed so far (ConvNet and VGG) use the fully connected layer-to-layer pattern.

ResNet34 introduced a new block layer and layer-connection pattern, residual blocks, and identity connection, respectively. The residual block in ResNet34 consists of blocks of two identical convolutional layers without a pooling layer. Each block has an identity connection that creates a parallel path between the input of the residual block and its output, as depicted in figure 3.11. As in VGG, each successive block doubles the number of filters. Pooling is done at the end of the sequence of blocks.

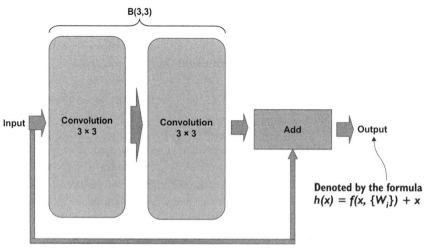

Figure 3.11   A residual block in which the input is a matrix added to the output of the convolution

One of the problems with neural networks is that as we add deeper layers (under the presumption of increasing accuracy), their performance can degrade. It can get worse, not better. This occurs for several reasons. As we go deeper, we are adding more parameters (weights). The more parameters, the more places that each input in the training data will fit to the excess parameters. Instead of generalizing, the neural network will simply learn each training example (rote memorization). The other issue is *covariate shift*: the distribution of the weights will widen (spread further apart) as we go deeper, resulting in making it more difficult for the neural network to converge. The former case causes a degradation in performance on the test (holdout) data, and the latter, on the training data as well as a vanishing or exploding gradient.

Residual blocks allow neural networks to be built with deeper layers without a degradation in performance on the test data. A ResNet block could be viewed as a VGG block with the addition of the identity link. While the VGG style of the block performs feature detection, the identity link retains the input for the next subsequent block, whereby the input to the next block consists of both the previous features' detection and input.

By retaining information from the past (previous input), this block design allows neural networks to go deeper than the VGG counterpart, with an increase in accuracy. Mathematically, we could represent the VGG and ResNet as follows. For both cases, we want to learn a formula for $h(x)$ that is the distribution (for example, labels) of the test data. For VGG, we are learning a function $f(x, \{W\})$, where $\{W\}$ represents the weights. For ResNet, we modify the equation by adding the term "+ x", which is the identity:

VGG: $h(x) = f(x, \{W\})$
ResNet: $h(x) = f(x, \{W\}) + x$

The following code snippet shows how a residual block can be coded in TF.Keras by using the functional API method approach. The variable x represents the output of a layer, which is the input to the next layer. At the beginning of the block, we retain a copy of the previous block/layer output as the variable shortcut. We then pass the previous block/layer output (x) through two convolutional layers, each time taking the output from the previous layer as input into the next layer. Finally, the last output from the block (retained in the variable x) is added (matrix addition) with the original value of x (shortcut). This is the identity link, which is commonly referred to as a *shortcut*:

```
shortcut = x                                    ◁────────┘   Remember the input to the block.
x = layers.Conv2D(64, kernel_size=(3, 3), strides=(1, 1), padding='same')(x)
x = layers.ReLU()(x)
x = layers.Conv2D(64, kernel_size=(3, 3), strides=(1, 1), padding='same')(x)
x = layers.ReLU()(x)                            ◁────────
x = layers.add([shortcut, x])    ◁──────┐     The output of the convolutional sequence

                                       Matrix addition of the input to the output
```

Let's now put the whole network together, using a procedural style. Additionally, we need to add the entry convolutional layer of ResNet and then the DNN classifier.

As we did for the VGG example, we define a procedure (function) for generating the residual block pattern, following the pattern we used in the preceding code snippet. For our procedure `residual_block()`, we pass in the number of filters for the block and the input layer (the output from the previous layer).

The ResNet architectures take as input a (224, 224, 3) vector—an RGB image (3 channels) of 224 (height) × 224 (width) pixels. The first layer is a basic convolutional layer, consisting of a convolution using a fairly large filter size of 7 × 7. The output (feature maps) is then reduced in size by a max pooling layer.

After the initial convolutional layer is a succession of groups of residual blocks. Each successive group doubles the number of filters (similar to VGG). Unlike VGG, though, there is no pooling layer between the groups that would reduce the size of the feature maps. Now, if we connect these blocks directly with each other, we have a problem. The input to the next block has a shape based on the previous block's filter size (let's call it *X*). The next block, by doubling the filters, will cause the output of that residual block to be double in size (let's call it 2*X*). The identity link would attempt to add the input matrix (*X*) and the output matrix (2*X*). Yikes—we get an error, indicating we can't broadcast (for the add operation) matrices of different sizes.

For ResNet, this is solved by adding a convolutional block between each "doubling" group of residual blocks. As depicted in figure 3.12, the convolutional block doubles the filters to reshape the size and doubles the stride to reduce the feature map size by 75% (performs feature pooling).

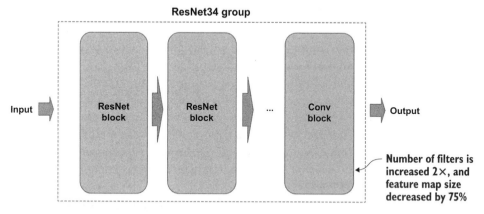

Figure 3.12   The convolution block performs pooling and doubles the number of feature maps for the next convolutional group.

The output of the last residual block group is passed to a pooling and flattening layer (`GlobalAveragePooling2D`), which is then passed to a single `Dense` layer of 1000 nodes (number of classes):

```
from tensorflow.keras import Model
import tensorflow.keras.layers as layers
```

←— **The residual block as a procedure**

```
def residual_block(n_filters, x):
    """ Create a Residual Block of Convolutions
        n_filters: number of filters
        x        : input into the block
    """
    shortcut = x
    x = layers.Conv2D(n_filters, (3, 3), strides=(1, 1), padding="same",
                      activation="relu")(x)
    x = layers.Conv2D(n_filters, (3, 3), strides=(1, 1), padding="same",
                      activation="relu")(x)
    x = layers.add([shortcut, x])
    return x
```

←— **The convolutional block as a procedure**

```
def conv_block(n_filters, x):
    """ Create Block of Convolutions without Pooling
        n_filters: number of filters
        x        : input into the block
    """
    x = layers.Conv2D(n_filters, (3, 3), strides=(2, 2), padding="same",
                      activation="relu")(x)
    x = layers.Conv2D(n_filters, (3, 3), strides=(2, 2), padding="same",
                      activation="relu")(x)
    return x
```

The input tensor —→

```
inputs = layers.Input(shape=(224, 224, 3))
```

First convolutional layer, where pooled feature maps will be reduced by 75%

```
x = layers.Conv2D(64, kernel_size=(7, 7), strides=(2, 2), padding='same',
                  activation='relu')(inputs)
x = layers.MaxPool2D(pool_size=(3, 3), strides=(2, 2), padding='same')(x)
```

```
for _ in range(2):
    x = residual_block(64, x)
```

First residual block group of 64 filters

```
x = conv_block(128, x)
```

←— **Doubles the size of filters and reduces feature maps by 75% (stride s = 2, 2) to fit the next residual group**

```
for _ in range(3):
    x = residual_block(128, x)
```

```
x = conv_block(256, x)
```

```
for _ in range(5):
    x = residual_block(256, x)
```

```
x = conv_block(512, x)
```

```
    x = residual_block(512, x)
```

```
x = layers.GlobalAveragePooling2D()(x)
```

```
outputs = layers.Dense(1000, activation='softmax')(x)
```

```
model = Model(inputs, outputs)
```

Let's now run `model.summary()`. We see that the total number of parameters to learn is 21 million. This is in contrast to the VGG16, which has 138 million parameters. So the ResNet architecture is six times computationally faster. This reduction is mostly achieved by the construction of the residual blocks. Notice that the DNN backend is just a single output `Dense` layer. In effect, there is no backend. The early residual block groups act as the CNN frontend doing the feature detection, while the latter residual blocks perform the classification. In doing so, unlike in VGG, there was no need for several fully connected dense layers, which would have substantially increased the number of parameters.

Unlike the previous example of pooling, in which the size of each feature map is reduced according to the size of the stride, `GlobalAveragePooling2D` is like a supercharged version of pooling: each feature map is replaced by a single value, which in this case is the average of all values in the corresponding feature map. For example, if the input is 256 feature maps, the output will be a 1D vector of size 256. After ResNet, it became the general practice for deep convolutional neural networks to use `Global-AveragePooling2D` at the last pooling stage, which benefited from a substantial reduction of the number of parameters coming into the classifier, without significant loss in representational power.

Another advantage is the identity link, which provided the ability to add deeper layers, without degradation, for higher accuracy.

ResNet50 introduced a variation of the residual block referred to as the *bottleneck residual block*. In this version, the group of two 3×3 convolutional layers is replaced by a group of 1×1, then 3×3, and then 1×1 convolutional layers. The first 1×1 convolution performs a dimensionality reduction, reducing the computational complexity, and the last convolution restores the dimensionality, increasing the number of filters by a factor of 4. The middle 3×3 convolution is referred to as the *bottleneck convolution*, like the neck of a bottle. The bottleneck residual block, depicted in figure 3.13, allows for deeper neural networks, without degradation, and further reduction in computational complexity.

Here is a code snippet for writing a bottleneck residual block as a reusable function:

```
def bottleneck_block(n_filters, x):
    """ Create a Bottleneck Residual Block of Convolutions
        n_filters: number of filters
        x        : input into the block
    """
    shortcut = x
    x = layers.Conv2D(n_filters, (1, 1), strides=(1, 1), padding="same",
                      activation="relu")(x)
    x = layers.Conv2D(n_filters, (3, 3), strides=(1, 1), padding="same",
                      activation="relu")(x)
    x = layers.Conv2D(n_filters * 4, (1, 1), strides=(1, 1), padding="same",
                      activation="relu")(x)
    x = layers.add([shortcut, x])
    return x
```

A 3×3 convolution for feature extraction

A 1×1 bottleneck convolution for dimensionality reduction

A 1×1 projection convolution for dimensionality expansion

Matrix addition of the input to the output

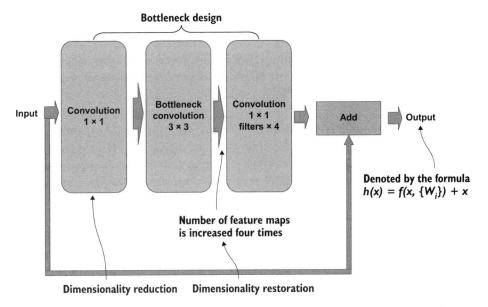

Figure 3.13   **The bottleneck design uses 1 × 1 convolutions for dimensionality reduction and expansion.**

Residual blocks introduced the concepts of representational power and representational equivalence. *Representational power* is a measure of how powerful a block is as a feature extractor. *Representational equivalence* is the idea that a block can be factored into a lower computational complexity, while maintaining representational power. The design of the residual bottleneck block was demonstrated to maintain representational power of the ResNet34 block, with a lower computational complexity.

3.4.2   *Batch normalization*

Another problem with adding deeper layers in a neural network is the *vanishing gradient* problem. This is actually about computer hardware. During training (the process of backward propagation and gradient descent), at each layer the weights are multiplied by very small numbers—specifically, numbers less than 1. As you know, two numbers less than 1 multiplied together make an even smaller number. When these tiny values are propagated through deeper layers, they continuously get smaller. At some point, the computer hardware can't represent the value anymore—hence, the *vanishing gradient.*

   The problem is further exacerbated if we try to use half-precision floats (16-bit floats) for the matrix operations versus single-precision floats (32-bit floats). The advantage of the former is that the weights (and data) are stored in half the amount of space—and using a general rule of thumb, by reducing the computational size in half, we can execute four times as many instructions per computing cycle. The problem, of course, is that with even smaller precision, we will encounter the vanishing gradient even sooner.

Batch normalization is a technique applied to the output of a layer (before or after the activation function). Without going into the statistics aspect, it normalizes the shift in the weights as they are being trained. This has several advantages: it smooths out (across a batch) the amount of change, thus slowing the possibility of getting a number so small that it can't be represented by the hardware. Additionally, by narrowing the amount of shift between the weights, convergence can happen sooner by using a higher learning rate and reducing the overall amount of training time. Batch normalization is added to a layer in TF.Keras with the `BatchNormalization` class.

In earlier implementations, batch normalization was implemented post-activation. The batch normalization would occur after the convolution and dense layers. At the time, it was debated whether the batch normalization should be before or after the activation function. This code example uses post-activation batch normalization both before and after an activation function, in both a convolution and dense layer:

```
from tensorflow.keras import Sequential
from tensorflow.keras.layers import Conv2D, ReLU, BatchNormalization, Flatten
from tensorflow.keras.layers import Dense

model = Sequential()

model.add(Conv2D(64, (3, 3), strides=(1, 1), padding='same',
                input_shape=(128, 128, 3)))
model.add(BatchNormalization())
model.add(ReLU())              ⟵─────┐  Adds batchnorm before
                                     │  the activation
model.add(Flatten())

model.add(Dense(4096))
model.add(ReLU())
                                     ┐  Adds batchnorm
model.add(BatchNormalization())  ⟵───┘  after the activation
```

3.4.3 ResNet50

ResNet50 is a well-known model, which is commonly reused as a stock model, such as for transfer learning, as shared layers in objection detection, and for performance benchmarking. The model has three versions: v1, v1.5 and v2.

ResNet50 v1 formalized the concept of a *convolutional group*. This is a set of convolutional blocks that share a common configuration, such as the number of filters. In v1, the neural network is decomposed into groups, and each group doubles the number of filters from the previous group.

Additionally, the concept of a separate convolution block to double the number of filters was removed and replaced by a residual block that uses *linear projection*. Each group starts with a residual block using linear projection on the identity link to double the number of filters, while the remaining residual blocks pass the input directly to the output for the matrix add operation. Additionally, the first 1×1 convolution in the residual block with linear projection uses a stride of 2 (feature pooling), which is also known as a *strided convolution*, reducing the feature map sizes by 75%, as depicted in figure 3.14.

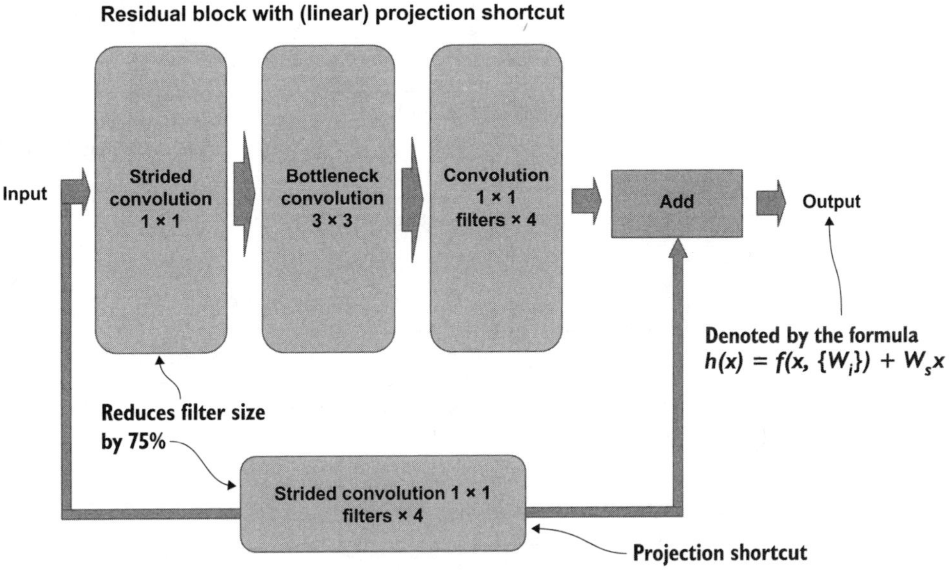

Figure 3.14 **The identity link is replaced with a 1 × 1 projection to match the number of feature maps on the convolutional output for the matrix add operation.**

The following is an implementation of ResNet50 v1 using the bottleneck block combined with batch normalization:

```
from tensorflow.keras import Model
import tensorflow.keras.layers as layers

def identity_block(x, n_filters):
    """ Create a Bottleneck Residual Block of Convolutions
        n_filters: number of filters
        x        : input into the block
    """
    shortcut = x

    x = layers.Conv2D(n_filters, (1, 1), strides=(1, 1))(x)
    x = layers.BatchNormalization()(x)
    x = layers.ReLU()(x)

    x = layers.Conv2D(n_filters, (3, 3), strides=(1, 1), padding="same")(x)
    x = layers.BatchNormalization()(x)
    x = layers.ReLU()(x)

    x = layers.Conv2D(n_filters * 4, (1, 1), strides=(1, 1))(x)
```

```
    x = layers.BatchNormalization()(x)

    x = layers.add([shortcut, x])
    x = layers.ReLU()(x)

    return x

def projection_block(x, n_filters, strides=(2,2)):
    """ Create Block of Convolutions with feature pooling
        Increase the number of filters by 4X
        x        : input into the block
        n_filters: number of filters
    """
    shortcut = layers.Conv2D(4 * n_filters, (1, 1), strides=strides)(x)
    shortcut = layers.BatchNormalization()(shortcut)


    x = layers.Conv2D(n_filters, (1, 1), strides=strides)(x)
    x = layers.BatchNormalization()(x)
    x = layers.ReLU()(x)

    x = layers.Conv2D(n_filters, (3, 3), strides=(1, 1), padding='same')(x)
    x = layers.BatchNormalization()(x)
    x = layers.ReLU()(x)

    x = layers.Conv2D(4 * n_filters, (1, 1), strides=(1, 1))(x)
    x = layers.BatchNormalization()(x)

    x = layers.add([x, shortcut])
    x = layers.ReLU()(x)

    return x

inputs = layers.Input(shape=(224, 224, 3))

x = layers.ZeroPadding2D(padding=(3, 3))(inputs)
x = layers.Conv2D(64, kernel_size=(7, 7), strides=(2, 2), padding='valid')(x)
x = layers.BatchNormalization()(x)
x = layers.ReLU()(x)
x = layers.ZeroPadding2D(padding=(1, 1))(x)
x = layers.MaxPool2D(pool_size=(3, 3), strides=(2, 2))(x)

x = projection_block(64, x, strides=(1,1))

for _ in range(2):
    x = identity_block(64, x)

x = projection_block(128, x)

for _ in range(3):
    x = identity_block(128, x)

x = projection_block(256, x)

for _ in range(5):
```

The projection block as a procedure

1 × 1 projection convolution on shortcut to match size of output

Each convolutional group after the first group starts with a projection block.

```
    x = identity_block(256, x)

x = projection_block(512, x)

for _ in range(2):
    x = identity_block(512, x)

x = layers.GlobalAveragePooling2D()(x)

outputs = layers.Dense(1000, activation='softmax')(x)

model = Model(inputs, outputs)
```

As depicted in figure 3.15, v1.5 introduced a refactoring of the bottleneck design and further reducing of computational complexity, while maintaining representational power. The feature pooling (strides = 2) in the residual block with linear projection is moved from the first 1×1 convolution to the 3×3 convolution, reducing computational complexity and increasing results on ImageNet by 0.5%.

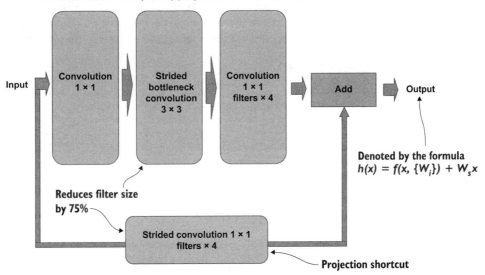

Figure 3.15 The dimensionality reduction moved from the 1 × 1 to the 3 × 3 convolution.

The following is an implementation of ResNet50 v1 residual block with a projection link:

```
def projection_block(x, n_filters, strides=(2,2)):
    """ Create Block of Convolutions with feature pooling
        Increase the number of filters by 4X
        x        : input into the block
        n_filters: number of filters
```

```
"""
shortcut = layers.Conv2D(4 * n_filters, (1, 1), strides=strides)(x)
shortcut = layers.BatchNormalization()(shortcut)


x = layers.Conv2D(n_filters, (1, 1), strides=(1, 1))(x)
x = layers.BatchNormalization()(x)
x = layers.ReLU()(x)

x = layers.Conv2D(n_filters, (3, 3), strides=(2, 2), padding='same')(x)
x = layers.BatchNormalization()(x)
x = layers.ReLU()(x)

x = layers.Conv2D(4 * n_filters, (1, 1), strides=(1, 1))(x)
x = layers.BatchNormalization()(x)

x = layers.add([x, shortcut])
x = layers.ReLU()(x)
return x
```

Bottleneck is moved to 3 × 3 convolution using a stride of 2

ResNet50 v2 introduced *preactivation batch normalization* (BN-RE-Conv), in which the batch normalization and activation functions are placed before (instead of after) the corresponding convolution or dense layer. This has now become a common practice, as depicted here for implementation of the residual block with the identity link in v2:

```
def identity_block(x, n_filters):
    """ Create a Bottleneck Residual Block of Convolutions
        n_filters: number of filters
        x               : input into the block
    """
    shortcut = x

    x = layers.BatchNormalization()(x)
    x = layers.ReLU()(x)
    x = layers.Conv2D(n_filters, (1, 1), strides=(1, 1))(x)

    x = layers.BatchNormalization()(x)
    x = layers.ReLU()(x)
    x = layers.Conv2D(n_filters, (3, 3), strides=(1, 1), padding="same")(x)

    x = layers.BatchNormalization()(x)
    x = layers.ReLU()(x)
    x = layers.Conv2D(n_filters * 4, (1, 1), strides=(1, 1))(x)

    x = layers.add([shortcut, x])
    return x
```

Batchnorm before the convolution

Summary

- A convolutional neural network can be described as adding a frontend to a deep neural network.
- The purpose of the CNN frontend is to reduce the high-dimensional pixel input to low-dimensional feature representation.
- The lower dimensionality of the feature representation makes it practical to do deep learning with real-world images.
- Image resizing and pooling are used to reduce the number of parameters in the model, without information loss.
- Using a cascading set of filters to detect features has similarities to the human eye.
- VGG formalized the concept of a convolutional pattern that is repeated.
- Residual networks introduced the concept of feature reuse and demonstrated the ability to obtain higher accuracy at the same number of layers as a VGG, and go deeper in layers for more accuracy.
- Batch normalization allowed models to go deeper in layers for more accuracy before being exposed to vanishing or exploding gradients.

Training fundamentals 4

This chapter covers

- Forward feeding and backward propagation
- Splitting datasets and preprocessing data
- Using validation data to monitor overfitting
- Using checkpointing and early stopping for more-economical training
- Using hyperparameters versus model parameters
- Training for invariance to location and scale
- Assembling and accessing on-disk datasets
- Saving and then restoring a trained model

This chapter covers the fundamentals of training a model. Prior to 2019, the majority of models were trained according to this set of fundamental steps. Consider this chapter as a foundation.

In this chapter, we cover methods, techniques, and best practices developed over time by experimentation and trial and error. We will start by reviewing forward feeding and backward propagation. While these concepts and practices pre-existed deep learning, numerous refinements over the years made model training practical—specifically, in the way we split the data, feed it, and then update weights using gradient descent during backward propagation. These technique refinements provided the means to train models to convergence, the point where the accuracy of the model to predict would plateau.

Other training techniques in data preprocessing and augmentation were developed to push convergence to higher plateaus, and aid models into better generalizing to data that the model was not trained on. Further refinements continued to make training more economical through hyperparameter search and tuning, along with checkpointing and early stopping, and more-efficient formats and methods of drawing data from disk storage during training. All these techniques combined led to making deep learning for real-world applications practical both computationally and economically.

4.1 Forward feeding and backward propagation

Let's start with an overview of supervised training. When training a model, you feed data forward through the model, and compute how incorrect the predicted results are—the *loss*. Then the loss is backward-propagated to make updates to the model's parameters, which is what the model is learning—the values for the parameters.

When training a model, you start with training data that's representative of the target environment where the model will be deployed. That data, in other words, is a sampling distribution of a population distribution. The training data consists of examples. Each example has two parts: the features, also referred to as *independent variables*; and corresponding labels, also referred to as the *dependent variable*.

The labels are also known as the *ground truths* (the "correct answers"). Our goal is to train a model that, once deployed and given examples without labels from the population (examples the model has never seen before), the model is generalized so that it can accurately predict the label (the "correct answer")—supervised learning. This step is known as *inference*.

During training, we feed *batches* (also called *samples*) of the training data to the model through the input layer (also referred to as the *bottom* of the model). The training data is then transformed by the parameters (weights and biases) in the layers of the model as it moves forward toward the output nodes (also referred to as the *top* of the model). At the output nodes, we measure how far away we are from the "correct" answers, which, again, is called the *loss*. We then backward-propagate the loss through the layers of the models and update the parameters to be closer to getting the correct answer on the next batch.

We continue to repeat this process until we reach *convergence*, which could be described as "this is as accurate as we can get on this training run."

4.1.1 Feeding

Feeding is the process of sampling batches from the training data and forward-feeding the batches through the model, and then calculating the loss at the output. A batch can be one or more examples from the training data chosen at random.

The size of the batch is typically constant, which is referred to as the (mini) *batch size*. All the training data is split into batches, and typically each example will appear in only one batch.

All of the training data is fed multiple times to the model. Each time we feed the entire training data, it is called an *epoch*. Each epoch is a different random permutation into batches—that is, no two epochs have the same ordering of examples—as depicted in figure 4.1.

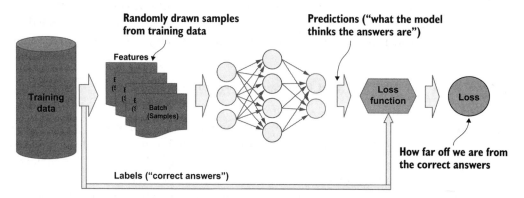

Figure 4.1   Mini-batches from the training data are fed forward through the neural network during training.

4.1.2   *Backward propagation*

In this section, we explore the importance of the discovery of backward propagation and how it is used today.

BACKGROUND

Let's take a step back in history to understand the importance of how backward propagation contributed to the success of deep learning. In early neural networks, like the perceptron and single-layer neurons, academic researchers experimented with ways to update weights to get the correct answer.

When they were working with just a few neurons and simple problems, the logical first tries were to just make random updates. Eventually, lo and behold, a random guess would work. Well, this was not scalable to large numbers of neurons (say, thousands) and real-world applications; making the correct random guess could take millions of years.

The next logical step tried was to make the random value proportional to how far off the prediction is. In other words, the further off, the larger the range of random values; and the closer, the smaller the range. Not bad—now we're down to maybe a thousand years on a real-world application to guess the right random values.

Eventually, academic researchers experimented with multilayer perceptrons (MLPs), and the technique of making the random values proportional to how far off they were from the correct answer—the loss—just didn't work. They found that when you have multiple layers, this technique has the effect of the left hand—one layer—undoing the work of the right hand—another layer.

These researchers discovered that while the updates to the weights of the output layer are relative to the loss in the prediction, updates to weights in earlier layers are relative to the updates in the next layer. Thus, the concept of backward propagation was formed. At this point, academic researchers went beyond using random distributions to calculate an update. Many things were tried, with no improvements, until a technique was developed to update weights not to the amount of change in the next layer, but relative to the rate of change—hence the discovery and development of gradient descent techniques.

BATCH-BASED BACKWARD PROPAGATION

After each batch of training data is forward-fed through the model and the loss is calculated, the loss is backward-propagated through the model. We go layer by layer updating the model's parameters (weights and parameters), starting at the top layer (output) and moving toward the bottom layer (input). How the parameters are updated is a combination of the loss, the values of the current parameters, and the updates made to the proceeding layer.

The general method for doing this is based on *gradient descent*. The optimizer is an implementation of gradient descent whose job is to update the parameters to minimize the loss (maximize getting closer to the correct answer) on subsequent batches. Figure 4.2 illustrates this process.

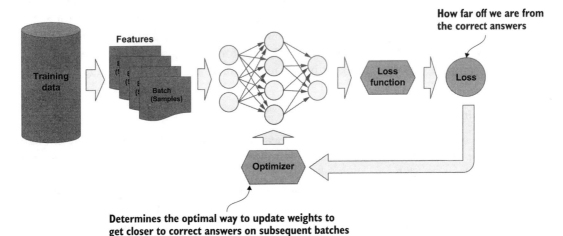

Figure 4.2   The calculated loss from a mini-batch is backward-propagated; the optimizer updates weights to minimize the loss on the next batch.

4.2   *Dataset splitting*

A *dataset* is a collection of examples that are large and diverse enough to be representative of the population being modeled (the sampling distribution). When a dataset meets this definition and is cleaned (not noisy), and in a format that's ready for machine learning training, we refer to it as a *curated dataset.* This book does not cover details of dataset cleaning, as it is a large and diverse topic that would be a book in its own right. We do touch on aspects of data cleaning throughout the book, where relevant.

A wide variety of curated datasets are available for academic and research purposes. Some of the well-known ones for image classification are MNIST (introduced in chapter 2), CIFAR-10/100, SVHN, Flowers, and Cats vs. Dogs. MNIST and CIFAR-10/100 (Canadian Institute for Advanced Research) are built into the TF.Keras framework. SVHN (Street View Home Numbers), Flowers, and Cats vs. Dogs are available with TensorFlow Datasets (TFDS). Throughout this section, we will be using these datasets for tutorial purposes.

Once you have a curated dataset, the next step is to split it into examples that will be used for training and those that will be used for testing (also called *evaluation* or *holdout*). We train the model with the portion of the dataset that is the training data. If we assume the training data is a good sampling distribution (representative of the population distribution), the accuracy of the training data should reflect the accuracy when deployed to the real-world predictions on examples from the population not seen by the model during training.

But how do we know whether this is true before we deploy the model? Hence the purpose for the test (holdout) data. We set aside a portion of the dataset that we will test against after the model is done training and see if we get comparable accuracy.

For example, let's say that when we are done training, we have 99% accuracy on the training data, but only 70% accuracy on the test data. Something went wrong (for example, overfitting). So how much do we set aside for training and testing? Historically, the rule of thumb has been 80/20: 80% for training and 20% for testing. That has changed, but we will start with this rule of thumb and in later chapters discuss the modern updates.

4.2.1   *Training and test sets*

What is important is that we are able to assume our dataset is sufficiently large enough that if we split it into 80% and 20%, and the examples are randomly chosen so that both datasets will be good sampling distributions representative of the population distribution, the model will make predictions (inference) after it's deployed. Figure 4.3 illustrates this process.

Let's start with the step-by-step process of training with a curated dataset. For our first step, we import the curated TF.Keras built-in MNIST dataset, as demonstrated in the following code. The TF.Keras built-in datasets have a `load_data()` method. This method loads into memory the dataset, already randomly shuffled and presplit into training and test data. Both training and test data are further separated into the features (the image

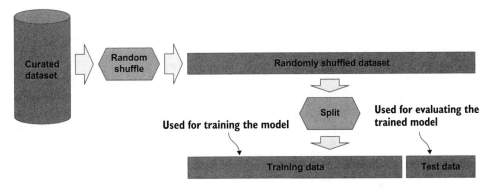

Figure 4.3   Training data is first randomly shuffled before being split into training and test data.

data, in this case) and the corresponding labels (the numerical values 0 to 9, representing each digit). It is a common convention to refer to the features and labels for training and testing as (x_train, y_train) and (x_test, y_test), respectively:

MNIST is a built-in dataset in the framework.

```
from tensorflow.keras.datasets import mnist

(x_train, y_train), (x_test, y_test) = mnist.load_data()
print(x_train.shape, y_train.shape)
print(x_test.shape, y_test.shape)yp
```

Built-in dataset is automatically randomly shuffled and presplit into training and testing data.

The MNIST dataset consists of 60,000 training and 10,000 test examples, with an even (balanced) distribution across the ten digits 0 to 9. Each example consists of a 28-×-28-pixel grayscale image (single channel). From the following output, you can see that the training data (x_train, y_train) consists of 60,000 examples of size 28 × 28 images and corresponding 60,000 labels, while the test data (x_test, y_test) consists of 10,000 examples and labels:

```
(60000, 28, 28) (60000,)
(10000, 28, 28) (10000,)
```

4.2.2   *One-hot encoding*

Let's build a simple DNN to train our curated dataset. In the next code example, we start by flattening the 28-×-28-image input into a 1D vector by using the Flatten layer, which is then followed by two hidden Dense() layers of 512 nodes each, each using the convention of a relu activation function. Finally, the output layer is a Dense layer with 10 nodes, one for each digit. Since this is a multiclass classifier, the activation function for the output layer is a softmax.

Next, we compile the model for the convention for multiclass classifiers by using categorical_crossentropy for the loss and adam for the optimizer:

```
from tensorflow.keras import Sequential
from tensorflow.keras.layers import Flatten, Dense        Flattens the 2D grayscale image
                                                          into 1D vector for a DNN
model = Sequential()
model.add(Flatten(input_shape=(28, 28)))      ◁─────────  The actual input layer of the
model.add(Dense(512, activation='relu'))      ◁─────────  DNN, once the image is flattened
model.add(Dense(512, activation='relu'))      ◁─────
model.add(Dense(10, activation='softmax'))    ◁─────────  A hidden layer
model.compile(loss='categorical_crossentropy',
              optimizer='adam',                           The output layer of the DNN
              metrics=['acc'])
```

The most basic way to train this model with this dataset is to use the fit() method. We will pass as parameters the training data (x_train, y_train). We will keep the remaining keyword parameters set to their defaults:

```
model.fit(x_train, y_train)
```

When you run the preceding code, you will see an error message:

```
ValueError: You are passing a target array of shape (60000, 1) while using
as loss 'categorical_crossentropy'. 'categorical_crossentropy' expects
targets to be binary matrices (1s and 0s) of shape (samples, classes).
```

What went wrong? This is an issue with the loss function we choose. It will compare the difference between each output node and corresponding output expectation. For example, if the answer is the digit 3, we need a 10-element vector (one element per digit) with a 1 (100% probability) in the 3 index and 0s (0% probability) in the remaining indexes. In this case, we need to convert the scalar-value labels into 10-element vectors with a 1 in the corresponding index. This is known as *one-hot encoding*, depicted in figure 4.4.

Let's fix our example by first importing the to_categorical() function from TF.Keras and then using it to convert the scalar-value labels to one-hot-encoded labels. Note that we pass the value 10 to to_categorical() to indicate the size of the one-hot-encoded labels (number of classes):

```
                                                         Method is used for
from tensorflow.keras.utils import to_categorical  ◁───  one-hot encoding
y_train = to_categorical(y_train, 10)
y_test = to_categorical(y_test, 10)       One-hot-encodes the
                                          training and testing labels
model.fit(x_train, y_train)
```

Now when you run this, your output will look something like this:

```
60000/60000 [==============================] - 5s 81us/sample - loss:
1.3920 - acc: 0.9078                ◁─────
                                          The accuracy on the training data is just over 90%.
```

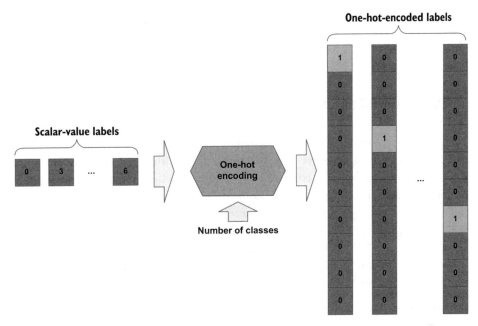

Figure 4.4 The size of a one-hot-encoded label is the same as the number of output classes.

That works, and we got 90% accuracy on the training data—but we can simplify this step. The compile() method has one-hot encoding built into it. To enable it, we just change the loss function from categorical_crossentropy to sparse_categorical_crossentry. In this mode, the loss function will receive the labels as scalar values and dynamically convert them to one-hot-encoded labels before performing the cross-entropy loss calculation.

We do this in the following example and additionally set the keyword parameter epoch to 10 to feed the entire training data to the model 10 times:

```
from tensorflow.keras import Sequential
from tensorflow.keras.layers import Flatten, Dense

model = Sequential()
model.add(Flatten(input_shape=(28, 28)))
model.add(Dense(512, activation='relu'))
model.add(Dense(512, activation='relu'))
model.add(Dense(10, activation='softmax'))
model.compile(loss='sparse_categorical_crossentropy', optimizer='adam',
              metrics=['acc'])

from tensorflow.keras.datasets import mnist
(x_train, y_train), (x_test, y_test) = mnist.load_data()

model.fit(x_train, y_train, epochs=10)
```

Loads MNIST dataset into memory

Trains MNIST model for 10 epochs

After the 10th epoch, you should see the accuracy on the training data at around 97%:

```
Epoch 10/10
60000/60000 [==============================] - 5s 83us/sample - loss:
0.0924 - acc: 0.9776
```

4.3   *Data normalization*

We can further improve on this. The image data loaded by the mnist() module is in raw format; each image is a 28 × 28 matrix of integer values from 0 to 255. If you were to inspect the parameters (weights and biases) within a trained model, they are very small numbers, typically from –1 to 1. Generally, when data feeds forward through the layer and the parameters of one layer are matrix-multiplied against parameters at the next layer, the result is a very small number.

The problem with our preceding example is that the input values are substantially larger (up to 255), which will produce large numbers initially as they are multiplied through the layers. This will result in taking longer for the parameters to learn their optimal values—if they learn them at all.

4.3.1   *Normalization*

We can increase the speed at which the parameters learn the optimal values and increase our chances of convergence (discussed subsequently) by squashing the input values into a smaller range. One simple way to do this is to squash them proportionally into a range from 0 to 1. We can do this by dividing each value by 255.

In the following code, we add the step of normalizing the input data by dividing each pixel value by 255. The load_data() function loads the dataset into memory in a NumPy format. *NumPy*, a high-performance array-handling module written in C with a Python wrapper (CPython), is highly efficient for feeding data during training of a model, when the entire training dataset is in memory. (Chapter 13 covers methods and formats when the training dataset is too large to fit into memory.)

A *NumPy array* is a class object that implements polymorphism on arithmetic operators. In our example, we show a single division operation (x_train / 255.0). The division operator is overridden for NumPy arrays and implements a broadcast operation—which means that every element in the array will be divided by 255.0.

By default, NumPy does floating-point operations as double precision (64 bits). By default, the parameters in a TF.Keras model are single-precision floating-point (32 bits). For efficiency, as a last step, we convert the result of the broadcasted division to 32 bits by using the NumPy astype() method. If we did not do the conversion, the initial matrix multiplication from the input-to-input layer would take double the number of machine cycles (64 × 32 instead of 32 × 32):

```
from tensorflow.keras import Sequential
from tensorflow.keras.layers import Flatten, Dense
import numpy as np
```

```
model = Sequential()
model.add(Flatten(input_shape=(28, 28)))
model.add(Dense(512, activation='relu'))
model.add(Dense(512, activation='relu'))
model.add(Dense(10, activation='softmax'))
model.compile(loss='sparse_categorical_crossentropy', optimizer='adam',
              metrics=['acc'])

from tensorflow.keras.datasets import mnist
(x_train, y_train), (x_test, y_test) = mnist.load_data()
x_train = (x_train / 255.0).astype(np.float32)      Normalizes the pixel
x_test  = (x_test  / 255.0).astype(np.float32)      data from 0 to 1

model.fit(x_train, y_train, epochs=10)
```

The following is the output from running the preceding code. Let's compare the output with a normalized input to the prior non-normalized input. In the prior input, we reached 97% accuracy after the 10th epoch. In our normalized input, we reach the same accuracy after just the second epoch, and almost 99.5% accuracy after the tenth. Thus, we learned faster and more accurately when we normalized the input data:

```
...
Epoch 2/10
60000/60000 [==============================] - 5s 84us/sample - loss:
0.0808 - acc: 0.9744
...
Epoch 10/10
60000/60000 [==============================] - 5s 81us/sample - loss:
0.0187 - acc: 0.9943
```

Let's now evaluate our model by using the evaluate() method on the test (holdout) data to see how well the model will perform on data it has never seen during training. The evaluate() method operates in inference mode: the test data is forward-fed through the model to make predictions, but there is no backward propagation. The model's parameters are not updated. Finally, evaluate() will output the loss and overall accuracy:

```
model.evaluate(x_test, y_test)
```

In the following output, we see that the accuracy is about 98%, compared to the training accuracy of 99.5%. This is expected. Some overfitting always occurs during training. What we are looking for is a very small difference between the training and testing, and in this case it's about 1.5%:

```
10000/10000 [==============================] - 0s 23us/sample - loss:
0.0949 - acc: 0.9790
```

4.3.2   Standardization

There are a variety of ways to squash the input data beyond the normalization used in the preceding example. For example, some ML practitioners prefer to squash the input values between −1 and 1 (instead of 0 and 1), so that the values are centered at 0. The following code is an example implementation that divides each element by one-half the maximum value (in this example, 127.5) and then subtracts 1 from the result:

```
x_train = ((x_train / 127.5) - 1).astype(np.float32)
```

Does squashing the values between −1 and 1 produce better results than between 0 and 1? I haven't seen anything in the research literature, or my own experience, that indicates a difference.

This and the previous method don't require any pre-analysis of the input data, other than knowing the maximum value. Another technique, called *standardization*, is considered to give a better result. However, it requires a pre-analysis (scan) over the entire input data to find its mean and standard deviation. You then center the data at the mean of the full distribution of the input data and squash the values between +/− one standard deviation. The following code, which implements standardization when the input data is in memory as a NumPy multidimensional array, uses the NumPy methods np.mean() and np.std():

Calculates the mean value for the pixel data

```
import numpy as np
mean = np.mean(x_train)
std = np.std(x_train)
x_train = ((x_train - mean) / std).astype(np.float32)
```

Calculates the standard
deviation for the pixel data

Standardization of
the pixel data using
the mean and
standard deviation

4.4   Validation and overfitting

This section demonstrates a case of overfitting and then shows how to detect overfitting during training and how we might tackle the problem. Let's revisit what *overfitting* means. Typically, to get higher accuracy, we build larger and larger models. One consequence is that the model can rote-memorize some or all of the examples. The model learns the examples instead of learning to generalize from the examples to accurately predict examples it never saw during training. In an extreme case, a model could achieve 100% training accuracy yet have random accuracy on the testing (for 10 classes, that would be 10% accuracy).

4.4.1   Validation

Let's say training the model takes several hours. Do you really want to wait until the end of training and then test on the test data to learn whether the model overfitted? Of course not. Instead, we set aside a small portion of the training data, which we call *validation data*.

We don't train the model with the validation data. Instead, after each epoch, we use the validation data to estimate the likely result on the test data. Like the test data, the validation data is forward-fed through the model without updating the model's parameters (inference mode), and we measure the loss and accuracy. Figure 4.5 depicts this process.

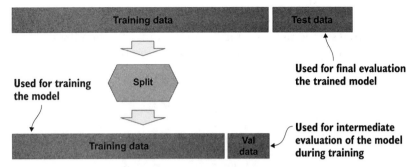

Figure 4.5 On each epoch, the validation data is used to estimate the likely accuracy on the test data.

If a dataset is very small, and using even less data for training has a negative impact, we can use *cross-validation*. Instead of setting aside at the outset a portion of the training data that the model will never be trained on, a random split is done for each epoch. At the beginning of each epoch, the examples for validation are randomly selected and not used for training for that epoch, and instead used for the validation test. But since the selection is random, some or all of the examples will appear in the training data for other epochs. Today's datasets are large, so you seldom see the need for this technique. Figure 4.6 illustrates cross-validation splitting of a dataset.

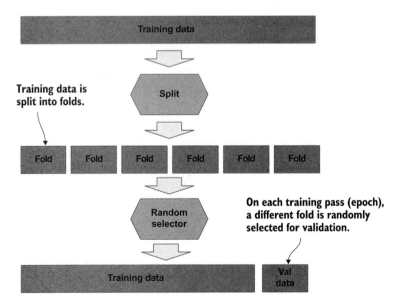

Figure 4.6 On each epoch, a randomly selected fold is selected for validation data.

Next, we will train a simple CNN to classify images from the CIFAR-10 dataset. Our dataset is a subset of this dataset of tiny images, of size $32 \times 32 \times 3$. It consists of 60,000 training and 10,000 test images covering 10 classes: airplane, automobile, bird, cat, deer, dog, frog, horse, ship, and truck.

In our simple CNN, we have one convolutional layer of 32 filters with kernel size 3×3, followed by a strided max pooling layer. The output is then flattened and passed to the final outputting dense layer. Figure 4.7 illustrates this process.

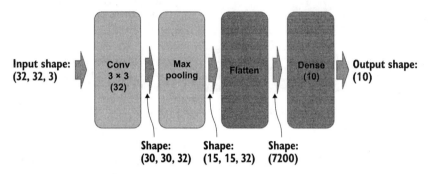

Figure 4.7   A simple ConvNet for classifying CIFAR-10 images

Here's the code to train our simple CNN:

```
from tensorflow.keras import Sequential
from tensorflow.keras.layers import Flatten, Dense, Conv2D, MaxPooling2D
import numpy as np

model = Sequential()
model.add(Conv2D(32, (3, 3), activation='relu', input_shape=(32, 32, 3)))
model.add(MaxPooling2D((2, 2)))
model.add(Flatten())
model.add(Dense(10, activation='softmax'))
model.compile(loss='sparse_categorical_crossentropy', optimizer='adam',
              metrics=['acc'])

from tensorflow.keras.datasets import cifar10
(x_train, y_train), (x_test, y_test) = cifar10.load_data()
x_train = (x_train / 255.0).astype(np.float32)
x_test  = (x_test  / 255.0).astype(np.float32)

model.fit(x_train, y_train, epochs=15, validation_split=0.1)
```

Uses 10% of training data for validation—not trained on

Here, we've added the keyword parameter `validation_split=0.1` to the `fit()` method to set aside 10% of the training data for validation testing after each epoch.

The following is the output after running 15 epochs. You can see that after the fourth epoch, the training and evaluation accuracy are essentially the same. But after the fifth epoch, we start to see them spread apart (65% versus 61%). By the 15th epoch, the spread is very large (74% versus 63%). Our model clearly started overfitting around the fifth epoch:

**After 4th epoch, accuracy on training data
and validation data is about the same.**

**After 5th epoch, accuracy
between train and validation
data start to spread apart.**

```
Train on 45000 samples, validate on 5000 samples
...
Epoch 4/15
45000/45000 [==============================] - 8s 184us/sample - loss: 1.0444
 ➡ - acc: 0.6386 - val_loss: 1.0749 - val_acc: 0.6374
Epoch 5/15
45000/45000 [==============================] - 9s 192us/sample - loss: 0.9923
 ➡ - acc: 0.6587 - val_loss: 1.1099 - val_acc: 0.6182
...
Epoch 15/15
45000/45000 [==============================] - 8s 180us/sample - loss: 0.7256
 ➡ - acc: 0.7498 - val_loss: 1.1019 - val_acc: 0.6382
```

**After 15th epoch, accuracy
between train and validation
data are far apart.**

Let's now work on getting the model to not overfit to the examples and instead generalize from them. As discussed in earlier chapters, we want to add some regularization—some noise—during training so the model cannot rote-memorize the training examples. In this code example, we modify our model by adding 50% dropout before the final dense layer. Because dropout will slow our learning (because of forgetting), we increase the number of epochs to 20:

```
from tensorflow.keras import Sequential
from tensorflow.keras.layers import Flatten, Dense, Conv2D
from tensorflow.keras.layers import MaxPooling2D, Dropout
import numpy as np

model = Sequential()
model.add(Conv2D(32, (3, 3), activation='relu', input_shape=(32, 32, 3)))
model.add(MaxPooling2D((2, 2)))
model.add(Flatten(input_shape=(28, 28)))
model.add(Dropout(0.5))
model.add(Dense(10, activation='softmax'))
model.compile(loss='sparse_categorical_crossentropy', optimizer='adam',
              metrics=['acc'])

from tensorflow.keras.datasets import cifar10
(x_train, y_train), (x_test, y_test) = cifar10.load_data()
x_train = (x_train / 255.0).astype(np.float32)
x_test  = (x_test  / 255.0).astype(np.float32)

model.fit(x_train, y_train, epochs=20, validation_split=0.1)
```

**Adds noise to training
to prevent overfitting**

We can see from the following output that while achieving comparable training accuracy requires more epochs, the training and test accuracy are comparable. Thus, the model is learning to generalize instead of rote-memorizing the training examples:

```
Epoch 18/20
45000/45000 [==============================] - 18s 391us/sample - loss:
    1.0029 - acc: 0.6532 - val_loss: 1.0069 - val_acc: 0.6600            ◁
Epoch 19/20
45000/45000 [==============================] - 17s 377us/sample - loss:
    0.9975 - acc: 0.6538 - val_loss: 1.0388 - val_acc: 0.6478            ◁
Epoch 20/20
45000/45000 [==============================] - 17s 381us/sample - loss:
    0.9891 - acc: 0.6568 - val_loss: 1.0562 - val_acc: 0.6502            ◁
```

**Adding noise by using dropout keeps the training
and validation accuracy from drifting apart.**

4.4.2   Loss monitoring

Up to now, we've been focusing on accuracy. The other metric you see outputted is the average loss across batches for both training and valuation data. Ideally, we would like to see a consistent increase in accuracy per epoch. But we might also see sequences of epochs for which the accuracy plateaus or even fluctuates +/− a small amount.

What is important is that we see a steady decrease in the loss. The plateau or fluctuations in this case occur because we are near or hovering over lines of linear separation or haven't fully pushed over a line, but are getting closer as indicated by the decrease in loss.

Let's look at this another way. Assume you're building a classifier for dogs versus cats. You have two output nodes on the classifier layer: one for cats and one for dogs. Assume that on a specific batch, when the model incorrectly classifies a dog as a cat, the output values (confidence level) are 0.6 for cat and 0.4 for dog. In a subsequent batch, when the model again misclassifies a dog as a cat, the output values are 0.55 (cat) and 0.45 (dog). The values are now closer to the ground truths, and thus the loss is diminishing, but they still have not passed the 0.5 threshold, so the accuracy has not changed yet. Then assume in another subsequent batch, the output values for the dog image are 0.49 (cat) and 0.51 (dog); the loss has further diminished, and because we crossed the 0.5 threshold, the accuracy has gone up.

4.4.3   Going deeper with layers

As mentioned in earlier chapters, simply going deeper with layers can lead to instability in the model, without addressing the issues with techniques such as identity links and batch normalization. For example, many of the values we are matrix-multiplying are small numbers less than 1. Multiply two numbers less than 1, and you get an even smaller number. At some point, numbers get so small that the hardware can't represent the value anymore, which is referred to as a *vanishing gradient*. In other cases, the parameters may be too close to distinguish from each other—or the opposite, spread too far apart, which is referred to as an *exploding gradient*.

The following code example demonstrates this by using a 40-layer DNN absent of methods to protect from numerical instability as we go deeper in layers, such as batch normalization after each dense layer:

```
model = Sequential()
model.add(Dense(64, activation='relu', input_shape=(28, 28))
for _ in range(40):
    model.add(Dense(64, activation='relu'))
model.add(Dense(10, activation='softmax'))
model.compile(loss='sparse_categorical_crossentropy', optimizer='adam',
              metrics=['acc'])

from tensorflow.keras.datasets import mnist
(x_train, y_train), (x_test, y_test) = mnist.load_data()
x_train = (x_train / 255.0).astype(np.float32)
x_test  = (x_test  / 255.0).astype(np.float32)

model.fit(x_train, y_train, epochs=10, validation_split=0.1)
```

Constructs a model with 40 hidden layers

In the following output, you can see in the first three epochs we have a consistent increase in accuracy in training and evaluation data, as well as a consistent decrease in corresponding loss. But afterward, the accuracy becomes erratic; the model is numerically unstable:

Model accuracy is stable in improvement to training and evaluation data.

```
Train on 54000 samples, validate on 6000 samples
Epoch 1/10
54000/54000 [==============================] - 9s 161us/sample - loss: 1.4461
 - acc: 0.4367 - val_loss: 0.8802 - val_acc: 0.7223
Epoch 2/10
54000/54000 [==============================] - 7s 134us/sample - loss: 0.8054
 - acc: 0.7202 - val_loss: 0.7419 - val_acc: 0.7727
Epoch 3/10
54000/54000 [==============================] - 7s 136us/sample - loss: 0.8606
 - acc: 0.7530 - val_loss: 0.6923 - val_acc: 0.8352
Epoch 4/10
54000/54000 [==============================] - 8s 139us/sample - loss: 0.8743
 - acc: 0.7472 - val_loss: 0.7726 - val_acc: 0.7617
Epoch 5/10
54000/54000 [==============================] - 8s 139us/sample - loss: 0.7491
 - acc: 0.7863 - val_loss: 0.9322 - val_acc: 0.7165
Epoch 6/10
54000/54000 [==============================] - 7s 134us/sample - loss: 0.9151
 - acc: 0.7087 - val_loss: 0.8160 - val_acc: 0.7573
Epoch 7/10
54000/54000 [==============================] - 7s 135us/sample - loss: 0.9764
 - acc: 0.6836 - val_loss: 0.7796 - val_acc: 0.7555
Epoch 8/10
54000/54000 [==============================] - 7s 134us/sample - loss: 0.8836
 - acc: 0.7202 - val_loss: 0.8348 - val_acc: 0.7382
Epoch 9/10
54000/54000 [==============================] - 8s 140us/sample - loss: 0.7975
 - acc: 0.7626 - val_loss: 0.7838 - val_acc: 0.7760
Epoch 10/10
54000/54000 [==============================] - 8s 140us/sample - loss: 0.7317
 - acc: 0.7719 - val_loss: 0.5664 - val_acc: 0.8282
```

Model accuracy becomes unstable for training and evaluation data.

4.5   Convergence

Early presumptions on training were that the more times you feed the training data into the model, the better the accuracy. What we've found, particularly on larger and more complex networks, is that at a certain point, accuracy will degrade. Today, we now look for convergence on an acceptable local optimum based on how the model will be used in an application. If we overtrain the neural network, the following can happen:

- The neural network becomes overfitted to the training data, showing increasing accuracy on the training data, but degrading accuracy on the testing data.
- In deeper neural networks, the layers will learn in a nonuniform manner and have different convergence rates. Thus, as some layers are working toward convergence, others may have convergence and thus start diverging.
- Continued training may cause the neural network to pop out of one local optimum and start converging on another that is less accurate.

Figure 4.8 shows what we ideally want to see in convergence when training a model. You start with a fairly fast reduction in loss across the early epochs, and as training homes in on a (near) optimal optimum, the rate of reduction slows, and then finally plateaus—at which point, you have convergence.

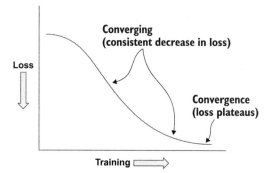

Figure 4.8   Convergence happens when the loss plateaus out.

Let's start with a simple ConvNet model in TF.Keras using the CIFAR-10 dataset to demonstrate the concept of convergence and then diverging. In this code, I have intentionally left out methods that prevent overfitting, like dropout or batch normalization:

```
from tensorflow.keras import Sequential
from tensorflow.keras.layers import Conv2D, MaxPooling2D
from tensorflow.keras.layers import Dropout, Flatten, Dense
from tensorflow.keras.datasets import cifar10
from tensorflow.keras.utils import to_categorical
import numpy as np

(x_train, y_train), (x_test, y_test) = cifar10.load_data()
```

```
height = x_train.shape[1]      | Calculates the height and width
width  = x_train.shape[2]      | of the images in the dataset

x_train = (x_train / 255.0).astype(np.float32)     | Normalizes the input data
x_test  = (x_test  / 255.0).astype(np.float32)

model = Sequential()
model.add(Conv2D(32, kernel_size=(3, 3),              Sets the input shape to the
                 activation='relu',                   model to the height and width
                 input_shape=(height, width, 3)))  <──┘ of the images in the dataset
model.add(Conv2D(64, (3, 3), activation='relu'))
model.add(MaxPooling2D(pool_size=(2, 2)))
model.add(Flatten())
model.add(Dense(128, activation='relu'))
model.add(Dense(10, activation='softmax'))
model.compile(loss='sparse_categorical_crossentropy', optimizer='adam',
              metrics=['accuracy'])

model.fit(x_train, y_train, epochs=20, validation_split=0.1)
```

The stats for the first six epochs follow. You can see a steady reduction in loss with each pass, which means the neural network is getting closer to fitting the data. Additionally, the accuracy on the training data is going up from 52.35% to 87.4%, and on the validation data it's increasing from 63.46% to 67.14%:

```
Train on 45000 samples, validate on 5000 samples        Initial loss on training data
Epoch 1/20
45000/45000 [==============================] - 53s 1ms/sample - loss: 1.3348
     - acc: 0.5235 - val_loss: 1.0552 - val_acc: 0.6346              <──
Epoch 2/20
45000/45000 [==============================] - 52s 1ms/sample - loss: 0.9527
     - acc: 0.6667 - val_loss: 0.9452 - val_acc: 0.6726
Epoch 3/20
45000/45000 [==============================] - 52s 1ms/sample - loss: 0.7789
     - acc: 0.7252 - val_loss: 0.9277 - val_acc: 0.6882
Epoch 4/20
45000/45000 [==============================] - 419s 9ms/sample - loss: 0.6328
     - acc: 0.7785 - val_loss: 0.9324 - val_acc: 0.6964
Epoch 5/20
45000/45000 [==============================] - 53s 1ms/sample - loss: 0.4855
     - acc: 0.8303 - val_loss: 1.0453 - val_acc: 0.6860
Epoch 6/20
45000/45000 [==============================] - 51s 1ms/sample - loss: 0.3575
     - acc: 0.8746 - val_loss: 1.2903 - val_acc: 0.6714
```
Steady decline on training data loss, but signs
of fitting to the data on validation loss

Let's now look at epochs 11 through 20. You can see that we've hit 98.46% on the training data, which means we are tightly fitted to it. On the other hand, our accuracy on the validation data plateaued at 66.58%. Thus, after six epochs, continued training provided no improvement, and we can conclude that by epoch 7, the model was overfitted to the training data:

Validation loss continues to climb while the model
becomes very overfitted to training data.

```
Epoch 11/20
45000/45000 [==============================] - 52s 1ms/sample - loss: 0.0966
⇒ - acc: 0.9669 - val_loss: 2.1891 - val_acc: 0.6694          ⟵
Epoch 12/20
45000/45000 [==============================] - 50s 1ms/sample - loss: 0.0845
⇒ - acc: 0.9712 - val_loss: 2.3046 - val_acc: 0.6666
....
Epoch 20/20
45000/45000 [==============================] - 1683s 37ms/sample - loss:
⇒ 0.0463 - acc: 0.9848 - val_loss: 3.1512 - val_acc: 0.6658
```

Validation loss is very high, and the model
is highly fitted to the training data.

The values of the loss function for the training and validation data also indicate that the model is overfitting. The loss function between epochs 11 and 20 for the training data continues to get smaller, but for the corresponding validation data, it plateaus and then gets worse (diverges).

4.6   Checkpointing and early stopping

This section covers two techniques for making training more economical: checkpointing and early stopping. Checkpointing is useful when a model overtrains and diverges, and we want to recover the model weights at the point of convergence without the additional cost of retraining. You can think of early stopping as an extension to checkpointing. We have a monitoring system detect divergence at the earliest moment that it occurs, and then we stop training, saving additional cost when recovering a checkpoint at the point of divergence.

4.6.1   Checkpointing

Checkpointing is periodically saving the learned model parameters and current hyperparameter values during training. There are two reasons for doing this:

- To be able to resume training of a model where you left off, instead of restarting the training from the beginning
- To identify a past point in training where the model gave the best results

In the first case, we might want to split training across sessions as a way of managing resources. For example, we might reserve (or be authorized) one hour a day for training. At the end of the one-hour training each day, the training is checkpointed. The following day, training is resumed by restoring from the checkpoint. For example, you might be working in a research organization that has a fixed budget for computing expenses, and your team is experimenting with training a model with substantial computing costs. To manage the budget, your team might be allocated a limit of daily computing expenses.

Why wouldn't saving the model's weights and biases be enough? In neural networks, some hyperparameter values will dynamically change, such as the learning rate and decay. We would want to resume at the same hyperparameter values at the time the training was paused.

In another scenario, we might implement continuous learning as a part of a continuous integration and delivery (CI/CD) process. In this scenario, new labeled images are continuously added to the training data, and we want to only incrementally retrain the model instead of retraining from scratch on each integration cycle.

In the second case, we might want to find the best result after a model has trained past the best optimum, and started to diverge and/or overfit. We would not want to start retraining from scratch with fewer epochs (or other hyperparameter changes), but instead identify the epoch that achieved the best results, and restore (set) the learned model parameters to those that were checkpointed at the end of that epoch.

Checkpointing occurs at the end of an epoch, but should we checkpoint after each epoch? Probably not. That can be expensive in terms of space. Let's presume that the model has 25 million parameters (for example, ResNet50), and each parameter is a 32-bit floating-point value (4 bytes). Each checkpoint would then require 100 MB to save. After 10 epochs, that would already be 1 GB of disk space.

We generally checkpoint after each epoch only if the number of model parameters is small and/or the number of epochs is small. In the following code example, a checkpoint is instantiated with the `ModelCheckpoint` class. The parameter `filepath` indicates the file path for the checkpoint. The file path can be either a complete file path or a formatted file path. In the former case, the checkpoint file would be overwritten each time.

In the following code, we use the format syntax `epoch:02d` to generate a unique file for each checkpoint, based on the epoch number. For example, if it's the third epoch, the file would be mymodel-03.ckpt:

```
from tensorflow.keras.callbacks import ModelCheckpoint    ⟵ Imports the
                                                             ModelCheckpoint class

filepath = "mymodel-{epoch:02d}.ckpt"    ⟵ Sets the file pathname
                                            to be unique per epoch

checkpoint = ModelCheckpoint(filepath)    ⟵ Creates a ModelCheckpoint object

model.fit(x_train, y_train, epochs=epochs, callbacks=[checkpoint])
```
Trains the model and uses the callbacks parameter to enable the checkpoint

A model can then be subsequently restored from a checkpoint by using the `load_model()` method:

```
from tensorflow.keras.models import load_model    ⟵ Imports the load_model method

model = load_model('mymodel-03.ckpt')    ⟵ Restores a model from a saved checkpoint
```

For models with a larger number of parameters and/or number of epochs, we can choose to save a checkpoint on every *n*th epoch with the parameter `period`. In this example, a checkpoint is saved on every fourth epoch:

```
from tensorflow.keras.callbacks import ModelCheckpoint

filepath = "mymodel-{epoch:02d}.ckpt"

checkpoint = ModelCheckpoint(filepath, period=4)
```
⟵⎯ **Creates a checkpoint for every fourth epoch**

```
model.fit(x_train, y_train, epochs=epochs, callbacks=[checkpoint])
```

Alternatively, we can save the current best checkpoint with the parameter save_best_only=True and the parameter monitor to the measurement to base the decision on. For example, if the parameter monitor is set to val_acc, it will write a checkpoint only if the validation accuracy is higher than the last saved checkpoint. If the parameter is set to val_loss, it will write a checkpoint only if the validation loss is lower than the last saved checkpoint:

File path for saving the best checkpoint
```
from tensorflow.keras.callbacks import ModelCheckpoint
```
⎿⟶
```
filepath = "mymodel-best.ckpt"
checkpoint = ModelCheckpoint(filepath, save_best_only=True,
   monitor='val_acc')
```
⟵⎯ **Saves the checkpoint only if validation loss is smaller than the last checkpoint**

```
model.fit(x_train, y_train, epochs=epochs, callbacks=[checkpoint])
```

4.6.2 *Early stopping*

An *early stop* is setting a condition upon which training is terminated earlier than the set limits (for example, number of epochs). This is generally set to conserve resources and/or prevent overtraining when a goal objective is reached, such as a level of accuracy or convergence on evaluation loss. For example, we might set a training for 20 epochs, which average 30 minutes each, for a total of 10 hours. But if the objective is met after 8 epochs, it would be ideal to terminate the training, saving 6 hours of resources.

An early stop is specified in a manner similar to a checkpoint. An EarlyStopping object is instantiated and configured with a target goal, and passed to the callbacks parameter of the fit() method. In this example, training will be stopped early only if the validation loss stops, reducing from the previous epoch:

Imports the EarlyStopping class
⎿⟶
```
from tensorflow.keras.callbacks import EarlyStopping

earlystop = EarlyStopping(monitor='val_loss')
```
⟵⎯ **Sets an early stop when the validation loss has stopped reducing**

⎡⟶
```
model.fit(x_train, y_train, epochs=epochs, callbacks=[earlystop])
```
Trains the model and uses early stop to stop training early if the validation loss stops decreasing

In addition to monitoring the validation loss for an early stop, we can monitor the validation accuracy with the parameter setting monitor="val_acc". Additional parameters exist for fine-tuning to prevent an inadvertent early stop; for example, where more train-ing will overcome being stuck on a saddle point—a plateau region in the loss curve. The parameter `patience` specifies a minimum number of epochs without improvement before early stopping, and `min_delta` specifies a minimum threshold to determine whether the model improved. In this example, the training will stop early if no improve-ment occurs in the validation loss after three epochs:

```
from tensorflow.keras.callbacks import EarlyStopping

earlystop = EarlyStopping(monitor='val_loss', patience=3)

model.fit(x_train, y_train, epochs=epochs, callbacks=[earlystop])
```

Sets an early stop when the validation loss has stopped reducing for three epochs

4.7 Hyperparameters

Let's start by explaining the difference between learned parameters and hyperparam-eters. *Learned parameters*, weights and biases, are learned during training. For neural networks, these typically are the weights on each neural network connection, and the biases on each node. For CNNs, learned parameters are the filters in each convolu-tional layer. These learned parameters stay as part of the model when the model is done training.

Hyperparameters are parameters used to train the model, but are not part of the trained model itself. After training, the hyperparameters no longer exist. Hyper-parameters are used to improve the training of the model, by answering questions such as these:

- How long does it take to train the model?
- How fast does the model converge?
- Does it find the global optimum?
- How accurate is the model?
- How overfitted is the model?

Another perspective of hyperparameters is that they are a means to measure the cost and quality of developing the model. We will delve into these questions and others as we explore hyperparameters further in chapter 10.

4.7.1 Epochs

The most basic hyperparameter is the number of epochs, though this is now being more commonly replaced with steps. The *epochs hyperparameter* is the number of times you will pass the entire training data through the neural network during training.

Training is very expensive in terms of computing time. It includes both the for-ward feeding to pass the training data through and the backward propagation to update (train) the model's parameters. For example, if a full pass of the data (epoch) takes 15 minutes, and we run 100 epochs, the training time will take 25 hours.

4.7.2   *Steps*

Another way to improve accuracy and reduce training time is by changing the sampling distribution of the training dataset. For epochs, we think of a sequential draw of batches from our training data. Even though we randomly shuffle the training data at the start of each epoch, the sampling distribution is still the same.

Let's now think of the entire population of the subject we want to recognize. In statistics, we call this the *population distribution* (figure 4.9).

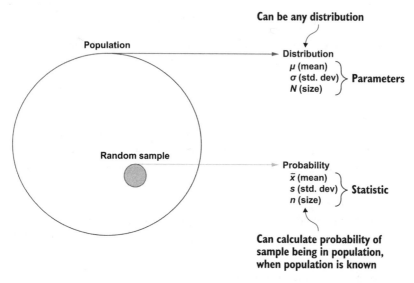

Figure 4.9   Difference between a population distribution and a random sample from within a population

But we will never have a dataset that is the actual entire population distribution. Instead, we have samples, which we refer to as a *sampling distribution of the population distribution* (figure 4.10).

Another way to improve our model is to additionally learn the best sampling distribution for training the model. Although our dataset may be fixed, we can use several techniques to alter the distribution, and thus learn the sampling distribution that best fits training the model. These methods include the following:

- Regularization/dropout
- Batch normalization
- Data augmentation

From this perspective, we no longer see feeding the neural network as sequential passes over the training data, but as making random draws from a sampling distribution. In this context, *steps* refers to the number of batches (draws) we will make from the sampling distribution of our training data.

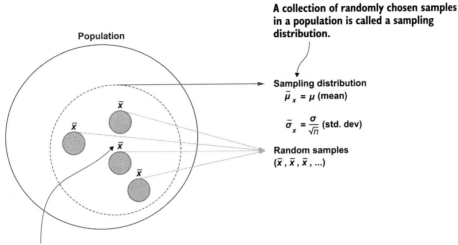

Figure 4.10 A sampling distribution is made up of random samples from the population.

When we add dropout layers to the neural networks, we are randomly dropping activations on a per-sample basis. In addition to reducing overfitting of a neural network, we are also changing the distribution.

With batch normalization, we are minimizing covariance shift between our batches of training data (samples). Just as we use standardization on our input, the activations are rescaled using standardization (we subtract the batch mean and divide by the batch standard deviation). This normalization reduces the fluctuations in updates to parameters in the model; this process is referred to as *adding more stability* to the training. In addition, this normalization mimics drawing from a sampling distribution that is more representative of the population distribution.

With data augmentation (discussed in chapter 13), we create new examples by modifying existing examples within a set of parameters. We then randomly select the modification, which also contributes to changing the distribution.

With batch normalization, regularization/dropout, and data augmentation, no two epochs will have the same sampling distribution. In this case, the practice now is to limit the number of random draws (steps) from each new sampling distribution, further changing the distribution. For example, if steps are set to 1000, then per epoch, only 1000 random batches will be selected and fed into the neural network for training.

In TF.Keras, we can specify both the number of epochs and steps as parameters to the fit() method, as the parameters epochs and steps_per_epoch:

```
model.fit(x_train, y_train, batch_size=batch_size, epochs=epochs,
          steps_per_epoch=1000)
```

4.7.3   *Batch size*

To understand how to set batch size, you should have a basic understanding of the three types of gradient descent algorithms: stochastic gradient descent, batch gradient descent, and mini-batch gradient descent. The algorithm is the means by which the model parameters are updated (learned) during training.

STOCHASTIC GRADIENT DESCENT

In *stochastic gradient descent* (SGD), the model is updated after each example is fed through during training. Since each example is randomly selected, the variance between examples can result in large swings in the gradient.

A benefit is that during training, we are less likely to converge on a local (that is, lessor) optimum, and more likely to find the global optimum to converge on. Another benefit is that the rate of change in loss can be monitored in real time, which may aid in algorithms that do automatic hyperparameter tuning. The downside is that this is more computationally expensive per epoch.

BATCH GRADIENT DESCENT

In *batch gradient descent*, the error loss per example is calculated as each example is fed through during training, but the updating of the model is done at the end of each epoch (after the entire training data is passed through). As a result, the gradient is smoothed out because it's calculated across the loss of all the examples, instead of a single example.

The benefits are that this is less computationally expensive per epoch, and the training more reliably converges. The downsides are that the model may converge on a less accurate local optimum, and an entire epoch needs to be run to monitor performance data.

MINI-BATCH GRADIENT DESCENT

The *mini-batch gradient descent* method is a tradeoff between stochastic and batch gradient descent. Instead of one example or all examples, the neural network is fed in mini-batches that are a subset of the entire training data. The smaller the mini-batch side, the more the training will resemble stochastic gradient descent, while larger batch sizes will resemble batch gradient descent.

For certain models and datasets, SGD works best. In general, it's a common practice to use the tradeoff of mini-batch gradient descent. The hyperparameter batch_ size indicates the size of the mini-batch. Because of hardware architectures, the most time/space-efficient batch sizes are multiples of 8, such as 8, 16, 32, and 64. The batch size that is most commonly tried first is 32, and then 128. For extremely large datasets on higher-end hardware (HW) accelerators (such as GPUs and TPUs), it is common to see batch sizes of 256 and 512. In TF.Keras, you can specify batch_size in the model fit() method:

```
model.fit(x_train, y_train, batch_size=32)
```

4.7.4 *Learning rate*

The *learning rate* is generally the most influential of the hyperparameters. It can have a significant impact on the length of time to train a neural network as well as on whether the neural network converges on a local (lessor) optimum, and whether it converges on the global (best) optimum.

When updating the model parameters during the backward propagation pass, the gradient descent algorithm is used to derive a value to add/subtract to the parameters in the model from the loss function for that pass. These additions and subtractions could result in large swings in parameter values. If a model has and continues to have large swings in parameter values, the model's parameters will be "all over the map" and never converge.

If you observe big swings in the amount of loss and/or accuracy, the training of your model is not converging. If the training is not converging, it won't matter how many epochs you run; the model will never finish training.

The learning rate provides us with a means to control the degree that the model parameters are updated. In the basic method, the learning rate is a fixed coefficient between 0 and 1 that is multiplied against the value to add/subtract, to reduce the amount being added or subtracted. These smaller increments add more stability during the training and increase the likelihood of convergence.

SMALL VS. LARGE LEARNING RATE

If we use a very small learning rate, like 0.001, we will eliminate large swings in the model parameters during updates. This will generally guarantee that the training will converge on a local optimum. But there is a drawback. First, the smaller we make the increments, the more passes of the training data (epochs) will be needed to minimize the loss. That means more time to train. Second, the smaller the increments, the less likely the training will explore other local optima, which might be more accurate than the one that the training is converging on; instead, it may converge on poor local optimum or get stuck on a saddle point.

A large learning rate, like 0.1, likely will cause big jumps in the model parameters during updates. In some cases, it might initially lead to faster convergence (fewer epochs). The drawback is that even if you are initially converging fast, the jumps may overshoot and start causing the convergence to swing back and forth, or hop across different local optima. At very high learning rates, the training may start to diverge (increasing loss).

Many factors help determine what the best learning rate will be at various times during the training. In best practices, the rate will range from 10e-5 to 0.1.

Here is a basic formula that adjusts weight by multiplying the learning rate by the amount calculated to add/subtract (the gradient):

```
weight += -learning_rate * gradient
```

DECAY

One common practice has been to start with a slightly larger learning rate, and then gradually decrease it, also referred to as *learning rate decay*. The larger learning rate would at first explore different local optima to converge on and make initial deep swings into the respective local optima. The rate of convergence and minimizing the loss function on the initial updates can be used to home in on the best (good) local optimum.

From that point, the learning rate is gradually decayed. As the learning rate decays, it is less likely for swings out of the good local optimum to occur, and the steadily decreasing learning rate will tune the convergence to approach the minimal point (albeit, the smaller and smaller learning rate will increase training time). So the decay becomes a tradeoff between small increases in final accuracy and the overall training time.

The following is a basic formula adding decay to the calculation of updating the weights. On each update, the learning rate is reduced by the decay amount (called the *fixed decay*):

```
weight += -learning_rate * gradient
learning_rate -= decay
```

In practice, the decay formulas are generally time-based, step-based, or cosine-based decays. These formulas can be expressed in simplified terms, and an iteration may be a batch or epoch. By default, TF.Keras optimizers use time-based decay. The formulas are as follows:

- Time-based decay

```
learning_rate *= (1 / (1 + decay * iteration))
```

- Step-based decay

```
learning_rate = initial_learning_rate * decay**iteration
```

- Cosine decay

```
learning_rate = c * (1 + cos(pi * (steps_per_epoch * interaction)/epochs))
# where c is typically in range 0.45 to 0.55
```

MOMENTUM

Another common practice is to accelerate or decelerate the rate of change based on prior changes. If we have large jumps in convergence, we risk jumping out of the local optimum, so we may want to decelerate the learning rate. If we have small to no changes in convergence, we may want to accelerate the learning rate to hop over a saddle point. Typically, values for momentum range from 0.5 to 0.99:

```
velocity = (momentum * velocity) - (learning_rate * gradient)
weight += velocity
```

ADAPTIVE LEARNING RATE

Many popular algorithms dynamically adapt the learning rate:

- Adadelta
- Adagrad
- Adam
- AdaMax
- AMSGrad
- Momentum
- Nadam
- Nesterov
- RMSprop

The explanation of these algorithms is beyond the scope of this section. For more information on these and other optimizers, see documentation for `tf.keras.optimizers` (http://mng.bz/Par9). For TF.Keras, these learning rate algorithms are specified when the optimizer is defined for minimizing the loss function:

```
from tensorflow.keras import optimizers

optimizer = optimizers.RMSprop(lr=0.001, rho=0.9, epsilon=None, decay=0.0)
model.compile(loss='mean_squared_error', optimizer=optimizer)
```

> **Specifies learning rate and decay for the optimizer**

> **Compiles the model, specifying the loss function and optimizer**

4.8   *Invariance*

So what's *invariance?* In the context of neural networks, it means that the outcome (the prediction) is unchanged when the input is transformed. In the context of training an image classifier, image augmentation can be used to train a model to recognize an object regardless of the object's size and location in the image, without the need for additional training data.

Let's consider a CNN that is an image classifier (this analogy can also be applied to object detection). We want the object being classified to be correctly recognized regardless of its location in the image. If we transform the input so that the object is shifted to a new location in the image, we want the outcome (the prediction) to remain unchanged.

For CNNs and imaging in general, the primary types of invariance we want the model to support are *translational* and *scale* invariance. Prior to 2019, translational and scale invariance were handled by image augmentation preprocessing upstream from the model training, using preprocessing of the image data on a CPU while the data was fed during training on a GPU. We will discuss these traditional techniques in this section.

One approach to training for translational/scale invariance is simply to have enough images per class (per object), so that the object is in different locations in the image, different rotations, different scales, and different view angles. Well, this may not be practical to collect.

It turns out there is a straightforward method of autogenerating translational/ scale invariant images using image augmentation preprocessing, which is performed efficiently using matrix operations. Matrix-based transforms can be done by a variety of Python packages, such as the TF.Keras `ImageDataGenerator` class, TensorFlow `tf.image` module, or OpenCV.

Figure 4.11 depicts a typical image augmentation pipeline when feeding training data to a model. For each batch drawn, a random subset of the images in the batch are selected for augmentation (for example, 50%). Then, this randomly selected subset of images is randomly transformed according to certain constraints, such as a randomly selected rotation value from –30 to 30 degrees. The modified batch (originals plus augmented) is then fed to the model for training.

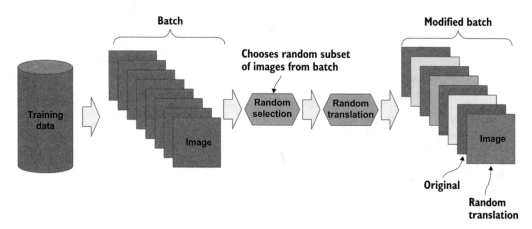

Figure 4.11   During image augmentation, a randomly selected subset of images in the batch is augmented.

4.8.1   *Translational invariance*

This subsection covers how to manually augment images in a training dataset such that the model learns to recognize the object in the image regardless of its location in the image. For example, we want the model to recognize a horse regardless of which direction the horse faces in the image, or an apple regardless of where in the background the apple is located.

Translational invariance in the context of image input includes the following:

- Vertical/horizontal location (object can be anywhere in the picture)
- Rotation (object can be at any rotation)

A vertical/horizontal transformation is typically performed either as a matrix roll operation or a crop. An orientation (for example, mirror) is typically performed as a matrix flip. A rotation is typically handled as a matrix transpose.

FLIP

A *matrix flip* transforms an image by flipping it either on the vertical or horizontal axis. Since the image data is represented as a stack of 2D matrices (one per channel), a flip can be done efficiently as a matrix transpose function without changes (such as interpolation) of the pixel data. Figure 4.12 compares an original and flipped versions of an image.

Original   Vertical flip   Horizontal flip

Figure 4.12 Comparison of an apple: original, vertical axis, and horizontal axis flips (image source: malerapaso, iStock)

Let's start by showing how to flip an image by using the popular imaging libraries in Python. The following code demonstrates how to flip an image vertically (mirror) and horizontally by using a matrix transpose method in Python's PIL imaging library:

```
from PIL import Image

image = Image.open('apple.jpg')    ◁—— Reads the image into memory

image.show()   ◁—— Displays the image in its original perspective

flip = image.transpose(Image.FLIP_LEFT_RIGHT)    | Flips the image on the
flip.show()                                      | vertical axis (mirror)

flip = image.transpose(Image.FLIP_TOP_BOTTOM)    | Flips the image on the horizontal
flip.show()                                      | axis (upside down)
```

Alternately, the flips can be done using the PIL class `ImageOps` module, as demonstrated here:

```
from PIL import Image, ImageOps

image = Image.open('apple.jpg')    ◁—— Reads in the image

flip = ImageOps.mirror(image)      | Flips the image on the
flip.show()                        | vertical axis (mirror)

flip = ImageOps.flip(image)v       | Flips the image on the
flip.show()                        | horizontal axis (upside down)
```

The following code demonstrates how to flip an image vertically (mirror) and horizontally by using a matrix transpose method in OpenCV:

```
import cv2
from matplotlib import pyplot as plt

image = cv2.imread('apple.jpg')

plt.imshow(image)
```
◁——— **Displays the image in its original perspective**

```
flip = cv2.flip(image, 1)
plt.imshow(flip)
```
Flips the image on the vertical axis (mirror)

```
flip = cv2.flip(image, 0)
plt.imshow(flip)
```
Flips the image on the horizontal axis (upside down)

This code demonstrates how to flip an image vertically (mirror) and horizontally by using a matrix transpose method in NumPy:

```
import numpy as np
import cv2
from matplotlib import pyplot as plt

image = cv2.imread('apple.jpg')
plt.imshow(image)
flip = np.flip(image, 1)
plt.imshow(flip)
```
Flips the image on the vertical axis (mirror)

```
flip = np.flip(image, 0)
plt.imshow(flip)
```
Flips the image on the horizontal axis (upside down)

ROTATE 90/180/270

In addition to flips, a *matrix transpose* operation can be used to rotate an image 90 degrees (left), 180 degrees, and 270 degrees (right). Like a flip, the operation is efficient, does not require interpolation of pixels, and does not have a side effect of clipping. Figure 4.13 compares the original and 90-degree rotation versions.

Figure 4.13   Comparison of an apple: 90-, 180-, and 270-degree rotations

This code demonstrates how to rotate an image 90, 180, and 270 degrees by using a matrix transpose method in Python's PIL imaging library:

```
from PIL import Image

image = Image.open('apple.jpg')

rotate = image.transpose(Image.ROTATE_90)
rotate.show()

rotate = image.transpose(Image.ROTATE_180)
rotate.show()

rotate = image.transpose(Image.ROTATE_270)
rotate.show()
```

rotate = image.transpose(Image.ROTATE_90)	**Rotates the image 90 degrees**
rotate = image.transpose(Image.ROTATE_180)	**Rotates the image 180 degrees**
rotate = image.transpose(Image.ROTATE_270)	**Rotates the image 270 degrees**

OpenCV does not have a transpose method for 90 or 270 degrees; you can do a 180 by using the flip method with a value of –1. (All other rotations using OpenCV are demonstrated in the following subsection, using the `imutils` module.)

```
import cv2
from matplotlib import pyplot as plt

image = cv2.imread('apple.jpg')

rotate = cv2.flip(image, -1)
plt.imshow(rotate)
```

Rotates the image 180 degrees

The next example demonstrates how to rotate an image 90, 180, and 270 degrees by using the NumPy method `rot90()`, whose first parameter is the image to rotate 90 degrees, and the second parameter (k) is the number of times to perform the rotation:

```
import numpy as np
import cv2
from matplotlib import pyplot as plt

image = cv2.imread('apple.jpg')

rotate = np.rot90(image, 1)
plt.imshow(rotate)

rotate = np.rot90(image, 2)
plt.imshow(rotate)

rotate = np.rot90(image, 3)
plt.imshow(rotate)
```

Rotates the image 90 degrees

Rotates the image 180 degrees

Rotates the image 270 degrees

When flipping the image 90 or 270 degrees, you are changing the orientation of the image, which is not a problem if the height and width of the image are the same. If not, the height and width will be transposed in the rotated image and will not match the input vector of the neural network. In this case, you should use the `imutils` module or other means to resize the image.

ROTATION

A *rotation* transforms an image by rotating it within –180 and 180 degrees. Generally, the degree of rotation is randomly selected. You may also want to limit the range of rotation to match the environment the model will be deployed in. Here are some common practices:

- If the images will be dead-on, use a range of –15 to 15 degrees.
- If the images may be on an incline, use a range of –30 to 30 degrees.
- For small objects, like packages or money, use the full range of –180 to 180 degrees.

Another issue with rotation is that if you rotate an image within the same-size boundaries, other than 90, 180, or 270, a portion of the image's edge will end up outside the boundary (clipped).

Figure 4.14 is an example of using the PIL method `rotate()` to rotate the image of the apple 45 degrees. You can see that part of the bottom of the apple and the leaf are clipped.

The correct way to handle a rotation is to rotate it within a larger bounding area, so that none of the image is clipped, and then resize the rotated image back to its original size. For this purpose, I recommend using the `imutils` module (created by Adrian Rosebrock, http://mng.bz/JvR0), which consists of a collection of convenience methods for OpenCV:

Figure 4.14   Example of image being clipped when rotated a non-multiple of 90 degrees

```
import cv2, imutils
from matplotlib import pyplot as plt

image = cv2.imread('apple.jpg')

shape = (image.shape[0], image.shape[1])    ⟵ Remembers the original
                                               height and width

rotate = imutils.rotate_bound(image, 45)    ⟵ Rotates the image

rotate = cv2.resize(rotate, shape, interpolation=cv2.INTER_AREA)  ⟵
plt.imshow(rotate)
                          Resizes the image back to its original shape
```

SHIFT

A *shift* will shift the pixel data in the image +/– in the vertical (height) or horizontal (width) axis. This will change the location in the image of the object being classified. Figure 4.15 shows the apple image shifted down 10% and up 10%.

Original   Shifted 10% down   Shifted 10% up

Figure 4.15   Comparison of an apple: original, 10% shift down, 10% shift up

The following code demonstrates shifting the image +/− 10% vertically and horizontally by using the NumPy np.roll() method:

```
import cv2
import numpy as np
from matplotlib import pyplot as plt

image = cv2.imread('apple.jpg')

height = image.shape[0]          | Gets the height and
Width  = image.shape[1]          | width of the image

roll = np.roll(image, height // 10, axis=0)      ◁——— Shifts the image down by 10%
plt.imshow(roll)

roll = np.roll(image, -(height // 10), axis=0)   ◁——— Shifts the image up by 10%
plt.imshow(roll)

roll = np.roll(image, width // 10, axis=1)       ◁——— Shifts the image right by 10%
plt.imshow(roll)

roll = np.roll(image, -(width // 10), axis=1)    ◁——— Shifts the image left by 10%
plt.imshow(roll)
```

A shift is efficient in that it is implemented as a roll operation of the matrix; the rows (height) or columns (width) are shifted. As such, the pixels that are shifted off the end are added to the beginning.

If the shift is too large, the image can become fractured into two pieces, with each piece opposing the other. Figure 4.16 shows the apple shifted by 50% vertically, leaving it fractured.

To avoid fracture, limiting the shift of the image to no more than 20% is a general practice. Alternatively, we could

Figure 14.16   When an image is shifted too much, it becomes fractured.

crop the image and fill the cut-off space with a black pad, as demonstrated here using OpenCV:

```
import cv2
from matplotlib import pyplot as plt

image = cv2.imread('apple.png')
image = cv2.cvtColor(image, cv2.COLOR_BGR2RGB)

height = image.shape[0]          Gets the height
width  = image.shape[1]          of the image

image = image[0: height//2,:,:]     ◁——— Drops the bottom (50%) of the image

image = cv2.copyMakeBorder(image, (height//4), (height//4), 0, 0,
                           cv2.BORDER_CONSTANT, 0)     ◁⌐
                                                          Makes black border to
                                                          refit the image back to
plt.imshow(image)                                         its original size
```

This code produces the output in figure 4.17.

Figure 4.17   Using a crop and fill to avoid fractures in an image

4.8.2   Scale invariance

This subsection covers how to manually augment images in a training dataset such that the model learns to recognize the object in the image regardless of the object's size. For example, we want the model to recognize an apple regardless whether it takes up most of the image or is a small fraction of the image overlaid on a background.

Scale invariance in the context of an image input includes the following:

- Zoom (object can be any size in the image)
- Affine (object can be viewed from any perspective)

ZOOM

Zoom transforms an image by zooming in from the center of the image, which is done with a resize-and-crop operation. You find the center of the image, calculate the crop-bounding box around the center, and then crop the image. Figure 4.18 is the apple image zoomed by a factor of 2.

When enlarging an image by using `Image.resize()` the `Image.BICUBIC` interpolation generally provides the best results. This code demonstrates how to zoom into an image by using Python's PIL imaging library:

Figure 4.18 The image is cropped after zooming in to maintain the same image size.

```
from PIL import Image
image = Image.open('apple.jpg')        Remembers the original
                                        height, width of the image
zoom = 2
height, width = image.size   ←┘
                                        Resizes (scale)
                                        the image
image = image.resize( (int(height*zoom),  proportional
    int(width*zoom)), Image.BICUBIC)  ←┘  to the zoom

center = (image.size[0]//2, image.size[1]//2)   ←
                                        Finds the center of
crop = (int(center[0]//zoom), int(center[1]//zoom))  the scaled image

box = ( crop[0], crop[1], (center[0] + crop[0]), (center[1] + crop[1]) )  ←┐

image = image.crop( box )  ←—— Crops the image    Calculates the crop
image.show()                                       bounding box
```
Calculates the crop upper-left corner

The next code example demonstrates how to zoom into an image by using the OpenCV imaging library. When enlarging an image by using `cv2.resize()` interpolation, `cv2.INTER_CUBIC` generally provides the best results. The interpolation `cv2.INTER_LINEAR` is faster and provides nearly comparable results. The interpolation `cv2.INTER_AREA` is generally used when reducing an image.

```
import cv2
from matplotlib import pyplot as plt

zoom = 2
                                        Remembers the original
height, width = image.shape[:2]   ←┘    height, width of the image

center = (image.shape[0]//2, image.shape[1]//2)
z_height = int(height // zoom)          Finds the center of
z_width  = int(width  // zoom)          the scaled image

image = image[(center[0] - z_height//2):(center[0] + z_height//2), center[1] -
            z_width//2:(center[1] + z_width//2)]
                                                   ←—————

image = cv2.resize(image, (width, height), interpolation=cv2.INTER_CUBIC)

    plt.imshow(image)                   Slices (cuts out) the zoomed image
                                        by forming a crop bounding box
```
**Resizes (enlarges) the cropped
image back to the original size**

4.8.3   *TF.Keras ImageDataGenerator*

The TF.Keras image-preprocessing module supports a wide variety of image augmentation with the class `ImageDataGenerator`. This class creates a generator for generating batches of augmented images. The class initializer takes as input zero or more parameters for specifying the type of augmentation. Here are a few of the parameters, which we will cover in this section:

- `horizontal_flip=True|False`
- `vertical_flip=True|False`
- `rotation_range=degrees`
- `zoom_range=(lower, upper)`
- `width_shift_range=percent`
- `height_shift_range=percent`
- `brightness_range=(lower, upper)`

FLIP

In the following code example, we do the following:

1. Read in a single image of an apple.
2. Create a batch of one image (the apple).
3. Instantiate an `ImageDataGenerator` object.
4. Initialize the `ImageDataGenerator` with our augmentation options (in this case, horizontal and vertical flips).
5. Use the `flow()` method of `ImageDataGenerator` to create a batch generator.
6. Iterate through the generator six times, each time returning a batch of one image in x.
    - The generator will randomly select an augmentation (including no augmentation) per iteration.
    - After transformation (augmentation), the pixel value type will be 32-bit float.
    - Change the data type of the pixels back to 8-bit integer, for displaying using Matplotlib.

Here is the code:

```
from tensorflow.keras.preprocessing.image import ImageDataGenerator
import cv2
import numpy as np
from matplotlib import pyplot as plt

image = cv2.imread('apple.jpg')      Makes a batch of        Creates a data
batch = np.asarray([image])          one image (apple)       generator for
                                                             augmenting
                                                             the data
datagen = ImageDataGenerator(horizontal_flip=True, vertical_flip=True)
```

```
step=0
for x in datagen.flow(batch, batch_size=1):
        step += 1
        if step > 6: break
        plt.figure()
        plt.imshow(x[0].astype(np.uint8))    ◁
```

Runs the generator, where every image is a random augmentation

The augmentation operation changes the pixel data to float, then changes it back to uint8 for displaying the image.

ROTATION

In the following code, we use the rotation_range parameter to set random rotations between –60 and 60 degrees. Note that rotate operation does not perform a bounds check and resize (like imutils.rotate_bound()), so part of the image may end up being clipped:

```
datagen = ImageDataGenerator(rotation_range=60)
```

ZOOM

In this code, we use the zoom_range parameter to set random values from 0.5 (zoom out) to 2 (zoom in). The value can be specified either as a tuple or list of two elements:

```
datagen = ImageDataGenerator(zoom_range=(0.5, 2))
```

SHIFT

In this code, we use width_shift_range and height_shift_range to set random values from 0 to 20% to shift horizontally or vertically:

```
datagen = ImageDataGenerator(width_shift_range=0.2, height_shift_range=0.2)
```

BRIGHTNESS

In the following code, we use the brightness_range parameter to set random values from 0.5 (darker) to 2 (brighter). The value can be specified either as a tuple or list of two elements:

```
datagen = ImageDataGenerator(brightness_range=(0.5, 2))
```

As a final note, transformations like brightness that add a fixed amount to the pixel value are done after normalization or standardization. If done before, normalization and standardization would squash the values into the same original range, undoing the transformation.

4.9   *Raw (disk) datasets*

So far, we have discussed training techniques for images that are stored and accessed directly from memory. This works for small datasets, such as those with tiny images, or for larger images in datasets that contain fewer than 50,000 images. But once we start training with larger-size images and large numbers of images, such as several hundred thousand images, your dataset will likely be stored on disk. This subsection covers common conventions for storing images on disk and accessing them for training.

Beyond the curated datasets used for academic/research purposes, the datasets we use in production are likely stored on disk (or a database, if structured data). In the case of image data, we need to do the following:

1 Read images and corresponding labels from disk into memory (assuming image data fits into memory).
2 Resize the images to match the input vector of the CNN.

Next we'll cover several common methods used to lay out image datasets on disk.

4.9.1   *Directory structure*

Placing images into a directory folder structure on a local disk is one of the most common layouts. In this layout, shown in figure 4.19, the root (parent) folder is a container for the dataset. Below the root level are one or more subdirectories. Each subdirectory corresponds to a class (label) and contains the images that correspond to that class.

Using our cats and dogs example, we would have a parent directory that might be named cats_n_dogs, with two subdirectories, one named cats and the other dogs. Within each subdirectory would be the corresponding class of images.

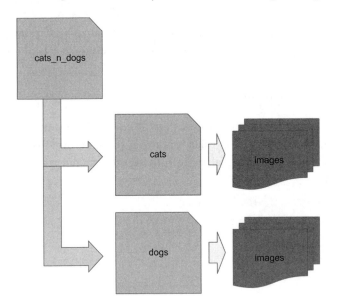

Figure 4.19   Directory folder layout by class

Alternatively, if the dataset has been previously split into training and test data, we'd first group the data by train/test, and then group the data by the two classes for cats and dogs, as depicted in figure 4.20.

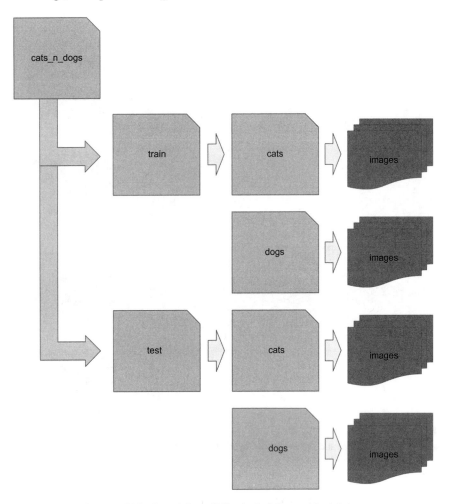

Figure 4.20   Directory folder layout for splitting by training and test data

When the dataset is hierarchically labeled, each top-level class (label) subfolder is further partitioned into child subfolders according to the class (label) hierarchy. Using our cats and dogs example, each image is hierarchically labeled by whether it's a cat or dog (species) and then by breed. See figure 4.21.

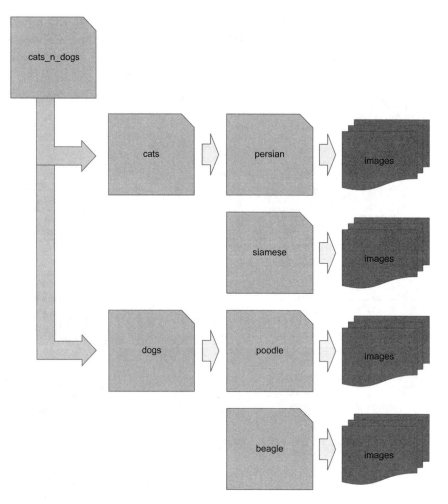

Figure 4.21   Hierarchical directory folder layout for hierarchical labeling

4.9.2   *CSV file*

Another common layout is to use a comma-separated values (CSV) file to identify the location and class (label) of each image. In this case, each row in the CSV file is a separate image, and the CSV file contains at least two columns, one for the location of the image, and the other for the class (label) of the image. The location might be a local path, a remote location, or the pixel data that's embedded as the value of the location:

- Local path example:

```
label,location
'cat', cats_n_dogs/cat/1.jpg
'dog',cats_n_dogs/dog/2.jpg
```

        ...

- Remote path example:

```
label,location
'cat','http://mysite.com/cats_n_dogs/cat/1.jpg'
 'dog','http://mysite.com/cats_n_dogs/dog/2.jpg'

...
```

- Embedded data example:

```
label,location
 'cat',[[...],[...],[...]]
 'dog',[[...], [...], [...]]
```

4.9.3   JSON file

Another common layout is to use a JavaScript Object Notation (JSON) file to identify the location and class (label) of each image. In this case, the JSON file is an array of objects; each object is a separate image, and each object has at least two keys, one for the location of the image, and the other for the class (label) of the image.

The location might be either a local path, a remote location, or pixel data embedded as the value of the location. Here is a local path example:

```
[
        {'label': 'cat', 'location': 'cats_n_dogs/cat/1.jpg' },
        {'label': 'dog', 'location': 'cats_n_dogs/dog/2.jpg'}
        ...
]
```

4.9.4   Reading images

When training on an on-disk dataset, the first step is to read an image from disk into memory. The image on disk will be in an image format such as JPG, PNG, or TIF. These formats define how the image is encoded and compressed for storage. An image can be read into memory by using the PIL `Image.open()` method:

```
from PIL import Image
image = Image.open('myimage.jpg')
```

In practice, you will have many images that need to be read in. Let's assume you want to read in all the images under a subdirectory (for example, cats). In the following code, we scan (get a list of) all the files in the subdirectory, read each one in as an image, and maintain a list of the read-in images as a list:

```
from PIL import Image
import os

def loadImages(subdir):          ◁──┐  Procedure to read all
        images = []                  │  images in a subfolder
                                     │  for a single class label

        files = os.scandir(subdir)   ◁──┐  Gets list of all files in
                                        │  the subdirectory cats
```

```
        for file in files:
                images.append(Image.open(file.path))
        return images

loadImages('cats')
```

Reads each image in and appends the in-memory image to a list

Reads all images in the subfolder cats

Note that `os.scandir()` was added in Python 3.5. If you are using Python 2.7 or an earlier version of Python 3, you can obtain a compatible version with `pip install scandir`.

Let's expand on the preceding example and assume that the image dataset is laid out as a directory structure; each subdirectory is a class (label). In this case, we would want to scan each subdirectory separately and keep a record of the subdirectory names for the classes:

```
import os

def loadDirectory(parent):
        classes = {}
        dataset = []

        for subdir in os.scandir(parent):
                if not subdir.is_dir():
                        continue

                classes[subdir.name] = len(dataset)

                dataset.append(loadImages(subdir.path))

                print("Processed:", subdir.name, "# Images",
                        len(dataset[len(dataset)-1]))

        return dataset, classes

loadDirectory('cats_n_dogs')
```

Procedure for reading all images of a dataset by class

Gets list of all subdirectories under the parent (root) directory of the dataset

Ignores any entry that is not a subdirectory (e.g., license file)

Maintains mapping of class (subdirectory name) to label (index)

Returns the dataset images and class mappings

Reads all images by class for the dataset cats_n_dogs

Let's now try an example in which the location of the image is remote (not local) and specified by a URL. In this case, we will need to make an HTTP request for the contents of the resource (image) specified by the URL and then decode the response into a binary byte stream:

```
from PIL import Image
import requests
from io import BytesIO

def remoteImage(url):
        try:
                response = requests.get(url)
                return Image.open(BytesIO(response.content))
        except:
                return None
```

Python package for HTTP requests

Python package for deserializing I/O into a byte stream

Reads the deserialized content into memory as an image

Requests the image content at the specified URL

After you've read in the images for training, you need to set the number of channels to match the input shape of your convolutional neural network, such as a single channel for grayscale or three channels for RGB images.

The number of channels is the number of color planes in your image. For example, a grayscale image will have one color channel. An RGB color image will have three color channels, one for each of red, green and blue. In most cases, this is either going to be a single channel (grayscale) or three channels (RGB), as depicted in figure 4.22.

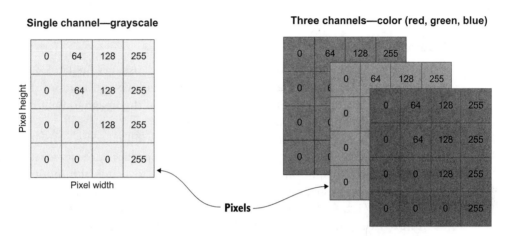

Figure 4.22   A grayscale image has one channel, and an RGB image has three channels.

The Image.open() method will read in the image according to the number of channels in the image stored on the disk. So if it's a grayscale image, the method will read it in as a single channel; if it's RGB, it will read it in as three channels; and if it's RGBA (+alpha channel), it will read it in as four channels.

In general, when working with RGBA images, the alpha channel can be dropped. It is a mask for setting the transparency of each pixel in the image, and therefore does not contain information that would otherwise contribute to the recognition of the image.

Once the image is read into memory, the next step is to convert the image to the number of channels that match the input shape of your neural network. So if the neural network takes grayscale images (single channel), we want to convert to grayscale; or if the neural network takes RGB images (three channels), we want to convert to RGB. The convert() method performs channel conversion. A parameter value of L converts to a single channel (grayscale), and RGB converts to three channels (RGB color). Here we've updated the loadImages() function to include channel conversion:

```
from PIL import Image
import os

def loadImages(subdir, channels):
        images = []
```

```
        files = os.scandir(subdir)
        for file in files:
                image = Image.open(file.path)
                if channels == 1:
                        image = image.convert('L')          Converts to grayscale
                else:
                        image = image.convert('RGB')        Converts to RGB
                images.append(image)
        return images

loadImages('cats', 3)        ◁──── Specifies conversion to RGB
```

4.9.5   *Resizing*

So far, you've seen how to read in the image from the disk, get the label, and then set the number of channels to match the number of channels in the input shape of the CNN. Next, we need to resize the height and width of the image to finalize matching the input shape for feeding images during training.

For example, a 2D convolutional neural network will take the shape of the form (height, width, channels). We dealt with the channel portion already, so next we need to resize the pixel height and width of each image to match the input shape. For example, if the input shape is (128, 128, 3), we want to resize the height and width of each image to (128, 128). The resize() method will do the resizing.

In most cases, you will be downsizing (downsampling) each image. For example, an 1024 × 768 image will be 3 MB in size. This is far more resolution than a neural network needs (see chapter 3 for more details). When the image is downsized, some resolution (details) will be lost. To minimize the effect when downsizing, it is a common practice to use the anti-aliasing algorithm in PIL. Finally, we will then want to convert our list of PIL images into a multidimensional array:

```
from PIL import Image
import os
import numpy as np

def loadImages(subdir, channels, shape):
        images = []

        files = os.scandir(subdir)
        for file in files:
                image = Image.open(file.path)
                if channels == 1:
                    image = image.convert('L')                     Resizes the image to the
                else:                                              target input shape
                    image = image.convert('RGB')

                images.append(image.resize(shape, Image.ANTIALIAS))   ◁
        return np.asarray(images)

loadImages('cats', 3, (128, 128))       ◁── Specifies target input size of 128 × 128.
```

Converts all the PIL images to NumPy arrays in a single invocation

Let's now repeat the preceding steps by using OpenCV. An image is read into memory by using the `cv2.imread()` method. One of the first advantages I find with this method is that the output is already in a multidimensional NumPy data type:

```
import cv2

image = cv2.imread('myimage.jpg')
```

Another advantage of OpenCV over PIL is that you can do the channel conversion at the time of reading in the image, instead of a second step. By default, `cv2.imread()` will convert the image to a three-channel RGB image. You can specify a second parameter that indicates which channel conversion to use. In the following example, we are doing the channel conversion at the time the image is read in:

Reads in image as a single-channel (grayscale) image

```
▷ if channel == 1:
          image = cv2.imread('myimage.jpg', cv2.IMREAD_GRAYSCALE)
▷ else:
          image = cv2.imread('myimage.jpg', cv2.IMREAD_COLOR)
```

Reads in image as a three-channel (color) image

In the next example, we read in the image from a remote location (`url`) and do the channel conversion at the same time. In this case, we use the method `cv2.imdecode()`:

```
try:
        response = requests.get(url)
        if channel == 1:
                return cv2.imdecode(BytesIO(response.content),
                              cv2.IMREAD_GRAYSCALE)
        else:
                return cv2.imdecode(BytesIO(response.content),
                              cv2.IMREAD_COLOR)
except:
        return None
```

Images are resized by using the `cv2.resize()` method. The second parameter is a tuple of the height and width for the resized image. The optional (keyword) third parameter is the interpolation algorithm to use when resizing. Since in most cases you will be downsampling, a common practice is to use the `cv2.INTER_AREA` algorithm for best results in preserving information and minimizing artifacts when downsampling an image:

```
image = cv2.resize(image, (128, 128), interpolation=cv2.INTER_AREA)
```

Let's now rewrite the `loadImages()` function by using OpenCV:

```
import cv2
import os
import numpy as np
```

```
def loadImages(subdir, channels, shape):
        images = []

        files = os.scandir(subdir)
        for file in files:
                if channels == 1:
                        image = cv2.imread(file.path, cv2.IMREAD_GRAYSCALE)
                else:
                        image = cv2.imread(file.path, cv2.IMREAD_COLOR)

                images.append(cv2.resize(image, shape, cv2.INTER_AREA))
        return np.asarray(images)

loadImages('cats', 3, (128, 128))
```

Resizes the image to the target input shape → `images.append(cv2.resize(image, shape, cv2.INTER_AREA))`

Specifies target input shape as 128 × 128 ← `loadImages('cats', 3, (128, 128))`

4.10 Model save/restore

In this subsection, we cover post-training: now that you've trained a model, what do you do next? Well, you would likely want to save the model architecture and corresponding learned weights and biases (parameters) and then subsequently restore the model for deployment.

4.10.1 Save

In TF.Keras, we can save both the model and the trained parameters (weights and biases). The model and weights can be saved separately or together. The save() method saves both the weights/biases and the model to a specified folder in Tensor-Flow SavedModel format. Here is an example:

```
model.fit(x_train, y_train, epochs=epochs, batch_size=batch_size)

model.save('mymodel')
```

Trains the model ← `model.fit(x_train, y_train, epochs=epochs, batch_size=batch_size)`

Saves the model and trained weights and biases ← `model.save('mymodel')`

The trained weights/biases and the model can be saved separately. The save_weights() method will save the model's parameters only to the specified folder in TensorFlow Checkpoint format. Here is an example:

```
model.fit(x_train, y_train, epochs=epochs, batch_size=batch_size)

model.save_weights('myweights')
```

Saves the trained weights and biases only ← `model.save_weights('myweights')`

4.10.2 Restore

In TF.Keras, we can restore a model architecture and/or the model parameters (weights and biases). Restoring a model architecture is generally done for loading a prebuilt model, while loading both the model architecture and model parameters is generally done for transfer learning (discussed in chapter 11).

Note that loading the model and model parameters is not the same as checkpointing, in that we are not restoring the current state of hyperparameters. Therefore, this approach should not be used for continuous learning:

```
from tensorflow.keras.models import load_model

model = load_model('mymodel')   ◁——— Loads a pretrained model
```

In the next code example, the trained weights/biases for a model are loaded into the corresponding prebuilt model, using the `load_weights()` method:

```
from tensorflow.keras.models import load_weights

model = load_model('mymodel')           ◁——— Loads a prebuilt model
model.load_weights('myweights')   ◁——— Loads pretrained weights for the model
```

Summary

- When a batch of images is fed forward, the difference between the predicted value and the ground truths is the loss. The loss is used by the optimizer to determine how to update the weights on backward propagation.
- A small amount of the dataset is held out, as test data, and not trained on. After training, the test data is used to observe how well the model generalized versus memorizing the data examples.
- Validation data is used after each epoch to detect model overfitting.
- Standardization of the pixel data is preferred over normalization because it contributes to slightly better speed of convergence.
- Convergence occurs when the loss plateaus during training.
- Hyperparameters are used to improve training the model, but are not part of the model.
- Augmentation allows training for invariance with fewer original images.
- Checkpointing is used to recover a good epoch without restarting training after training has diverged.
- Early stopping saves training time and cost by detecting that the model will not improve with further training.
- Small datasets can be trained from in-memory storage and access, but large datasets are trained from on-disk storage and access.
- After training, you save the model architecture and learned parameters and then subsequently restore the model for deployment.

Part 2

Basic design pattern

In this second part, you'll learn how to design and code models using the procedural reuse design pattern. I will show you how simple and easy it is to apply procedural reuse, which is a fundamental principle in software engineering, to deep learning models. You'll see how to decompose the model into its standard three components—stem, learner, and task—along with the interface between the components, and how to apply a procedural reuse pattern for coding each piece.

Next, you'll see how to apply this design pattern to a variety of seminal state-of-the-art (SOTA) computer vision models as well as several examples from structured data and NLP. I'll walk you through coding a progression of SOTA models, and cover their contributions to the development of deep learning: VGG, ResNet, ResNeXt, Inception, DenseNet, WRN, Xception, and SE-Net. Then we will turn our attention to mobile models for memory-constrained devices, such as a mobile phones or IoT sensors. We'll look at the progression in design principles that were developed to make models run in memory-constrained devices, starting with MobileNet, then SqueezeNet and ShuffleNet. Again, we'll code each of these mobile models with the procedural reuse design pattern, and then you'll see how to deploy and serve these models using TensorFlow Lite.

Most of the chapters in part 2 focus on models for supervised learning, where the data is labeled. But the final chapter introduces autoencoders, which do unsupervised learning—training a model with data that has not been labeled by a human. You learn to design and code autoencoders for compression, image denoising, super resolution, and pretext tasks.

5

Procedural
design pattern

This chapter covers

- Introducing a procedural design pattern for a convolutional neural network

- Decomposing the architecture of the procedural design pattern into macro- and micro-components

- Coding former SOTA models with the procedural design pattern

Prior to 2017, the majority of renditions of neural network models were coded in a batch scripting style. As AI researchers and experienced software engineers became increasingly involved in research and design, we started to see a shift in the coding of models that reflected software engineering principles for reuse and design patterns.

One of the earliest versions of using design patterns for neural network models was the use of a procedural style for reuse. A design pattern implies that there is a current best practice for constructing and coding a model that can be reapplied across a wide range of cases, such as image classification, object detection and tracking, facial recognition, image segmentation, super resolution, and style transfer.

So how did the introduction of design patterns aid in the advancement of CNNs (as well as in other architectures, such as transformers for NLP)? First, it aided other researchers in understanding and reproducing a model's architecture. Decomposing a model into its reusable components, or patterns, provided a means for other practitioners to observe, understand, and then perform efficient device experiments.

We can see this happening as early as the transition in AlexNet to VGG. The authors of AlexNet (http://mng.bz/1ApV) had insufficient resources to run the Alex-Net model on a single GPU. They designed a CNN architecture to run in parallel on two GPUs. To solve this problem, they came up with a design of having two mirrored convolution paths, a design that won the 2012 ILSVRC competition for image classification. Soon other researchers seized on the idea of having a convolutional pattern that is repeated, and they began studying the effects of the convolutional pattern in addition to analyzing the overall performance. In 2014, both GoogLeNet (https://arxiv.org/abs/1409.4842) and VGG (https://arxiv.org/pdf/1409.1556.pdf) based their models, and corresponding research papers, on using a convolutional pattern that is repeated in the model; these innovations became the winner and first runner-up, respectively, of the 2014 ILSVRC competition.

Understanding the architecture of the procedural design pattern is crucial if you are going to apply it to any model you are building. In this chapter, I will first show you how this pattern is built, by decomposing it into its macro-architectural components, then its micro-architectural groups and blocks. Once you see how the parts work, individually and together, you'll be ready to start working with the code that builds these parts.

To show how the procedural design pattern makes it easier to reproduce model components, we will then apply it to several formerly SOTA models: VGG, ResNet, ResNeXt, Inception, DenseNet, and SqueezeNet. This should give you both a deeper understanding of how these models work, as well as practical experience reproducing them. Some notable highlights of these architectures are as follows:

- *VGG*—2014 winner of image classification in ImageNet ILSVRC challenge
- *ResNet*—2015 winner of image classification in ImageNet ILSVRC challenge
- *ResNeXt*—2016, authors improve accuracy with introduction of wide convolutional layer
- *Inception*—2014 winner for object detection in ImageNet ILSVRC challenge
- *DenseNet*—2017, authors introduced feature map reuse
- *SqueezeNet*—2016, authors introduce concept of a configurable component

We will briefly cover one procedural design pattern based on the Idiomatic design pattern for CNN models.

5.1   *Basic neural network architecture*

The *Idiomatic design pattern* views the model as consisting of an overall macro-architecture pattern, and then each macro-component, in turn, consisting of a micro-architecture design. The concept of a macro- and micro-architecture for a model was introduced in the research paper for SqueezeNet in 2016 (https://arxiv.org/abs/1602.07360). For a CNN, the macro architecture follows the convention of consisting of three macro components: a stem, a learner, and a task, as depicted in figure 5.1.

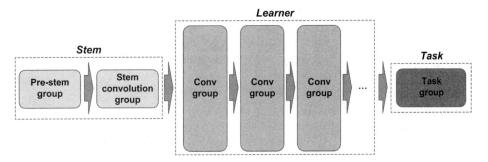

Figure 5.1   The CNN macro-architecture is made up of three components: the stem, the learner, and the task.

As you can see, the *stem* component takes the input (the image) and does the initial coarse-level feature extraction, which becomes the input to the learner component. In this example, the stem includes a pre-stem group that does data preprocessing, and a stem convolution group that does coarse-level feature extraction.

The *learner*, which may be composed of any number of convolutional groups, then does the detailed feature extraction and representational learning from the extracted coarse features. The output from the learner component is referred to as the *latent space*.

The *task* component learns the task (classification, for example) from the representation of the input in the latent space.

While this book focuses on CNNs, this macro-architecture of stem, learner, and task components can be applied to other neural network archit+architectures, such as transformer networks with attention mechanisms in natural-language processing.

Looking at a skeleton template for the Idiomatic design pattern using the functional API, you can see the data flow between components at a high level. We will be using this template (in the following code block), and building on it, throughout the chapters that use the Idiomatic design pattern. The skeleton consists of two main components:

- Function (procedural) input/output definitions of the major components: stem, learner, and task
- The input (tensor) flows through the major components

Here's the skeleton template:

```
def stem(input_shape):          ⟵⎤ Constructs the
    ''' stem layers               ⎦ stem component
        Input_shape : the shape of the input tensor
    '''
    return outputs
                                ⎤ Constructs the
def learner(inputs):   ⟵────────⎦ learner component
    ''' leaner layers
        inputs : the input tensors (feature maps)
    '''
    return outputs
                                ⎤ Constructs the task
def task(inputs, n_classes):   ⟵⎦ component for a classifier
    ''' classifier layers
        inputs    : the input tensors (feature maps)
        n_classes : the number of output classes
    '''
    return outputs
                                              ⎤ Defines the
inputs = Input(input_shape=(224, 224, 3))  ⟵──⎦ input tensor
outputs = stem(inputs)
outputs = learner(outputs)
outputs = task(x, n_classes=1000)
model = Model(inputs, outputs)    ⟵─── Assembles the model
```

In this example, the Input class defines the input tensor to the model; in the case of a CNN, it consists of the shape of the image. The tuple (224, 224, 3) refers to a 224 × 224 RGB (three-channel) image. The Model class is the final step when coding the neural network using the TF.Keras functional API. This step is the final build step (referred to as the compile() method) of the model. The parameters to the Model class are the model input(s) tensor and output(s) tensor. In our example, we have a single input and single output tensor. Figure 5.2 depicts these steps.

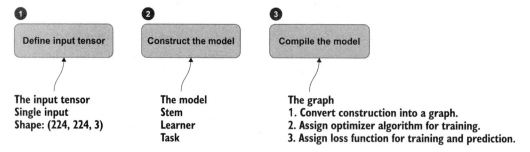

Figure 5.2   The steps for building a CNN model: define input, construct components, compile into a graph

Now let's take a closer look at the three macro-components.

5.2 Stem component

The *stem component* is the entry point to the neural network. Its primary purpose is to perform the first (coarse-level) feature extraction while also reducing the feature maps to a size designed for the learner component. The number of feature maps and the feature map sizes outputted by the stem component are designed by balancing two criteria at the same time:

- Maximize the feature extraction for coarse-level features. The goal here is to give the model enough information to learn finer-level features, within the model's capacity.
- Minimize the number of parameters in the downstream learner component. Ideally, you want to minimize the size of the feature maps and the time it takes to train the model, but without affecting the model's performance.

This initial task is performed by the *stem convolution group*. Let's now look at some variations of stem groups from a select number of well-known CNN models: VGG, ResNet, ResNeXt, and Inception.

5.2.1 VGG

The VGG architecture, winner of the 2014 ImageNet ILSVRC contest for image classification, is considered the father of modern CNNs, while AlexNet is considered the grandfather. VGG formalized the concept of constructing a CNN into components and groups by using a pattern. Prior to VGG, CNNs were constructed as ConvNets, whose usefulness did not go beyond academic novelties.

VGGs were the first to have practical applications in production. For several years after its development, researchers continued to compare more modern SOTA architecture developments to the VGG and to use VGGs for the classification backbone of early SOTA object-detection models.

The VGG, along with Inception, formalized the concept of having a first convolutional group that did a coarse-level feature extraction, which we now refer to as the *stem component*. Subsequent convolutional groups would then do finer levels of feature extraction and feature learning, which we now refer to as *representational learning*, and hence the term *learner* for this second major component.

Researchers eventually discovered a drawback of a VGG stem: it retained the size of the input (224 × 224) in the extracted coarse feature maps, resulting in an unnecessary number of parameters entering the learner. The quantity of parameters both increased the memory footprint as well as reduced performance for training and prediction. Researchers subsequently addressed this problem in later SOTA models by adding pooling in the stem component, reducing the output size of the coarse-level feature maps. This change decreased memory footprint while increasing performance, without a loss in accuracy.

The convention of outputting 64 coarse-level feature maps continues today, though the stem of some modern CNNs may output 32 feature maps.

The VGG stem component, depicted in figure 5.3, was designed to take as an input a 224 × 224 × 3 image and to output 64 feature maps, each 224 × 224 in size. In other words, the VGG stem group did not do any size reduction of the feature maps.

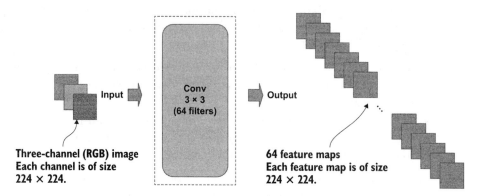

Figure 5.3   The VGG stem group uses a 3 × 3 filter for coarse-level feature extraction.

Now take a look at a code sample for coding the VGG stem component in the Idiomatic design pattern, which consists of a single convolutional layer (Conv2D). This layer uses a 3 × 3 filter for coarse-level feature extraction for 64 filters. It does not do any reduction in size of the feature maps. With a (224, 224, 3) image input (ImageNet dataset), the output from this stem group will be (224, 224, 64):

```
def stem(inputs):
    """ Construct the Stem Convolutional Group
        inputs : the input tensor
    """
    outputs = Conv2D(64, (3, 3), strides=(1, 1), padding="same",
                     activation="relu")(inputs)
    return outputs
```

A complete code rendition using the Idiomatic procedure reuse design pattern for VGG is located on GitHub (http://mng.bz/qe4w).

5.2.2   *ResNet*

The ResNet architecture, winner of the 2015 ImageNet ILSVRC contest for image classification, was one of the first to incorporate the conventional steps of both maximizing coarse-level feature extraction and minimizing parameters with feature map reduction. When comparing their model to VGG, the authors of ResNet found they could reduce the size of the extracted feature maps by a whopping 94% in the stem component, reducing memory footprint and increasing the model performance without affecting the accuracy.

NOTE The process of comparing a newer model to the previous SOTA model is called an *ablation study*, and is common practice in the machine learning field. Basically, the researchers replicate the study of the previous model, and then use the same configuration (say, image augmentation or learning rate) for their new model. This allows them to make direct apple-to-apple comparisons with the earlier models.

The ResNet authors also chose to use an extremely large coarse filter of size 7×7, which covered an area of 49 pixels. Their reasoning here was that the model needed a very large filter to be effective. The drawback was a substantial increase in matrix multiply, or matmul, operations in the stem component. Eventually, researchers subsequently found in later SOTA models a 5×5 filter to be as effective and more efficient. In conventional CNNs, the 5×5 filter is generally replaced with a stack of two 3×3 filters, with the first convolution being unstrided (no pooling) and the second convolution being strided (with feature pooling).

For several years, the ResNet v1 and refined v2 became the de facto architecture used in production for image classification, and the backbone in object-detection models. Beyond its improved performance and accuracy, public versions of pretrained ResNets for image classification, object detection, and image segmentation tasks were widely available, so this architecture became the standard for transfer learning as well. Even today, in high-profile model zoos, like TensorFlow Hub, pretrained ResNet v2 continues to be highly prevalent as the image-classification backbone. The more modern convention today for a pretrained image classification, however, is the smaller, faster, and more accurate EfficientNet. Figure 5.4 depicts the layers in a ResNet stem component.

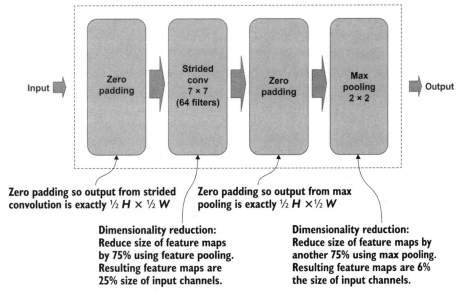

Figure 5.4 The ResNet stem component aggressively reduces the feature map sizes with a strided convolution and max pooling.

In ResNet, the stem component consists of one convolutional layer for coarse feature extraction. The model uses a 7 × 7 filter size to obtain coarse features over a wider window, under the theory it would extract larger features. The 7 × 7 filter covers 49 pixels (in contrast to a 3 × 3, which covers 9 pixels). Using a much larger filter size also substantially increases the number of computations (matrix multiplies) per filter step (as the filter is slid across the image). On a per pixel basis, the 3 × 3 has 9 matrix multiplications, and the 7 × 7 has 49. After ResNet, the convention of using 7 × 7 to obtain larger coarse-level features was not pursued anymore.

Note that both the VGG and ResNet stem components output 64 initial feature maps. This continues to be a fairly common convention, learned through trial and error by researchers.

For feature map reduction, the ResNet stem group does both a feature pooling step (strided convolution) and downsampling (max pooling).

The convolutional layer uses no padding when sliding the filter across the image. Thus, when the filter reaches the edge of the image, it stops. Since the last pixels before an edge do not have their own slide by the filter, the output size is smaller than the input size, as depicted in figure 5.5. The consequence is that the size of the input and output feature maps are not preserved. For example, in a convolution of stride 1, filter size of 3 × 3, and input feature map size 32 × 32, the output feature maps will be 30 × 30. Calculating the loss in size is straightforward. If the filter size is $N \times N$, the loss in size will be $N - 1$ pixels. In TF.Keras, this is specified with the keyword parameter `padding='valid'` to the `Conv2D` layer.

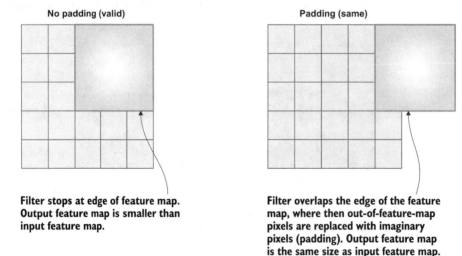

No padding (valid)

Padding (same)

Filter stops at edge of feature map. Output feature map is smaller than input feature map.

Filter overlaps the edge of the feature map, where then out-of-feature-map pixels are replaced with imaginary pixels (padding). Output feature map is the same size as input feature map.

Figure 5.5   Options for padding and no padding result in different stopping locations for the filter.

Alternatively, we can slide the filter over the edge until the last row and column are covered. But part of the filter would hang over imaginary pixels. This way, the last pixels before an edge have their own slide by the filter, and the size of the output feature map is preserved.

Several strategies exist for padding the imaginary pixels. The most common convention today is to pad the imaginary pixels with the same pixel value at the edge, as depicted in figure 5.5. In TF.Keras, this is specified with the keyword parameter `padding='same'` to the `Conv2D` layer.

ResNet predated this convention and padded the imaginary pixels with zero values; this is why you see in the stem group the `ZeroPadding2D` layers, where a zero padding is placed around the image. Today we typically pad the image with the same padding and defer feature map size reduction to pooling or feature pooling. Through trial and error, researchers learned that this approach gave a better result in maintaining feature extraction information at the edge of the image.

Figure 5.6 shows a convolution with padding on an image of size $H \times W \times 3$ (three channels for RGB). With a single filter, we would output a feature map of size $H \times W \times 1$.

3 × 3 kernel is moved across each channel (e.g., 3 × 3 × 3) of image of size *H* × *W*

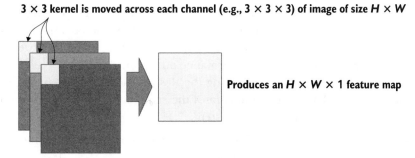

Produces an *H* × *W* × 1 feature map

Figure 5.6   A padded convolution with a single filter produces the least variability of feature extraction.

Figure 5.7 shows a convolution with padding on an image of size $H \times W \times 3$ (three channels for RGB) with multiple filters *C*. Here, we would output a feature map of size $H \times W \times C$.

X (e.g., 256) 3 × 3 kernels are moved across each channel (e.g., 3 × 3 × 3 × 256)

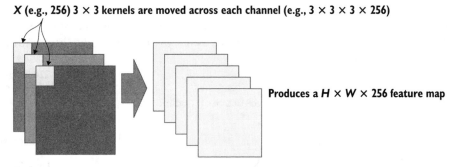

Produces a *H* × *W* × 256 feature map

Figure 5.7   A padded convolution with multiple filters proportionality increases the variability in feature extraction.

Would you ever see a stem convolution with only a single outputted feature map, as depicted in figure 5.6? The answer is no. That's because a single filter can learn to extract only a single coarse feature. That's not going to work for images! Even if our images are simple sequences of parallel lines (a single feature) and we just want to count the lines, it still won't work: we can't control which feature a filter will learn to extract. A certain amount of randomness remains in the process, so we need some redundancy to guarantee that enough of the filters will learn to extract the important features.

Would you ever output a single feature map, somewhere else in a CNN? The answer is yes. That would be an aggressive reduction by a 1 × 1 bottleneck convolution. A 1 × 1 bottleneck convolution is typically used for feature reuse between different convolutions in a CNN.

Once again, it involves a tradeoff. On the one hand, you want to combine the benefits of feature extraction/learning at one place in the CNN with another place in the CNN (feature reuse). The problem is that reusing the entire previous feature maps, in number and size, would create a potential explosion in parameters. That resulting increase in memory footprint and reduction in speed offsets the benefit. The ResNet authors settled on the amount of feature reduction as the best tradeoff between accuracy on the one hand, and size and performance on the other.

Next, take a look at a sample for coding the ResNet stem component in the Idiomatic design pattern. The code demonstrates the sequential flow through the layers illustrated previously in figure 5.3 for the stem:

- The `Conv2D` layer uses 7 × 7 filter size for coarse-level feature extraction and `strides=(2, 2)` for feature pooling.
- `MaxPooling` layers perform downsampling for further feature map reduction.

It's also worth noting that the ResNet was one of the first models to use the convention of batch normalization (`BatchNormalization`). Early conventions, now denoted as Conv-BN-RE, had the batch normalization follow the convolutional and dense layers. To remind you, batch normalization stabilizes neural networks by redistributing the outputs in a layer into a normal distribution. This allows the neural network to go deeper in layers without being prone to a vanishing or exploding gradient. For more details, see "Batch Normalization: Accelerating Deep Network Training by Reducing Internal Covariate Shift" by Sergey Ioffe and Christian Szegedy (https://arxiv.org/abs/1502.03167).

```
def stem(inputs):
    """ Construct the Stem Convolutional Group
        inputs : the input vector
    """

    outputs = ZeroPadding2D(padding=(3, 3))(inputs)   ◁

    outputs = Conv2D(64, (7, 7), strides=(2, 2), padding='valid')(outputs)   ◁
    outputs = BatchNormalization()(outputs)
```

The 224 × 224 images are zero padded (black—no signal) to be 230 × 230 images prior to the first convolution.

First convolutional layer, which uses a large (coarse) filter

```
outputs = ReLU()(outputs)

outputs = ZeroPadding2D(padding=(1, 1))(outputs)      ◁
outputs = MaxPooling2D((3, 3), strides=(2, 2))(outputs)
return outputs
```

Pooled feature maps will be reduced by 75% with a stride of 2 × 2.

A complete code rendition using the Idiomatic procedure reuse design pattern for ResNet is located on GitHub (http://mng.bz/7jK9).

5.2.3 *ResNeXt*

Models that came after ResNet used the convention of same padding, which reduces the layers to a single strided convolution (feature pooling) and strided max pooling (downsampling), while maintaining the same computational complexity. The ResNeXt model (https://arxiv.org/abs/1512.03385) by Facebook AI Research (figure 5.8), along with Inception by Google Inc, introduced using wide residual blocks in the learner component. Don't worry if you don't know the ramifications of wide and deep residual blocks; I'll explain those in chapter 6. Here I just want you to know that the appearance of padding within the convolution emerged with the early SOTA wide residual models. As far as use in production, ResNeXt architectures and other wide CNNs seldom appear outside of memory-constrained devices; subsequent developments for size, speed, and accuracy are more prominent.

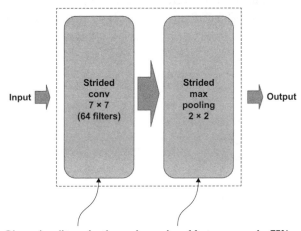

Dimensionality reduction reduces size of feature maps by 75%.

Figure 5.8 The ResNeXt stem component does aggressive feature map reduction with combined features and max pooling.

Note that by using the convention of same padding, there was no need to use Zero-Padding layers to maintain feature map sizes.

The following is a code sample for coding the ResNeXt stem group in the Idiomatic design pattern. In this example, you can see the contrast with the ResNet stem group; the ZeroPadding layers are absent, and replaced with padding='same' for the Conv2D and MaxPooling layer:

```
def stem(inputs):
    """ Construct the Stem Convolution Group
        inputs : input vector
    """
    outputs = Conv2D(64, (7, 7), strides=(2, 2), padding='same')(inputs)
    outputs = BatchNormalization()(outputs)
    outputs = ReLU()(outputs)
    outputs = MaxPooling2D((3, 3), strides=(2, 2), padding='same')(outputs)
    return outputs
```

Uses padding='same' instead of a ZeroPadding2D as in VGG

In subsequent models, the 7×7 filter size was replaced with a smaller 5×5 filter, which had lower computational complexity. A common convention today is the 5×5 filter refactored into two 3×3 filters, which have the same representational power with lower computational complexity.

A complete code rendition using the Idiomatic procedure reuse design pattern for ResNeXt is available on GitHub (http://mng.bz/my6r).

5.2.4 *Xception*

The current convention replaces a single 5×5 with two 3×3 convolutional layers. The Xception (https://arxiv.org/abs/1610.02357) stem component shown in figure 5.9 is an example. The first 3×3 convolution is strided (feature pooling) and produces 32 filters, and the second 3×3 convolution is not strided and doubles the number of output feature maps to 64. However, outside of its novelty in academics, the architecture of Xception was not adopted in production nor developed further by subsequent researchers.

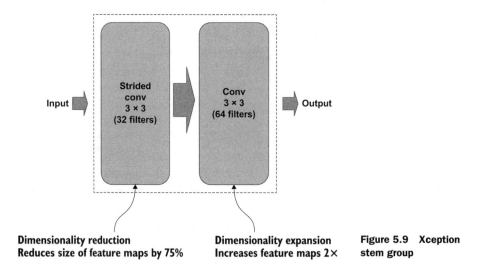

Dimensionality reduction
Reduces size of feature maps by 75%

Dimensionality expansion
Increases feature maps 2×

Figure 5.9   Xception stem group

In this example, for coding the Xception stem group in the Idiomatic design pattern, you see the two 3×3 convolutions (refactored 5×5), with the first convolution strided (feature pooling). Both convolutions are followed by the Conv-BN-RE form of batch normalization:

```
def stem(inputs):
        """ Create the stem entry into the neural network
            inputs : input tensor to neural network
        """

        outputs = Conv2D(32, (3, 3), strides=(2, 2))(inputs)
        outputs = BatchNormalization()(outputs)
        outputs = ReLU()(outputs)


        outputs = Conv2D(64, (3, 3), strides=(1, 1))(outputs)
        outputs = BatchNormalization()(outputs)
        outputs = ReLU()(outputs)
        return outputs
```

A 5 × 5 convolution refactored as two 3 × 3 convolutions

A complete code rendition using the Idiomatic procedure reuse design pattern for Xception is on GitHub (http://mng.bz/5WzB).

5.3 *Pre-stem*

In 2019, we started to see the emergence of adding a *pre-stem group* to the stem component. The purpose of a pre-stem is to move into the graph (model) some or all of the data preprocessing that was performed upstream. Before the development of the pre-stem component, the data preprocessing took place in a separate module and then had to be replicated when the model was deployed for inference (for prediction) on future examples. Generally, this was done on a CPU. Many of the data preprocessing steps can be replaced by graph operations, however, and then executed more efficiently on a GPU, where the model typically is deployed.

Pre-stems are also plug-and-play in that they can be added or removed from existing models and reused. I'll present the technical details of pre-stems later. Here I just want to provide a summary of functions typically performed by a pre-stem group:

- Preprocessing
  - Adapting a model to a different input size
  - Normalization
- Augmentation
  - Resizing and cropping
  - Translational and scale invariance

Figure 5.10 depicts how a pre-stem group is added to an existing model. To attach a pre-stem, you create a new empty wrapper model, add the pre-stem, and then add the existing model. In the latter step, the output shape from the pre-stem group must match the input shape of the stem component of the existing model.

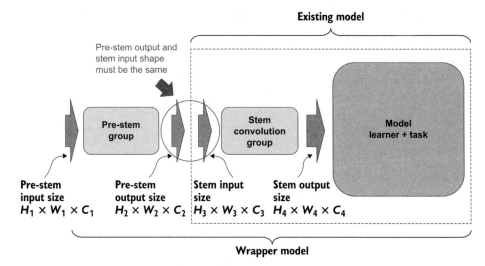

Figure 5.10 Pre-stem added to an existing model, which forms a new wrapper model

The following is an example of a typical approach to adding a pre-stem group to an existing model. In this code, an empty `Sequential` wrapper model is instantiated. The prestem group is then added, followed by the existing model. This will work as long as the output tensors match the input tensors of the model (for example, $(224, 224, 3)$):

```
from tf.keras.layers.experimental.preprocessing import Normalization

def prestem(input_shape):
    ''' pre-stem layers '''
    outputs = Normalization(input_shape=input_shape)
    return outputs

wrapper_model = Sequential()          ⟵┐ Creates an empty
                                        ┘ wrapper model

                                                        ┌ Starts the wrapper model
wrapper_model.add(prestem(input_shape=(224, 224, 3))    ⟵┘ with the pre-stem

wrapper_model.add(model)    ⟵———— Adds the existing model to the wrapper model
```

Next we will explain the design of the learner component, which the stem component will connect to.

5.4   *Learner component*

The *learner component* is where we generally perform feature learning through moredetailed feature extraction. This process is also referred to as *representational* or *transformational* learning (as transformational learning is dependent on the task). The learner component consists of one or more convolutional groups, and each group consists of one or more convolutional blocks.

The convolutional blocks get assembled into groups based on a common model configuration attribute. The most common attributes for convolutional groups in conventional CNNs are the number of input or output filters, or the size of the input or output feature maps. For example, in ResNet, the configurable attributes for a group are the number of convolutional blocks, and the number of filters per block.

Figure 5.11 shows a configurable convolutional group. As you can see, the convolutional blocks correspond to the metaparameter for the number of blocks in the group. All but the last group in most SOTA architectures have the same number of output feature maps, which corresponds to the metaparameter for the number of input filters. The last block may change the number of feature maps outputted by the group (for example, by doubling), which corresponds to the metaparameter for the number of output filters. The final layer (labeled *[Feature] pooling block* in the image) refers to groups that have delayed downsampling, which corresponds to the metaparameter for the type of pooling.

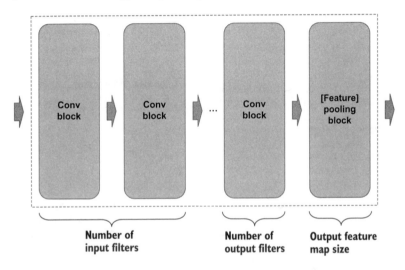

Figure 5.11 Convolutional group metaparameters for number of input/output filters and output feature map size

The following code is a skeleton template (and example) for coding the learner component. In this example, the configuration attribute for the groups is passed as a list of dictionary values, one per group. The `learner()` function iterates through the list of group configuration attributes; each iteration is the group parameters (group_ params) for the corresponding group.

Correspondingly, the `group()` function iterates through the block parameters (block_params) for each block in the group. The `block()` function then constructs the block according to the block-specific configuration parameters that have been passed down to it.

As depicted in figure 5.11, the configurable attributes passed to the block() method as keyword arguments lists would be the number of input filters (in_filters), output filters (out_filters), and number of convolutional layers (n_layers). If the number of input and output filters is the same, a single keyword argument typically is used (n_filters):

```
def learner(inputs, groups):
    ''' leaner layers
        inputs : the input tensors (feature maps)
        groups : the block parameters for each group
    '''
    outputs = inputs
    for group_parmas in groups:              Iterates through the
        outputs = group(outputs, **group_params)   dictionary values for
    return outputs                           each group attribute

def group(inputs, **blocks):
    ''' group layers
        inputs : the input tensors (feature maps)
        blocks : the block parameters for each block
    '''
    outputs = inputs
    for block_parmas in blocks:              Iterates through the
        outputs = block(**block_params)      dictionary values for
    return outputs                           each block attribute

def block(inputs, **params):
    ''' block layers
        inputs : the input tensors (feature maps)
        params : the block parameters for the block
    '''
    ...
    return outputs                           Assembles the learner component
                                             by specifying the number of groups
outputs = learner(outputs, [ {'n_filters: 128'},   and filters per group
                    {'n_filters: 128'},
                    {'n_filters: 256'} ]
```

5.4.1   ResNet

In ResNet50, 101, and 151, the learner component consists of four convolutional groups. The first group uses a nonstrided convolutional layer for the projection short-cut in the first convolutional block, which takes input from the stem component. The other three convolutional groups use a strided convolutional layer (feature pooling) in the projection shortcut for the first convolutional block. Figure 5.12 shows this arrangement.

Now we'll look at an example application of the skeleton template for coding the learner component of a ResNet50. Note that in the learner() function, we popped off the first group of configuration attributes. In this application, we did this because the first group starts with a nonstrided projection shortcut residual block, while all the

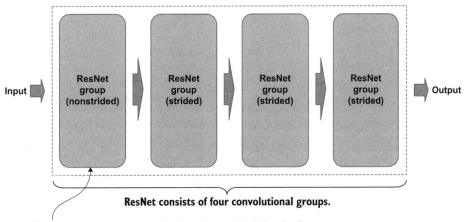

ResNet consists of four convolutional groups.

The first group uses a nonstrided projection block for the first block, while subsequent groups use a strided projection block.

Figure 5.12 In the ResNet learner component, the first group starts with a nonstrided projection shortcut block.

remaining groups use a strided projection shortcut. Alternatively, we could have used a configuration attribute to indicate whether the first residual block is strided or not, and eliminated the special case (coding a separate block construction).

```
def learner(inputs, groups):
    """ Construct the Learner
        inputs: input to the learner
        groups: group parameters per group
    """
    outputs = inputs

    group_params = groups.pop(0)                                    First residual group
    outputs = group(outputs, **group_params, strides=(1, 1))        is not strided.

                                                                    Remaining
                                                                    residual groups
                                                                    are strided
    for group_params in groups:                                     convolutions.
        outputs = group(outputs, **group_params, strides=(2, 2))
    return outputs
```

While ResNets continue to be used today as a stock model for the image classification backbone, the 50-layer ResNet50, depicted in figure 5.13, is the standard. At 50 layers, the model gives high accuracy at reasonable size and performance. The larger ResNets at 101 and 151 layers provide only minor increases in accuracy but at substantial increase in size and reduction in performance.

Each group starts with a residual block with a linear projection shortcut, followed by one or more residual blocks with an identity shortcut. All the residual blocks in a group have the same number of output filters. Each group successively doubles the number of output filters, and the residual block with a linear projection shortcut doubles the number of filters from the input to the group.

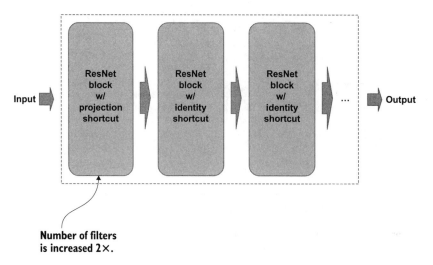

Figure 5.13   In the ResNet group macro-architecture, the first block uses a projection shortcut, and the remaining blocks use an identity link.

The ResNets (for example, 50, 101, 152) consist of four convolutional groups; the output filters for the four groups follow the doubling convention, starting at 64, then 128, 256, and finally 512. The number convention (50) refers to the number of convolutional layers, which determines the number of convolutional blocks in each convolutional group.

The following is an example application of the skeleton template for coding the convolutional group of a ResNet50. For the group() function, we pop off the first block's configuration attributes, which we know for a ResNet is a projection block, and then iterate through the remaining blocks as identity blocks:

```
def group(inputs, blocks, strides=(2, 2)):
    """ Construct a Residual Group
        inputs    : input into the group
        blocks    : block parameters for each block
        strides   : whether the projection block is a strided convolution
    """
    outputs = inputs

    block_params = blocks.pop(0)
    outputs = projection_block(outputs, strides=strides, **block_params)

    for block_params in blocks:
        outputs = identity_block(outputs, **block_params)
    return outputs
```

First block in residual group uses linear projection shortcut link.

Remaining blocks use an identity shortcut link.

A complete code rendition using the Idiomatic procedure reuse design pattern for ResNet is on GitHub (http://mng.bz/7jK9).

5.4.2 DenseNet

The learner component in a DenseNet (https://arxiv.org/abs/1608.06993) consists of four convolutional groups, as shown in figure 5.14. Each group, with the exception of the last group, delays pooling to the end of the group, in what is called the *transitional block*. The last convolutional group has no transitional block, since no group follows. The feature maps will be pooled and flattened by the task component, so it is unnecessary (redundant) to pool at the end of the group. This pattern of deferring final pooling in the last group to the task component continues to be a common convention today.

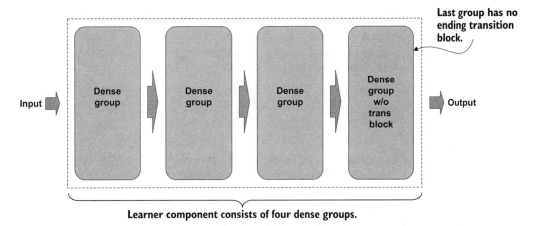

Learner component consists of four dense groups.

Figure 5.14 DenseNet learner component consists of four convolutional groups with delayed pooling.

The following is an example implementation of using the skeleton template for coding the learner component of a DenseNet. Note that we pop off the last group configuration attributes before iterating through the groups. We treat the last group as a special case, as the group does not end in a transition block. Alternatively, we could have used a configuration parameter to indicate whether or not a group contains a transition block, eliminating the special case (that is, coding a separate block construction). The parameter `reduction` specifies the amount of feature map size reduction during delayed pooling:

```
def learner(inputs, groups, reduction):
    """ Construct the Learner
        inputs    : input to the learner
        groups    : set of number of blocks per group
        reduction : the amount to reduce (compress) feature maps by
    """
    outputs = inputs

    last = groups.pop()

    for group_params in groups:
```

Pops off the last dense group parameters and saves for the end

Constructs all but the last dense group with an interceding transition block

```
        outputs = group(outputs, reduction, **group_params)
    outputs = group(outputs, last, reduction=None)
    return outputs
```

Adds the last dense group without a transition block

Let's look at a convolutional group in a DenseNet (figure 5.15). It consists of only two types of convolutional blocks. The first blocks are DenseNet blocks for feature learning, and the last block is a transitional block for reducing the size of the feature maps prior to the next group, which is referred to as the *compression factor*.

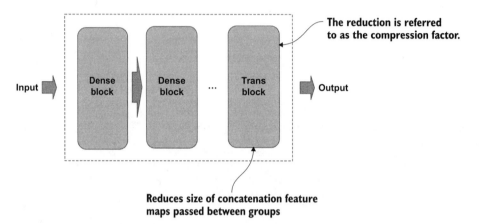

The reduction is referred to as the compression factor.

Input   Dense block   Dense block   ...   Trans block   Output

Reduces size of concatenation feature maps passed between groups

Figure 5.15 A DenseNet group consists of a sequence of dense blocks and a final transition block for dimensionality reduction in outputted feature maps.

A DenseNet block is essentially a residual block, except that in place of adding (matrix add operation) the identity link to the output, it is concatenated. In a ResNet, the information from previous inputs is passed only one block forward. Using concatenation, the information from the feature maps accumulates, and each block passes all the accumulative information forward to all subsequent blocks.

This concatenation of feature maps would result in a continued growth in size of feature maps and corresponding parameters as we go deeper in layers. To control (reduce) the growth, the transitional block at the end of each convolutional block compresses (reduces) the size of the concatenated feature maps. Otherwise, without the reduction, the number of parameters to learn would grow substantially as we grow deeper, resulting in taking longer to train without a benefit in increased accuracy.

The following is an example implementation for coding a DenseNet convolutional group:

```
def group(inputs, reduction=None, **blocks):
    """ Construct a Dense Group
        inputs    : input tensor to the group
```

```
        reduction : amount to reduce feature maps by
        blocks    : parameters for each dense block in the group
    """
    outputs = inputs                               Constructs a group of densely
                                                   connected residual blocks
    for block_params in blocks:            <──┘
        outputs = residual_block(outputs, **block_params)

    if reduction is not None:              <──┐   Constructs interceding
        outputs = trans_block(outputs, reduction)  transition block
    return outputs                               
```

A complete code rendition using the Idiomatic procedure reuse design pattern for DenseNet is on GitHub (http://mng.bz/6N0o). Next we will explain the design of the task component, which the learner component will connect to.

5.5 Task component

The *task component* is where we generally perform task learning. In large conventional CNNs for image classification, this component typically consists of two layers:

- *Bottleneck layer*—Performs dimensionality reduction of final feature maps into latent space
- *Classifier layer*—Performs the task the model is learning

The output from the learner component is the final reduced size of the feature maps (for example, 4×4 pixels). The bottleneck layer does the final dimensionality reduction of the final feature maps, which is then inputted to the classifier layer for classification.

For the remainder of this section, we will describe the task component in the context of an image classifier; we refer to this as the *classification component*.

5.5.1 ResNet

For a ResNet50, the number of feature maps is 2048. The first layer in the classifier component is both flattening the feature maps into a 1D vector and reducing the size, using GlobalAveragePooling2D, for example. This flattening/reduction layer is also referred to as the bottleneck layer, as stated previously. Following the bottleneck layer is a Dense layer that does the classification.

Figure 5.16 depicts the ResNet50 classifier. The input to the classifier component is the final feature maps from the learner component (latent space), which is then passed through GlobalAveragePooling2D, which reduces the size of each feature map to a single pixel and flattens it into a 1D vector (bottleneck). The output from this bottleneck layer is passed through the Dense layer, where the number of nodes corresponds to the number of classes. The output is the probability distribution for all classes, squashed to add up to 100% by a softmax activation.

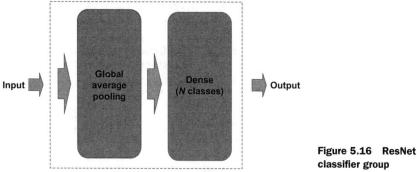

Figure 5.16   ResNet classifier group

The following is an example of coding this approach to a classifier component, consisting of `GlobalAveragePooling2D` for flattening and dimensionality reduction, followed by the `Dense` layer for classification:

```
def classifier(inputs, n_classes):
    """ The output classifier
        inputs    : input tensor to the classifier
        n_classes : number of output classes
    """
    outputs = GlobalAveragePooling2D()(inputs)

    outputs = Dense(n_classes, activation='softmax')(outputs)
    return outputs
```

Uses global average pooling to reduce and flatten the feature maps (latent space) into a 1D feature vector (bottleneck layer)

The fully connected Dense layer for the final classification of the input

A complete code rendition using the Idiomatic procedure reuse design pattern for ResNet is available on GitHub (http://mng.bz/7jK9).

5.5.2 *Multilayer output*

In earlier deployed ML production systems, models were treated as independent algorithms, and we would be interested only in the final output (the prediction). Today, we build not models, but applications that are an amalgamation, or composition, of models. As a result, we no longer treat the task component as a single output.

Instead, we see it as having four outputs, depending on how the model is connected to other models in the application. These outputs are as follows:

- Feature extraction
  - High dimensionality (encoding)
  - Low dimensionality (embedding)—feature vector
- Prediction
  - Prediction pre-activation (probabilities)—soft targets
  - Post-activation (outputs)—hard targets

Later chapters cover the purposes of these outputs (chapter 9 on autoencoders, chapter 11 on transfer learning, and chapter 14 for pretext tasks in training pipelines), and you will see that each layer in the classifier has two parallel outputs. In the multi-output of a conventional classifier depicted in figure 5.17, you can see that the input to the task component is also an independent output of the model, referred to as the *encoding*. The encoding is then passed through a global average pooling for dimensionality reduction, further reducing the size of the features extracted by the learner component. The output from the global average pooling is also an independent output of the model, referred to as the *embedding*.

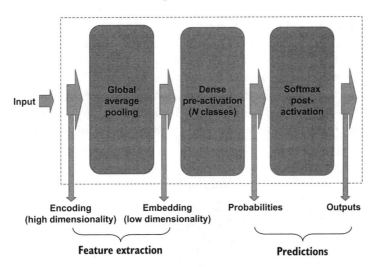

Figure 5.17 Multi-output classifier group with four outputs—two for feature extraction sharing and two for probability distribution

The embedding is then passed to a pre-activation dense layer (prior to the softmax activation). The output from the pre-activation layer is also an independent output of the model, referred to as the *pre-activation probability distribution*. This probability distribution is then passed through a softmax for the post-activation probability distribution, making the fourth independent output of the model. All these outputs can then be used by downstream tasks.

Let's describe a simple real-world example for using a multi-output task component: estimating the cost of repairs from a photo of a vehicle. We want estimates on two categories: costs for minor damage like dings and scratches, and costs for major damage like collision damage. We could attempt to do this in a single task component that acts as a regressor to output a real value (dollar value), but we would really be overloading the task component during training because it's learning both tiny values (minor damage) and large values (major damage). During training, the wide distribution in the values likely will keep the model from converging.

The approach is to solve this as two separate task components: one for minor and one for major damage. The minor damage task component will learn only tiny values, and the major damage task component will learn only large values—so both task components should converge during training.

Next, we consider which output level we share with each of the two tasks. For the minor damage, we are looking at tiny objects. While we are not covering object detection, the historical problem with object classification with small objects was that the cropped feature maps after being pooled contained too little spatial information. The fix was to do the object classification from feature maps at an earlier convolution; the feature maps would then be of sufficient size, so that when a tiny object is cropped out, enough spatial information remains for object classification.

We have a comparable issue in our example. For minor damage, the objects (each ding) will be very small, and we need larger feature maps to detect them. So for this purpose, we connect the high-dimensional encoding, prior to averaging and pooling, to the task that performs minor damage estimating. On the other hand, major collision damage does not require much detail. If the fender has a dent, it has to be replaced no matter the size or location of the dent, for instance. So for this purpose, we connect the low-dimensional embedding, after averaging and pooling, to the task that performs major damage estimating. Figure 5.18 illustrates this example.

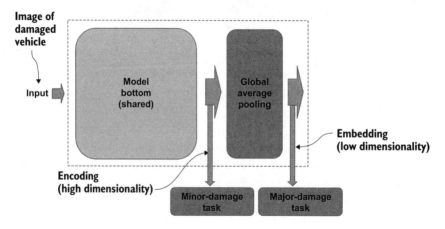

Figure 5.18   Multitask component using multi-outputs from shared model top for estimating vehicle repair costs

The following is an example implementation of coding the multi-outputs to a classifier component. The feature extraction and prediction outputs are implemented by capturing the tensor inputs to each layer. At the end of the classifier, we replace returning a single output with returning a tuple of all four outputs:

```
def classifier(inputs, n_classes):
    """ The output classifier
        inputs    : input tensor to the classifier
        n_classes : number of output classes
    """
    encoding = inputs          High-dimensionality feature
                               extraction (encoding)
```

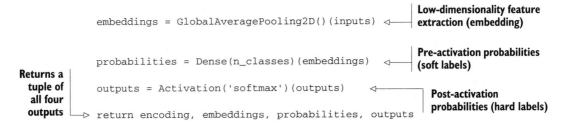

Returns a tuple of all four outputs

```
embeddings = GlobalAveragePooling2D()(inputs)          Low-dimensionality feature
                                                        extraction (embedding)

probabilities = Dense(n_classes)(embeddings)            Pre-activation probabilities
                                                        (soft labels)

outputs = Activation('softmax')(outputs)                Post-activation
                                                        probabilities (hard labels)
return encoding, embeddings, probabilities, outputs
```

5.5.3 SqueezeNet

In compact models, particularly for mobile devices, GlobalAveraging2D followed by a Dense layer is replaced with a Conv2D using a softmax activation. The number of filters in Conv2D is set to the number of classes, and then followed by GlobalAveraging2D for the flattening into the number of classes. The "SqueezeNet" paper by Forrest Iandola et al. (https://arxiv.org/pdf/1602.07360.pdf) explains the reasoning for replacing the dense layer with a convolution layer: "Note the lack of fully connected layers in SqueezeNet; this design choice was inspired by the NiN (Lin et al., 2013) architecture."

Figure 5.19 is a coding example of a SqueezeNet that uses this approach to the classifier component. SqueezeNet was developed in 2016 by DeepScale, the University of California at Berkeley, and Stanford University for mobile devices, and was SOTA at the time.

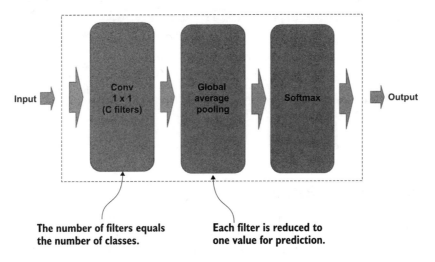

Figure 5.19 SqueezeNet classifier group

You can see that instead of a dense layer, it uses a 1×1 convolution, in which the number of filters corresponds to the number of classes (C). In this way, the 1×1 convolution is learning a probability distribution for the classes instead of a projection of the input feature maps. The resulting (C) feature maps are then each reduced into a single real value for the probability distribution and flattened into a 1D output vector. For example, if each feature map outputted by the 1 × 1 convolution is 3 × 3 in size (9 pixels), the pixel with the highest value is chosen as the probability for the corresponding class. The 1D vector is then squashed by a softmax activation so all the probabilities add up to 1.

Let's contrast this to the global average pooling and dense layer approach we've discussed in large SOTA models. Let's assume the size of the final feature maps is 3 × 3 (9 pixels). We then average the 9 pixels to a single value and do a probability distribution based on a single average value per feature map. In the method used by SqueezeNet, the convolutional layer that does the probability distribution sees the 9-pixel feature map (versus an averaged single pixel) and has more pixels to learn the probability distribution. This was likely chosen by SqueezeNet's authors to offset the lesser amount of feature extraction/learning with a smaller model bottom.

The following is a sample for coding the SqueezeNet classifier component. In this example, the number of filters for the `Conv2D` is the number of classes (n_classes), which is then followed by `GlobalAveragePooling2D`. Since this layer is a static (not learned) layer, it has no activation parameter, so we must explicitly follow it with a softmax activation layer:

```
def classifier(inputs, n_classes):
    ''' Construct the Classifier
        inputs   : input tensor to the classifier
        n_classes: number of output classes
    '''
    encoding = Conv2D(n_classes, (1, 1), strides=1,          ◁─── Sets the number of filters
                      activation='relu', padding='same')(inputs)      equal to the number of
                                                                       output classes

    embedding = GlobalAveragePooling2D()(outputs)    ◁─── Reduces each feature
    outputs = Activation('softmax')(outputs)              map (class) to a single
    return outputs                                        value (soft label)
```

Uses softmax to squash all the class probabilities to add up to 100%

A complete code rendition using the Idiomatic procedure reuse design pattern for SqueezeNet is located on GitHub (http://mng.bz/XYmv).

5.6 *Beyond computer vision: NLP*

As mentioned in chapter 1, the design patterns I explain in the context of computer vision have comparable principles and patterns in natural language processing and structured data. To see how a procedural design pattern can be applied to NLP, let's look at an example from a type of NLP, natural-language understanding (NLU).

5.6.1 *Natural-language understanding*

Let's start by taking a look at the general model architecture for NLU in figure 5.20. In NLU, the model learns to understand the text and learns to perform a task based

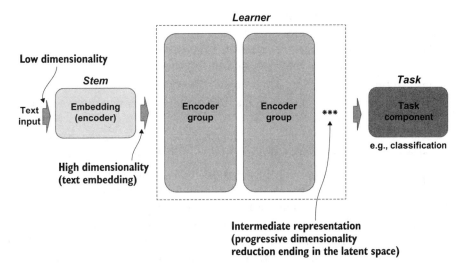

Figure 5.20 As with all deep learning models, NLU models consist of stem, learner, and task components. The differences lie inside each component.

on that understanding. Examples of tasks include classifying the text, sentiment analysis, and entity extraction.

We might be classifying medical documents by type; for example, identifying each as a prescription, doctor's note, claim submission, or other document. For sentiment analysis, the task might be determining whether a review was favorable or unfavorable (binary classification) or ranking from unfavorable to favorable (multiclass classification). For entity extraction, our task might be extracting health vitals from lab results and doctor/nurse notes.

An NLU model is decomposed into the same components that make up all deep learning models: stem, learner, and task. The differences lie in what happens in each component.

In an NLU model, the stem consists of an encoder. Its purpose is to convert the string representation of the text into a numeric-based vector, referred to as an *embedding*. This embedding is of a higher dimensionality than the string input and contains richer contextual information about the words, or characters, or sentences. The stem encoder is actually another model that has been pretrained. Think of the stem encoder as a dictionary. For each word, the low dimensionality, it outputs all the possible meanings, the high dimensionality. A common example of an embedding is a vector of N dimensions, in which each element represents another word, and the value indicates how closely this word is related to the other word.

Next, the embeddings are passed to the learner component. In an NLU model, the learner consists of one or more encoder groups, which consist, in turn, of one or more encoder blocks. Each of these blocks is based on a design pattern, such as an attention block in a transformer model, and the assembly of the blocks and groups is based on design principles for encoder patterns.

You probably notice that both the stem and learner refer to an encoder. *They are not the same type of encoder in each component.* Having the same name for two different things can be a bit confusing, so I'll clarify. When we talk about the encoder that generates embeddings, we will refer to it as the *stem encoder*; otherwise, we are referring to the encoder in the learner.

The purpose of the encoder in the learner is to convert the embeddings to a lower-dimensionality representation of the meaning of the text, which is called an *intermediate representation.* This is comparable to learning the essential features in an image in a CNN.

The task component is remarkably similar to the computer vision counterpart. The intermediate representation is flattened into a 1D vector and pooled. The pooled representation, for classification and semantic analysis, is passed to a softmax dense layer to predict a probability distribution across the classes or semantic rankings.

As for entity extraction, the task component is comparable to the task component for an object detection model; you are learning two tasks: classifying the extracted entity, and fine-tuning the location boundary in the text of the extracted entity.

5.6.2 *Transformer architecture*

Let's now look at another aspect of modern (NLU) models that's comparable to the SOTA in computer vision. As mentioned in chapter 1, a major change in NLU occurred with the introduction of the Transformer model architecture by Google Brain in 2017, and the corresponding paper "Attention is All You Need" by Ashishh Vaswani et al. (https://arxiv.org/abs/1706.03762). The Transformer architecture addressed a challenging problem in NLU: how to handle text sequences that are essentially comparable to a time-series—that is, the meaning is dependent on the sequence ordering of the words. Previously to the Transformer architecture, NLU models were implemented as recurrent neural networks (RNNs), which would retain the sequence ordering of the text and learn the importance (long memory) or non-importance (short memory) of the words.

What the Transformer model did is introduce a new mechanism called *attention* that transformed NLU models from a time-series to a spatial model. Instead of looking at words, or characters, or sentences as a sequence, we take a chunk of words and represent them spatially, like an image. The model learns to extract essential context—the features. The attention mechanism acts similarly to the identity link in a residual network. It adds attention—weight—to the contexts that are more important.

Figure 5.21 shows an attention block in a transformer architecture. The input to the block is a set of context maps, comparable to feature maps, from the previous block. The attention mechanism adds weight to portions of the context block that are more important to the contextual understanding (indicating to pay attention here). The attention context maps are then passed to a feed-forward layer that outputs the next set of context maps.

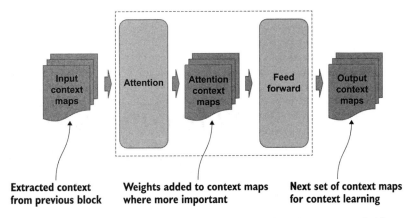

Extracted context   **Weights added to context maps**   **Next set of context maps**
from previous block   **where more important**   **for context learning**

**Figure 5.21   An attention block adds weight to the portion of the context that is
more important to the understanding of the text.**

In the next chapter, we will cover wide convolutional neural networks, a design pattern that focuses on wider layers instead of deeper layers.

Summary

- Using a design pattern to design and code a CNN makes models more understandable, saves time, ensures that the model represents best SOTA practices, and is easy for others to reproduce.
- The procedural design pattern uses the software engineering principle of reuse that is widely practiced by software engineers.
- The macro-architecture consists of stem, learner, and task components that define the flow through the model and where/what type of learning occurs.
- The micro-architecture consists of group and block design patterns that define how the model performs learning.
- The purpose of a pre-stem group is to extend existing (pretrained) models for upstream data preprocessing, image augmentation, and adaptations to other deployed environments. Implementing pre-stems as plug-and-play provides ML ops to deploy models without accompanying upstream code.
- The purpose of the task component is to learn a model-specific task from the latent space, encoding learning during feature extraction and representational learning.
- The purpose of a multiple-layer output is to extend interconnectivity between models for complex tasks in the most efficient way while maintaining performance objectives.
- The attention mechanism in a transformer provided the method to sequentially learn the essential features in a manner comparable to computer vision, without the need for a recurrent network.

Wide convolutional neural networks

This chapter covers

- Introducing the wide convolutional layer design pattern
- Understanding the advantages of wide versus deep layers
- Refactoring micro-architecture patterns to decrease computational complexity
- Coding former SOTA wide convolutional models with the procedural design pattern

Up to now, we've focused on networks with deeper layers, block layers, and shortcuts in residual networks for image-related tasks such as classification, object localization, and image segmentation. Now we are going to take a look at networks with wide, rather than deep, convolutional layers. Starting in 2014 with Inception v1 (GoogLeNet) and 2015 with ResNeXt and Inception v2, neural network designs moved into wide layers, reducing the need for going deeper in layers. Essentially, a wide-layer design means having multiple convolutions in parallel and then concatenating their outputs. In contrast, deeper layers have sequential convolutions and aggregate their outputs.

So what led to the experimentation with wide-layer design patterns? At the time, researchers understood that for models to gain in accuracy, they needed more capacity. More specifically, they needed to have overcapacity for redundancy.

Early work with VGG (https://arxiv.org/pdf/1409.1556.pdf) and ResNet v1 (https://arxiv.org/abs/1512.03385) demonstrated that the capacity added by deeper layers did indeed increase accuracy. For example, AlexNet (2012) was the first convolutional neural network submission as well as the winner in the ILSVRC challenge, achieving a top-5 category error of 15.3%, which was 10% better than the 2011 winner. ZFNet built on AlexNet and became the 2013 winner with a top-5 error of 14.8%. Then, in 2014, VGG pushed deeper in layers, becoming first runner-up with a top-5 error rate of 7.3%, while ResNet went even deeper in 2015, and took first place with a top-5 error rate of 3.57%.

But these designs all hit roadblocks that limited the depth of the layers, and thus the ability to add more capacity. A major problem was vanishing and exploding gradients. As deeper layers were added to the models, the weights in these deeper layers were more likely to either get too small (vanishing) or too large (exploding). During training, the models would crash, much like a computer program crashes.

The introduction of batch normalization in 2015 partially solved this problem. The authors of the seminal paper (https://arxiv.org/abs/1502.03167) hypothesized that redistributing the weights during training at each layer into a normal distribution would solve the problem of weights getting too small or too big in deeper layers. Other researchers validated the hypothesis, and batch normalization became a convention that continues today.

But another problem still remained with going deeper with layers: memorization. It turned out that deeper layers, which added the overcapacity for higher accuracy, were more likely to memorize the data than the shallower layers. That is, with overcapacity, the examples from the training data could snap into the nodes instead of generalizing from the training data. When you see increasing accuracy during training on the training data, but plummeting accuracy on examples not seen during training, we say the model is *overfitting*. And it was overfitting that indicated the models were memorizing rather than learning. Adding some noise in the deeper layers, like dropout and Gaussian noise, reduced memorization but did not eliminate it.

But what if we added capacity by making convolutions in the shallower layers wider instead? That added capacity would reduce the need to go deeper in layers, where memorization occurred. Take, for example, ResNeXt, which was first runner-up in the 2016 ILSVRC competition. It replaced the sequential convolution in a residual block with a parallel convolution to add capacity in shallow layers.

This chapter covers the evolution in design of wide layers, starting with the principle of the naive inception module, which was resigned in Inception v1, and then the wide-layer block refinements in Inception v2 and v3. We will also look at the parallel evolution in the design of wide layers in ResNeXt by Facebook AI Research and Wide Residual Network by Paris Tech.

6.1   *Inception v1*

Inception v1 (https://arxiv.org/abs/1409.4842), which won the 2014 ILSVRC contest for object detection under its original name, GoogLeNet, introduced the *inception module.* This convolutional layer has parallel convolutions of different filter sizes, with the outputs from each convolution getting concatenated together. The idea here was that instead of trying to pick the best filter size for a layer, each layer has multiple filter sizes in parallel, and the layer "learns which size is the best."

For example, assume you've designed a model with multiple layers of convolutions, but you don't know what filter size will give you the best result. Say you want to know which of three sizes—3 × 3, 5 × 5, or 7 × 7—would give you the best accuracy. To compare the accuracy, you would have to make three versions of the model, one for each filter size, and train each one. But say you now want to know the best filter size on each layer. Perhaps the first layer should be a 7 × 7, the next 5 × 5, and the remainder 3 × 3 (or some other combination). Depending on the depth, this could mean hundreds or even thousands of possible combinations. Training each combination would be an enormous undertaking.

Instead, the inception module design solved the problem by having every feature map pass through parallel convolutions of different filter sizes at each convolutional layer. This innovation allowed the model to learn the appropriate filter size with a single version and training of a model instance.

6.1.1   *Naive inception module*

Figure 6.1 shows the *naive inception module,* which demonstrates this approach.

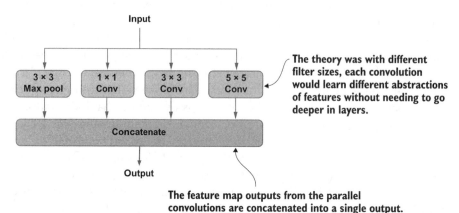

Figure 6.1   The naive inception module that was the theoretical base for experimenting with various variants of the inception module

The native inception module is a convolutional block. Input to the block is passed through four branches: a pooling layer for dimensionality reduction, and 1 × 1, 3 × 3, and 5 × 5 convolutional layers. The outputs from the pooling and the other convolutional layers are then concatenated together.

The different filter sizes capture different levels of detail. The 1 × 1 convolution captures fine details of features, while the 5 × 5 captures more-abstract features. You can see this process in the example implementation of a naive inception module. The input from a previous block (layer) x is branched and passed through a max pooling layer, 1 × 1, 3 × 3, and 5 × 5 convolutions, which are then concatenated together:

**The inception branches,
where x is the previous layer**

```
x1 = MaxPooling2D((3, 3), strides=(1,1), padding='same')(x)
x2 =Conv2D(64,(1,1),strides=(1,1),padding='same',activation='relu')(x)
x3 =Conv2D(96,(3,3),strides=(1,1),padding='same',activation='relu')(x)
x4 =Conv2D(48,(5,5),strides=(1,1),padding='same',activation='relu')(x)

output = Concatenate()([x1, x2, x3, x4])
```
Concatenates the outputs from the four branches together

By setting padding='same', the height and width dimensions of the input are preserved. This allows concatenating the corresponding outputs from each branch together. For example, if the input was 256 feature maps of size 28 × 28, the dimensions at the branch layers would be as follows, where ? is a placeholder for the batch size:

```
x1 (pool)      :   (?, 28, 28, 256)
x2 (1x1)       :   (?, 28, 28, 64)
x2 (3x3)       :   (?, 28, 28, 96)
x3 (5x5)       :   (?, 28, 28, 48)
```

After the concatenation, the output would be as follows:

```
x (concat)     :   (?, 28, 28, 464)
```

Let's now see how we got to these numbers. First, both the convolution and max pooling are nonstrided (meaning they have a stride of 1), so there is no downsampling of the feature maps. Second, since we set padding='same', we won't have any loss in pixel width/height for the edges. So the size of the feature maps outputted will be the same as the input, hence the 28 × 28 in the output.

Now, let's look at the max pooling branch, which outputs the same number of feature maps that come in, so that's why we get 256. The number of feature maps for the three convolutional branches is equal to the number of filters, so that would be 64, 96, 48. Then if we add up all the feature maps from the branches for the concatenation, we get 464.

A summary() for a naive inception module shows 544,000 parameters to train:

```
max_pooling2d_1 (MaxPooling2D (None, 28, 28, 256)  0        input_1[0][0]

conv2d_1 (Conv2D)             (None, 28, 28, 64)   16448    input_1[0][0]

conv2d_2 (Conv2D)             (None, 28, 28, 96)   221280 input_1[0][0]

conv2d_3 (Conv2D)             (None, 28, 28, 48)   307248 input_1[0][0]

concatenate_1 (Concatenate) (None, 28, 28, 464)  0        max_pooling2d_1[0][0]
conv2d_1[0][0]
conv2d_2[0][0]
conv2d_3[0][0]
==========================================================================
Total params: 544,976
Trainable params: 544,976
```

If the padding='same' argument were to be left out (defaults to padding='valid'), the shapes would be as follows instead:

```
x1 (pool)    :   (?, 26, 26, 256)
x2 (1x1)     :   (?, 28, 28, 64)
x2 (3x3)     :   (?, 26, 26, 96)
x3 (5x5)     :   (?, 24, 24, 48)
```

Since the width and height dimensions do not match, if you tried to concatenate these layers, you would get the following error:

```
ValueError: A Concatenate layer requires inputs with matching shapes except
➥ for the concat axis. Got inputs shapes: [(None, 26, 26, 256), (None, 28,
➥ 28, 64), (None, 26, 26, 96), (None, 24, 24, 48)]
```

The naive inception module was a theoretical principle of the Inception v1 authors. When the authors went to the ILSVRC contest, they refactored the module by using a bottleneck residual block design, referred to as the Inception v1 module. This module maintained accuracy and was computationally less expensive to train.

6.1.2 *Inception v1 module*

Inception v1 introduced a further dimensionality reduction by adding a 1 × 1 bottleneck convolution to the pooling, 3 × 3, and 5 × 5 branches. This dimension reduction reduced the overall computational complexity by nearly two-thirds.

At this point, you may be asking, why use a 1 × 1 convolution? How can a 1-pixel filter being scanned across each channel learn any feature? The use of a 1 × 1 convolution acts like glue code. The 1 × 1 convolutions are either used to expand or reduce the number of channels in the output while preserving the channel size (shape). Expanding the number of channels is referred to as a *linear projection*; we discussed this in section 5.3.1.

Reducing, also known as a *bottleneck,* is used to reduce the number of channels between the input to a block and the input to a convolutional layer. The linear projection and bottleneck convolutions are analogous to upsampling and down-sampling, except that we are not expanding or reducing the *size* of the channels, but the *number* of them. In this case, as we are reducing the number of channels, we could say we are compressing the data—and that's why we use the term *dimensionality reduction*. We could do this using a static algorithm, or, as in this case, we *learn the optimal method to reduce the number of channels*. This is analogous to max pooling and feature pooling; in max pooling, we use a static algorithm to reduce the size of the channels, and with feature pooling, we *learn the optimal method to reduce the size*.

Figure 6.2 shows the Inception v1 block (module). The 3 × 3 and 5 × 5 branches are preceded by a 1 × 1 bottleneck convolution, and the pooling branch is followed by a 1 × 1 bottleneck convolution.

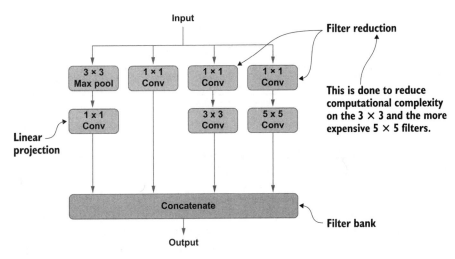

Figure 6.2   The design of the Inception v1 block (module), which was used in the 2014 ILSVRC submission

And here is an example of an Inception v1 block (module), where the pooling, 3 × 3, and 5 × 5 convolution branches have an additional 1 × 1 bottleneck convolution:

```
x1 = MaxPooling2D((3, 3), strides=(1,1), padding='same')(x)
x1 = Conv2D(64, (1, 1), strides=(1, 1), padding='same',
➥ activation='relu')(x1)
x2 = Conv2D(64, (1, 1), strides=(1, 1), padding='same', activation='relu')(x)
x3 = Conv2D(64, (1, 1), strides=(1, 1), padding='same', activation='relu')(x)
x3 = Conv2D(96, (3, 3), strides=(1, 1), padding='same',
➥ activation='relu')(x3)
x4 = Conv2D(64, (1, 1), strides=(1, 1), padding='same', activation='relu')(x)
x4 = Conv2D(48, (5, 5), strides=(1, 1), padding='same',
➥ activation='relu')(x4)

x = Concatenate([x1, x2, x3, x4])
```

The inception branches, where x is the previous layer

Concatenates the feature maps from the branches together

A `summary()` for these layers shows 198,000 parameters to train, in contrast to 544,000 parameters in the native inception module with the use of the bottleneck convolution for dimensionality reduction. The model's designers were able to maintain the same accuracy level as the naive inception module, but with faster training and improved performance on prediction (inference):

```
max_pooling2d_1 (MaxPooling2D (None, 28, 28, 256)   0            input_1[0][0]
_____
conv2d_1 (Conv2D)             (None, 28, 28, 64)    16448        input_1[0][0]
_____
conv2d_2 (Conv2D)             (None, 28, 28, 64)    16448        input_1[0][0]
_____
conv2d_3 (Conv2D)             (None, 28, 28, 64)    16448        max_pooling2d_1[0][0]
_____
conv2d_4 (Conv2D)             (None, 28, 28, 64)    16448        input_1[0][0]
_____
conv2d_5 (Conv2D)             (None, 28, 28, 96)    55392        conv2d_4[0][0]
_____
conv2d_6 (Conv2D)             (None, 28, 28, 48)    76848        conv2d_2[0][0]
_____
concatenate_430 (Concatenate) (None, 28, 28, 272)   0            conv2d_3[0][0]
conv2d_1[0][0]
conv2d_5[0][0]
conv2d_6[0][0]
================================================================================
Total params: 198,032
Trainable params: 198,032
```

As you can see in figure 6.3, the Inception v1 architecture, when retrofitted into the procedural design pattern, consists of four components: stem, learner, classifier, and auxiliary classifier. Overall, the macro-architecture represented by the procedural design pattern is the same as previous SOTA models I've shown, except for the addition

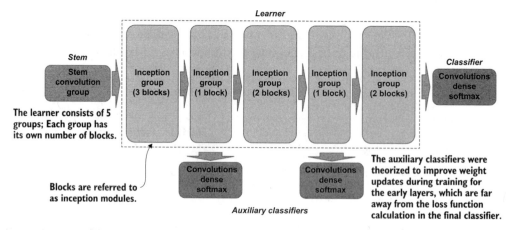

Figure 6.3   In the Inception v1 macro-architecture, the auxiliary classifiers were added after the second and fourth inception groups.

of the auxiliary classifiers. As the diagram shows, the learner component consists of five convolutional groups, and each group has a different number of convolutional blocks. The second and fourth convolutional groups are the only groups with a single convolutional block, and are the groups connected with an auxiliary classifier.

The fact that Inception v1 won first place in the 2014 ILSVRC challenge for object detection demonstrated the utility of exploring design patterns for wide layers in conjunction with deeper layers.

Note that I've been referring to modules as blocks, which is the term used in this design pattern. Next, we will explore each component in more detail.

6.1.3 *Stem*

The stem is the entry point into the neural network. The inputs (images) are processed by a sequential (deep) set of convolutions and max pooling, much like a conventional ConvNet.

Let's dive a little deeper into the stem so you can see how its construction differed from conventional SOTA stems of the time (figure 6.4). Inception used a very coarse 7 × 7 initial filter followed by a very aggressive feature map reduction consisting of two strided convolutions and two max poolings. On the other hand, it progressively increased the number of feature maps from 64 to 192. Inception was coded without the benefit of being able to move the filter past the edge in a convolutional. So to preserve the reducing height and width by half during the reduction, zero padding was added.

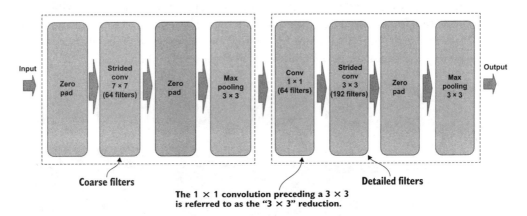

Figure 6.4   The Inception v1 stem consists of a coarse 7 × 7 filter followed by a detailed 3 × 3 filter, along with dimensionality reduction after each convolution with max pooling.

6.1.4 *Learner*

The learner is a set of nine inception blocks in five groups, shown previously in figure 6.3 and again in figure 6.5. The wider groups in the diagram represent a group of two or three inception blocks, and the thinner ones are a single inception block, for a total of nine inception blocks. The fourth and seventh blocks (single blocks) are separated out to highlight they have an additional component, the auxiliary classifier.

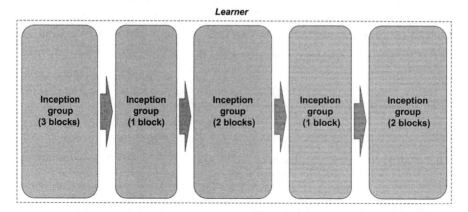

Figure 6.5   The group configuration and number of blocks in the Inception v1 learner component.

6.1.5   *Auxiliary classifiers*

The auxiliary classifiers are a set of two classifiers, acting as auxiliaries (aids) in training the neural network. Each auxiliary classifier consists of a convolutional layer, a dense layer, and a final softmax activation function (figure 6.6). Softmax (as you may already know) is an equation from statistics that takes as input a set of independent probabilities (from 0 to 1) and squashes the set such that all the probabilities add up to 1. In a final dense layer with one node per class, each node makes an independent prediction (from 0 to 1), and by passing the values through a softmax function, the sum of the predicted probabilities for all classes will add up to 1.

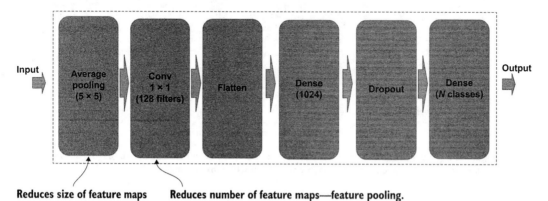

Reduces size of feature maps   Reduces number of feature maps—feature pooling.

Figure 6.6   Inception v1/v2 auxiliary classifier group

The Inception v1 architecture introduced the concept of an auxiliary classifier. The principle here is that as a neural network gets deeper in layers (as the front layers get further away from the final classifier), the front layers are more exposed to a vanishing gradient and increased time (increased number of epochs) to train the weights in the frontmost layers. Figure 6.7 illustrates this process. As updates to weights are propagated from the back layers, the updates tend to get progressively smaller.

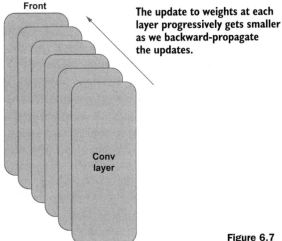

Front

The update to weights at each layer progressively gets smaller as we backward-propagate the updates.

Conv layer

Back

Figure 6.7 Weight updates get progressively smaller through layers during backward propagation.

As theorized by the Inception v1 authors, this can lead to two problems they wanted to fix. First, if the updates get too small, the multiplication operation may result in a number too small to be represented by the floating-point computer hardware (this is referred to as the *vanishing gradient*).

The other problem is that if the updates to the early layers are much smaller than the later layers, they will take longer to converge and increase training time. Additionally, if the later layers converge early and early layers converge later, then the later layers may start memorizing the data while the early layers are still learning to generalize.

The Inception v1 authors' theory is that at the semi-deep layers, there is some information to predict, or classify, the input, albeit with less accuracy than the final classifier. These earlier classifiers are closer to the front layers and thus less prone to a vanishing gradient. During training, the cost function becomes a combination of the losses of the auxiliary classifiers and the final classifier. In other words, the authors thought that combining the losses from the auxiliary and final classifier would result in more uniform updates to the weights across all layers, alleviating the vanishing gradient and decreasing training time.

The auxiliary classifier depicted in figure 6.6 is used in both Inception v1 and Inception v2. Subsequent to Inception, the practice of using an auxiliary classifier was not pursued for two reasons. First, as models went even deeper in layers, the issue of vanishing (and exploding) gradients became more pronounced in the deeper layers than the front layers, so the theory did not pan out in deeper neural networks. Second, the introduction of batch normalization in 2015 uniformly addressed this issue across all layers.

When compared to the VGG design, Inception v1 eliminated adding additional dense layers in the classifier (in both the auxiliary and final classifier), in contrast to VGG, which had two additional 4096-node dense layers. The authors theorized that the additional dense nodes were unnecessary for training the final dense layer for classification. This substantially reduced the computational complexity without reduction in accuracy on the classifier. In subsequent SOTA models, researchers found they could eliminate all preceding dense layers between the bottleneck and final classifier layer, without reduction in accuracy.

Inception was one of the last SOTA models that used a dropout layer in the classifiers for regularization to reduce overfitting. After the subsequent introduction of batch normalization, researchers observed that the normalization added a small amount of regularization on a per layer basis, and was more effective at generalization than dropout. Eventually, researchers would introduce explicit layer-by-layer regularization known as *weight regularization*, further improving regularization. Thus, subsequently the use of dropout was phased out.

6.1.6   *Classifier*

Figure 6.8 depicts the final (non-auxiliary) classifier in both training the neural network and in prediction. Note that for prediction, the auxiliary classifiers are removed. The classifier implements a global average pooling step as two layers; the first layer (AveragePooling2D) does an average pooling of each feature map into 1×1 feature maps, which is then followed by a flatten layer to flatten into a 1D vector. Prior to the Dense layer for classification, a Dropout layer was used for regularization—which was a common practice of the time.

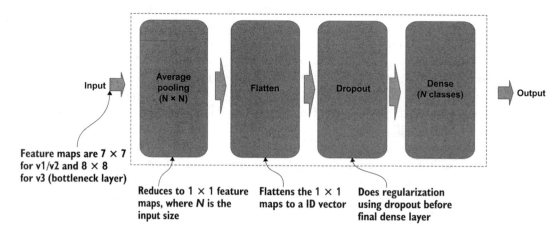

Figure 6.8   In the Inception final classifier, the pooling into 1 × 1 pixel maps and flattening is done as two steps.

A complete code rendition using the Idiomatic procedure reuse design pattern for Inception v1 is on GitHub (http://mng.bz/oGnd).

Next, let's see how Inception v2 introduced the concept of factorization of computationally expensive convolutions.

6.2   *Inception v2: Factoring convolutions*

The larger a filter (kernel) size is in a convolution, the more computationally expensive it is. The paper that presented the *Inception v2* architecture calculated that the 5 × 5 convolution in the inception module was 2.78 times more computationally expensive than a 3 × 3. In other words, a 5 × 5 filter requires almost three times more matmul operations, requiring more time for training and prediction. The authors' goal was to find a way to replace 5 × 5 filters with a 3 × 3 filter to reduce training/prediction time without sacrificing the model's accuracy.

Inception v2 introduced *factorization* for the more expensive convolutions in an inception module to reduce computational complexity, and reduce information loss from representational bottlenecks. Figure 6.9 depicts representational loss. In this depiction, we show a 5 × 5 filter that covers an area of 25 pixels. During each slide of the filter, the area of 25 pixels is replaced (represented by) a single pixel. This single pixel in the corresponding feature map in a subsequent pooling operation will be reduced by one-half. The representational loss is the ratio of compression, in this case 50 (25 to 0.5). For a smaller 3 × 3 filter, the representational loss is 18 (9 to 0.5).

In the Inception v2 module, the 5 × 5 filter is replaced by a stack of two 3 × 3 filters, which results in a reduction of computational complexity of the replaced 5 × 5 filter by 33%.

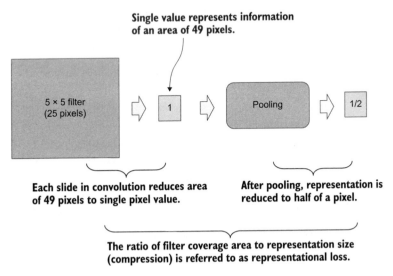

Figure 6.9   **Representational loss between filter and outputted pixel value after subsequent pooling**

Additionally, representational bottleneck loss occurs when large differences in filter sizes exist. By replacing the 5 × 5 with two 3 × 3 filters, all the non-bottleneck filters are now of the same size, and the overall accuracy of the Inception v2 architecture increases over Inception v1.

Figure 6.10 illustrates the Inception v2 block: the 5 × 5 convolution in v1 is replaced by two 3 × 3 convolutions.

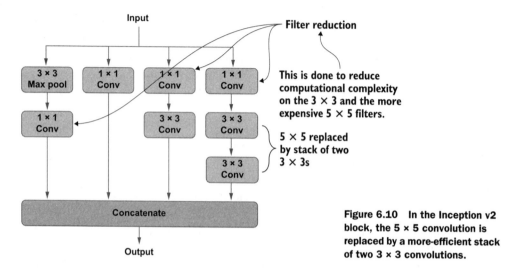

Figure 6.10   In the Inception v2 block, the 5 × 5 convolution is replaced by a more-efficient stack of two 3 × 3 convolutions.

Inception v2 also added using a post-activation batch normalization (Conv-BN-ReLU) for each convolutional layer. Since batch normalization was not introduced until 2015, the 2014 Inception v1 did not have the benefit of using this technique. Figure 6.11 shows the difference between the previous convolution without a batch normalization (Conv-ReLU) and a post-activation batch normalization.

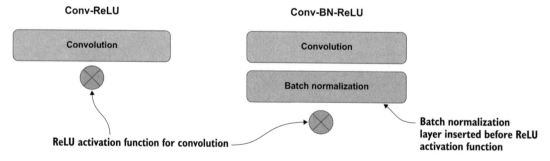

Figure 6.11   A comparison between convolutional layer and activation before and after the convention of adding batch normalization

The following is a code example of an Inception v2 module, which differs from v1 as follows:

- Each convolution layer is followed by a batch normalization.
- The v1 5 × 5 convolution is replaced by two 3 × 3 convolutions, and the factorization of the more-expensive 5 × 5 to less-expensive pair of 3 × 3 convolutions reduced computational complexity and information loss from representational bottlenecks.

**Uses post-activation
batch normalization**

```
x1 = MaxPooling2D((3, 3), strides=(1,1), padding='same')(x)
x1 = Conv2D(64, (1, 1), strides=(1, 1), padding='same')(x1)
x1 = BatchNormalization()(x1)
x1 = ReLU()(x1)

x2 = Conv2D(64, (1, 1), strides=(1, 1), padding='same')(x)
x2 = BatchNormalization()(x2)
x2 = ReLU()(x2)

x3 = Conv2D(64, (1, 1), strides=(1, 1), padding='same')(x)
x3 = BatchNormalization()(x3)
x3 = ReLU()(x3)
x3 = Conv2D(96, (3, 3), strides=(1, 1), padding='same')(x3)
x3 = BatchNormalization()(x3)
x3 = ReLU()(x3)

x4 = Conv2D(64, (1, 1), strides=(1, 1), padding='same')(x)
x4 = BatchNormalization()(x4)
x4 = ReLU()(x4)
x4 = Conv2D(48, (3, 3), strides=(1, 1), padding='same')(x4)
x4 = BatchNormalization()(x4)
x4 = ReLU()(x4)
x4 = Conv2D(48, (3, 3), strides=(1, 1), padding='same')(x4)
x4 = BatchNormalization()(x4)
x4 = ReLU()(x4)

x = Concatenate([x1, x2, x3, x4])
```

The Inception branches, where x is the previous layer

Concatenates the feature maps from the branches together

A `summary()` for these layers shows 169,000 parameters to train, when compared to 198,000 for the inception v1 module.

A complete code rendition using the Idiomatic procedure reuse design pattern for Inception v2 is located on GitHub (http://mng.bz/oGnd). Next, we will describe how the Inception architecture was redesigned in Inception v3.

6.3 *Inception v3: Architecture redesign*

The *Inception v3* introduced a new design to the macro-architecture, as well as redesigning the stem group and using only a single auxiliary classifier. Christian Szegedy et al. referred to this arrangement in the title of their paper, "Rethinking the Inception Architecture" (https://arxiv.org/abs/1512.00567).

The authors noted that substantial strides had been made in recent years in improving accuracy and lowering parameter size by going both deeper and wider. AlexNet had 60 million parameters, and VGG had three times that many, whereas Inception v1 had only 5 million. The authors emphasized the need for efficient architectures that could move models into real-world use and provide further efficiency in parameters while achieving higher accuracy gains.

In their opinion, the Inception v1/v2 architecture was too complex for this purpose. For example, doubling the size of the filter banks for more capacity would increase the number of parameters by four times. The motivation for the redesign was to simplify the architecture, while maintaining computational gains when scaled and improving on the accuracy of existing SOTA models of the time.

In the redesign, the convolutional blocks were refactored so the architecture could be scaled up efficiently. Figure 6.12 shows the macro-architecture: the learner component is composed of three groups (A, B, and C) for feature learning, as well as two grid reduction groups for feature map reduction. In addition, the number of auxiliary classifiers is reduced from two to one.

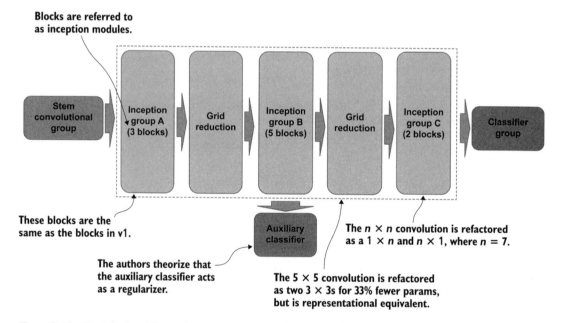

Figure 6.12   The redesigned Inception v3 macro-architecture simplified the Inception v1 and v2 architecture.

Let's spend the next few sections looking more closely at these redesigned components.

6.3.1 *Inception groups and blocks*

Four design principles shaped the redesign of the Inception architecture:

1. Avoid representational loss.
2. Higher-dimensional representations are easier to process locally within a network.
3. Spatial aggregation can be done over lower-dimensional embeddings without much loss in representational power.
4. Balance the width and depth of the network.

The micro-architecture of the Inception reflected the first design principle, of reducing information loss from representational bottlenecks, by achieving a more gradual reduction in feature map size. It also addressed principle 4, balancing the width and depth of the convolutional layers. The authors observed that the optimal improvement occurred when the increase in width and depth was done in parallel, and the computational budget is balanced between the two. Consequently, the model increases both width and depth in order to contribute to higher-quality networks.

Let's zoom in even more now, and look at the redesigns for groups A, B, and C. The blocks in group A remain the same as in the earlier versions, while group B and C differ. The output feature map sizes for groups A, B, and C are 35×35, 17×17, and 8×8, respectively. Note the gradual reduction in feature map sizes, as each group reduces by half the $H \times W$. This gradual reduction across the three groups reflects design principle 1, reducing representational loss, as the network goes deeper.

Figures 6.13 and 6.14 show the blocks in groups B and C, respectively. In these two groups, some of the $N \times N$ convolutions are factored into spatial separable convolutions of $N \times 1$ and $1 \times N$. This adjustment reflected design principle 3, which states that

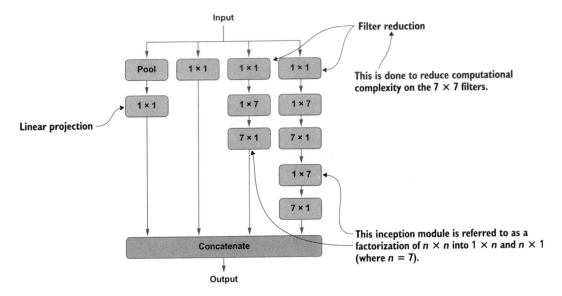

Figure 6.13 Inception v3 block 17 × 17 (group B) using a spatial separable convolution

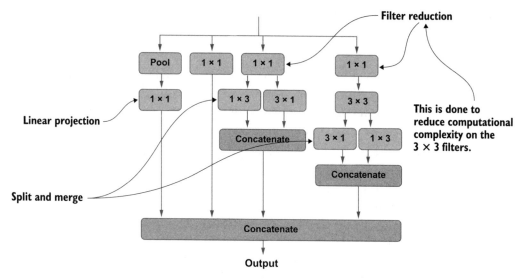

Figure 6.14   Inception v3 block 8 × 8 (group C) using a parallel spatial separable convolution

spatial separable convolutions, when done on lower dimensionality of the feature maps, do not lose representational power.

In the earlier versions of Inception, the feature maps between convolutional groups were pooled, in order to reduce dimensionality, and doubled in number, which, the researchers argued, caused representational loss (design principle 1). They proposed that the feature map reduction stage between groups could be done instead with parallel convolutions and pooling, as depicted in figure 6.15. However, after Inception v3, this approach for eliminating representational loss during reduction was not further pursued.

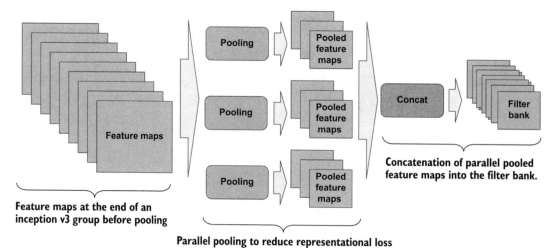

Figure 6.15   Using parallel pooling of feature maps to reduce representational loss

The parallel pooling after groups A and B is shown in figures 6.16 and 6.17, respectively. Termed *grid reduction*, these pooling blocks reduce the number of feature maps (or channels) from the output of the previous group to match the input of the next group. Thus, grid reduction block A reduces from 35×35 to 17×17, and grid reduction block B reduces from 17×17 to 8×8 (satisfying design principle 1).

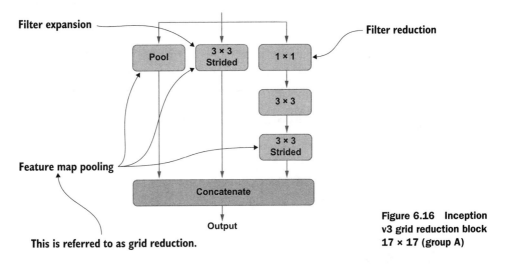

Figure 6.16 Inception v3 grid reduction block 17×17 (group A)

Additionally, reflecting design principle 3, the 7×7 convolution, along with some of the 3×3 convolutions in groups B and C, and grid reduction in group B are replaced by a spatial convolution of $(7 \times 1, 1 \times 7)$ and $(3 \times 1, 1 \times 3)$, respectively.

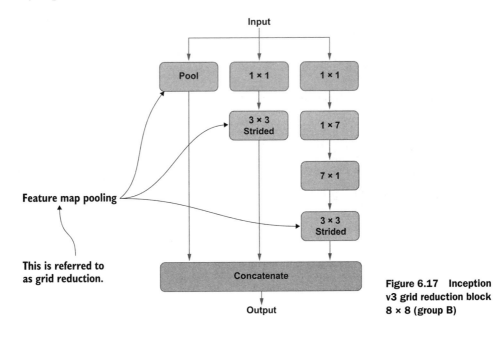

Figure 6.17 Inception v3 grid reduction block 8×8 (group B)

Now let's compare a normal convolution from Inception v1 and v2, which we have been calling simply a normal convolution, to a spatially separable convolution from v3.

6.3.2 *Normal convolution*

In a *normal convolution*, the kernel (for example, 3×3) is applied across the height (H), width (W) and depth (D) channels. Each time the kernel is moved, the number of matrix multiply operations equals the number of pixels as $H \times W \times D$.

For example, an RGB image (which has three channels) with a 3×3 kernel applied across all three channels uses $3 \times 3 \times 3 = 27$ matrix multiply (matmul) operations, producing an $N \times M \times 1$ (for example, $8 \times 8 \times 1$) feature map (per kernel), where N and M are the resulting height and width of the feature map; see figure 6.18

3×3 kernel is moved across each channel (e.g., $3 \times 3 \times 3$) of image of size $H \times W$

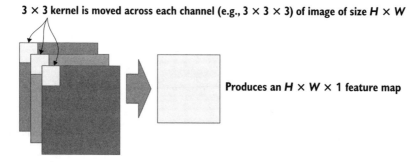

Produces an $H \times W \times 1$ feature map

Figure 6.18   A padded convolution with a single filter

If we specify 256 filters for the output of the convolution, we have 256 kernels to train. In the RGB example using 256 3×3 kernels, that means 6912 matrix multiply operations each time the kernels move; see figure 6.19. Thus, even with a small kernel size of 3×3, normal convolutions become computationally expensive as we increase the number of output feature maps for more representational power.

X (e.g., 256) 3×3 kernels are moved across each channel (e.g., $3 \times 3 \times 3 \times 256$)

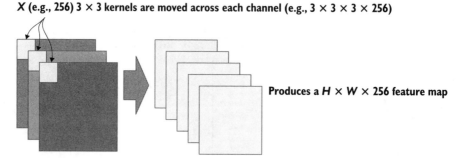

Produces a $H \times W \times 256$ feature map

Figure 6.19   Padded convolution with multiple filters

6.3.3 *Spatial separable convolution*

In contrast, a *spatial separable convolution* factors a 2D kernel (for example, 3 × 3) into two smaller 1D kernels. If we represent the 2D kernel as $H \times W$, the factored two smaller 1D kernels would be $H \times 1$ and $1 \times W$. This factorization reduces the total number of computations by one-third. While this factorization does not always maintain representational equivalence, the researchers demonstrated they were able to maintain representational equivalence in Inception v3. Figure 6.20 compares a normal convolution to a separable convolution.

In the RGB example with a 3 × 3 kernel, a normal convolution would be 3 × 3 × 3 (channels) = 27 matrix multiply operations each time the kernel is moved. In the same RGB example with a factored 3 × 3 kernel, a spatial separable convolution would be (3 × 1 × 3) + (1 × 3 × 3) = 18 matrix multiply operations each time the kernel is moved. Thus, the number of matrix multiply operations is reduced by a third (18 / 27).

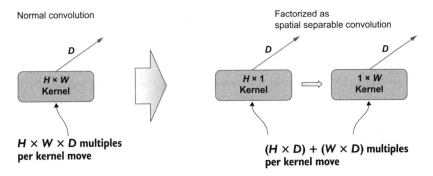

Figure 6.20   Normal vs. spatial separable convolution

In the RGB example using 256 3 × 3 kernels, we have 4608 matrix multiply operations each time the kernels move, in contrast to a normal convolution, which would have 6912 matrix multiply operations.

6.3.4 *Stem redesign and implementation*

By the time Inception v3 was designed, it was a common practice to replace coarse 5 × 5 filters with a stack of two 3 × 3 filters, which is computationally less (18 versus 25 matrix matmul operations) and retains representational power. Using the same principle, the authors theorized that a 7 × 7 coarse-level convolution, which is computationally expensive (49 matmul per move), could be replaced by a stack of three 3 × 3 convolutions (27 matmul per move). This reduced the number of parameters in the stem component while retaining representational power.

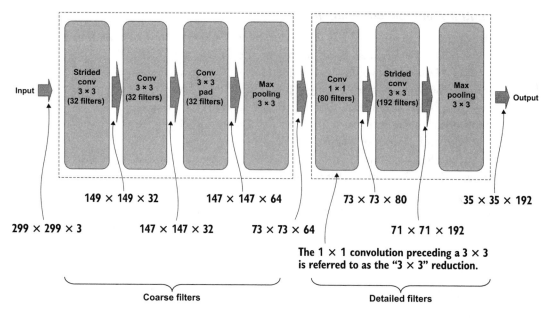

Figure 6.21 Inception v3 stem group consisting of a stack of three 3 × 3 convolutions replacing the 7 × 7 convolution in v1/v2

Figure 6.21 shows how the 7 × 7 convolution in the stem convolution group was factorized and replaced by a stack of three 3 × 3 convolutions, as follows:

1 The first 3 × 3 is a strided convolution (strides=2, 2) which performs a feature map reduction.
2 The second 3 × 3 is a regular convolution.
3 The third 3 × 3 doubles the number of filters.

Inception v3 would be one of the last SOTA models based on a factorized (or unfactorized) 7 × 7 coarse filter. Today's current practice is factorized (or unfactorized) 5 × 5. And the next code example is an implementation of the Inception v3 stem group, which consists of the following:

1 Stack of three 3 × 3 convolutions (factorized 7 × 7), in which first convolution is strided for feature pooling (25% size of input shape).
2 A max pooling layer for further dimensionality reduction of the feature maps (6% size of input shape).
3 1 × 1 linear projection convolution to expand the number of feature maps from 64 to 80.
4 A 3 × 3 convolution for further dimensionality expansion to 192 feature maps.
5 A second max pooling layer for further dimensionality reduction of the feature maps (1.5% size of input shape).

```
x = Conv2D(32, (3, 3), strides=(2, 2), padding='same')(input)
x = BatchNormalization()(x)
x = ReLU()(x)
x = Conv2D(32, (3, 3), strides=(1, 1), padding='same')(x)
x = BatchNormalization()(x)
x = ReLU()(x)
x = Conv2D(64, (3, 3), strides=(1, 1), padding='same')(x)
x = BatchNormalization()(x)
x = ReLU()(x)

# max pooling layer
x = MaxPooling2D((3, 3), strides=(2, 2), padding='same')(x)

x = Conv2D(80, (1, 1), strides=(1, 1), padding='same')(x)
x = BatchNormalization()(x)
x = ReLU()(x)

x = Conv2D(192, (3, 3), strides=(1, 1), padding='same')(x)
x = BatchNormalization()(x)
x = ReLU()(x)

x = MaxPooling2D((3, 3), strides=(2, 2), padding='same')(x)
```

Inception v3 stem, 7 × 7 is replaced by a stack of 3 × 3 convolutions

A 1 × 1 linear projection convolution

Feature map expansion (dimensionality expansion)

Feature map pooling (dimensionality reduction)

A summary() for the stem group shows 614,000 parameters to train with input (229, 229, 3).

6.3.5 *Auxiliary classifier*

Another change to Inception v3 was to reduce the two auxiliary classifiers to a single auxiliary, and to further simplify it, as depicted in figure 6.22. The authors explained that they made these changes because they "found that auxiliary classifiers did not

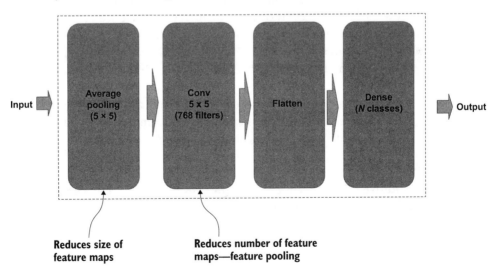

Figure 6.22 Inception v3 auxiliary group

result in improved convergence early in the training." By retaining a single classifier, it appears they shot for the midpoint.

Likewise, they adopted the convention of the time to remove additional dense layers before the final classifier, further reducing parameters. Earlier researchers had established that removing additional dense layers (prior to the dense layer for classification) resulted in no loss in accuracy.

The auxiliary classifier was further simplified to the following:

- An average pooling (`AveragePooling2D`) layer, which reduces each feature map to a single 1×1 matrix
- A 3×3 convolution (`Conv2D`) layer, which outputs 768 1×1 feature maps
- A flattening layer to flatten (`Flatten`) the feature maps to a 768-element 1D vector
- A final dense (`Dense`) layer for classification

A complete code rendition using the Idiomatic procedure reuse design pattern for Inception v3 is on GitHub (http://mng.bz/oGnd).

6.4   *ResNeXt: Wide residual neural networks*

Facebook AI Research's *ResNeXt*, which was the first runner-up of the 2016 ILSVRC competition for ImageNet, introduced a wide residual block that uses a split-transform-merge pattern for parallel convolutions. This architecture for parallel convolutions is referred to as a *group convolution.*

The number of parallel convolutions constitutes the width, and is called the *cardinality.* For example, in the 2016 competition, the ResNeXt architecture used a cardinality of 32, meaning each ResNeXt layer consisted of 32 parallel convolutions.

The idea here was that adding parallel convolutions would help a model gain in accuracy without the necessity of going deeper, which is more prone to memorization. In their ablation study (https://arxiv.org/abs/1611.05431), Saining Xie et al. compared ResNeXt with 50, 101, and 200 layers with ResNet, and 101 and 200 layers with Inception v3 on the ImageNet dataset. In all cases, ResNeXt architecture at the same depth layer achieved higher accuracy.

If you look at pretrained model repositories, such as TensorFlow Hub, you can see that the SE-ResNeXt variant has slightly higher computational and more accuracy, and is favored as the image classification backbone.

6.4.1   *ResNeXt block*

At each ResNeXt layer, the input from the previous layer is split across the parallel convolutions, and the output (feature maps) from each convolution is concatenated back together. Finally, the input to the layer is matrix-added to the concatenated output (identity link) to form the residual block. This set of layers is referred to as *split-transform-merge and scale* operations. Defining these terms will help clarify the operation:

- *Split* refers to the splitting of the feature maps into groups based on the cardinality.
- *Transform* is what happens in the parallel convolutions for each group.
- *Merge* refers to the concatenation operation of the resulting feature maps.
- *Scale* indicates the add operation in the identity link.

The goal of the split-transform-merge operation was to increase accuracy without increasing parameters. It did this by converting an elementary transformation ($w \times x$) into a network-in-neuron aggregated transformation.

Now for the architecture that implements these concepts. As you can see in figure 6.23, the wide residual block group of ResNeXt consists of the following:

- A first bottleneck convolution (1×1 kernel)
- A split-branch-concatenate convolution of cardinality N (group convolution)
- A final bottleneck convolution (1×1 kernel)
- An identity link (shortcut) between the input and the final convolution output

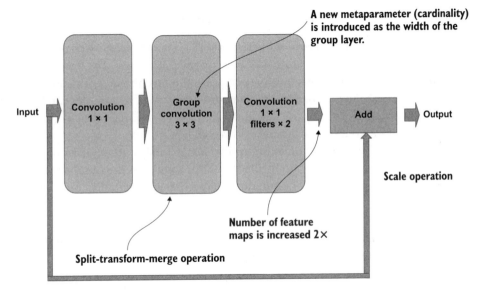

Figure 6.23 Residual next block with identity shortcut that implements the split-transform-merge and scale operations

Let's take a closer look at the split-transform-merge operation of the group convolution (figure 6.24). Here's how the three major steps get applied:

1. Split: The input (feature maps) are evenly split into N groups (where N is the cardinality).
2. Transform: Each group is passed through a separate 3×3 convolution.
3. Merge: All the transformed groups are concatenated back together.

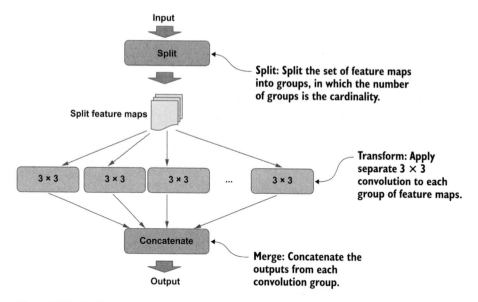

Figure 6.24   ResNeXt group convolution that implements the split-transform-merge operation

The first bottleneck convolution performs dimensionality reduction by reducing (compressing) the number of input feature maps. We saw a similar use for the bottleneck convolution when we looked at the bottleneck residual block in chapter 5 and at the inception module in sections 6.1 through 6.3.

After the bottleneck convolution, the feature maps are split among the parallel convolutions according to the cardinality. For example, if the number of input feature maps (or channels) is 128 and the cardinality is 32, each parallel convolution will get 4 feature maps, which is the number of feature maps divided by the cardinality, or 128 divided by 32.

The outputs from the parallel convolutions are then concatenated back into a full set of feature maps, which are then passed through a final bottleneck convolution for another dimensionality reduction. As in the residual block, there is an identity link between the input to and output from the ResNeXt block, which is then matrix-added.

The following coding example of a ResNeXt block consists of four code sequences:

1 The block input (shortcut) is passed through a 1 × 1 bottleneck convolution for dimensionality reduction.
2 The split-transform operation (group convolution).
3 The merge operation (concatenation).
4 The input is matrix-added to the output from the merge operation (identity link) as the scale operation.

Calculates the number of channels per group by dividing by cardinality (width) size

```
    shortcut = x

    x = Conv2D(filters_in, (1, 1), strides=(1, 1), padding='same')(shortcut)
    x = BatchNormalization()(x)
    x = ReLU()(x)

    filters_card = filters_in // cardinality
```

Shortcut link is a 1 × 1 bottleneck convolution for dimensionality reduction

```
    groups = []
    for i in range(cardinality):
        group = Lambda(lambda z: z[:, :, :, i * filters_card:i *
                             filters_card + filters_card])(x)
        groups.append(Conv2D(filters_card, (3, 3), strides=(1, 1),
                       padding='same')(group))
```

Performs the split-transform step

```
    x = Concatenate()(groups)
    x = BatchNormalization()(x)
    x = ReLU()(x)
```

Performs the merge step by concatenating the outputs from the group convolutions

```
    x = Conv2D(filters_out, (1, 1), strides=(1, 1), padding='same')(x)
    x = BatchNormalization()(x)
```

1 × 1 linear projection for dimensionality restoration

```
    x = Add()([shortcut, x])
    x = ReLU()(x)
    return x
```

Adds the shortcut to the output of the block

NOTE In this code listing, the `Lambda()` method performs the splitting of the feature maps. The sequence `z[:, :, :, i * filters_card:i * filters_card + filters_card]` is a sliding window that splits the input feature maps along the fourth dimension; the fourth dimensions are the channels $B \times H \times W \times C$.

6.4.2 ResNeXt architecture

The architecture, depicted in figure 6.25, starts with a stem convolution group for the input, consisting of a 7×7 convolution that is then passed through a max pooling layer for reducing the data.

Following the stem are four groups of ResNeXt blocks. Each group progressively doubles the number of filters outputted as compared to the input. Between each block is a strided convolution, which serves two purposes:

- It reduces the data by 75% (feature pooling).
- It doubles the filters from the output of the previous layer, so when the identity link is made between the input of this layer and its output, the number of filters match for the matrix addition operation.

After the final ResNeXt group, the output is passed to the classifier component. The classifier consists of a max pooling layer and a flattening layer, which flattens the input into a 1D vector, and then passes it to a single dense layer for classification.

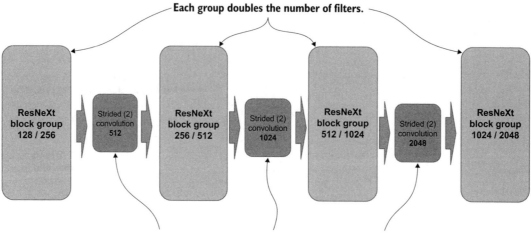

Figure 6.25   ResNeXt learner component showing feature pooling between convolution groups

A complete code rendition using the Idiomatic procedure reuse design pattern for ResNeXt is on GitHub (http://mng.bz/my6r).

6.5   *Wide residual network*

The *wide residual network* (WRN), introduced in 2016 by researchers at ParisTech, took another approach to wide convolutional neural networks. The researchers operated from the theory that as a model goes deeper in layers, feature reuse is diminished and therefore training takes longer. They did a study using residual networks and added a parameter for a multiplier on the number of filters (width) per residual block. This decreased the depth. When they tested this design, they found that a WRN with just 16 layers could outperform other SOTA architectures.

Soon, a design called DenseNet would demonstrate another alternative for dealing with feature reuse in deeper layers. As with the WRN, DenseNet worked on the assumption that increasing feature reuse would lead to more representational power and higher accuracy. DenseNet, however, achieved the reuse with a feature map concatenation of the input with the output of each residual block.

In their ablation study, "Wide Residual Networks" (https://arxiv.org/pdf/1605.07146.pdf), Sergey Zagoruyko and Nikos Komodakis applied their widening principal to a ResNet50, which they called a WRN-50-2, and they found that it outperformed an even deeper ResNet101. Today's SOTA models adopt the principle of using both wide and deep layers to achieve higher performance, faster training, and less memorization.

6.5.1 WRN-50-2 architecture

This WRN model used the following design considerations:

1 Use pre-activation batch normalization (BN-RE-Conv) for faster training, as in the ResNet v2.

2 Use two 3×3 convolutionals (B(3, 3)), as in ResNet34, instead of the less representational expressive bottleneck residual block (B(1,3,1)) in ResNet50. The rationale here is based on the fact that the bottleneck design helped reduce parameters for increasing accuracy, *as networks went deeper.* By going *wider* for accuracy, the network is shallower, and can therefore retain the more representational expressive stack.

3 Denote l as the number of convolutional layers per group and k as the width factor to multiply the number of filters.

4 Move the dropout operation from the top layers (which was the convention) to in between each convolutional layer in the residual blocks and after the ReLU. The reasoning here was to perturb the batch normalization.

In the macro-architecture in figure 6.26, you can see three of these principles at work, so that each convolutional group doubles the number of output features. Each convolution uses a pre-activation batch normalization (design principle 1). Each residual block within the group uses a B(3,3) residual block (design principle 2). And metaparameter k is used for the width multiplier on the number of filters per convolution (design principle 3). Not depicted is the dropout in the residual blocks (design principle 4).

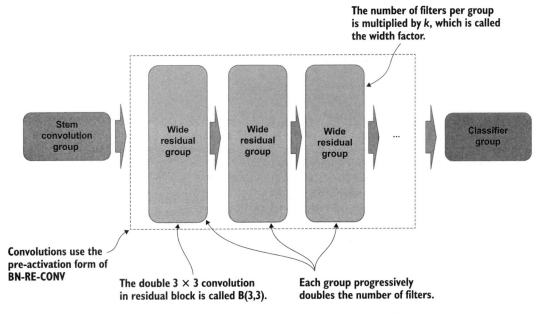

Figure 6.26 In the WRN macro-architecture, each convolution group progressively doubles the number of output feature maps.

6.5.2   *Wide residual block*

Let's focus on the wide residual block, which is composed of the various residual groups. Figure 6.27 shows that both 3×3 convolutions (B(3,3)) have their number of filters multiplied by a configurable width factor (k). Between the 3×3 convolution is a dropout layer for block-level regularization. Otherwise, the wide residual block design is identical to the ResNet34 residual block.

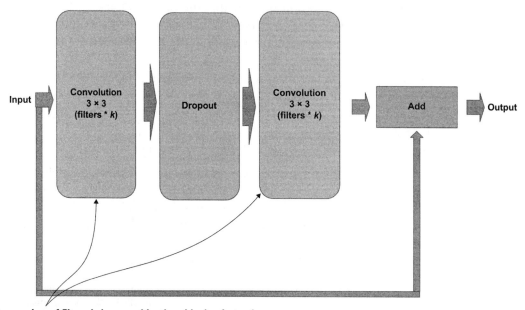

The number of filters is increased by the widening factor *k*.

Figure 6.27   Wide residual block with identity shortcut

And here is a coding example of a wide residual block:

```
shortcut = x ⟵ Remembers the input        First 3 × 3 convolution
                                           using pre-activation
x = BatchNormalization()(x)      ⟵        batch normalization
x = ReLU()(x)
x = Conv2D(filters_out, (3, 3), strides=(1, 1), padding='same')(x)

x = BatchNormalization()(x)   ⟵   Second 3 × 3 convolution using
x = ReLU()(x)                      pre-activation batch normalization
x = Dropout(rate)(x)
x = Conv2D(filters_out, (3, 3), strides=(1, 1), padding='same')(x)   ⟵

  ⟶ x = Add()([shortcut, x])                    Dropout after the
    return x                                    ReLU to perturb the
                                                batch normalization
  Identity link, adds the input
  to the output of the block
```

A complete code rendition using the Idiomatic procedure reuse design pattern for WRN is on GitHub (http://mng.bz/n2oa).

6.6   *Beyond computer vision: Structured data*

Let's take a look at how wide and deep layer concepts evolved in models for structured data. Prior to 2016, most applications for structured data continued to use classical machine learning methods, as opposed to deep learning. Unlike the unstructured data used in computer vision, structured data has a diversity of inputs, including numeric, categorical, and feature engineered. This range of inputs meant that going deep in layers of dense layers was not so effective in getting models to learn the non-linear relationships between the input features and the corresponding labels.

Figure 6.28 depicts the pre-2016 approach of applying deep learning to structural data. In this approach, all the feature inputs are processed by a sequence of dense layers—going deep, where the hidden dense layers are essentially the learner. The output from the last dense layer is then passed to the task component. The task component is comparable to the task component in computer vision. The output from the last dense layer is already a 1D vector. There may be some additional pooling of the vector, which is then passed to a final dense layer with an activation function that corresponds to the task: linear or ReLU for regression, sigmoid for binary classification, and softmax for multiclass classification.

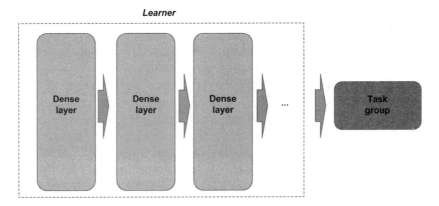

Figure 6.28   The approach to structured-data models before 2016 used a deep-layer DNN.

For structured data, you want to learn both *memorization* and *generalization.* Memorization is learning the co-occurrences of feature values (the covariant relationships). Generalization is learning new feature combinations that are not seen in the training data distribution but that would be seen in the data distribution when deployed.

I will use face detection to illustrate the difference between memorization and generalization. In memorization, portions of the network learn to lock in on patterns for specific clusters of samples (for example, specific eye patterns or skin tones).

When locked in, this part of the network will signal extremely high confidence on similar examples, but low confidence on comparable examples. As more and more of the neural network becomes locked in, the neural network degenerates into a decision tree. This is comparable to the set of rules in classical AI for an expert system. If an example matches a pattern that the expert coded, it is recognized. Otherwise, it can't be recognized.

For example, let's assume the neural network is locked in on patterns such as eyes, skin tone, piercings, glasses, hats, hair occlusion, and facial hair. We then submit an image of a child with face paint and the model doesn't recognize a face. You could then retrain with images of face paint, but with lock-in, you need to further increase the parameter capacity of the model to memorize the new pattern. And then there is another and another pattern—hence the problem with expert systems.

In generalization, redundant clusters of nodes weakly signal recognition of a pattern and collectively act as an ensemble within the model. The more redundant weakly signaling clusters in the model, the more likely the model will generalize to recognize a pattern it was not trained on.

Then, in 2016, Google Research published the model architecture wide-and-deep network and corresponding paper, "Wide & Deep Learning for Recommender Systems" by Heng-Tze Cheng et al. (https://arxiv.org/pdf/1606.07792.pdf). While the paper was specific to improving recommender models, this model has been widely used across different structured-data model types. Recommendation was an interesting challenge because it makes use of both generalization and memorization. The goal was to make niche recommendations with high-value conversions that required generalization, in addition to memorization for widespread common co-occurrences. The wide-and-deep architecture combines both memorization and generalization in one model. It is essentially two models that combine at the task component.

Figure 6.29 shows the wide-and-deep architecture. This architecture is also a *multimodal* architecture, in that it takes two separate inputs of different types.

Let's dive a little deeper into this architecture. The learner component consists of two sections, a multilayer deep neural network and a single-layer wide dense layer. The wide dense layer acts as a linear regressor and memorizes high-frequency co-occurrences. The deep neural network learns the nonlinearity and generalizes to the low-frequency (sparse) co-occurrences and co-occurrences not seen in the training data. The input to the wide dense layer are the base features (non-cross-features), which have been feature preprocessed, and transformed features (for example, one-hot encoding of categorical features). They are inputted directly into the wide dense layer, and as such there is no stem. The inputs to the multilayer dense neural network are the base features and the cross-features. In this case, a stem component converts the combined features into an embedding by using an encoder.

The output from both the wide dense layer and the multilayer deep neural networks are then combined in the task component and may be additionally pooled. The task component is essentially the same as in a computer vision model. Both the wide dense layer and the multilayer deep neural network layers are trained together.

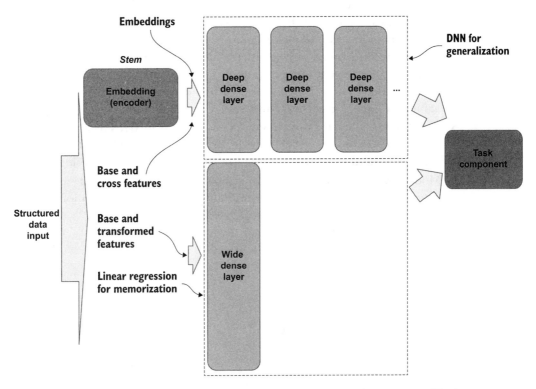

Figure 6.29 The inputs are divided between the wide and deep layers, and the outputs of the layers are combined for the task component.

Summary

- One approach to reducing exposure to memorization in deeper layers was to use parallel convolutions. This allowed for shallower convolutional neural networks to address the overcapacity.
- Representational equivalence occurs when a convolution design pattern can be refactored into another pattern that is computationally less expensive and smaller (in the number of parameters). With factorization, the model maintains the same level of information (or feature) extraction with less computational requirements. This allows models to be smaller, train faster, and reduce latency in prediction.
- The concept of refactoring a normal convolution into a computationally smaller spatial separable convolution was introduced in the Inception design. Inception demonstrates representational equivalence in preserving performance objectives on the ImageNet dataset.
- ResNeXt introduced the split-transform-merge pattern in parallel group convolutions. This pattern increased accuracies from prior residual networks without going deeper in layers.

- The purpose of moving batch normalization from post- to pre-activation in WRN was to increase model accuracy. Pre-activation batch normalization further reduced the need to go deeper, which in turn reduced the need for regularization to prevent memorization. The pre-activation method increased training speed enough that slightly a higher learning rate could be used to achieve comparable convergence.
- A width multiplier for widening layers was added to WRN as a metaparameter for finding a width in a shallow wide residual network. The result was a model that would perform as well (in terms of accuracy) as a deeper residual network.
- Modern deep learning models for structured data use both wide and deep layers; wide layers do memorization, and deep layers do generalization.

Alternative connectivity patterns

This chapter covers

- Understanding alternative connectivity patterns for deeper and wider layers
- Increasing accuracy with feature map reuse, further refactoring convolutions, and squeeze-excitation
- Coding alternatively connected models (DenseNet, Xception, SE-Net) with the procedural design pattern

So far, we've looked at convolutional networks with deep layers and convolutional networks with wide layers. In particular, we've seen how the corresponding connectivity patterns both between and within convolutional blocks addressed issues of vanishing and exploding gradients and the problem of memorization from overcapacity.

Those methods of increasing deep and wide layers, along with regularization (adding noise to reduce overfitting) at the deeper layers, reduced the problem with memorization but certainly did not eliminate it. So researchers explored other connectivity patterns within and between residual convolutional blocks to further reduce memorization without substantially increasing the number of parameters and compute operations.

We'll cover three of those alternative connectivity patterns in this chapter: DenseNet, Xception, and SE-Net. These patterns all had similar goals: reducing compute complexity in the connectivity component. But they differed in their approaches to the problem. Let's first get an overview of those differences. Then we'll spend the rest of the chapter looking at the specifics of each pattern.

In 2017, researchers from Cornell University, Tsinghua University, and Facebook AI Research argued that the residual link in conventional residual blocks only partially allowed deeper layers to use feature extraction from earlier layers. By doing a matrix addition of the input to the output, the feature information from the input is gradually diluted as it progresses to deeper layers. The authors proposed using a feature map concatenation, which they referred to as *feature reuse*, in place of the matrix addition. Their reasoning was that the feature maps at the output of each residual block would be reused at all the remaining (deeper) layers. To keep the model parameters exploding in size as feature maps accumulate through deeper layers, they introduced an aggressive feature map dimensionality reduction between convolutional groups. In their ablation study, DenseNet obtained better performance than previous residual block networks.

In the same year, François Chollet, who created Keras, introduced Xception, which redesigned the Inception v3 model into a new flow pattern. The new pattern consisted of entry, middle, and exit, as opposed to the previous Inception designs. While other researchers did not adopt this new flow pattern, they did adopt Chollet's further refactoring of normal and separable convolutions into depthwise separable convolutions. This process reduces the number of matrix operations, while maintaining representational equivalence (more on this shortly). This refactoring continues to appear in many SOTA models—particularly those designed for memory and computationally constrained devices, such as mobile devices.

Later in 2017, researchers from the Chinese Academy of Sciences and Oxford University introduced another connectivity pattern for residual blocks, which could be retrofitted into conventional residual networks. The connectivity pattern of SE-Net, as it became known, inserted a micro-block (referred to as an *SE link*) between the output of the residual block and the matrix add operation with the block input. This micro-block did an aggressive dimensionality reduction, or *squeeze*, on the output feature maps, followed by a dimensionality expansion, or *excitation*. The researchers hypothesized that this squeeze-and-excitation step would cause the feature maps to become more generalized. They inserted the SE links into ResNet and ResNeXt and showed performance improvements averaging 2% on examples not seen during testing (holdout data).

Now that we have the big picture, let's look at the details of how these three patterns address the problem of reducing complexity at the connection level.

7.1   DenseNet: Densely connected convolutional neural network

The *DenseNet* model introduced the concept of a densely connected convolutional network. The corresponding paper, "Densely Connected Convolutional Networks," by Gao Huang et al. (https://arxiv.org/abs/1608.06993), won the Conference on Computer Vision and Pattern Recognition (CVPR) 2017 Best Paper Award. The design is based on the principle that the output of each residual block layer is connected to the input of every subsequent residual block layer.

This extends the concept of identity links in residual blocks (covered in chapter 4). This section provides details on the macro-architecture, group and block components, and corresponding design principles.

7.1.1   Dense group

Prior to DenseNet, an identity link between the input and output of a residual block was combined by matrix addition. In contrast, in a dense block, the input to the residual block is concatenated to the output of the residual block. This change introduced the concept of *feature (map) reuse.*

In figure 7.1, you can see the difference in connectivity between a residual block and a dense residual block. In a residual block, the values in input feature maps are added to the output feature maps. While this retained some of the information in the block, it can be seen as being diluted by the addition operation. In the DenseNet residual block version, the input feature maps are fully retained, so no dilution occurs.

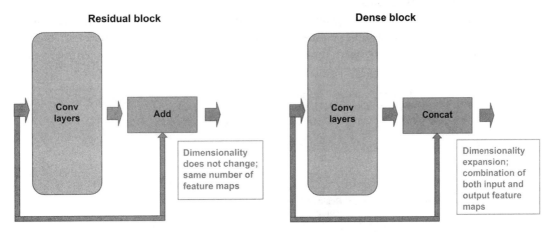

Figure 7.1   Residual block vs. dense block: the dense block uses a matrix concatenation instead of a matrix add operation.

The replacing of the matrix addition with concatenation has these advantages:

- Further alleviating the vanishing gradient problem over deeper layers
- Further reducing the computational complexity (parameters) with narrower feature maps

With concatenation, the distance between the output (classifier) and the feature maps is shorter. The shortened distance reduces the vanishing gradient problem, allowing for deeper networks that could produce higher accuracy.

The reuse of feature maps has representational equivalence with the former operation of a matrix addition, but with substantially fewer filters. The authors refer to this arrangement as *narrower* layers. With the narrower layers, the overall number of parameters to train is reduced. The authors theorized that the feature reuse allowed the model to go deeper in layers for more accuracy, without being exposed to vanishing gradients or memorization.

Here is an example for comparison. Let's assume the outputs of a layer are feature maps of size 28 × 28 × 10. After a matrix addition, the outputs continue to be 28 × 28 × 10 feature maps. The values within them are the addition of the residual block's input and output, and thus do not retain the original values—in other words, they have been merged. In the dense block, the input feature maps are concatenated—not merged—to the residual block output, thus preserving the original value of the identity link. In our example, with input and output of 28 × 28 × 10, the output, after the concatenation, will be 28 × 28 × 20. Continuing to the next block, the output will be 28 × 28 × 40.

In this way, the output of each layer is concatenated into the input of each subsequent layer, giving rise to the phrasing *densely connected* to describe these kinds of models. Figure 7.2 depicts the general construction and identity linking between residual blocks in a dense group.

As you can see, a dense group consists of multiple dense blocks. Each dense block consists of a residual block (without an identity link) and the identity link from the input to the residual block to the output. The input and output feature maps are then

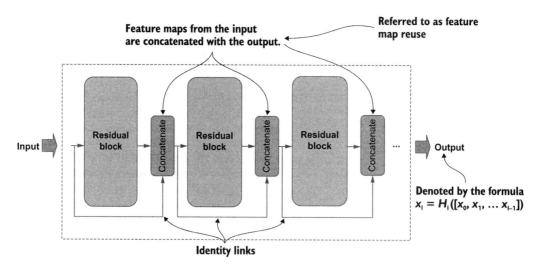

Figure 7.2 In this dense group micro-architecture, a matrix concatenation operation is used between the output of the residual block and the input (identity link).

concatenated into a single output, which becomes the input to the next dense block. This way, the feature maps outputted from each dense block are reused (shared) with every subsequent dense block.

The DenseNet researchers introduced a metaparameter k, which specified the number of filters in each convolutional group. They tried $k = 12, 24$, and 32. For ImageNet, they used $k = 32$ with four dense groups. They found that they could get comparable results with ResNet networks with half the parameters. For example, they trained a DenseNet with comparable parameters to a ResNet50, with 20 million parameters, and got comparable results to a deeper ResNet101, with 40 million parameters.

The following code is an example implementation of a dense group. The number of dense residual blocks is specified by the parameter n_blocks, the number of output filters by n_filters, and the compression factor by compression. For the last group, the lack of a transition block (we'll look at those next) is indicated by setting the parameter compression set to None:

```
def group(x, n_blocks, n_filters, compression=None):
    """ Construct a Dense Group
        x             : input to the group
        n_blocks      : number of residual blocks in dense block
        n_filters     : number of filters in convolution layer in residual
    block
        compression : amount to reduce feature maps by
    """
    for _ in range(n_blocks):
        x = dense_block(x, n_filters)

    if compression is not None:
        x = trans_block(x, reduction)
    return x
```

Constructs a group of densely connected residual blocks ⟶ (annotation pointing to the `for` loop)

Constructs the interceding transition block ⟵ (annotation pointing to the `if compression is not None:` line)

Let's discuss again why DenseNet and other SOTA models have no final pooling of the feature maps before the task component (for example, the classifier). These models do feature extraction within the blocks and feature summarization at the end of the group, a process we refer to as *feature learning*. Each group summarizes the features it has learned to reduce the computational complexity for further processing of the feature maps by subsequent groups. The final (nonpooled) feature maps of the last group are optimized in size for representing the features as a high-dimensional encoding in the latent space. Recall here that in multitask models, such as in object detection, it is the latent space that is shared between tasks (or in the case of model amalgamation, between model interfaces).

Once the final feature maps enter the task component, they are pooled one final time—but they are pooled in a manner that is optimal for learning the task instead of feature summarization. This last pooling step in the task component is the bottleneck layer, and the output is referred to as *the low-dimensional embedding* of the latent space, which may also be shared with other tasks and models.

The DenseNet architecture has four dense groups, and each consists of a configurable number of dense blocks. Let's now look into the construction and design of a dense block.

7.1.2 *Dense block*

The residual block in DenseNet uses the B(1, 3) pattern, which is a 1 × 1 convolution followed by a 3 × 3 convolution. However, the 1 × 1 convolution is a linear projection instead of a bottleneck: the 1 × 1 expands the number of output feature maps (filters) by an expansion factor of 4. The 3 × 3 then performs a dimensionality reduction, restoring the number of output feature maps to the same number as the input feature maps.

Figure 7.3 depicts the dimensionality expansion and reduction of feature maps in the residual dense block. Note that the number and size of the input and output feature maps stay the same. Within the block, the 1 × 1 linear projection expands the number of feature maps, while the subsequent 3 × 3 convolution does both feature extraction and feature map reduction. It is this last convolutional that restores the number and size of feature maps at the output to be the same as the input—a process called *dimensionality restoration*.

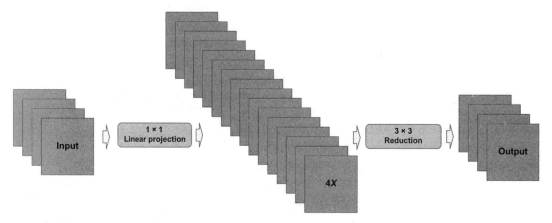

Figure 7.3   In dimensionality expansion and reduction in convolution layers of a residual dense block, the number and size of feature maps at the input and output are the same.

Figure 7.4 illustrates the residual dense block, which consists of the following:

- A 1 × 1 linear projection convolution that increases the number of feature maps by four times
- A 3 × 3 convolution that both performs feature extraction and restores the number of feature maps
- An operation that concatenates the residual block's input feature maps and its output

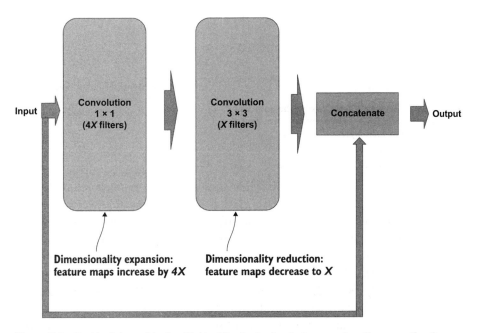

Figure 7.4 Residual dense block with identity shortcut using a concatenation operation for feature reuse

DenseNet also adopted the modern convention of using a pre-activation batch normalization (BN-ReLU-Conv) to improve accuracy. In a post-activation, the ReLU activation and batch normalization occur *after* the convolution. In pre-activation, the batch normalization and ReLU occur *before* the convolution.

Previous researchers had found that by moving from a post- to a pre-activation, models gained from 0.5 to 2 percent in accuracy. (For example, the ResNet v2 researchers, as presented in "Identity Mappings in Deep Residual Networks" [https://arxiv.org/abs/1603.05027].)

The following code is an example implementation of a dense residual block, which consists of these steps:

1. Saving a copy of the input feature maps in the variable `shortcut`.
2. A pre-activation 1 × 1 linear projection that increases the number of feature maps by four times
3. A pre-activation 3 × 3 convolution for feature extraction and restoring the number of feature maps
4. A concatenation of the saved input feature maps with the output feature maps for feature reuse

```
shortcut = x                    ⟵  Remembers the input
x = BatchNormalization()(x)
x = ReLU()(x)                                     Dimensionality expansion,
x = Conv2D(4 * n_filters, (1, 1), strides=(1, 1))(x)   expands filters by 4 (DenseNet-B)
```

```
x = BatchNormalization()(x)
x = ReLU()(x)
x = Conv2D(n_filters, (3, 3), strides=(1, 1), padding='same')(x)
```

3 × 3 bottleneck convolution with padding='same' to preserve shape of feature maps

```
x = Concatenate()([shortcut, x])
```

Concatenates the input (identity) with the output of the residual block, where concatenation provides feature reuse between layers

7.1.3 DenseNet macro-architecture

In the learner component, a *transition block* is inserted between each dense group to further reduce computational complexity. The transition block is a strided convolution, also referred to as *feature pooling*, used to reduce the overall size of the concatenated feature maps (feature reuse) as they move from one dense group to the next. Without the reduction, the overall size of the feature maps would progressively double per dense block, which would have resulted in an explosion in the number of parameters to train. By reducing the number of parameters, a DenseNet can go deeper in layers with only a linear increase in the number of parameters.

Before we look at the architecture of the transition block, let's first see where it fits into the learner component. You can see, in figure 7.5, that the learner component consists of four dense groups, and the transition block is between each of the dense groups.

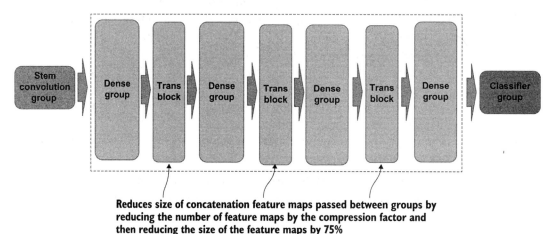

Reduces size of concatenation feature maps passed between groups by reducing the number of feature maps by the compression factor and then reducing the size of the feature maps by 75%

Figure 7.5 DenseNet macro-architecture showing transition blocks between dense groups

Now let's look up close at a transition block between each dense group.

7.1.4 Dense transition block

The transition block consists of two steps:

- A 1 × 1 bottleneck convolution that reduces the number of output feature maps (channels) by a compression factor *C*.
- A strided average pooling that follows the bottleneck and reduces the size of each feature map by 75%. When we say *strided*, we generally mean a stride of 2. And a stride of 2 will reduce the height and width dimensions of the feature by one-half, which reduces the number of pixels by one-quarter (25%).

Figure 7.6 depicts this process. Here, filters / *C* represents the feature map compression in the 1 × 1 bottleneck convolution that reduces the *number* of feature maps. The average pooling that follows is strided, which reduces the *size* of those reduced number of feature maps.

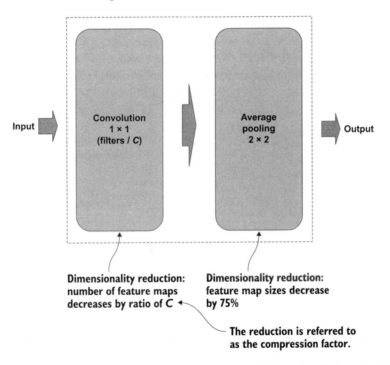

Figure 7.6   In the dense transition block, feature map dimensionality is reduced by both the 1 × 1 bottleneck convolution and the strided average pooling layer.

Now, how does that compression actually work? As you can see in figure 7.7, we start with input of eight feature maps, each of size $H \times W$, which, in total, can be represented as $H \times W \times 8$. The compression ratio in the 1 × 1 bottleneck convolution is 2. So the bottleneck takes the input and then outputs half the number of feature maps, which is 4 in this example. We can represent that as $H \times W \times 4$. The strided average

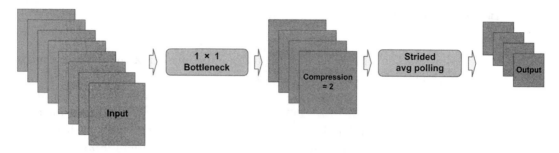

Figure 7.7   Demonstrating the progress of reducing feature maps (compression) in a transition block

pooling then reduces the dimension of the 4 feature maps by one-half, resulting in a final output size of $0.5H \times 0.5W \times 4$.

To compress the number of feature maps, we need to know the number of feature maps (channels) coming into the transition block. In the following code example, this is obtained by x.shape[-1]. We use an index of –1 to refer to the last dimension in the shape of the input tensor (B, H, W, C), which is the number of channels. The number of feature maps in the input tensor is then multiplied by the compression factor (which is from 0 to 1). Note that in Python, multiplication operations are done as floating-point values, so we cast the result back to an integer:

```
n_filters = int(x.shape[-1]) * compression )
x = BatchNormalization()(x)
x = Conv2D(n_filters, (1, 1), strides=(1, 1))(x)
x = AveragePooling2D((2, 2), strides=(2, 2))(x)
```

Calculates the reduction (compression) of the number of feature maps (DenseNet-C)

1 × 1 bottleneck convolution using BN-LI-Conv form of batch normalization

Uses mean value (average) when pooling to reduce by 75%

A complete code rendition using the Idiomatic procedure reuse design pattern for DenseNet is available on GitHub (http://mng.bz/6N0o).

7.2   *Xception: Extreme Inception*

The *Xception* (*Extreme Inception*) architecture, as noted previously, was introduced by Keras creator François Chollet at Google in 2017 as a proposed further improvement over the Inception v3 architecture. In his paper, "Xception: Deep Learning with Depthwise Separable Convolutions" (https://arxiv.org/pdf/1610.02357.pdf), Chollet argued that the success of the Inception-style module was based on a factorization that substantially decoupled the spatial correlations from the channel correlations. This decoupling resulted in fewer parameters while still maintaining representational power. He proposed that we could reduce parameters even more, maintaining representational power, by fully decoupling the spatial and channel correlations. Don't worry if these ideas on decoupling seem a bit complicated; you'll find a more detailed explanation in section 7.2.5.

Chollet made another important statement in his paper: he claimed that his redesign of the architecture for Xception was actually simpler than Inception's architecture, and could be coded in only 30 to 40 lines using a high-level library such as Keras.

Chollet based his conclusion on experiments comparing the accuracy of Inception v3 to Xception on ImageNet and Google's internal Joint Foto Tree (JFT) datasets. He used the same number of parameters in both models, so he believed any accuracy improvement was due to *more-efficient use of the parameters*. The JFT dataset consists of 350 million images, and 17,000 categories; Xception outperformed Inception by 4.3% on the JFT dataset. In his experiments on ImageNet, which consists of 1.2 million images and 1000 categories, the difference in accuracy was negligible.

There were two major changes from Inception v3 to Xception:

- Reorganization of the Inception architecture's use of three inception-style residual groups (A, B, and C) into an entry, middle, and exit flow instead. Under this new approach, the stem group becomes part of the entry, and the classifier becomes part of the exit, which reduces the structural complexity of the Inception-style residual blocks.
- The factorization of a convolution into a spatial separable convolution in an Inception v3 block is replaced with a depthwise separable convolution, which reduces the number of matrix multiply operations by 83%.

Like Inception v3, Xception uses a post-activation batch normalization (Conv-BN-ReLU).

Let's take a look at the overall macro-architecture, and then look at the details of the redesigned components (the entry, exit, and middle flow). At the end of this section, we'll come back to where we started, and I'll explain the factorization of spatial convolutions into depthwise separable convolutions.

7.2.1 Xception architecture

Chollet took the traditional stem-learner-classifier arrangement and regrouped it into an entry flow, middle flow, and exit flow. You can see this in figure 7.8, which shows the Xception architecture, regrouped and retrofitted into the procedural reuse design pattern. The entry and middle represent the feature learning, and the exit flow represents the classification learning.

While I have read Chollet's paper multiple times, I can't find a justification for describing the architecture as having an entry, middle, and exit flow. I think it would be clearer to just call these three *styles* of residual groups in the learner component, maintaining the convention of referencing them as A, B, and C. The paper seems to hint that his decision was an attempt to simplify what he referred to as the complex architecture of Inception. He wanted this simplification so the architecture could be written in 30 to 40 lines of a high-level library, like Keras or TensorFlow-Slim, while maintaining the comparable number of parameters. In any case, subsequent researchers have not adopted Chollet's terminology of entry, middle, and exit flow.

The stem component is
incorporated into the entry flow.

The classifier component is
incorporated into the exit flow.

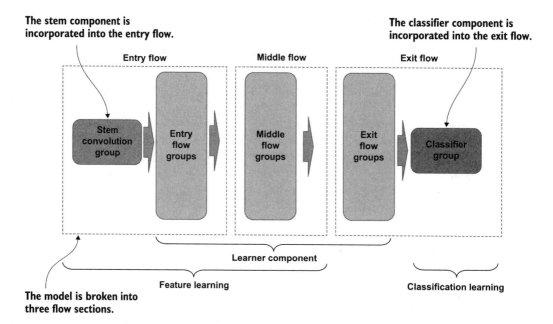

The model is broken into
three flow sections.

Figure 7.8 The Xception macro-architecture regrouped the major components into entry, middle, and exit flow. Here's how they fit into the stem, learner, and task components.

As you can see, the stem component is incorporated into the entry flow, and the classifier component into the exit flow. The residual convolutional groups from the entry to exit flow collectively form the equivalent of the learner component.

The skeleton implementation of the Xception architecture shows how the code is partitioned into an entry flow, middle flow, and exit flow section. The entry flow is further subpartitioned into a stem and body, and the exit flow is further subpartitioned into a classifier and body. These partitions are denoted in the code template with three top-level functions: entryFlow(), middleFlow(), and exitFlow(). The entry-Flow() function has the nested stem() to denote the inclusion of the stem in the entry flow, and the exitFlow() has the nested function classifier() to denote the inclusion of the classifier in the exit flow.

I've left the function body details out for brevity. A complete code rendition using the Idiomatic procedure reuse design pattern for Xception is available on GitHub (http://mng.bz/5WzB).

```
def entryFlow(inputs):
    """ Create the entry flow section
        inputs : input tensor to neural network
    """
    def stem(inputs):                                 The stem component is
        """ Create the stem entry into the neural network   part of the entry flow.
            inputs : input tensor to neural network
        """
```

```
                        ◁——— Code removed for brevity
        return x

    x = stem(inputs)    ◁——| The stem component is
                            | part of the entry flow.

    for n_filters in [128, 256, 728]:   ◁——┐
        x = projection_block(x, n_filters)  | Constructs three residual blocks
                                            | using linear projection
    return x

def middleFlow(x):
    """ Create the middle flow section
        inputs : input tensor into section
    """
    for _ in range(8):         ◁——┐
        x = residual_block(x, 728)  | Middle flow constructs 8
    return x                        | identical residual blocks.

def exitFlow(x, n_classes):
    """ Create the exit flow section
        x          : input to the exit flow section
        n_classes : number of output classes
    """                                        ┌ The classifier component
    def classifier(x, n_classes):      ◁———————┘ is part of the exit flow.
        """ The output classifier
            x          : input to the classifier
            n_classes : number of output classes
        """
                         ◁——— Code removed for brevity
        return x
                         ◁——— Code removed for brevity

    x = classifier(x, n_classes)
    return x
                                      ┌ Creates the input vector
inputs = Input(shape=(299, 299, 3))  ◁┘ of shape (229, 229, 3)

x = entryFlow(inputs)   ◁——— Constructs the entry flow

x = middleFlow(x)   ◁——— Constructs the middle flow

outputs = exitFlow(x, 1000)   ◁——┐ Constructs the exit
                                 | flow for 1000 classes
model = Model(inputs, outputs)
```

Middle flow constructs 8 identical residual blocks.

7.2.2 Entry flow of Xception

The entry flow component consists of the stem convolutional group, followed by three Xception entry-flow-style residual blocks, successively outputting 128, 256, and 728 feature maps. Figure 7.9 shows the entry flow and how the stem group fits into it as a subcomponent.

The stem consists of a stack of two 3 × 3 convolutions, as shown in figure 7.10. The second 3 × 3 doubles the number of output feature maps (dimensionality expansion),

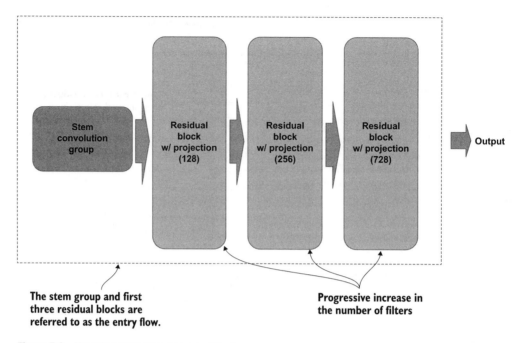

The stem group and first
three residual blocks are
referred to as the entry flow.

Progressive increase in
the number of filters

Figure 7.9   Xception entry flow micro-architecture

and one of the convolutions is strided for feature pooling (dimensionality reduction). For Xception, the number of filters for the stack is 32 and 64, respectively, which is a common convention. The first convolution in the stack, which is strided, would've been chosen to reduce the number of parameters to the second 3 × 3 convolution in the stack. The other convention is with the second 3 × 3 convolution, which is strided for feature summarization, and forgoes the reduction in parameters.

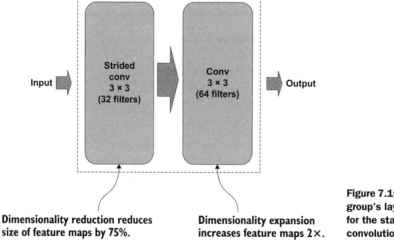

Dimensionality reduction reduces
size of feature maps by 75%.

Dimensionality expansion
increases feature maps 2×.

**Figure 7.10   Xception stem
group's layer construction
for the stack of two 3 × 3
convolutions.**

Next is the entry-flow-style residual block, shown in figure 7.11. The entry flow style uses a B(3, 3) residual block followed by a max pooling and 1 × 1 linear projection on the identity link. The 3 × 3 convolutions are depthwise separable convolutions (Separable-Conv2D), in contrast to Inception v3, which used a combination of normal and spatially separable convolutions. The max pooling uses a 3 × 3 pooling size, thus outputting the maximum value from a 9-pixel window (versus 4 pixels for 2 × 2). Note that the 1 × 1 linear projection is also strided, reducing the size of the feature maps, to match the size of reduction of the feature maps from the residual path by the max pooling layer.

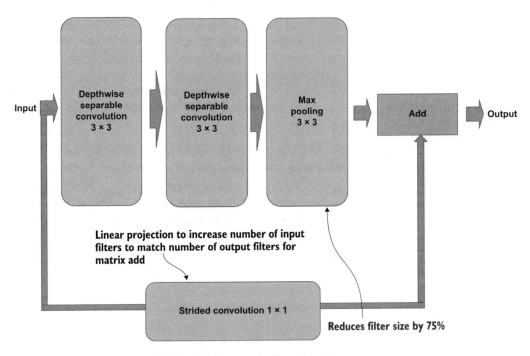

Figure 7.11 Xception residual block with linear projection shortcut

Now let's look at an example implementation of the entry-flow-style residual block. This codes for the following:

1. A 1 × 1 linear projection to increase the number of feature maps and reduce the size to match output from the residual path (shortcut)
2. Two 3 × 3 depthwise separable convolutions
3. A matrix add operation of the feature maps from the linear projection link (shortcut) to the output of the residual path

```
def projection_block(x, n_filters):
    """ Create a residual block using Depthwise Separable Convolutions with
        Projection shortcut
        x        : input into residual block
        n_filters: number of filters
```

```
            """
            shortcut = Conv2D(n_filters, (1, 1), strides=(2, 2), padding='same')
                       (x)
            shortcut = BatchNormalization()(shortcut)
       ┌─▷ x = SeparableConv2D(n_filters, (3, 3), padding='same')(x)
       │    x = BatchNormalization()(x)
       │    x = ReLU()(x)
       │
       │
       ├─▷ x = SeparableConv2D(n_filters, (3, 3), padding='same')(x)
       │    x = BatchNormalization()(x)
       │    x = ReLU()(x)
       │
            x = MaxPooling2D((3, 3), strides=(2, 2), padding='same')(x) ◁─┐
       │
            x = Add()([x, shortcut])   ◁──┐
            return x
```

First depthwise separable convolution

Second depthwise separable convolution

Projection shortcut uses strided convolution to reduce the size of feature maps while doubling the number of filters to match output of block for the matrix add operation.

Adds the projection shortcut to the output of the block

Reduces size of feature maps by 75%

7.2.3 *Middle flow of Xception*

The middle flow consists of eight middle-flow-style residual blocks, each outputting 728 feature maps. It is the convention to maintain the same number of input/output feature maps across blocks in a group; while between groups, the number of feature maps progressively increases. In contrast, with Xception, the number of output feature maps in the entry and middle flow stayed the same, instead of increasing.

The middle-flow-style residual block, shown in figure 7.12, uses eight B(3, 3, 3) residual blocks. Unlike the entry-flow residual block, there is no 1 × 1 strided linear projection on the identity link, since the number of input and output feature maps stays the same across all blocks, and no pooling occurs.

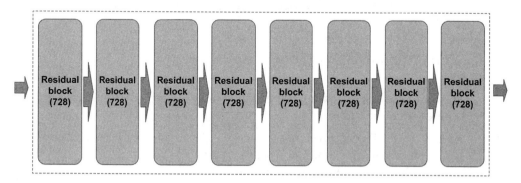

Figure 7.12   The Xception middle flow micro-architecture has a sequence of eight identical residual blocks.

Now let's take a look at what's happening in each of those residual blocks. Figure 7.13 shows the three 3 × 3 convolutions, which are depthwise separable convolutions (`SeparableConv2D`). (Again, we'll soon get to what exactly a depthwise separable convolution is.)

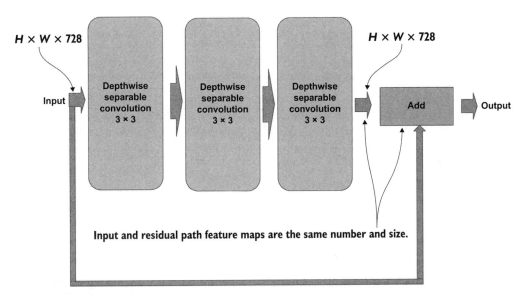

Figure 7.13 Residual block middle flow with identity shortcut: the number and size of both the input feature maps and the residual path are the same for the matrix add operation.

The following code is an example implementation of the middle-flow-style residual block, where the B(3, 3, 3) style is implemented using depthwise separable convolutions (SeparableConv2D):

```
def residual_block(x, n_filters):
    """ Create a residual block using Depthwise Separable Convolutions
        x        : input into residual block
        n_filters: number of filters
    """

    shortcut = x

    x = SeparableConv2D(n_filters, (3, 3), padding='same')(x)
    x = BatchNormalization()(x)
    x = ReLU()(x)

    x = SeparableConv2D(n_filters, (3, 3), padding='same')(x)
    x = BatchNormalization()(x)
    x = ReLU()(x)

    x = SeparableConv2D(n_filters, (3, 3), padding='same')(x)
    x = BatchNormalization()(x)
    x = ReLU()(x)

    x = Add()([x, shortcut])
    return x
```

Sequence of three 3 × 3 depthwise separable convolutions

Adds the identity link to the output of the block

7.2.4   *Exit flow of Xception*

Now for the exit flow. It consists of a single exit-flow-style residual block, followed by a convolutional (nonresidual) block, and then the classifier. The classifier group, as shown in figure 7.14, is a subcomponent of the exit flow.

The exit flow takes as input 728 feature maps, and output from the middle flow, and progressively increases the number of feature maps to 2048 before the classifier. Compare this with the convention for large CNNs, such as Inception v3 and ResNet, which generate 2048 final feature maps before the bottleneck layer, creating what's known as *high-dimensional encoding*.

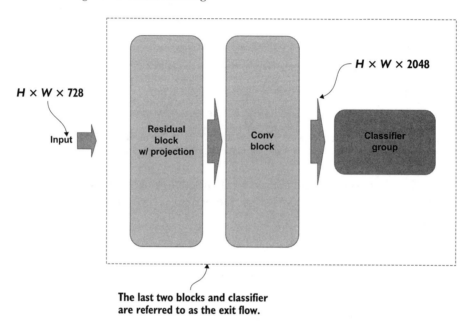

Figure 7.14   The Xception exit flow progressively increases the number of feature maps.

Let's take a close-up look at that single exit-flow-style residual block, in figure 7.15. This residual block is a B(3,3) with the two convolutions outputting 728 and 1024 feature maps, respectively. The two convolutions are followed by a max pooling with a pooling size of 3 × 3, and then a 1 × 1 linear projection for the identity link. In contrast to the middle flow, the exit-flow block increases the number of feature maps and delays pooling between the single residual and convolution block in the exit flow.

Note that the exit flow residual block structure is identical to the entry flow, except the exit flow style does a dimensionality expansion with the block, going from 728 to 1024 feature maps, while the entry flow does not do any dimensionality expansion.

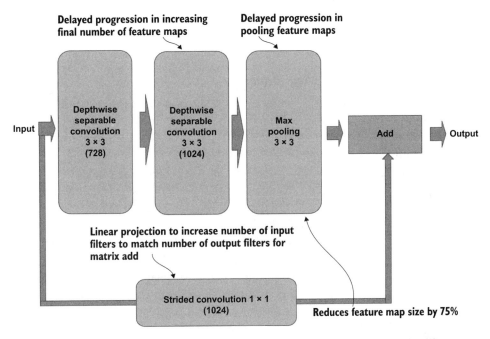

Figure 7.15 The Xception exit flow residual block with linear projection shortcut delays the progression of increasing the final number of feature maps and pooling.

Now for the exit flow convolutional block, which follows the residual block, and is shown in figure 7.16. This block consists of two 3 × 3 depthwise separable convolutions, each doing a dimensionality expansion. That expansion increases the number of feature maps to 1156 and 2048, respectively, which completes the delayed progression of increasing the final number of feature maps before the bottleneck layer.

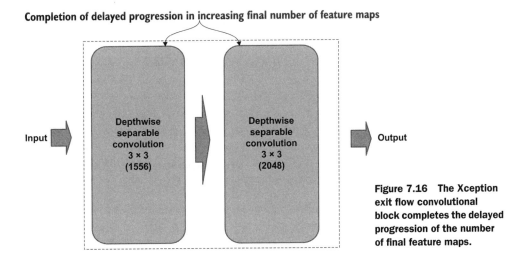

Figure 7.16 The Xception exit flow convolutional block completes the delayed progression of the number of final feature maps.

The final group in the exit flow is the classifier, composed of a `GlobalAverage-Pooling2D` layer, which pools and flattens the final feature maps into a 1D vector, followed by a `Dense` layer with softmax activation for the classification.

7.2.5   *Depthwise separable convolution*

As promised, we are finally going to get to the bottom of the depthwise separable convolution in the Xception architecture. Since their introduction, depthwise separable convolutions have been frequently used in convolutional neural networks, because of their ability to be computationally less expensive while maintaining representational power. Originally proposed by Laurent Sifre and Stephane Mallat in 2014 while working at Google Brain (see https://arxiv.org/abs/1403.1687), depthwise separable convolutions have since been studied and adopted in a variety of SOTA models, including Xception, MobileNet, and ShuffleNet.

Put simply, a depthwise separable convolution factors a 2D kernel into two 2D kernels; the first is a depthwise convolution, and the second is a pointwise convolution. To fully understand this, we first need to understand two related concepts: depthwise convolution and pointwise convolution, from which a depthwise convolution is constructed.

7.2.6   *Depthwise convolution*

In a *depthwise convolution*, the kernel is split into a single $H \times W \times 1$ kernel, one per channel, with each kernel operating on a single channel instead of across all channels. In this arrangement, the cross-channel relationships are decoupled from the spatial relationships. As Chollet suggested, fully decoupling the spatial and channel convolutions results in fewer matmul operations, and accuracy comparable to that of models with no decoupling and normal convolution, as well as of models with partial decoupling and spatial separable convolution.

So, in the RGB example with a 3×3 kernel shown in figure 7.17, a depthwise convolution would be three $3 \times 3 \times 1$ kernels. The number of multiply operations as the kernel is moved is the same as in the normal convolution (for example, 27 for 3×3 on three channels). The output, however, is a D-depth feature map, rather than a 2D (`depth=1`) feature map.

A separate 3 × 3 × 1 kernel is moved across each channel.

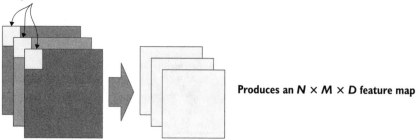

Produces an N × M × D feature map

Figure 7.17   In this depthwise convolution, the kernel gets split into single *H* x *W* x 1 kernels.

7.2.7 *Pointwise convolution*

The output from a depthwise convolution is then passed as the input to a *pointwise convolution*, which forms a depthwise separable convolution. The pointwise convolution performs the decoupled spatial convolution. The pointwise convolution combines the outputs of the depthwise convolution and expands the number of feature maps to match the specified number of filters (feature maps). The combination outputs the same number of feature maps as a normal or separable convolution (89), but with fewer matrix multiply operations (83% reduction).

A pointwise convolution, shown in figure 7.18, has a $1 \times 1 \times D$ (number of channels). It will iterate through each pixel producing an $N \times M \times 1$ feature map, which replaces the $N \times M \times D$ feature map.

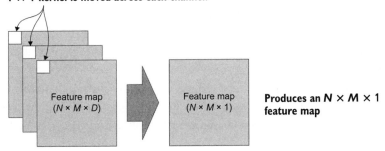

1 × 1 kernel is moved across each channel.

Feature map
($N \times M \times D$)

Feature map
($N \times M \times 1$)

Produces an $N \times M \times 1$ feature map

Figure 7.18   Pointwise convolution

In the pointwise convolution, we use $1 \times 1 \times D$ kernels, one for each output. As in the previous example in figure 7.17, if our output is 256 filters (feature maps), we will use 256 $1 \times 1 \times D$ kernels.

In the RGB example using a $3 \times 3 \times 3$ kernel for the depthwise convolution in figure 7.17, we have 27 multiply operations each time the kernel moves. This would be followed by a $1 \times 1 \times 3 \times 256$ (where 256 is the number of output filters)—which is 768. The total number of multiply operations would be 795, instead of 6912 for a normal convolution and 4608 for a spatial separable convolution.

In the Xception architecture, the spatial separable convolutions in the inception module are replaced with a depthwise separable convolution, reducing computational complexity (number of multiply operations) by 83%. A complete code rendition using the Idiomatic procedure reuse design pattern for Xception is on GitHub (http://mng.bz/5WzB).

7.3   *SE-Net: Squeeze and excitation*

Now we will turn to another alternative connectivity design, the *squeeze-excitation-scale pattern*, or *SE-Net*, which can be added to existing residual networks to increase accuracy by adding only a few parameters.

Introducing the pattern in "Squeeze-and-Excitation Networks" (https://arxiv.org/abs/1709.01507), Jie Hu et al. explained that previous improvements to models focused on spatial relationships between convolutional layers. So they decided to take a different tack and investigate a new network design based on the relationship between *channels*. Their idea was that the feature recalibration could use global information to selectively emphasize important features and de-emphasize less-important features.

To achieve the ability to selectively emphasize features, the authors came up with the concept of adding a *squeeze-excitation* (SE) *link* inside a residual block. This block would go between the output of the convolution layer (or layers), and the matrix add operation with the identity link. This concept won the 2017 ILSVRC competition for ImageNet.

Their ablation study indicated several benefits of the SE-Net approach, including these:

- Can be added to existing SOTA architectures, such as ResNet, ResNeXt, and Inception.
- Adds a minimal increase in parameters while achieving higher accuracy results. For example:
  - ImageNet top-5 error rate was 7.48% for ResNet50 and 6.62% for SE-ResNet50
  - ImageNet top-5 error rate was 5.9% for ResNeXt50 and 5.49% for SE-ResNeXt50
  - ImageNet top-5 error rate was 7.89% for Inception and 7.14% for SE-Inception

7.3.1   *Architecture of SE-Net*

SE-Net architecture, shown in figure 7.19, consists of an existing residual network that is then retrofitted by inserting an SE link into the residual blocks. The retrofitted ResNet and ResNeXt architectures are referred to as *SE-ResNet* and *SE-ResNeXt*, respectively.

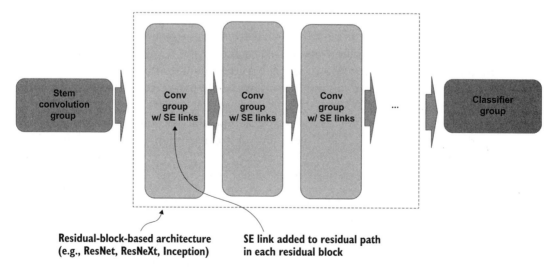

Residual-block-based architecture   SE link added to residual path
(e.g., ResNet, ResNeXt, Inception)   in each residual block

Figure 7.19   SE-Net macro-architecture showing addition of SE-Link to each residual block

7.3.2   *Group and block of SE-Net*

If we break down the macro-architecture, we find that each convolutional group in figure 7.19 consists of one or more residual blocks, composing a residual group. Each residual block has an SE link. This close-up look at the residual group is depicted in figure 7.20.

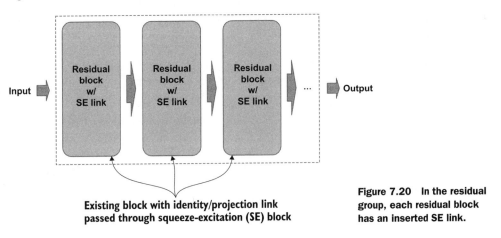

Existing block with identity/projection link passed through squeeze-excitation (SE) block

Figure 7.20   In the residual group, each residual block has an inserted SE link.

Now let's break down the residual group. Figure 7.21 shows how the SE link is inserted into a residual block, between the convolution layer(s) output and the matrix add operation.

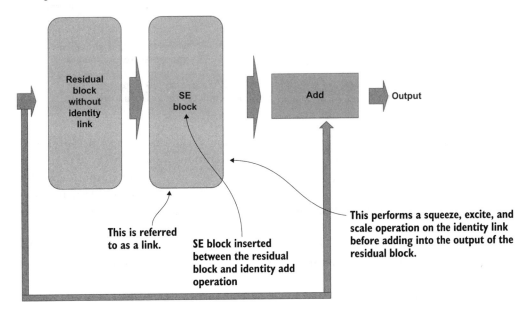

This is referred to as a link.

SE block inserted between the residual block and identity add operation

This performs a squeeze, excite, and scale operation on the identity link before adding into the output of the residual block.

Figure 7.21   Residual block showing how the SE link is inserted between the residual path and the matrix add operation (denoted as *Add*) for the identity link

The following code is an example implementation of adding an SE link to a ResNet residual block. At the end of the block, a call to `squeeze_excite_link()` is inserted between the output from the B(3,3) output and the matrix add operation (`Add()`). In the `squeeze_excite_link()` function, we implement the SE link (detailed in the next subsection).

The parameter `ratio` is the amount (ratio) of dimensionality reduction on the squeeze operation on the input prior to the subsequent dimensionality restoration by the excitation operation.

```
def identity_block(x, n_filters, ratio=16):
    """ Create a Bottleneck Residual Block with Identity Link
        x        : input into the block
        n_filters: number of filters
        ratio    : amount of filter reduction during squeeze
    """
    shortcut = x


    x = Conv2D(n_filters, (1, 1), strides=(1, 1))(x)        ◁─── 1 × 1 convolution for
    x = BatchNormalization()(x)                                  dimensionality reduction
    x = ReLU()(x)
                                                            3 × 3 convolution for bottleneck layer

    x = Conv2D(n_filters, (3, 3), strides=(1, 1), padding="same")(x)   ◁───
    x = BatchNormalization()(x)
    x = ReLU()(x)                                           1 × 1 convolution
                                                            increases filters
    x = Conv2D(n_filters * 4, (1, 1), strides=(1, 1))(x)    ◁─── by 4 times for
    x = BatchNormalization()(x)                                  dimensionality
                                                                 restoration

    x = squeeze_excite_link(x, ratio)    ◁───
                                             Passes the output through the
                                             squeeze-and-excitation link
    x = Add()([shortcut, x])    ◁───
    x = ReLU()(x)
    return x                    Adds the identity link (input) to
                                the output of the residual block
```

7.3.3 SE link

Now, let's go into detail on the SE link (figure 7.22). The link consists of three layers. The first two layers perform the squeeze operation. A global average pooling is used to reduce each input feature map (channel) to a single value, outputting a 1D vector of size C (channels), which is then reshaped into a 1-×-1-pixel 2D matrix of size C (channels). The dense layer then further reduces the output by the reduction ratio r, resulting in a 1-×-1-pixel 2D matrix of size C / r (channels).

The squeezed output is then passed to the third layer, which performs the excitation by restoring to the number of channels (C) inputted to the link. Note that this is comparable to using a 1×1 linear projection convolution, but is instead done with a dense layer.

The final step is a scale operation that consists of an identity link from the input, where the $1 \times 1 \times C$ vector from the squeeze-excitation operation is matrix-multiplied

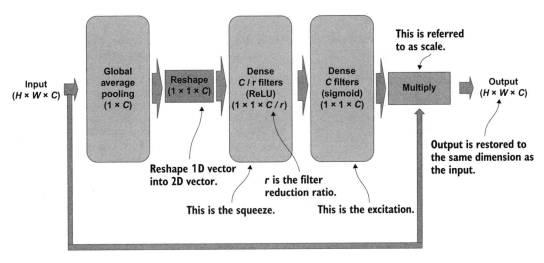

Figure 7.22 Squeeze-excitation block showing the squeeze, excitation, and then scale operation

against the input ($H \times W \times C$). After the scale operation, the output dimension (number and size of feature maps) is restored to the original dimension of the input (scale).

Now let's see an example implementation of the SE link, consisting of the squeeze, excitation, and scale operations. Note the `Reshape` operation after `GlobalAverage-Pooling2D` to convert the pooled 1D vector into a 1-×-1-pixel 2D vector for the subsequent two `Dense` layers, which perform the squeeze and excitation operations, respectively. The $1 \times 1 \times C$ matrix produced by the excitation is then matrix-multiplied with the input (`shortcut`), for the scale operation:

Squeeze operation for dimensionality reduction using global average pooling, which will output a 1D vector

```
def squeeze_excite_link(x, ratio=16):
    """ Create a Squeeze and Excite link
        x     : input to the link
        ratio : amount of filter reduction during squeeze
    """
    shortcut = x
    n_filters = x.shape[-1]
    x = GlobalAveragePooling2D()(x)
    x = Reshape((1, 1, n_filters))(x)
    x = Dense(n_filters // ratio, activation='relu')(x)
    x = Dense(n_filters, activation='sigmoid')(x)
    x = Multiply()([shortcut, x])
    return x
```

Gets the number of feature maps (filters) in the input to the SE link

Reshapes the output into 1 × 1 feature maps (1 × 1 × C)

Reduces the number of filters (1 × 1 × C / r) by the reduction ratio

Excitation operation for dimensionality restoration by restoring the number of filters (1 × 1 × C)

Scale operation, multiply the squeeze/excitation output with the input (W × H × C)

A complete code rendition using the Idiomatic procedure reuse design pattern for SE-Net is on GitHub (http://mng.bz/vea7).

Summary

- Feature reuse in DenseNet replaces the matrix addition with a feature map concatenation of the input to the output from a residual block. This classification increases accuracy over existing SOTA models.

- Using 1×1 convolutions in DenseNet to learn is the best way to upsample and downsample feature maps for a specific dataset.

- Further refactoring a spatial separable convolution to a depthwise separable convolution in Xception further reduces computational cost while maintaining representational equivalence.

- Adding a squeeze-excite-scale pattern in SE-Net to existing residual networks increases the accuracy while adding only a few parameters.

Mobile convolutional neural networks

This chapter covers

- Understanding the design principles and unique requirements for mobile convolutional networks

- Examining the design patterns for MobileNet v1 and v2, SqueezeNet, and ShuffleNet

- Coding examples of these models by using the procedural design pattern

- Making models more compact by quantizing models and then executing them using TensorFlow Lite (TF Lite)

You have now learned several key design patterns for large models without memory constraints. Now let's turn to design patterns such as the popular FaceApp from Facebook that are optimized for memory-constrained devices, such as mobile phones and IoT devices.

In contrast to their PC or cloud equivalents, compact models have a special challenge: they need to operate in substantially less memory, and therefore cannot benefit from the use of overcapacity to achieve high accuracy. To fit into these constrained memory sizes, models need to have substantially fewer parameters for inference or prediction. The architecture for compact models relies on a tradeoff between accuracy and latency. The more of the device's memory the model occupies, the higher the accuracy, but the longer the response time latency.

In early SOTA mobile convolutional models, researchers found ways to address this tradeoff with methods that substantially reduced parameters and computational complexity while maintaining minimal loss of accuracy. Those methods relied on further refactoring of convolutions, such as the depthwise separable convolution (MobileNet) and pointwise group convolutions (ShuffleNet). These refactoring techniques provided the means to increase capacity for accuracy, which would otherwise be lost by the more extreme refactoring methods.

This chapter presents two of those refactoring approaches, used in two different models: MobileNet and SqueezeNet. We'll also look at another novel approach for memory-constrained devices in a third model, ShuffleNet. We'll finish the chapter by exploring other strategies to further reduce the memory footprint, such as parameter compression and quantization to make models more compact.

Before we start looking at the particulars of the three models, let me briefly compare the methods they use to deal with limited memory. MobileNet's researchers explored strategies of thinning the model to adjust to various memory sizes and latency requirements, and the effects that thinning had on accuracy.

SqueezeNet researchers proposed a block pattern, known as a *fire module,* that would sustain accuracy after the model size is reduced by up to 90%. The fire module uses deep compression. This method for compressing the size of a neural network was introduced in "Deep Compression," by Song Han et al. (https://arxiv.org/abs/1510.00149) presented at the 2015 International Conference on Learning Representations (ICLR).

Meanwhile, ShuffleNet researchers focused on increasing representational power for models deployed on extremely low-power computational devices (for example, 10 to 150 MFLOPs). They proposed a twofold approach: a channel shuffle within a highly factorized group, along with pointwise convolution.

Now we can get into the details of each.

8.1   MobileNet v1

MobileNet v1 is an architecture introduced by Google in 2017 for producing smaller networks that can fit on mobile and IoT devices, while maintaining accuracy close to their larger network counterparts. The MobileNet v1 architecture, explained in "MobileNets" by Andrew G. Howard et al. (https://arxiv.org/abs/1704.04861), replaces normal convolutions with depthwise separable convolutions to further reduce computational complexity. (As you remember, we covered the theory behind the refactoring of normal convolutions into depthwise separable convolutions when we looked at the Xception model in chapter 7.) Let's see how MobileNet put this approach to work on a compact model.

8.1.1 Architecture

The MobileNet v1 architecture incorporated several design principles for constrained memory devices:

- The stem convolutional group introduced an additional parameter, known as a *resolution multiplier,* for a more aggressive reduction in the *size* of the feature maps feeding into the learner component. (This is labeled *A* in figure 8.1.)
- Similarly, the learner component added a *width multiplier* parameter for a more aggressive reduction in the *number* of feature maps within the learner component (B).
- The model uses depthwise convolutionals (as in Xception) to reduce computational complexity while maintaining representational equivalence (C).
- The classifier component uses a convolutional layer in place of a dense layer for final classification (D).

You can see these innovations implemented in the macro-architecture in figure 8.1, with letters A, B, C, and D marking the corresponding feature.

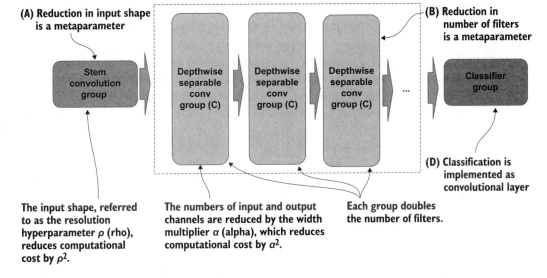

Figure 8.1 The MobileNet v1 macro-architecture uses metaparameters in the stem and learner (A and B), along with depthwise convolutions in the learner (C), and a convolutional layer instead of a dense layer in the classifier (D).

Unlike the models we've covered so far, MobileNets are categorized not by their number of layers, but by the input resolution. For example, a MobileNet-224 has input (224, 224, 3). The convolutional groups follow the convention of doubling the number of filters from the previous group.

Let's first look at the two new hyperparameters, the width multiplier and resolution multiplier, to see how and where they help thin the network. Then we'll go through the stem, learner, and classifier components step-by-step.

8.1.2   *Width multiplier*

The first hyperparameter introduced was the *width multiplier* α (alpha), which thinned a network uniformly at each layer. Let's take a quick look at the pros and cons of thinning a network.

We know that by thinning it, we are reducing the number of parameters between layers, and exponentially reducing the number of matmul operations. Using dense layers, for example, if, prior to thinning, the output of one dense layer and the corresponding input is 100 parameters each, we would have 10,000 matrix multiply (matmul) operations. In other words, two 100-node dense layers fully connected to one another would have 100 x 100 matmul operations per 1D vector that passes through the two layers.

Now let's thin it by one-half. That is 50 output parameters and 50 input parameters. We've now reduced the number of matmul operations to 2500. The result would be a 50% reduction in memory size and 75% reduction in computation (latency). The downside is we are further removing overcapacity for accuracy, and will need to explore other strategies to compensate for it.

At each layer, the number of input channels is αM, and the number of output channels is αN, where M and N are the number of channels (feature maps) of a non-thinned MobileNet. Let's now look at how to calculate the reduction in parameters by thinning the network layers. The value of α (alpha) is from 0 to 1, and will reduce the computational complexity of a MobileNet by α^2 (the number of parameters). A value of $\alpha < 1$ is referred to as a *reduced MobileNet*. Typically, values are 0.25 (6% of non-thinned), 0.50 (25%), and 0.75 (56%). Let's go ahead and do the computation. If the α factor is 0.25, the resulting complexity is 0.25×0.25, which computes to 0.0625.

In tests results reported in the paper, a nonthinned MobileNet-224 had a 70.6% accuracy on ImageNet with 4.2 million parameters and 569 million matrix multiply-add operations, while a 0.25 (width multiplier) MobileNet-224 had 50.6% accuracy with 0.5 million parameters and 41 million matrix multiply-add operations. These results show that the loss of overcapacity by aggressive thinning was not being effectively offset by the design of the model. So the researchers looked to reducing the resolution, which turned out to be more effective in maintaining accuracy.

8.1.3   *Resolution multiplier*

The second hyperparameter introduced was the *resolution multiplier* ρ (rho), which thins the input shape and consequently the feature map sizes at each layer.

When we reduce the input resolution without altering the stem component, the size of the feature maps entering the learner component is correspondingly reduced. For example, if the height and width of an input image is reduced by one-half, the number of input pixels is reduced by 75%. If we maintain the same coarse-level filters and number of filters, the outputted feature maps would be reduced by 75%. Since the feature maps are reduced, this will have a downstream effect of reducing the number of parameters per convolution (model size) and number of matmul operations (latency). Note this is in contrast to the width thinning that would reduce the number of feature maps while maintaining their size.

The downside is that if we reduce too aggressively, the size of the feature maps by the time we get to the bottleneck may be 1×1 pixels and in essence lose the spatial relationships. We could offset this by reducing the number of intermediate layers so the feature maps are bigger than 1×1, but then we are removing more overcapacity for accuracy.

In tests results reported in the paper, a 0.25 (resolution multiplier) MobileNet-224 had 64.4% accuracy with 4.2 million parameters and 186 million matrix multiply-add operations. Let's go ahead and do the computation, given the value of ρ (rho) is from 0 to 1, and will reduce computational complexity of a MobileNet by ρ^2. If the ρ factor is 0.25, the resulting complexity is 0.25×0.25, which computes to 0.0625.

The following is a skeleton template for a MobileNet-224. Note the use of parameters `alpha` and `rho` for the width and resolution multiplier:

```
def stem(inputs, alpha):
    """ Construct the stem group
        inputs : input tensor
        alpha  : with multiplier
    """

    return outputs

def learner(inputs, alpha):
    """ Construct the learner group
        inputs : input to the learner
        alpha  : with multiplier
    """

    return outputs

def classifier(inputs, alpha, dropout, n_classes):
    """ Construct the classifier group
        inputs : input to the classifier
        alpha  : with multiplier
        Dropout: percent of dropout
        n_classes: number of output classes
    """

    return outputs

inputs = Input((224*rho, 224*rho, 3))
outputs = stem(inputs, alpha)
outputs = learner(outputs, alpha)
outputs = classifier(outputs, alpha, dropout, n_classes)
model = Model(inputs, outputs)
```

Width multiplier used on all layers in the model

Code removed for brevity

Resolution multiplier used only on input tensor

8.1.4 Stem

The stem component consists of a strided 3 × 3 convolution, for feature pooling, followed by a single depthwise separable block of 64 filters. The number of filters in both the strided convolution and the depthwise block are further reduced by the hyperparameter α (alpha). The reduction of the input size by the hyperparameter ρ (rho) is not done in the model, but upstream in the input preprocessing function.

Let's discuss how this differed from a conventional stem at the time for a large model. Typically, the first convolutional layer would start with a coarse 7 × 7, or 5 × 5, or refactored stack of two 3 × 3 convolutions with 64 filters. The coarse convolution would be strided for reduction in size of feature maps and then followed by a max pooling layer for another reduction in feature map size.

In the MobileNet v1 stem, the convention of using 64 filters and a stack of two 3 × 3 convolutions is continued, but with three significant changes:

- The first convolution outputs one-half (32) the number of feature maps as the second one. This acts as a bottleneck, reducing computational complexity in the dual 3 × 3 stack.
- The second convolutional is replaced by a depthwise separable convolution, further reducing computational complexity in the stem.
- Without max pooling, there is only one feature map size reduction with the first strided convolution.

The tradeoff here is that the sizes of the feature maps are kept larger—double the *H* × *W*. This offsets the representational loss from aggressive reduction in computational complexity in the first coarse-level feature extraction.

Figure 8.2 illustrates the stem component, which consists of a stack of two 3 × 3 convolutions. The first is a normal convolution that does feature pooling (strided).

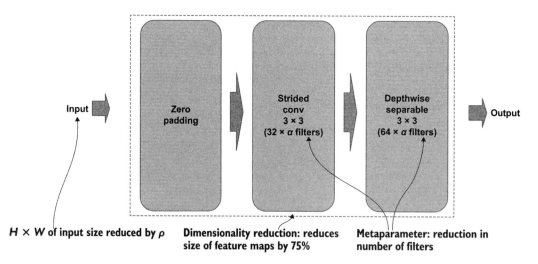

Figure 8.2   MobileNet stem group thins the network in the stack of 3 × 3 convolutions.

The second is a depthwise convolution, which maintains the size of the feature maps (non-strided). The strided 3×3 convolution did not use padding. To maintain feature map reduction of 75% $(0.5H \times 0.5W)$, a zero padding is added to the input prior to the convolution. Note the use of the metaparameter ρ on the input size for resolution reduction and α on the dual stack of 3×3 convolutions for network thinning.

The following is an example implementation of the stem component. As you can see, a post-activation batch normalization (Conv-BN-RE) is used for convolutional layers, so the model did not have the benefit of using a pre-activation batch normalization, which was found to increase accuracy from 0.5 to 2%:

```
def stem(inputs, alpha):
    """ Construct the stem group
        inputs : input tensor
        alpha  : with multiplier
    """
    x = ZeroPadding2D(padding=((0, 1), (0, 1)))(inputs)
    x = Conv2D(32 * alpha, (3, 3), strides=(2, 2), padding='valid')(x)
    x = BatchNormalization()(x)
    x = ReLU(6.0)(x)

    x = depthwise_block(x, 64, alpha, (1, 1))
    return x
```

> **Convolutional block with zero padding of input feature maps** (points to `x = ZeroPadding2D(...)`)
>
> **Depthwise separable convolution block** (points to `x = depthwise_block(...)`)

Note that ReLU in this example takes an optional parameter with the value of 6.0. This is the max_value argument to ReLU, which defaults to None. Its purpose is to clip any value above max_value. Thus in the preceding examples, all the outputs will be in the range of 0 to 6.0. It is common practice to clip the output from ReLU in mobile networks, if the weights are later quantized.

Quantizing in this context is computing using a lower-bit representation; I'll explain the details of this process in section 8.5.1. Quantized models have been found to maintain better accuracy when the output from ReLU has a constrained range. The general practice is to set it to 6.0.

Let's briefly discuss the reasoning behind the choice of the value of 6. The concept was introduced in Alex Krizhevsky's 2010 paper, "Convolutional Deep Belief Networks on CIFAR-10" (www.cs.utoronto.ca/~kriz/conv-cifar10-aug2010.pdf). Krizhevsky proposed it as a solution to the problem of exploding gradients in deeper layers.

When the output of an activation got very large, it could dominate the outputs of surrounding activations. As a result, that area of the network would exhibit symmetry, meaning that it would reduce down, as if there were only a single node. Through experimentation, Krizhevsky found the value 6 to be the best.

Remember, this was before we were aware of the benefit of batch normalization, which would not be introduced until 2015. With batch normalization, the activations would be squashed at each successive depth, so the need for clipping went away.

The idea of clipping the ReLU returned when quantization was introduced. In brief, when weights are quantized, we are decreasing the number of bits that represent a value. If we mapped the weights to, say, an 8-bit integer range, we have to "bucketize" the entire output range into 256 bins, based on the actual distribution of output values. The longer the range, the more stretched thin the floating-point-value mappings to the buckets, making each bucket less distinctive.

The theory here is that values that would be 98, 99, and 99.5% confidence are essentially the same, and lower values are more distinctive—that is, output is 70% confident. But with clipping, we are treating everything above 6 as essentially 100% and bucketizing only the distribution between 0 and 6, and those values are more meaningful for inference.

8.1.5   *Learner*

The learner component in the MobileNet-224 consists of four groups, and each group has two or more convolutional blocks. Each group will double the number of filters from the preceding group, and the first block in each group uses a strided convolution (feature pooling) to reduce the feature map sizes by 75%.

The construction of a MobileNet group follows the same principles as its large convolutional network groups. Both typically have the following:

1 A progression in the number of filters per group, such as doubling the number of filters

2 A reduction in the outputted feature map sizes either by using a strided convolution or deferred max pooling

You can see in figure 8.3 that the MobileNet group uses a strided convolution for the first block, to reduce the feature map (principle 2). Though not shown in the diagram, each group in the learner doubles the number of filters (principle 1) starting at 128.

Figure 8.4 zooms in on a depthwise convolutional block in the learner group. In v1, the model's authors used a convolutional block design instead of a residual block

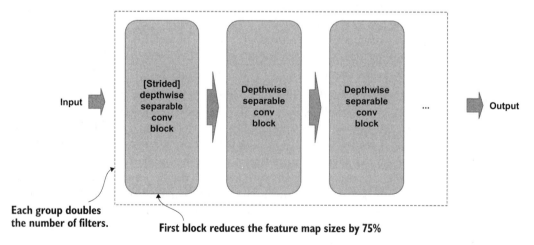

Figure 8.3   In a MobileNet v1 learner component, each group is a sequence of depthwise convolutional blocks.

design; there is no identity link. Each block is essentially a single depthwise separable convolution constructed as two separate convolutional layers. The first layer is a 3×3 depthwise convolution followed by the 1×1 pointwise convolution. When combined, these form the depthwise separable convolution. The number of filters, which corresponds to the number of feature maps, can be further reduced for network thinning by the metaparameter α.

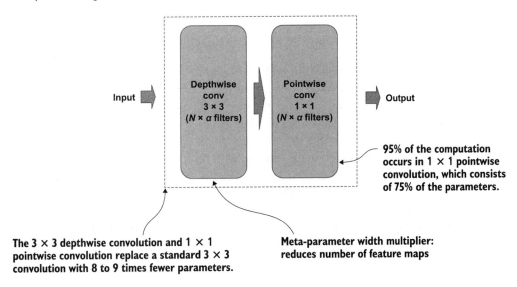

Figure 8.4 MobileNet v1 convolutional block

Next is an example implementation of a depthwise separable convolutional block. The first step is to calculate the number of reduced `filters` for network thinning, after applying the width multiplier `alpha`. For the first block in the group, the feature map sizes are reduced (feature pooling) using a strided convolution (`strides=(2, 2)`). This corresponds to the convolutional group design principle 2 mentioned earlier, where the first block in a group typically does a dimensionality reduction on the size of the input feature maps.

```
def depthwise_block(x, n_filters, alpha, strides):
    """ Construct a Depthwise Separable Convolution block
        x          : input to the block
        n_filters : number of filters
        alpha     : width multiplier
        strides   : strides
    """
    filters = int(n_filters * alpha)

    if strides == (2, 2):
        x = ZeroPadding2D(padding=((0, 1), (0, 1)))(x)
        padding = 'valid'
    else:
```

Applies the width filter to the number of feature maps

Adds zero padding when a strided convolution, for matching the number of filters

```
          padding = 'same'                                        The depthwise
x = DepthwiseConv2D((3, 3), strides, padding=padding)(x)   ◁──┘  convolution
x = BatchNormalization()(x)
x = ReLU(6.0)(x)

x = Conv2D(filters, (1, 1), strides=(1, 1), padding='same')(x)   ◁──┐
x = BatchNormalization()(x)
x = ReLU(6.0)(x)                          The pointwise convolution    │
return x
```

8.1.6   *Classifier*

The classifier component differed from the conventional classifier for large models in that it used a convolutional layer in place of a dense layer for the classification step. Like other classifiers of the time, to prevent memorization, it added a dropout layer prior to the classification for regularization.

You can see in figure 8.5 that the classifier component contains a GlobalAverage-Pooling2D layer to flatten the feature maps and reduce the high-dimensional encoding to a lower-dimensional encoding (1 pixel per feature map). Then a Reshape layer reshapes the 1D vector for a 2D convolution, using a softmax activation, in which the number of filters is the number of classes. Then comes another Reshape to reshape the output back to a 1D vector (one element per class). Prior to the 2D convolution is the Dropout layer for regularization.

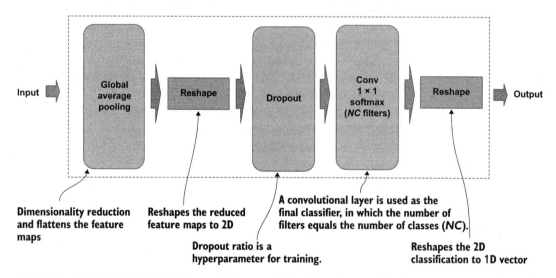

Figure 8.5   MobileNet v1 classifier group using a convolutional layer for classification

The following is an example implementation of the classifier component. The first Reshape layer reshapes the 1D vector from GlobalAveragePooling2D to a 2D vector of size 1 × 1. The second Reshape layer reshapes the 2D 1 × 1 output from Conv2D into a 1D vector for the softmax probability distribution (classification):

```
def classifier(x, alpha, dropout, n_classes):
    """ Construct the classifier group
        x          : input to the classifier
        alpha      : width multiplier
        dropout    : dropout percentage
        n_classes  : number of output classes
    """
    x = GlobalAveragePooling2D()(x)

    shape = (1, 1, int(1024 * alpha))
    x = Reshape(shape)(x)

    x = Dropout(dropout)(x)

    x = Conv2D(n_classes, (1, 1), padding='same', activation='softmax')(x)

    x = Reshape((n_classes, ))(x)
    return x
```

Flattens the feature maps into 1D feature maps (α, N)

Reshapes the flattened feature maps to (α, 1, 1, 1024)

Performs dropout for preventing overfitting

Uses convolution for classifying (emulates a fully connected layer)

Reshapes the resulting output to 1D vector of number of classes

A complete code rendition using the Idiomatic procedure reuse design pattern for MobileNet v1 is located on GitHub (http://mng.bz/Q2rG).

8.2 MobileNet v2

After improving version 1, Google introduced *MobileNet v2* in "MobileNetV2: Inverted Residuals and Linear Bottlenecks" by Mark Sandler et al. in 2018 (https://arxiv.org/abs/1801.04381). The new architecture replaces convolutional blocks with inverted residual blocks to improve performance. The paper summarizes the benefits of the inverted residual blocks:

- Significantly decreasing the number of operations while retaining the same accuracy as convolutional block
- Significantly reducing the memory footprint needed for inference

8.2.1 Architecture

The MobileNet v2 architecture incorporated several design principles for constrained memory devices:

- It continued using the hyperparameter (alpha) as a width multiplier, as in v1, for network thinning in the stem and learner components.
- Continued using depthwise separable convolutions in place of normal convolutions, as in v1, for substantial reduction in computational complexity (latency), while maintaining nearly comparable representational power.
- Replaced using convolutional blocks with residual blocks, allowing deeper layers for more accuracy.
- Introduced a new design for residual blocks, which the authors called *inverted residual blocks.*
- Replaced using 1 × 1 nonlinear convolutions with 1 × 1 linear convolutions.

The reason for the last modification, using 1×1 linear convolutions, according to the authors: "Additionally, we find that it is important to remove nonlinearities in the narrow layers in order to maintain representational power." In their ablation study, they compared using a 1×1 nonlinear convolution (with `ReLU`) to a 1×1 linear convolution (without `ReLU`) and got a 1% top-1 accuracy improvement on ImageNet by removing the ReLU.

The authors describe their main contribution as a novel layer module: the inverted residual with linear bottleneck. I describe the inverted residual block in detail in section 8.2.3.

Figure 8.6 depicts the MobileNet v2 architecture. In the macro-architecture, the learner component consists of four inverted residual groups, followed by a final 1×1 linear convolution, which means that the activation function is linear. Each inverted residual group increases the number of filters from the previous group. The number of filters per group is thinned by the metaparameter width multiplier α (alpha). The final 1×1 convolution does a linear projection, increasing the final number of feature maps four times, to 2048.

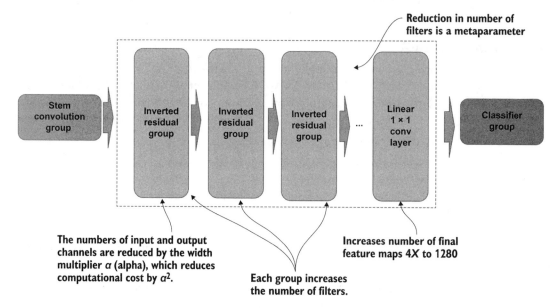

Figure 8.6   MobileNet v2 macro-architecture

8.2.2   Stem

The stem component is similar to v1, except after the initial 3×3 convolutional layer, it is not followed by a depthwise convolutional block as in v1 (figure 8.7). As such, the coarse-level feature extraction would have less representational power than the dual stack of 3×3 in v1. The authors don't state why the reduction in representational power did not impact the model, which outperformed v1 in accuracy.

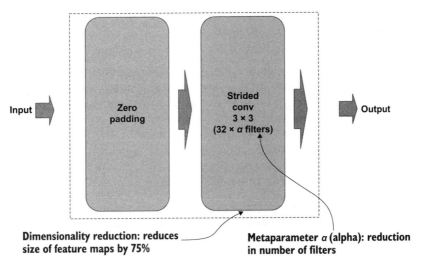

Input | Zero padding | Strided conv 3 × 3 (32 × *α* filters) | Output

Dimensionality reduction: reduces size of feature maps by 75%

Metaparameter *α* (alpha): reduction in number of filters

Figure 8.7   MobileNet v2 stem group

8.2.3   *Learner*

The learner component consists of seven inverted residual groups, followed by a 1 × 1 linear convolution. Each inverted residual group consists of two or more inverted residual blocks. Each group progressively increases the number of filters, also known as *output channels*. Each group starts with a strided convolutional, reducing the size of the feature maps (channels) as each group progressively increases the number of feature maps.

Figure 8.8 depicts a MobileNet v2 group, in which the first inverted residual block is strided for reducing the size of the feature maps to offset the progressive increase in the number of feature maps per group. As noted in the diagram, only groups 2, 3, 4, and 6, start with a strided inverted residual block. In other words, groups 1, 5, and 7

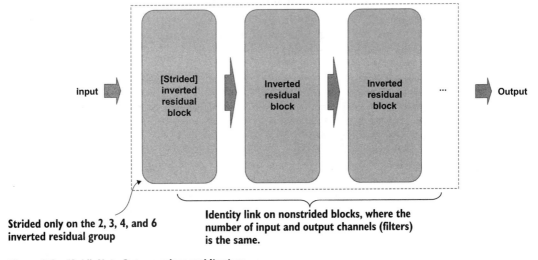

input | [Strided] inverted residual block | Inverted residual block | Inverted residual block | ... | Output

Strided only on the 2, 3, 4, and 6 inverted residual group

Identity link on nonstrided blocks, where the number of input and output channels (filters) is the same.

Figure 8.8   MobileNet v2 group micro-architecture

start with a nonstrided residual block. Additionally, each nonstrided block has an identity link, and the strided blocks do not have an identity link.

The following is an example implementation of a MobileNet v2 group. The group follows the convention whereby the first block does a dimensionality reduction to reduce the size of feature maps. In this case, the first inverted block is strided (feature pooling), and the remaining blocks are not strided (no feature pooling).

```
def group(x, n_filters, n_blocks, alpha, expansion=6, strides=(2, 2)):
    """ Construct an Inverted Residual Group
        x          : input to the group
        n_filters  : number of filters
        n_blocks   : number of blocks in the group
        alpha      : width multiplier
        expansion  : multiplier for expanding the number of filters
        strides    : whether the first inverted residual block is strided.
    """
    x = inverted_block(x, n_filters, alpha, expansion, strides=strides)
    for _ in range(n_blocks - 1):
        x = inverted_block(x, n_filters, alpha, expansion, strides=(1, 1))
    return x
```

Constructs the remaining blocks

The first inverted residual block in the group may be strided.

The block is referred to as an *inverted residual block* because it reverses (inverts) the relationship of the dimensionality reduction and expansion surrounding the middle convolution layer from a conventional residual block, such as in a ResNet50. Instead of starting with a 1 × 1 bottleneck convolution for dimensionality reduction and ending with a 1 × 1 linear projection convolution for dimensionality restoration, the order is reversed. An inverted block starts with a 1 × 1 projection convolution for dimensionality expansion, and ends with a 1 × 1 bottleneck convolution for dimensionality restoration (figure 8.9).

In their ablation study comparing the bottleneck residual block design in MobileNet v1 to the inverted residual block design in v2, the authors achieved a 1.4% improvement in top-1 accuracy on ImageNet. The inverted residual block design is also more efficient, reducing the total number of parameters from 4.2 million to 3.4 million, and the number of matmul operations from 575 million to 300 million.

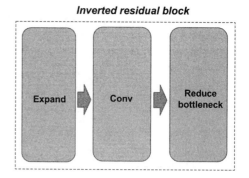

Figure 8.9   Conceptual difference between residual bottleneck block and inverted residual block

Next, we will dive deeper into the mechanics behind the inversion. MobileNet v2 introduced a new metaparameter expansion for the initial 1 × 1 projection convolution. The 1 × 1 projection convolution performs the dimensionality expansion, and the metaparameter specifies the amount to expand the number of filters. In other words, the 1 × 1 projection convolution expands the number of feature maps to a high-dimensional space.

The middle convolution is a 3 × 3 depthwise convolution. This is followed by a linear pointwise convolution that reduces the feature maps (also called *channels*), restoring them to the original number. Note that restoration convolutions use a linear activation instead of a nonlinear (ReLU). The authors found it important to remove nonlinearities in the narrow layers in order to maintain representational power.

The authors also found that a ReLU activation loses information in low-dimensional space, but makes up for it when there are lots of filters. The assumption here is that the input to the block is in a lower-dimensional space but expands the number of filters, thus the reason to maintain using the ReLU activation in the first 1 × 1 convolution.

The MobileNet v2 researchers referred to the amount of expansion as the *expressiveness* of the block. In their main experiments, they tried expansion factors between 5 and 10 and observed little difference in accuracy. Since an increase in expansion results in an increase in the number of parameters, while observing little gain in accuracy, the authors used a ratio of 6 for expansion in their ablation study.

Figure 8.10 shows the inverted residual block. You can see how its design changes took another step forward in reducing memory footprint while maintaining accuracy.

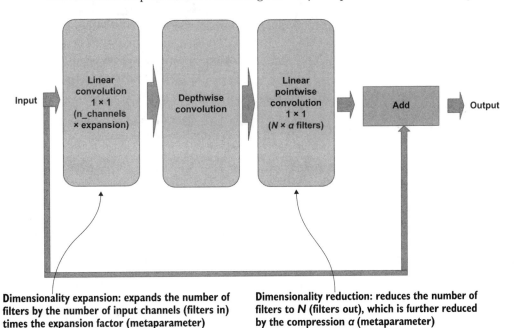

Figure 8.10 Inverted residual block with identity shortcut inverts the relationships of the 1 × 1 convolutions from v1.

The following is an example implementation of an inverted residual block. For context, remember that the input to the inverted residual block is the output from a prior block, or stem group, in a low-dimensional space. The input is then projected into a higher-dimensional space by the 1×1 projection convolution, where the 3×3 depthwise convolution is performed. The pointwise 1×1 linear convolution then restores the output to the lower dimensionality of the input.

Here are some notable steps:

- The width factor is applied to the number of output filters for the block: `filters = int(n_filters * alpha)`.
- The number of input channels (feature maps) is determined by `n_channels = int(x.shape[-1])`.
- The 1×1 linear projection is applied when the `expansion` factor is greater than 1.
- The `Add()` operation is done on every block, except the first block in the first group: `if n_channels == filters and strides == (1, 1)`.

```
def inverted_block(x, n_filters, alpha, expansion=6, strides=(1, 1)):
    """ Construct an Inverted Residual Block
        x          : input to the block
        n_filters  : number of filters
        alpha      : width multiplier
        expansion  : multiplier for expanding number of filters
        strides    : strides
    """
    shortcut = x   # Remember input

    filters = int(n_filters * alpha)              Applies the width multiplier to
                                                  the number of feature maps for
                                                  the pointwise convolution
    n_channels = int(x.shape[-1])
                                          Does dimensionality expansion when
                                          not the first block in a group
    if expansion > 1:
        # 1x1 linear convolution
        x = Conv2D(expansion * n_channels, (1, 1), padding='same')(x)
        x = BatchNormalization()(x)
        x = ReLU(6.)(x)                   Adds zero padding to feature map
                                          when strided convolution (feature
    if strides == (2, 2):                 pooling)
        x = ZeroPadding2D(padding=((0, 1), (0, 1)))(x)
        padding = 'valid'
    else:
        padding = 'same'                                        3 × 3
                                                                depthwise
    x = DepthwiseConv2D((3, 3), strides, padding=padding)(x)    convolution
    x = BatchNormalization()(x)
    x = ReLU(6.)(x)                            1 × 1 linear pointwise convolution

    x = Conv2D(filters, (1, 1), strides=(1, 1), padding='same')(x)
    x = BatchNormalization()(x)
                                              Adds the identity link to
                                              output when the number
    if n_channels == filters and strides == (1, 1):    of input filters matches the
        x = Add()([shortcut, x])                        number of output filters
    return x
```

8.2.4 *Classifier*

In v2, the researchers used the conventional approach of a `GlobalAveragePooling2D` layer followed by a `Dense` layer, which we covered in section 5.4 in chapter 5 on large SOTA models. Early ConvNets, such as AlexNet, ZFNet, and VGG flatten the bottleneck layer (final feature maps), which was then followed by one or more hidden dense layers, before the final dense layer for classification. For example, VGG used two layers of 4096 nodes before the final dense layer for classification.

As representational learning improved, starting with ResNet and Inception, the need for hidden layers in the classifier became unnecessary, as did the need for a flattening layer without a reduction into a lower-dimensionality bottleneck layer. MobileNet v2 followed the practice that when the latent space had strong enough representational information, we could further reduce it to a lower-dimensionality space—the bottleneck layer. With the high representational information, the model can then pass the lower dimensionality, also known as the *embedding* or *feature vector*, straight to the classifier's dense layer without the need for intermediate hidden dense layers. Figure 8.11 illustrates the classifier component.

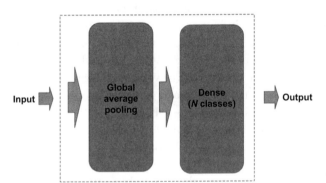

Figure 8.11 MobileNet v2 classifier group

In the authors' ablation study, they compare MobileNet v1 to v2 with the ImageNet classification task. MobileNet v2 achieved 72% top-1 accuracy compared to v1, which achieved 70.6%. A complete code rendition using the Idiomatic procedure reuse design pattern for MobileNet v2 is on GitHub (http://mng.bz/Q2rG).

Next, we will cover SqueezeNet, which introduced the fire module and the terminology of macro- and micro-architecture and metaparameters for configuring the micro-architecture attributes. While other researchers of the time explored this concept, the SqueezeNet authors coined the terms for this innovative stepping-stone to later advances in macro-architecture search, machine design, and model amalgamation. For myself, when I first read their paper and these concepts, it was like a light bulb went off.

8.3   *SqueezeNet*

SqueezeNet is an architecture introduced by joint research of DeepScale, the University of California at Berkeley, and Stanford University in 2016. In the corresponding "SqueezeNet" paper ("SqueezeNet: AlexNet-Level Accuracy with 50x Fewer Parameters and <0.5MB Model Size"; https://arxiv.org/abs/1602.07360), Forrest N. Iandola et al. introduced a new type of module, the *fire module*, as well as terminology for micro-architecture, macro-architecture, and metaparameters. The authors' goal was to find a CNN architecture with fewer parameters but equivalent accuracy compared to the well-known AlexNet model.

The fire module design was based on their research on the micro-architecture to achieve this goal. The *micro-architecture* is the design of modules, or groups, and the *macro-architecture* is how the modules, or groups, are connected. The introduction of the term *metaparameters* aided in better distinguishing what a hyperparameter is (discussed in detail in chapter 10).

Generally, the weights and biases that are learned during training are the model parameters. The term *hyperparameters* can be confusing. Some researchers/practitioners used the term to refer to the tunable parameters for training the model, while others used the term to also include the model architecture (for example, layers and width). In the SqueezeNet paper, the authors used *metaparameters* to refer to the structure of the model architecture that is configurable—such as the number of blocks per group, and the number of filters per convolutional layer in a block, and the amount of dimensionality reduction at the end of a group.

The authors tackled several issues in their paper. First, they wanted to demonstrate a CNN architecture design that would fit on a mobile device and still retain accuracy comparable to that of AlexNet on the ImageNet 2012 dataset. On this point, the authors achieved the same results empirically as AlexNet with a 50 times reduction in parameters.

Second, they wanted to demonstrate a small CNN architecture that would maintain accuracy when compressed. Here the authors achieved the same results without compression after compressing with the Deep Compression algorithm, which reduced the size of the model from 4.8 MB to 0.47 MB. Getting the model size down to under 0.5 MB while maintaining the accuracy of AlexNet demonstrated the practicality of placing models on extremely memory-constrained IoT devices such as microcontrollers.

In their SqueezeNet paper, the authors refer to their design principles for achieving their objectives as strategies 1, 2, and 3:

- *Strategy 1*—Use mostly 1×1 filters, which give a 9 times reduction in the number of parameters, instead of the more common convention of 3×3 filters. The v1.0 version of SqueezeNet used a 2:1 ratio of 1×1 to 3×3 filters.
- *Strategy 2*—Reduce the number of input filters to the 3×3 layers to further reduce the number of parameters. They refer to this component of the fire module as the *squeeze layer*.

- *Strategy 3*—Delay downsampling of feature maps to as late as possible in the network. This contrasts the convention of downsampling early to preserve accuracy. The authors used a stride of 1 on the early convolution layers and delayed using a stride of 2.

The authors stated this justification for their strategies:

Strategies 1 and 2 are about judiciously decreasing the quantity of parameters in a CNN while attempting to preserve accuracy. Strategy 3 is about maximizing accuracy on a limited budget of parameters.

The authors named their architecture after their design of the fire block, which uses a squeeze operation followed by an expand operation.

8.3.1 Architecture

The SqueezeNet architecture consists of a stem group, three fire groups comprising a total of eight fire blocks (referred to as *modules* in the paper), and a classifier group. The authors did not explicitly state why they chose three fire groups and eight fire blocks, but described a macro-architecture exploration that demonstrated a cost-effective method of designing a model for a specific memory footprint and accuracy range merely by training different combinations of numbers of blocks per group and the input-to-output filter sizes.

Figure 8.12 shows the architecture. In the macro-architecture view, you see the three fire groups. The feature learning is done in the stem group and first two fire groups. The last fire group overlaps feature learning and classification learning with the classification group.

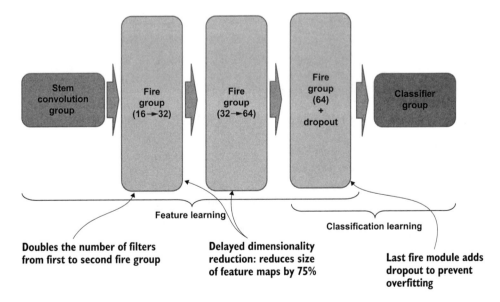

Figure 8.12   SqueezeNet macro-architecture

The first two fire groups double the number of feature maps from the input to the output, starting at 16, doubling to 32, and then doubling again to 64. Both the first and second fire groups delay dimensionality reduction to the end of the group. The last fire group does not do any doubling of the feature maps or dimensionality reduction, but does add a dropout for regularization at the end of the group. This last step differed from the convention of the time, whereby the dropout layer would otherwise be placed in the classifier group after the bottleneck layer (after the feature maps were reduced and flattened to a 1D vector).

8.3.2   *Stem*

The stem component uses a coarse-level 7 × 7 convolutional layer, which was the convention of the time, in contrast to the current convention of using a 5 × 5 or refactored stack of two 3 × 3 convolutional layers. The stem performs an aggressive feature map reduction, which continues to be the present convention.

The coarse 7 × 7 convolution is strided (feature pooling) for a 75% reduction, followed by a max pooling layer for a further 75% reduction, resulting in feature maps that are 6% the size of the input channels. Figure 8.13 depicts the stem component.

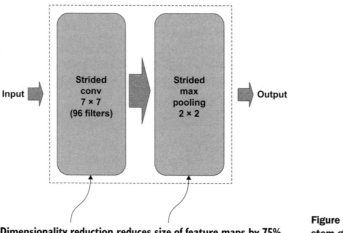

Dimensionality reduction reduces size of feature maps by 75%

Figure 8.13   SqueezeNet stem group

8.3.3   *Learner*

The learner consists of three fire groups. The first fire group has an input of 16 filters (channels) and an output of 32 filters (channels). Recall that the stem outputs 96 channels, so the first fire group does a dimensionality reduction on the input by reducing to 16 filters. The second fire group doubles that with input of 32 filters (channels) and output of 64 filters (channels).

Both the first and second fire groups consist of multiple fire blocks. All but the last fire block use the same number of input filters. The last fire block doubles the number of filters for the output. Both fire groups delay downsampling of the feature maps to the end of the group with a `MaxPooling2D` layer.

The third fire group consists of a single fire block of 64 filters followed by a dropout layer for regularization, prior to the classifier group. This is slightly different from the convention of the time, as SqueezeNet's dropout layer appears prior to the bottleneck layer in the classifier, versus appearing after the bottleneck layer. Figure 8.14 depicts a fire group.

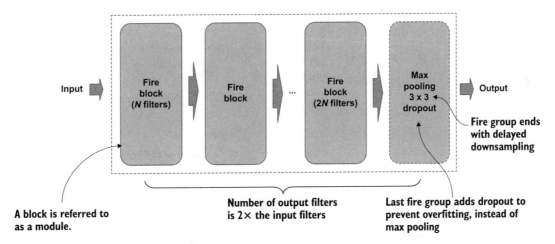

Figure 8.14 In the SqueezeNet group micro-architecture, the last fire group uses dropout instead of max pooling.

The following is an example implementation for the first and second fire group. Note that the parameter `filters` is a list, in which each element corresponds to a fire block and the value is the number of filters for that block. For example, consider the first fire group, which consists of three fire blocks; the input is 16 filters, and the output is 32 filters. The parameter `filters` would be the list [16, 16, 32].

After all the fire blocks have been added for the group, a `MaxPooling2D` layer is added for the delayed downsampling:

```
def group(x, filters):
    ''' Construct a Fire Group
        x      : input to the group
        filters: list of number of filters per fire block (module)
    '''
    for n_filters in filters:
        x = fire_block(x, n_filters)
    x = MaxPooling2D((3, 3), strides=(2, 2))(x)
    return x
```

Adds the fire blocks (modules) for the group

Adds the delayed downsampling at the end of the group

Figure 8.15 illustrates the fire block, which consists of two convolutional layers. The first layer is the squeeze layer, and the second layer is the expand layer. The *squeeze layer* reduces, or squeezes, the number of input channels to a lower dimensionality by using a 1 × 1 bottleneck convolution, while maintaining sufficient information for the subsequent convolution in the expand layer. The squeeze operation substantially

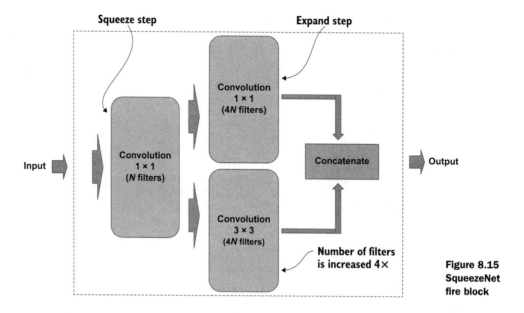

Figure 8.15 SqueezeNet fire block

lowers the number of parameters and corresponding matmul operations. In other words, the 1 × 1 bottleneck convolution learns the best way to maximize squeezing the number of feature maps into fewer feature maps, while still being able to perform feature extraction in the subsequent *expand layer*.

The *expand layer* is a branch of two convolutions: a 1 × 1 linear projection convolution and a 3 × 3 convolution, where the feature extraction occurs. The outputs (feature maps) from the convolutions are then concatenated. The expand layer expands the number of feature maps by a factor of 8.

Let's take an example. The input to the first fire block from the stem is 96 feature maps (channels), and the squeeze layer reduces it to 16 feature maps. The expand layer then expands by a factor of 8, so the output is 96 feature maps again. The next (second) fire block once again squeezes it to 16 feature maps, and so forth.

The following is an example implementation of a fire block. The block starts with a 1 × 1 bottleneck convolution for the squeeze layer. The output squeeze from the squeeze layer is branched to the two parallel expansion convolutions expand1x1 and expand3x3. Finally, the output from the two expansion convolutions is concatenated together.

```
def fire_block(x, n_filters):
    ''' Construct a Fire Block
        x        : input to the block
        n_filters: number of filters
    '''
    squeeze = Conv2D(n_filters, (1, 1), strides=1, activation='relu',
                    padding='same')(x)

    expand1x1 = Conv2D(n_filters * 4, (1, 1), strides=1, activation='relu',
```

Squeeze layer with 1 × 1 bottleneck convolution

```
                        padding='same')(squeeze)
      expand3x3 = Conv2D(n_filters * 4, (3, 3), strides=1, activation='relu',
                        padding='same')(squeeze)
```

Expansion layer branches into 1 × 1 and 3 × 3 convolutions and doubles the number of filters.

```
      x = Concatenate()([expand1x1, expand3x3])
      return x
```

The branched output from the excitation layer is concatenated together.

8.3.4 Classifier

The classifier does not follow the conventional practice of a `GlobalAveraging-Pooling2D` layer followed by a `Dense` layer in which the number of output nodes equals the number of classes. Instead, it uses a convolutional layer, and the number of filters equals the number of classes, followed by a `GlobalAveragingPooling2D` layer. This arrangement reduces each prior filter (class) to a single value. The outputs from the `GlobalAveragingPooling2D` layer are then passed through a softmax activation to get a probability distribution across all the classes.

Let's revisit a conventional classifier. In a conventional classifier, the final feature maps are reduced and flattened to a lower dimensionality at the bottleneck layer, generally with `GlobalAveragingPooling2D`. We would now have 1 pixel per feature map as a 1D vector (embedding). This 1D vector is then passed to a dense layer, where the number of nodes is equal to the number of output classes.

Figure 8.16 shows the classifier component. In SqueezeNet, the final feature maps are passed through a 1 × 1 linear projection, which learns to project the final feature maps to a new set that is exactly equal to the number of output classes. Now, these projected feature maps, each corresponding to a class, are reduced to a single pixel per feature map and flattened, becoming a 1D vector whose length is exactly equal to the number of output classes. The 1D vector is then passed through a softmax for prediction.

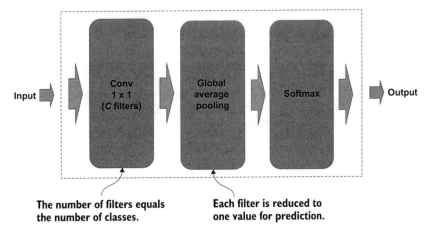

The number of filters equals the number of classes.   **Each filter is reduced to one value for prediction.**

Figure 8.16 SqueezeNet classifier group using a convolution instead of a dense layer for classification

What's the fundamental difference? In a conventional classifier, the dense layer learns the classification. In this mobile version, the 1 × 1 linear projection learns the classification.

The following is an example implementation of the classifier. In this example, the inputs, which are the final feature maps, are passed through a `Conv2D` layer that does the 1 × 1 linear projection into the number of output classes. The subsequent feature maps are then reduced to a single pixel 1D vector with `GlobalAveragePooling2D`:

```
def classifier(x, n_classes):
    ''' Construct the Classifier        Sets the number of
        x          : input to the classifier    filters equal to the
        n_classes: number of output classes     number of classes
    '''
    x = Conv2D(n_classes, (1, 1), strides=1, activation='relu',
               padding='same')(x)               ◁

    x = GlobalAveragePooling2D()(x)      Reduces each filter (class) to a
    x = Activation('softmax')(x)         single value for classification
    return x
```

Next, let's look deeper into the classifier design by constructing it with the conventional approach of large SOTA models. Figure 8.17 depicts the conventional approach. The final feature maps are globally pooled into a 1 × 1 matrix (a single value) each. The matrices are then flattened into a 1D vector that's the length of the number of feature maps (such as 2048 in ResNet). The 1D vector is then passed through a dense layer with a softmax activation that outputs a probability for each class.

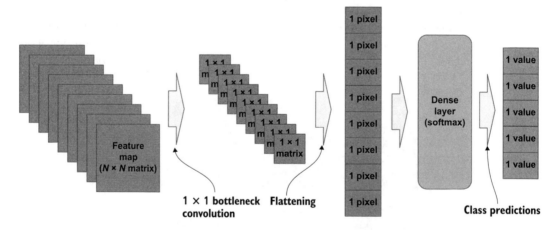

Figure 8.17 Feature map processing in a conventional, large SOTA classifier

Figure 8.18 depicts the approach in SqueezeNet. The feature maps are processed by a 1 × 1 bottleneck convolution, which reduces the number of feature maps to the number of classes. In essence, this is the class prediction step—except we don't have a single value, but an $N \times N$ matrix. The $N \times N$ matrix predictions are then globally pooled into

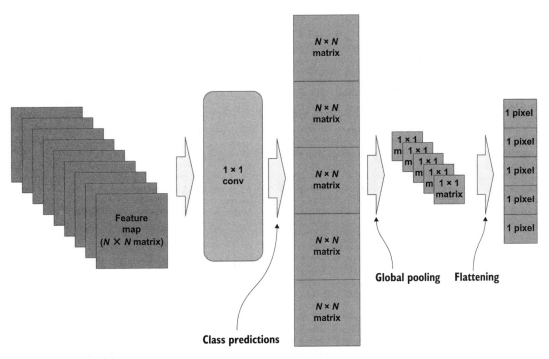

Figure 8.18 **Using a convolution instead of dense layer for classification**

1 × 1 matrices, which are then flattened into a 1D vector, in which each element is the probability for the corresponding class.

8.3.5   *Bypass connections*

In their ablation study, the authors experimented with micro-architecture search of a block using an identity link, introduced in ResNet, which they referred to as *bypass connections*. SqueezeNet, they said in their paper, resided "in a broad and largely unexplored design space of CNN architectures." Part of their exploration included what they called the *micro-architecture design space*. They indicated they were inspired by the ResNet authors' A/B comparison on a ResNet34 with and without bypass connections and obtained a 2% performance improvement with a bypass connection.

The authors experimented with what they called a simple bypass and a complex bypass. In the *simple bypass*, they gained a 2.9% increase on top-1, and 2.2% on top-5, accuracy for ImageNet without increasing computational complexity. Thus their improvements were comparable to those observed by the ResNet authors.

In the *complex bypass*, they observed a lesser improvement, with a gain of only 1.3% accuracy with an increase in model size from 4.8 MB to 7.7 MB. In the simple bypass, there was no increase in model size. The authors concluded the simple bypass was sufficient.

SIMPLE BYPASS

In the simple bypass, the identity link occurs only in the first fire block (entry into the group) and the fire block prior to the doubling of filters. Figure 8.19 illustrates a fire group with simple bypass connection. The first fire block in the group has the bypass connection (identity link), and then the fire block preceding the fire block doubles the number of output channels (feature maps).

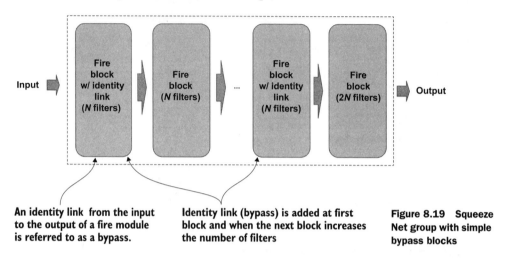

An identity link from the input to the output of a fire module is referred to as a bypass.

Identity link (bypass) is added at first block and when the next block increases the number of filters

Figure 8.19   Squeeze Net group with simple bypass blocks

Now let's take a close-up look at a fire block with a simple bypass (identity link) connection. This is depicted in figure 8.20. Note that the input to the block is added to the output of the concatenation operation.

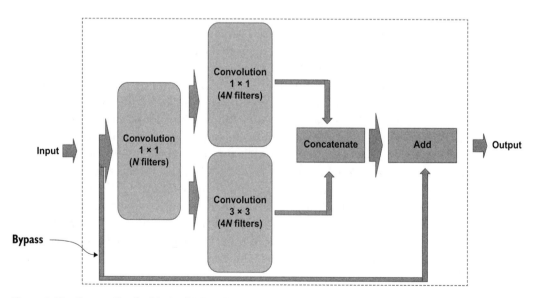

Figure 8.20   SqueezeNet fire block with identity link

Let's walk through this. First, we know that with a matrix add operation, the number of feature maps on the input must match the number of outputs from the concatenation operation. For a multitude of fire blocks, this is true. For example, from the stem group, we have 96 feature maps as input, which are reduced to 16 in the squeeze layer, and then expanded by 8 times (back to 96) through the expand layer. Since the number of feature maps on the input equals the output, we can add an identity link. But this isn't the case for all the fire blocks, and thus why only a subset have the bypass connection.

The following is an example implementation of a fire block with a simple bypass connection (identity link). In this implementation, we pass the additional parameter bypass. If it is true, we add a final layer at the end of the block that does a matrix add (`Add()`) to the output from the concatenation:

```
def fire_block(x, n_filters, bypass=False):
    ''' Construct a Fire Block
        x       : input to the block
        n_filters: number of filters in the block
        bypass  : whether block has an identity shortcut
    '''

    shortcut = x

    squeeze = Conv2D(n_filters, (1, 1), strides=1, activation='relu',
                     padding='same')(x)


    expand1x1 = Conv2D(n_filters * 4, (1, 1), strides=1, activation='relu',
                     padding='same')(squeeze)
    expand3x3 = Conv2D(n_filters * 4, (3, 3), strides=1, activation='relu',
                     padding='same')(squeeze)


    x = Concatenate()([expand1x1, expand3x3])

    if bypass:
        x = Add()([x, shortcut])

    return x
```

When bypass is True, the input (shortcut) is matrix-added to the output of the fire block.

COMPLEX BYPASS

In the authors' next micro-architecture search, they explored adding a linear projection to the remaining fire blocks without an identity link (simple bypass). The linear projection would project the number of input features to be equal to the number of output feature maps after the concatenation operation. They referred to this as the *complex bypass.*

The intent was to see if this would further increase top-1/top-5 accuracy, though at the expense of increasing model size. As I noted earlier, their experiments showed that using the complex bypass was detrimental to the objective. Figure 8.21 depicts a

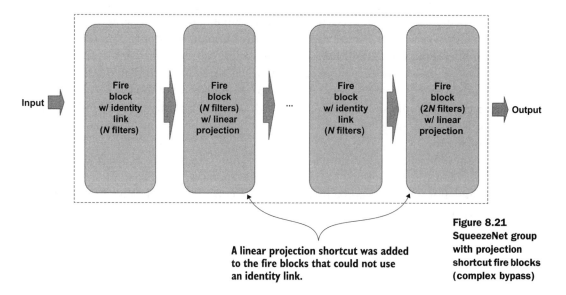

A linear projection shortcut was added to the fire blocks that could not use an identity link.

Figure 8.21
SqueezeNet group with projection shortcut fire blocks (complex bypass)

fire group in which the remaining fire blocks without a simple bypass (identity link) have a complex bypass (linear projection link).

Now for a closer look at a fire block with a complex bypass, shown in figure 8.22. Note that the 1×1 linear projection on the identity link increases the number of filters (channels) by 8. This is to match the output size of the concatenation of outputs from the branched 1×1 and 3×3, both of which increased the output size by 4 ($4 + 4 = 8$). Using a 1×1 linear projection on the identity link is what distinguished the complex from the simple bypass.

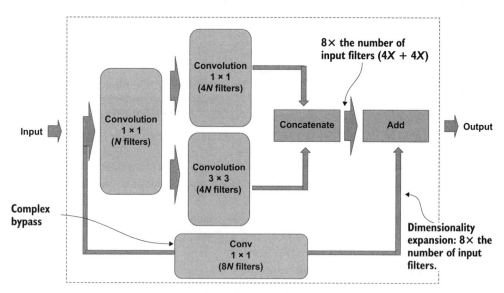

Figure 8.22   SqueezeNet fire block with projection shortcut (complex bypass)

In the ablation study, the use of a simple bypass increased accuracy from the vanilla SqueezeNet on ImageNet from 57.5% to 60.4%. For the complex bypass, the accuracy increased to only 58.8%. The authors made no conclusion about why, other than to say it was interesting. A complete code rendition using the Idiomatic procedure reuse design pattern for SqueezeNet is on GitHub (http://mng.bz/XYmv).

Next, we will cover ShuffleNet, which introduced pointwise group convolutions and channel shuffle (transpose) operations to increase the number of feature maps without increasing computational complexity and size.

8.4　*ShuffleNet v1*

One of the challenges of large networks is that they need many feature maps, typically in the thousands, which means they have a high computational cost. So in 2017, Xiangyu Zhang et al. at Face++ introduced a way to have a large number of feature maps at a substantial reduction in compute costs. This new architecture, called *ShuffleNet v1* (https://arxiv.org/abs/1707.01083), was designed specifically for low-compute devices typically found on mobile phones, drones, and robots.

The architecture introduced new layer operations: groupwise point convolutions and channel shuffle. When compared to MobileNet, the authors found that Shuffle-Net achieves superior performance by a significant margin: absolute 7.8% lower ImageNet top-1 error at a level of 40 MFLOPs. While the authors reported gains in accuracy over the MobileNet counterparts, MobileNets continued to be favored for production, though they're now being replaced by EfficientNets.

8.4.1　*Architecture*

The ShuffleNet architecture consists of three shuffle groups, which the paper refers to as *stages*. The architecture followed the conventional practice, with each group doubling the number of output channels or feature maps from the previous group. Figure 8.23 depicts the ShuffleNet architecture.

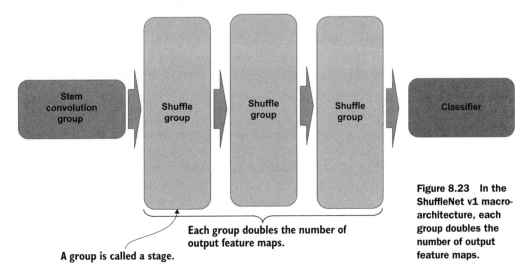

Each group doubles the number of output feature maps.

A group is called a stage.

Figure 8.23 In the ShuffleNet v1 macro-architecture, each group doubles the number of output feature maps.

8.4.2   *Stem*

The stem component uses a less coarse 3 × 3 convolutional layer when compared to other mobile SOTA models at the time, which typically used a 7 × 7 or stack of two 3 × 3 convolutional layers. The stem, depicted in figure 8.24, performs an aggressive feature map reduction, which continues to be the present convention. The 3 × 3 convolution is strided (feature pooling) for a 75% reduction, followed by a max pooling layer for a further 75% reduction, resulting in feature maps that are 6% the size of the input channels. Reducing the channel size from the input to 6% continues to be the conventional practice.

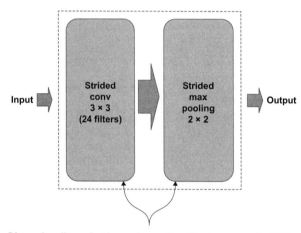

Dimensionality reduction reduces size of feature maps by 75%.

Figure 8.24 **The ShuffleNet stem group combines feature and max pooling for an output feature map reduction to 6% of the size of the input.**

8.4.3   *Learner*

Each group in the learner component consists of a strided shuffle block (referred to as a *unit* in the paper), followed by one or more shuffle blocks. The strided shuffle block doubles the number of output channels while reducing the size of each channel by 75%. The progressive doubling of the number of filters, and hence output feature maps, per feature was the convention of the time and continues today. It has also been a convention that when a group doubles the number of output feature maps, their sizes are reduced to prevent an explosion in parameter growth as you go deeper into layers.

GROUP

Like MobileNet v1/v2, the ShuffleNet group does the feature map reduction at the beginning of the group, with the strided shuffle block. This is in contrast to SqueezeNet and large SOTA models that delay the feature map reduction to the end of the group. By reducing the size at the beginning of the group, the number of parameters and matmul operations are substantially reduced, but at the cost of less representational power.

Figure 8.25 illustrates a shuffle group. The group starts with the strided shuffle block, which does the feature map size reduction at the beginning of the group, and

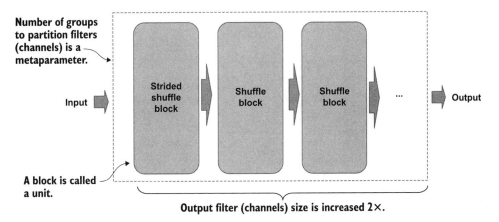

Figure 8.25 ShuffleNet group micro-architecture

then one or more shuffle blocks follows. The strided and subsequent shuffle blocks double the number of filters from the previous group. For example, if the previous group had 144 filters, the current group would double to 288.

The following is an example implementation of a shuffle group. The parameter n_blocks is the number of blocks in the group, and n_filters is the number of filters for each block. The parameter reduction is a metaparameter for dimensionality reduction in the shuffle block (discussed subsequently), and the parameter n_partitions is the metaparameter used for partitioning the feature maps for the channel shuffle (discussed subsequently). The first block is a strided shuffle block, and the remaining blocks are not strided: for _ in range(n_blocks-1).

```
def group(x, n_partitions, n_blocks, n_filters, reduction):
    ''' Construct a Shuffle Group
        x              : input to the group
        n_partitions : number of groups to partition feature maps (channels)
        ➥ into.
        n_blocks       : number of shuffle blocks for this group
        n_filters      : number of output filters
        reduction      : dimensionality reduction
    '''
    x = strided_shuffle_block(x, n_partitions, n_filters, reduction)

    for _ in range(n_blocks-1):
        x = shuffle_block(x, n_partitions, n_filters, reduction)
    return x
```

First block in a group is a strided shuffle block.

Adds the remaining nonstrided shuffle blocks

BLOCK

The shuffle block is based on a B(1, 3, 1) residual block, where the 3×3 convolution is a depthwise convolution (as in MobileNet). The authors noted that architectures such as Xception and ResNeXt become less efficient in extremely small networks because of the costly dense 1×1 convolutions. To address this, they replaced the 1×1

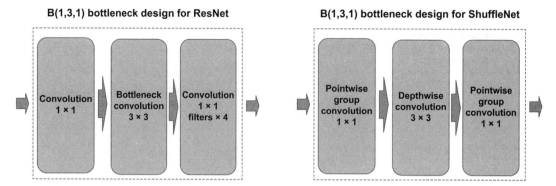

Figure 8.26   Comparing ResNet and ShuffleNet B(1,3,1) designs

pointwise convolutions with pointwise group convolutions to reduce computational complexity. Figure 8.26 shows the difference in design.

The first pointwise group convolution also performs a dimensionality reduction on the number of input filters to the block, when the parameter reduction is < 1 (reduction * n_filters), and then it is restored in the output channels with the second pointwise group convolution, for matching the input with the residual for the matrix add operation.

They also deviated from the practice in Xception of using a ReLU after the depthwise convolution, to use a linear activation. Their reasoning for this change is not clear, nor is the advantage of using a linear activation. The paper merely states, "The usage of batch normalization (BN) and nonlinearity is similar to [ResNet, ResNeXt], except that we do not use ReLU after depthwise convolution as suggested by [Xception]." Between the first pointwise group convolution and the depthwise convolution is the channel shuffle operation, both of which will be discussed subsequently.

Figure 8.27 shows a shuffle block. You can see how the channel shuffle has been inserted in the B(1,3,1) residual block design before the 3 × 3 depthwise convolution, where the feature extraction occurs. The B(1, 3, 1) residual block is a bottleneck design comparable to MobileNet v1, in which the first 1 × 1 convolution does a dimensionality reduction, and the second 1 × 1 convolution does a dimensionality expansion. The block continued with the convention in MobileNet of pairing a 3 × 3 depthwise convolution with a 1 × 1 pointwise group convolution to form a depthwise separable convolution. It differs from MobileNet v1, though, by changing the first 1 × 1 bottleneck convolution into a 1 × 1 bottleneck pointwise group convolution.

The following is an example implementation of a shuffle block. The block starts with a pointwise 1 × 1 group convolution defined in the function pw_group_conv(), where the parameter value int(reduction * n_filters) specifies the dimensionality reduction. Next is the channel shuffle defined in the function channel_shuffle(), followed by the depthwise convolution (DepthwiseConv2D). Next is the final pointwise

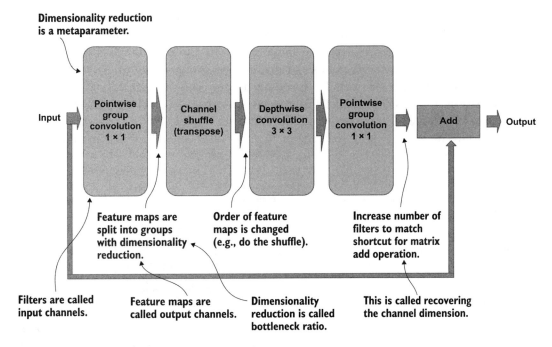

Figure 8.27 ShuffleNet block using Idiomatic design

group 1 × 1 convolution, which restores the dimensionality. Finally, the input to the block is matrix-added (Add()) to the output from the pointwise group convolution.

```
def shuffle_block(x, n_partitions, n_filters, reduction):
    ''' Construct a shuffle Shuffle block
        x              : input to the block
        n_partitions: number of groups to partition feature maps (channels)
     into.
        n_filters    : number of filters
        reduction    : dimensionality reduction factor (e.g, 0.25)
    '''

    shortcut = x

    x = pw_group_conv(x, n_partitions, int(reduction * n_filters))
    x = ReLU()(x)

    x = channel_shuffle(x, n_partitions)

    x = DepthwiseConv2D((3, 3), strides=1, padding='s
    x = BatchNormalization()(x)

    x = pw_group_conv(x, n_partitions, n_filters)

    x = Add()([shortcut, x])
    x = ReLU()(x)
    return x
```

The first pointwise group convolution does a dimensionality reduction.

The channel shuffle

3 × 3 depthwise convolution

The second group convolution does a dimensionality restoration.

Adds the input (shortcut) to the output of the block

POINTWISE GROUP CONVOLUTION

The following is an example implementation of a pointwise group convolution. The function starts by determining the number of input channels (in_filters = x.shape[-1]). Next, the number of channels per group is determined by dividing the number of input channels by the number of groups (n_partitions). The feature maps are then proportionally split across the groups (lambda), and each group is passed through a separate 1 × 1 pointwise convolution. Finally, the outputs from the group convolutions are concatenated together and passed through a batch normalization layer.

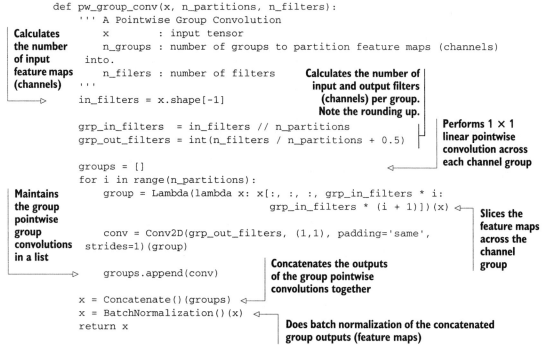

```
def pw_group_conv(x, n_partitions, n_filters):
    ''' A Pointwise Group Convolution
        x        : input tensor
        n_groups : number of groups to partition feature maps (channels)
    into.
        n_filers : number of filters
    '''
    in_filters = x.shape[-1]

    grp_in_filters  = in_filters // n_partitions
    grp_out_filters = int(n_filters / n_partitions + 0.5)

    groups = []
    for i in range(n_partitions):
        group = Lambda(lambda x: x[:, :, :, grp_in_filters * i:
                           grp_in_filters * (i + 1)])(x)

        conv = Conv2D(grp_out_filters, (1,1), padding='same',
    strides=1)(group)
        groups.append(conv)
    x = Concatenate()(groups)
    x = BatchNormalization()(x)
    return x
```

Annotations:
- Calculates the number of input feature maps (channels) → in_filters = x.shape[-1]
- Calculates the number of input and output filters (channels) per group. Note the rounding up.
- Performs 1 × 1 linear pointwise convolution across each channel group
- Maintains the group pointwise group convolutions in a list → groups.append(conv)
- Slices the feature maps across the channel group
- Concatenates the outputs of the group pointwise convolutions together
- Does batch normalization of the concatenated group outputs (feature maps)

STRIDED SHUFFLE BLOCK

The strided shuffle block differs as follows:

- The dimensionality of the shortcut link (input to the block) is reduced by a 3 × 3 average pooling operation.
- The residual and shortcut feature maps are concatenated instead of using a matrix add in the nonstrided shuffle block.

As for the use of concatenation, the authors reasoned to "replace the element-wise addition with channel concatenation, which makes it easy to enlarge channel dimension with little extra computation cost."

Figure 8.28 depicts a strided shuffle block. You can see the two differences from the nonstrided shuffle block. On the shortcut link, an average pooling has been added that does a dimensionality reduction by reducing the feature maps to $0.5H \times 0.5W$. This is

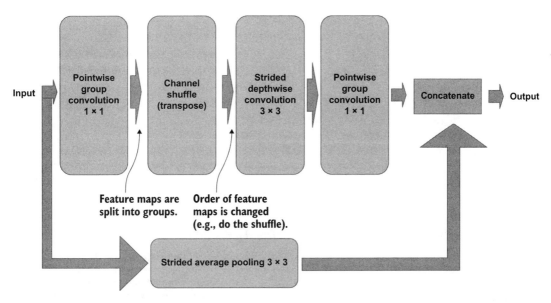

Figure 8.28 Strided shuffle block

done to match the size of the feature pooling that is done by the strided 3×3 depthwise convolution, so they can be concatenated together—instead of a matrix addition in the nonstrided shuffle block.

The following is an example implementation of a strided shuffle block. The parameter n_filters is the number of filters for the convolution layers in the block. The parameter reduction is the metaparameter for further thinning of the network, and the parameter n_partitions specifies the number of groups to partition the feature maps into for the pointwise group convolution.

The function starts by creating the projection shortcut. The input is passed through a strided AveragePooling2D layer, which reduces the size of the feature maps in the projection shortcut to $0.5H \times 0.5W$.

The input is then passed through the 1×1 pointwise group convolution (pw_group_conv()). Note that the network thinning occurs in the first pointwise group convolution (int(reduction * n_filters)). The input is channel-shuffled (channel_shuffle()), and then passed through the 3×3 strided depthwise convolution that does the feature extraction and feature pooling; note there is no ReLU activation.

The output from DepthwiseConv2D() is then passed through the second 1×1 pointwise group convolution, whose output is then concatenated with the projection shortcut.

```
def strided_shuffle_block(x, n_partitions, n_filters, reduction):
    ''' Construct a Strided Shuffle Block
        x            : input to the block
        n_partitions: number of groups to partition feature maps (channels)
        ➡ into.
```

```
      n_filters    : number of filters
      reduction    : dimensionality reduction factor (e.g, 0.25)
   '''
   # projection shortcut
   shortcut = x
shortcut = AveragePooling2D((3, 3), strides=2, padding='same')(shortcut)
   n_filters -= int(x.shape[-1])

   x = pw_group_conv(x, n_partitions, int(reduction * n_filters))
   x = ReLU()(x)

   x = channel_shuffle(x, n_partitions)

   x = DepthwiseConv2D((3, 3), strides=2, padding='same')(x)
   x = BatchNormalization()(x)

   x = pw_group_conv(x, n_partitions, n_filters)

   x = Concatenate()([shortcut, x])
   x = ReLU()(x)
   return x
```

Uses average pooling for a bottleneck shortcut

On the first block, the number of output filters of the entry pointwise group convolution is adjusted to match the exit pointwise group convolution.

Concatenates the projection shortcut to the output of the block

CHANNEL SHUFFLE

The *channel shuffle* was designed to overcome side effects with the group convolutions, thus helping information to flow across the output channels. The group convolution significantly reduces computation cost by ensuring that each convolution operates only on the corresponding input channel group. As the authors point out, if multiple group convolutions are stacked together, one side effect results: outputs from a certain channel are derived from only a small fraction of input channels. In other words, each group convolution is limited to learning the next feature extraction level for its filter, based only on a single feature map (channel) instead of from all, or portion of, all the input feature maps.

Figure 8.29 depicts splitting channels into groups and then shuffling the channels. In essence, a shuffle consists of constructing new channels, as each shuffled channel has a portion from every other channel—thus increasing information flow across the output channels.

Let's take a closer look at this process. We start with a group of input channels, which I gray-shaded in the diagram to denote that they are different channels (not copies). Next, based on the partition setting, the channels are split into equal-size partitions, which we call *groups*. In our depiction, each group has three separate channels. We construct three shuffled versions of the three channels. Through the gray shading, we denote that each shuffled channel is formed from a portion of each unshuffled channel, and the portion differs for each shuffled channel.

For example, the first shuffled channel is constructed from the first one-third of the feature maps of the three unshuffled channels. The second shuffled channel is

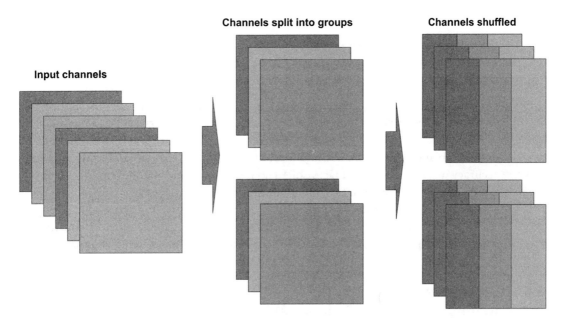

Figure 8.29   Channel shuffle

constructed from the first one-third of the feature maps of the three unshuffled channels, and so forth.

The following is an example implementation of a channel shuffle. The parameter
n_partitions specifies the number of groups to partition the input feature map,
parameter x, into. We use the shape of the input to determine $B \times H \times W \times C$ (where C
is channels), and then calculate the number of channels per group (grp_in_channels).

The next three Lambda operations do the following:

1 Reshapes the input from $B \times H \times W \times C$ to $B \times W \times W \times G \times Cg$. A fifth dimension,
   G (groups), is added, and C is reshaped into $G \times Cg$, where Cg is the subset of
   channels per group.
2 The k.permute_dimesions() performs the channel shuffle depicted in figure 5.27.
3 The second reshape reconstructs the shuffled channels back into the shape
   $B \times H \times W \times C$.

```
def channel_shuffle(x, n_partitions):
    ''' Implements the channel shuffle layer
        x              : input tensor
        n_partitions : number of groups to partition feature maps (channels)
        into.
    '''
    batch, height, width, n_channels = x.shape        ← Gets dimensions of
                                                         the input tensor

    grp_in_channels  = n_channels // n_partitions     ← Derives the number of input
                                                         filters (channels) per group
```

```
    x = Lambda(lambda z: K.reshape(z, [-1, height, width, n_partitions,
                                   grp_in_channels]))(x)
```
Separates out the channel groups

```
    x = Lambda(lambda z: K.permute_dimensions(z, (0, 1, 2, 4, 3)))(x)
```

```
    x = Lambda(lambda z: K.reshape(z, [-1, height, width, n_channels]))(x)
    return x
```
Restores the output shape

Transposes the order (shuffle) of the channel groups (i.e., 3, 4 => 4, 3)

In their ablation study, the authors found that the best tradeoff in complexity versus accuracy was for a reduction factor of 1 (no reduction), and the number of group partitions set to 8. A complete code rendition using the Idiomatic procedure reuse design pattern for ShuffleNet is located on GitHub (http://mng.bz/oGop).

Next, we will cover shrinking the size of the model for a memory-constrained device with quantization, and converting/predicting using the TensorFlow Lite Python package, for the deployment of a mobile model.

8.5 Deployment

We will wrap up this chapter by covering the basics for deploying a mobile convolutional model. We will look first at quantization, which reduces the parameter size and hence the memory footprint. Quantization happens prior to deploying the model. Next, we will see how to use TF Lite to execute the model on a memory-constrained device. In our examples, we use a Python environment as a proxy. We won't dive into specifics related to Android or iOS.

8.5.1 Quantization

Quantization is a process for reducing the number of bits that represent a number. For memory-constrained devices, we want to store the weights at a lower bit representation without significant loss of accuracy.

Because neural networks are fairly resilient to small errors in calculations, they do not need as high of a precision for inference as for training. This provides the opportunity to reduce the precision of the weights in a mobile neural network. The conventional reduction is to replace the 32-bit floating-point weight values with a discrete approximation as 8-bit integer values. The primary advantage is that the reduction from 32 to 8 bits requires only one-quarter of the memory space for the model.

During inference (prediction), the weights are scaled back to their approximate 32-bit floating-point values for the matrix operations, which are then passed through the activation function. Modern hardware accelerators have been designed to optimize this rescaling operation so that there is nominal compute overhead.

In the conventional reduction, the 32-bit floating-point weights are divided into buckets (bins) across the integer range. For an 8-bit value, this would be 256 buckets, as depicted in figure 8.30.

To perform the quantization in this example, the floating-point range of the weights is first determined, which we refer to as [rmin, rmax], for the minimum and

Conceptually, an infinite unbounded (dynamic) range (e.g., 32-bit IEEE representation)

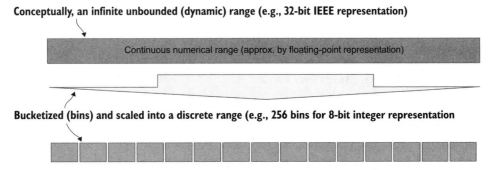

Bucketized (bins) and scaled into a discrete range (e.g., 256 bins for 8-bit integer representation

Figure 8.30 Quantization categorizes a floating-point range into a fixed set of bins represented by an integer type.

maximum value. The range is then linearly divided by the number of buckets (256 in the case of 8-bit integers).

Depending on the hardware accelerator, we may additionally see an execution speedup from two to three times on a CPU (and TPU). Integer operations are not supported on a GPU.

For a GPU that natively supports float16 (half precision), quantization is done by converting the float32 values to float16. This reduces the model's memory footprint in half and typically speeds up execution by four times.

Additionally, quantization works best when the floating-point range of the weights is constrained (shrunk). The current convention for mobile models is to use a max_ value of 6.0 for the ReLU for this purpose.

We should be careful of quantizing very small models. Large models benefit from the redundancy of weights and are immune to loss of accuracy when quantized to 8-bit integers. The SOTA mobile models have been designed to limit the amount of accuracy loss when quantized. If we design smaller models and quantize them, they may degrade significantly in accuracy.

Next, we will cover TF Lite for executing models in memory constrained devices.

8.5.2 *TF Lite conversion and prediction*

TF Lite is an execution environment for TensorFlow models in memory-constrained devices. Unlike the native TensorFlow runtime environment, the TF Lite runtime environment is much smaller and easier to fit into memory-constrained devices. While optimized for this purpose, it does come with some tradeoffs. For instance, some TF graph ops are not supported, and some operations require additional steps. We won't cover the unsupported graph ops, but we will go over the required additional steps.

The following code demonstrates using TensorFlow Lite to quantize an existing model, where the model is a trained TF.Keras model. The first step is to convert the model in SavedModel format into a TF Lite model format. This is done by instantiating a TFLiteConverter and passing it an in-memory or on-disk model in SavedModel format, and then invoking the convert() method:

```
import tensorflow as tf

converter = tf.lite.TFLiteConverter.from_saved_model(model)

tflite_model = converter.convert()
```

Creates an instance of the converter for TF.Keras (SavedModel format) model

Converts the model to the TF Lite format

The TF Lite version of the model is not a TensorFlow SavedModel format. You cannot directly use methods like `predict()`. Instead, we use the TF Lite interpreter. You must first set up the interpreter for the TF Lite model as follows:

1 Instantiate a TF Lite interpreter for the TF Lite model.
2 Instruct the interpreter to allocate input and output tensors for the model.
3 Get detail information about the model's input and output tensors that will need to be known for prediction.

The following code demonstrates these steps:

Instantiates an interpreter for the TF Lite model

```
interpreter = tf.lite.Interpreter(model_content=tflite_model)
interpreter.allocate_tensors()

input_details = interpreter.get_input_details()
output_details = interpreter.get_output_details()
input_shape = input_details[0]['shape']
```

Allocates the input and output tensors for the model

Gets input and output tensor details needed for prediction

The `input_details` and `output_details` are returned as a list; the number of elements corresponds to the number of input and output tensors, respectively. For example, a model with a single input (for example, image) and a single output (multiclass classifier) would have one element for both the input and output tensors.

Each element contains a dictionary with corresponding details. In the case of an input tensor, the key `shape` returns a tuple that is the shape of the input. For example, if the model took as input (32, 32, 3) images (for example, CIFAR-10), the key would return (32, 32, 3).

To make a single prediction, we do the following:

1 Prepare the input to be a batch of size 1. For our CIFAR-10 example, that would be (1, 32, 32, 3).
2 Assign the batch to the input tensor.
3 Invoke the interpreter to perform the prediction.
4 Get the output tensor from the model (for example, softmax outputs in a multiclass model).

The following code demonstrates these steps:

```
import numpy as np

data = np.expand_dims(x_test[1], axis=0)

interpreter.set_tensor(input_details[0]['index'], data)
```

Converts the single input to a batch of size 1

Assigns the batch to the input tensor

```
interpreter.invoke()          ◁——┤ Executes (invoke) the interpreter
                                  │ to perform the prediction
                                                                        ┤ Gets the output
softmax = interpreter.get_tensor(output_details[0]['index'])   ◁——┘ from the model

label = np.argmax(softmax)——┤ Multiclass example, determine the label
                            │ predicted from the softmax output
```

For batch prediction, we need to modify (resize) the interpreter's input and output tensors for the batch size. The following code resizes the batch size for the interpreter to 128 for a (32, 32, 3) input (CIFAR-10), prior to allocating the tensors:

```
Instantiates an interpreter                                    Resizes the input and
for the TF Lite model                                       output tensors for a
  └▷ interpreter = tf.lite.Interpreter(model_content=tflite_model)    batch of 128

interpreter.resize_tensor_input(input_details[0]['index'], (128, 32, 32, 3))
interpreter.resize_tensor_input(output_details[0]['index'], (128, 10))   ◁——┘

interpreter.allocate_tensors()   ◁——— Allocates the input and output tensors for the model
```

Summary

- Refactoring using depthwise convolutions and network thinning in MobileNet v1 demonstrated the ability to run models on memory-constrained devices with AlexNet accuracy.
- Redesigning the residual block in MobileNet v2 to an inverted residual block further reduced the memory footprint and increased accuracy.
- SqueezeNet introduced the concept of computationally efficient macro-architecture search using metaparameters to configure group and block attributes.
- Refactoring and channel shuffle in ShuffleNet v1 demonstrated the ability to run models on extremely constrained memory devices, such as microcontrollers.
- Quantization techniques provided a means to reduce memory footprint by 75% with little or no loss of accuracy for inference.
- Use TF Lite to convert from SavedModel format to quantized TF Lite format and do predictions for deployment to a memory-constrained device.

Autoencoders

Up to now, we've discussed only models for supervised learning. An *autoencoder model* falls into the category of unsupervised learning. As a reminder, in supervised learning our data consists of the features (for example, image data) and labels (for example, classes), and we train the model to learn to predict the labels from the features. In unsupervised learning, we either have no labels or don't use them, and we train the model to find correlating patterns in the data. You might ask, what can we do without labels? We can do a lot of things, and autoencoders are one type of model architecture that can learn from unlabeled data.

Autoencoders are the fundamental deep learning models for unsupervised learning. Even without human labeling, autoencoders can learn image compression, representational learning, image denoising, super-resolution and pretext tasks—and we'll cover each of these in this chapter.

So how does unsupervised learning work with autoencoders? Even though we don't have labels for the image data, we can manipulate images to be both the input data and output label, and train the model to predict the output label. For example, the output label could simply be the input image—here, the model would be learning the identity function. Or we could make a copy of the image and add noise to it, and then use the noisy version as the input and the original image as the output label—this is how our model could learn to denoise the image. In this chapter, we will cover these and several other techniques for manipulating the input image into output labels.

9.1 Deep neural network autoencoders

We will start this chapter on autoencoders with the classic deep neural network version. While you can learn interesting things using just a DNN, it does not scale well when it comes to image data, so in subsequent sections we will move onto using CNN autoencoders.

9.1.1 Autoencoder architecture

An example of how DNN autoencoders can be useful is when reconstructing images. One of my favorite reconstructions, typically used as a pretext task, is the jigsaw puzzle. In this case, the input image is divided into nine tiles and then randomly shuffled. The reconstruction task is to predict the order that the tiles were shuffled. Since this task is essentially a multivalue regressor output, it works well with a traditional CNN, where the multiclass classifier is replaced with a multivalue regressor.

An autoencoder is composed of two basic components: an encoder and a decoder. For image reconstruction, the *encoder* learns an optimal (or nearly optimal) method to progressively pool the image data into the latent space, and the *decoder* learns an optimal (or nearly optimal) method to progressively unpool the latent space for image reconstruction. The reconstruction task determines the type of representational and transformational learning. For example, in the identity function, the reconstruction task is reconstructing the input image. But you could also reconstruct an image without noise (by denoising) or an image of higher resolution (super-resolution). These types of reconstructions work well with an autoencoder.

Let's see how the encoders and decoders work together in an autoencoder to do these kinds of reconstructions. The basic autoencoder architecture, shown in figure 9.1, actually has three key components, with latent space between the encoder and decoder. The encoder performs representational learning on the input to learn a function $f(x) = x'$. That x' is referred to as the *latent space*, which is the learned representation from x at a lower dimensionality. Then the decoder performs transformational learning from the latent space to perform some form of reconstruction of the original image.

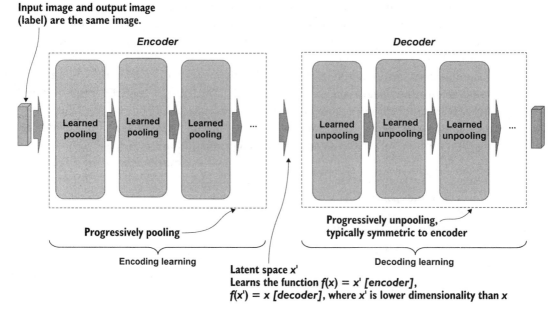

Figure 9.1   Learning the identity function for image input/output in the autoencoder macro-architecture

Let's say the autoencoder in figure 9.1 learns the identity function $f(x) = x$. Since the latent space x' is of lower dimensionality, we typically describe this form of an autoencoder as learning the optimal way to compress images in a dataset (encoder) and then decompress the images (decoder). We could also describe this as the sequence of functions: $encoder(x) = x'$, $decoder(x') = x$.

In other words, the dataset represents a distribution, and for that distribution the autoencoder learns the optimal method to compress the images to a lower dimensionality and learns the optimal decompression to reconstruct the image. Let's take a closer look at the encoder and decoder, and then see how we'd train this kind of model.

9.1.2   Encoder

The basic form of an autoencoder for learning the identity function uses dense layers (hidden units). Pooling is performed by having each layer in the encoder progressively reduce the number of nodes (hidden units), and unpooling is learned by having each layer progressively increase the number of nodes. The number of nodes in the final unpooling dense layer is the same as the number of pixels in the input.

For the identity function, the image itself is the label. You do not need to know what the image depicts, whether it is a cat, dog, horse, airplane, or whatever. When the model is trained, the images are both the independent variables (features) and the dependent variables (labels).

The following code is an example implementation of the encoder for an autoencoder to learn the identity function. It follows the process depicted in figure 9.1, progressively pooling the number of nodes (hidden units) through the parameter layers. The output from the encoder is the latent space.

We start by flattening the image input to a 1D vector. The parameter layers is a list; the number of elements is the number of hidden layers, and the element value is the number of units at that layer. Since we are progressively pooling, each subsequent element value is progressively smaller. While an encoder tends to be shallow in layers when compared to a CNN used for classification, we add batch normalization for its regularizing effect:

```
def encoder(x, layers):
    ''' Construct the Encoder
        x     : input to the encoder
        layers: number of nodes per layer
    '''
    x = Flatten()(x)              ◁——— Flattening of the input image

    for layer in layers:          ◁——┐ Progressive unit pooling
        n_nodes = layer['n_nodes']     │ (dimensionality reduction)
        x = Dense(n_nodes)(x)
        x = BatchNormalization()(x)
        x = ReLU()(x)

    return x        ◁——— The encoding (latent space)
```

9.1.3 *Decoder*

Now let's look at an example implementation of a decoder for an autoencoder. Again, following the process depicted in figure 9.1, we progressively unpool the number of nodes (hidden units) through the parameter layers. The output from the decoder is the reconstructed image. For symmetry with the encoder, we iterate through the layers parameter in the reverse direction. The activation function for the final Dense layer is a sigmoid. Why? Each node represents a reconstructed pixel. Since we've normalized the image data between 0 and 1, we want to squash the output into the same range of 0 to 1.

Finally, to reconstruct the image, we do a Reshape to reshape the 1D vector from the final Dense layer into an image format ($H \times W \times C$):

```
def decoder(x, layers, input_shape):
    ''' Construct the Decoder
        x     : input to the decoder (encoding)
        layers: nodes per layer
    input_shape: input shape for reconstruction
    '''
    for _ in range(len(layers)-1, 0, -1):  ◁——┐ Progressive unit unpooling
        n_nodes = layers[_]['n_nodes']           │ (dimensionality expansion)
        x = Dense(n_nodes)(x)
        x = BatchNormalization()(x)
        x = ReLU()(x)

    units = input_shape[0] * input_shape[1] * input_shape[2]  ◁——┐ Last
    x = Dense(units, activation='sigmoid')(x)                       │ unpooling
```

```
outputs = Reshape(input_shape)(x)          Reshapes back into the
                                           image input shape
return outputs          The decoded image
```

9.1.4   Training

The autoencoder wants to learn a representation (which we call the *latent space*) of a lower dimensionality and then learn a transformation to reconstruct the image according to a predefined task; in this case, the identity function.

The following code example will train the preceding autoencoder to learn an identity function for the MNIST dataset. The example creates an autoencoder with hidden units 256, 128, 64 (latent space), 128, 256, and 784 (for pixel reconstruction).

Typically, a DNN autoencoder will consist of three or sometimes four layers in both the encoder and decoder component. Since DNNs have limited effectiveness, adding more capacity as in layers generally will not improve on learning the identity function.

Another convention you see here for DNN autoencoders is that each layer in the encoder reduces the number of nodes by one-half and, conversely, the decoder doubles the number of nodes, with the exception of the last layer. The last layer reconstructs the image, so the number of nodes is the same as the number of pixels in the input vector; in this case, 784. The choice of starting with 256 nodes in the example is somewhat arbitrary; other than starting with a large size that would increase capacity, it would aid little, or not at all, in improving learning the identity function.

For the dataset, we expand the image shape from (28, 28) to (28, 28, 1) since the TF.Keras models expect the number of channels to be explicitly specified—even when there is just one channel. Finally, we train the autoencoder with the fit() method and pass x_train as both the training data and the corresponding labels (identity function). Likewise, when evaluating, we pass x_test as both the test data and corresponding labels. Figure 9.2 shows an autoencoder learning the identity function.

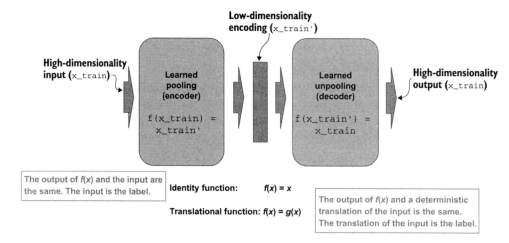

Figure 9.2   An The autoencoder learns two functions: the encoder learns to convert a high-dimensional representation to a low-dimensional representation, and then a decoder learns to reconstruct back to a high-dimensional representation that is a translation of the input.

The following code demonstrates the construction and training of an autoencoder, as depicted in figure 9.2, where the training data is the MNIST dataset:

**Metaparameter for number
of filters per layer**

```
layers = [ {'n_nodes': 256 }, { 'n_nodes': 128 }, { 'n_nodes': 64 } ]

inputs = Input((28, 28, 1))     ⟵─── Constructs the autoencoder
encoding = encoder(inputs, layers)
outputs = decoder(encoding, layers, (28, 28, 1))
ae = Model(inputs, outputs)

from tensorflow.keras.datasets import mnist
import numpy as np
(x_train, y_train), (x_test, y_test) = mnist.load_data()
x_train = (x_train / 255.0).astype(np.float32)
x_test  = (x_test  / 255.0).astype(np.float32)
x_train = np.expand_dims(x_train, axis=-1)
x_test  = np.expand_dims(x_test, axis=-1)
```

**Unsupervised training,
where the input and
labels are the same**

```
ae.compile(loss='binary_crossentropy', optimizer='adam',
      metrics=['accuracy'])
ae.fit(x_train, x_train, epochs=10, batch_size=32, validation_split=0.1,
      verbose=1)                                              ⟵─
ae.evaluate(x_test, x_test)
```

Let's summarize. The autoencoder wants to learn a representation (the latent space) of a lower dimensionality and then learn a transformation to reconstruct the image according to a predefined task, such as the identity function.

A complete code rendition using the Idiomatic procedure reuse design pattern for a DNN autoencoder is available on GitHub (http://mng.bz/JvaK). Next, we will describe designing and coding an autoencoder by using convolutional layers in place of dense layers.

9.2 *Convolutional autoencoders*

With the small images in the MNIST or CIFAR-10 datasets, the DNN autoencoders work fine. But when we work with larger images, autoencoders using nodes (which are the hidden units) for (un)pooling are computationally expensive. For larger images, deep convolutional (DC) autoencoders are more efficient. Instead of learning to (un)pool nodes, they learn to (un)pool feature maps. To do this, they use convolutions in the encoder, and *deconvolutions*, also known as *transpose convolutions*, in the decoder.

While a strided convolution, which does feature pooling, learns the optimal method to downsample a distribution, a strided deconvolution (feature unpooling) does the opposite and learns the optional method to upsample a distribution. Both feature pooling and unpooling are depicted in figure 9.3.

Let's describe this process by using the same context as for the DNN autoencoder for MNIST. In that example, the encoder and decoder each had three layers, and the

Feature pooling
(strided convolution)

Feature unpooling
(strided deconvolution)

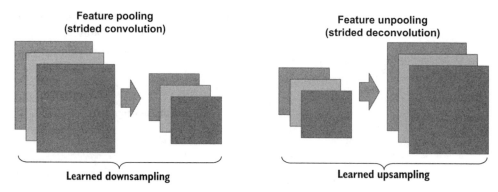

Learned downsampling   **Learned upsampling**

Figure 9.3   Contrasting feature pooling with feature unpooling

encoder started with 256 feature maps. The corresponding equivalent for a CNN autoencoder would be an encoder with three convolution layers of 256, 128, and 64 filters, respectively, and the decoder with three deconvolution layers of 128, 256, and C, where C is the number of channels of the input, respectively.

9.2.1   *Architecture*

The macro-architecture for a deep convolutional autoencoder (DC-autoencoder) can be decomposed as follows:

- *Stem*—Does coarse-level feature extraction
- *Learner*—Does representational and transformational learning
- *Task* (*reconstruction*)—Does projection and reconstruction

Figure 9.4 shows the macro-architecture for a DC-autoencoder.

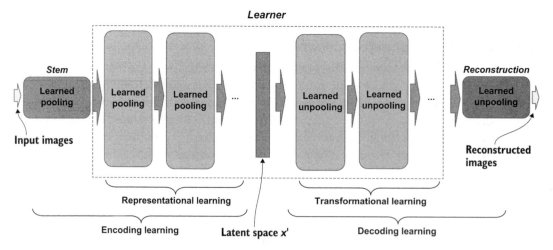

Figure 9.4   The DC-autoencoder macro-architecture distinguishes between representational learning and transformational learning.

9.2.2 Encoder

The *encoder* in a deep convolutional autoencoder (shown in figure 9.5) progressively reduces the number of feature maps (via feature reduction) and the size of the feature maps (via feature pooling) using strided convolutions.

As you can see, the encoder progressively reduces the number of filters, also known as *channels*, and corresponding size. The output from the encoder is the latent space.

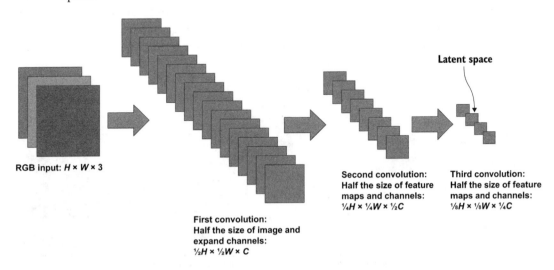

Figure 9.5 Progressive reduction in number and size of output feature maps in a CNN encoder

Now take a look at an example code implementation of an encoder. The parameter `layers` is a list, in which the number of elements is the number of convolutional layers and the element value is the number of filters per convolution. Since we are progressively pooling, each subsequent element value is progressively smaller. Additionally, each convolutional layer further pools the feature maps by reducing their size using a stride of 2.

For the convolutions, we use the Conv-BN-RE convention in this implementation. You may want to try to see if you get better results using BN-RE-Conv.

```
def encoder(inputs, layers):
    """ Construct the Encoder
        inputs : the input vector
        layers : number of filters per layer
    """
    outputs = inputs

    for n_filters in layers:
        outputs = Conv2D(n_filters, (3, 3), strides=(2, 2), padding='same')
                  (outputs)
```

Progressive feature pooling
(dimensionality reduction)

```
        outputs = BatchNormalization()(outputs)
        outputs = ReLU()(outputs)

    return outputs    ⟵——— The encoding (latent space)
```

9.2.3   *Decoder*

Now for the decoder, shown in figure 9.6. The decoder progressively increases the number of feature maps (via feature expansion) and the size of the feature maps (via feature unpooling) by using strided deconvolutions (transpose convolutions). The last unpooling layer projects the feature maps according to the reconstruction task. For the identity function example, the layer would project the feature maps into the shape of the input images to the encoder.

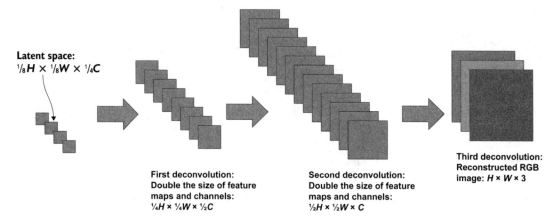

Figure 9.6   Progressive expansion in number and size of output feature maps in a CNN decoder

Here's an implementation of a decoder for the identity function. In this example, the output is an RGB image; therefore, there are three filters on the last transpose convolution, each one corresponding to an RGB channel:

```
def decoder(inputs, layers):
    """ Construct the Decoder
      inputs : input to decoder
      layers : the number of filters per layer (in encoder)
    """
    outputs = inputs
    for _ in range(len(layers)-1, 0, -1):      ⟵—— Progressive feature unpooling
                                                    (dimensionality expansion)
        n_filters = layers[_]
        outputs = Conv2DTranspose(n_filters, (3, 3), strides=(2, 2),
                                  padding='same')(outputs)
        outputs = BatchNormalization()(outputs)
        outputs = ReLU()(outputs)

    outputs = Conv2DTranspose(3, (3, 3), strides=(2, 2), padding='same')
                             (outputs)
```

Last unpooling and restore to image input shape ⟶ (annotation pointing to last Conv2DTranspose)

```
outputs = BatchNormalization()(outputs)
outputs = Activation('sigmoid')(outputs)

return outputs   ◁——— The decoded image
```

Now let's assemble the encoder with the decoder.

In this example, the convolutional layers will progressively feature pool from 64, to 32, to 16 filters, and the deconvolutional layers will progressively feature unpool from 32, to 64, and then 3 for reconstruction of the image. The image size for CIFAR is very small ($32 \times 32 \times 3$), so if we add more layers, the latent space would be too small for reconstruction, and if we widen the layers with more filters, we risk memorization (overfitting) by the additional parameter capacity.

```
layers = [64, 32, 16]       ◁————————┐  Metaparameter for the number of
                                      │  filters per layer in the encoder
inputs = Input(shape=(32, 32, 3))

encoding = encoder(inputs, layers)
                                         Constructs the
outputs = decoder(encoding, layers)      autoencoder

model = Model(inputs, outputs)
```

A complete code rendition using the Idiomatic procedure reuse design pattern for a CNN autoencoder is on GitHub (http://mng.bz/JvaK).

9.3   *Sparse autoencoders*

The size of the latent space is a tradeoff. If we go too big, the model may overfit to the representational space of the training data and not generalize. If we go too small, it may underfit so that we are unable to perform the transformation and reconstruction for the designated tasks (for example, identity function).

We want to find that "sweet spot" between the two. One method to increase the likelihood of the autoencoder to not under- or overfit is to add a *sparsity constraint*. The concept of the sparsity constraint is to limit the activation of the neurons on the bottleneck layer that outputs the latent space. This acts as both a squashing function and a regularizer, which helps the autoencoder generalize the latent space representation.

The sparsity constraint is typically described as activating only the units with large activation values and making the rest output zero. In other words, activations that are close to zero are set to zero (sparseness).

Mathematically, we could state this as follows: we want the activation of any unit (σ_i) to be constrained within the vicinity of the average activation value (σ_μ):

$$\sigma_i \approx \sigma_\mu$$

To achieve this, we add a penalty term that penalizes an activation σ_i when it deviates significantly from σ_μ.

In TF.Keras, we add the sparsity constraint with the `activity_regularizer` parameter to the last layer in the encoder. The value specifies the threshold for which an activation within +/− of zero is changed to zero. A typical value is 1e-4.

Here's the implementation of a DC-autoencoder using a sparsity constraint. The parameter `layers` is a list of progressively pooling the number of feature maps. We start by popping off the end of the list, which is the last layer in the encoder. We then proceed to build the remaining layers. We then use the number of feature maps in the popped (last) layer to construct the last layer, where we add the sparsity constraint. This last convolutional layer is the latent space:

```
from tensorflow.keras.regulaziers import l1

def encoder(inputs, layers):
    """ Construct the Encoder
        inputs : the input vector
        layers : number of filters per layer
    """
    outputs = inputs

    last_filters = layers.pop()        ◁─── Sets aside the last layer

    for n_filters in layers:           ◁─── Feature pooling
        outputs = Conv2D(n_filters, (3, 3), strides=(2, 2), padding='same')
                         (outputs)
        outputs = BatchNormalization()(outputs)
        outputs = ReLU()(outputs)

    outputs = Conv2D(last_filters, (3, 3), strides=(2, 2), padding='same',   ◁─┐
            activity_regularizer=l1(1e-4))(outputs)
    outputs = BatchNormalization()(outputs)                    Adds sparsity constraint
    outputs = ReLU()(outputs)                                  to last layer in encoder

    return outputs
```

9.4 *Denoising autoencoders*

Another way to use an autoencoder is to train it as an image denoiser. We input a noisy image, and then output a denoised version of the image. Think of this process as learning the identity function with some noise. If we represent this process as an equation, assume x is the image and e is the noise. The function learns to return x:

$$f(x + e) = x$$

We don't need to change the autoencoder architecture for this purpose; instead, we change our training data. Changing the training data requires three basic steps:

1 Construct a random generator that will output a random distribution with the value range of the noise you want to add to the training (and test) images.
2 When training, add the noise to the training data.
3 For labels, use the original images.

Here's code for training an autoencoder to denoise. We set the noise to be within a normal distribution centered at 0.5 with a standard deviation of 0.5. We then add the random noise distribution to a copy of the training data (x_train_noisy). We use the fit() method to train the denoiser, where the noisy training data is the training data and the original (denoised) training data is the corresponding labels:

Generates the noise as a normal distribution centered at 0.5 and standard deviation of 0.5

```
noise = np.random.normal(loc=0.5, scale=0.5, size=x_train.shape)
x_train_noisy = x_train + noise
```

Adds the noise to a copy of the image training data

```
model.fit(x_train_noisy, x_train, epochs=epochs, batch_size=batch_size,
          verbose=1)
```

Trains the encoder by feeding the noisy images as the training data and the original images as the labels

9.5 Super-resolution

Autoencoders were also used to develop models for *super-resolution* (SR). This process takes a low-resolution (LR) image and upscales it to improve the details to a high-resolution (HR) image. Instead of learning an identity function, such as in compression, or a noisy identity function as in denoising, we want to learn a representational mapping between a low-resolution image and a high-resolution image. Let's use a function to express this mapping that we want to learn:

$$f(x_{lr}) = x_{hr}$$

In this equation, $f()$ represents the transformation function that is being learned by the model. The term x_{lr} represents the low-resolution image input to the function, and the term x_{hr} is the transformed high-resolution predicted output from the function.

Although very advanced models now do super-resolution, early versions (~2015) used variations of autoencoders to learn a mapping from a low-resolution representation and a high-resolution representation. One example is the super-resolution convolutional neural network (SRCNN) model, which was presented in "Image Super-Resolution Using Deep Convolutional Networks" by Chao Dong et al. (https://arxiv.org/pdf/1501.00092.pdf). In this approach, the model learns a representation (latent space) of the low-resolution image in a high-dimensional space. Then it learns a mapping from the high-dimensional space of the low-resolution image to a high-resolution image, to reconstruct the high-resolution image. Note, this is opposite of a typical autoencoder, which learns a representation in a low-dimensional space.

9.5.1 Pre-upsampling SR

The creators of the SRCNN model introduced the use of a fully convolutional neural network for image super-resolution. This approach is called a *pre-upsampling SR approach*, depicted in figure 9.7. We can decompose the model into four components: a low-resolution feature extraction, a high-dimensional representation, an encoder to a low-dimensional representation, and a convolutional layer for reconstruction.

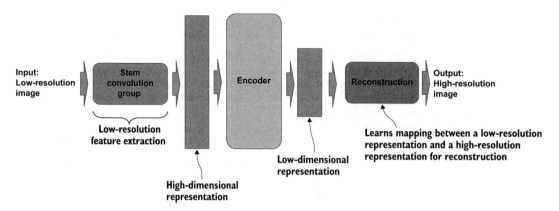

Figure 9.7 **A pre-upsampling super-resolution model learns to reconstruct a high-resolution image from a low-resolution image.**

Let's dive into more detail. Unlike in an autoencoder, there is no feature pooling (or downsampling) in the low-resolution feature extraction component. Instead, the size of the feature maps stays the same as the size of the channels in the low-input image. For example, if the input shape is (16, 16, 3), the $H \times W$ of the feature maps will stay 16×16.

In the stem convolution, the number of feature maps is substantially increased from the number of channels (3) in the input, which gives us the high-dimensionality representation of the low-resolution image. An encoder then reduces the high-dimensionality representation into a low-dimensionality representation. A final convolution reconstructs the image as a high-resolution image.

Typically, you would train this approach to a super-resolution model by using an existing image dataset that becomes the HR images. You then make a copy of the training data, where each image has been resized smaller and then resized back to its original size. To do both resizings, you use a static algorithm, like bicubic interpolation. The LR images will be the same size as the HR images, but because of the approximations done during the resizing operations, the LR images will be of lower quality than the original images.

What exactly is interpolation, and, more specifically, *bicubic interpolation*? Think of it this way: if we have 4 pixels and replace them with 2 pixels, or vice versa, you need a mathematical method that makes a good estimate for the replacement representation—this is what *interpolation* is. *Cubic interpolation* is a specific method for doing this with a vector (1D), and *bicubic* is a variation used for a matrix (2D). For image reduction, bicubic interpolation tends to give a better estimation than other interpolation algorithms.

Here's a code example to demonstrate this training data preparation using the CIFAR-10 dataset. In this example, the NumPy array x_train contains the training data images. We then make a mirror list x_train_lr for the low-resolution pairs by sequentially first resizing each image in x_train to one-half the $H \times W$ (16, 16), and then resize the image back to the original $H \times W$ (32, 32), and place it at the same index location in x_train_lr. Finally, we normalize the pixel data in both sets of images:

```
from tensorflow.keras.datasets import cifar10
import numpy as np
import cv2

(x_train, y_train), (x_test, y_test) = cifar10.load_data()
```
← **Downloads into memory the CIFAR-10 dataset as the high-resolution images**

```
x_train_lr = []
for image in x_train:
    image = cv2.resize(image, (16, 16), interpolation=cv2.INTER_CUBIC)
    x_train_lr.append(cv2.resize(image, (32, 32),
                      interpolation=cv2.INTER_CUBIC))
x_train_lr = np.asarray(x_train_lr)
```
Makes a low-resolution pairing of the training images

```
x_train = (x_train / 255.0).astype(np.float32)
x_train_lr = (x_train_lr / 255.0).astype(np.float32)
```
Normalizes the pixel data for training

Now let's look at code for a pre-upsampling SR model for HR reconstruction quality on small images like CIFAR-10. To train it, we treat the original CIFAR-10 32 × 32 images (x_train) as the HR images, and the mirrored pairing images (x_train_lr) as the LR images. For training, the LR images are the input, and the paired HR images are the corresponding label.

This example gets fairly good reconstruction results on CIFAR-10 in just 20 epochs with an 88% reconstruction accuracy. As you can see in the code, the stem() component does the low-resolution feature extraction using a coarse 9 × 9 filter and outputs 64 feature maps for the high-dimensional representation. The encoder() consists of a convolution to reduce the low-resolution representation from a high to a low dimensionality using a 1 × 1 bottleneck convolution and reducing the number of feature maps to 32. A final convolution using a coarse 5 × 5 filter learns the mapping from the low-resolution representation to a high resolution for reconstruction:

```
from tensorflow.keras import Input, Model
from tensorflow.keras.layers import Conv2D, BatchNormalization
from tensorflow.ketas.layers import ReLU, Conv2DTranspose, Activation
from tensorflow.keras.optimizers import Adam

def stem(inputs):    ←──── The low-resolution feature extraction

    x = Conv2D(64, (9, 9), padding='same')(inputs)
    x = BatchNormalization()(x)
    x = ReLU()(x)
    return x
```
The high-dimensional representation

```
def encoder(x):
    x = Conv2D(32, (1, 1), padding='same')(x)
    x = BatchNormalization()(x)
    x = ReLU()(x)
```
1 × 1 bottleneck convolution as the encoder

```
x = Conv2D(3, (5, 5), padding='same')(x)
x = BatchNormalization()(x)
outputs = Activation('sigmoid')(x)
return outputs
```
5 × 5 convolution for the
reconstruction into HR image

```
inputs = Input((32, 32, 3))
x = stem(inputs)
outputs = encoder(x)

model = Model(inputs, outputs)
model.compile(loss='mean_squared_error', optimizer=Adam(lr=0.001),
              metrics=['accuracy'])

model.fit(x_train_lr, x_train, epochs=25, batch_size=32, verbose=1,
          validation_split=0.1)
```

Let's see some actual images now. Figure 9.8 shows a set of the same image of a peacock from the CIFAR-10 training data. The first two images are the low- and high-resolution pair used in training, and the third is the super-resolution reconstruction of the same peacock image after the model was trained. Notice that the low-resolution image has more artifacts—regions that are boxy, without smoothness in color transitions around contours—than the high-resolution image. The reconstructed SR image shows a smoother color transition around contours, similar to that of the high-resolution image.

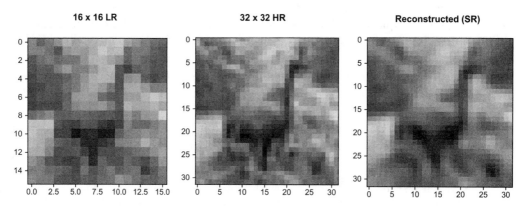

Figure 9.8 Comparison of LR, HR pairing and reconstructed SR image for pre-upsampling SR

9.5.2   *Post-upsampling SR*

Another example of an SRCNN style of model is a post-upsampling SR model, depicted in figure 9.9. We can decompose this model into three components: a low-resolution feature extraction, a high-dimensional representation, and a decoder for reconstruction.

Let's dive into more detail. Again, unlike in an autoencoder, there is no feature pooling (or downsampling) in the low-resolution feature extraction component. Instead, the size of the feature maps stays the same as the size as the channels in the

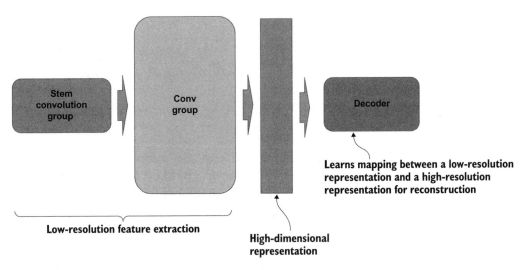

Figure 9.9   A post-upsampling super-resolution model

low-input image. For example, if the input shape is (16, 16, 3), the $H \times W$ of the feature maps will stay 16×16.

During the convolutions, we progressively increase the number of feature maps—which is where we get the high-dimensional space. For example, we might go from the three-channel input to 16, then 32, and then 64 feature maps. So you may be asking why the higher dimensionality? We want the abundance of different low-resolution feature extraction representations to aid us in learning a mapping from them to a high resolution so we can do a reconstruction using a deconvolution. But if we have too many feature maps, we might be exposing the model to memorizing mappings in the training data.

Typically, we train a super-resolution model using an existing image dataset that will be the HR images, and then make a copy of the training data in which each image has been resized smaller for the LR image pairs.

The following code example demonstrates this training data preparation using the CIFAR-10 dataset. In this example, the NumPy array x_train contains the training data images. We then make a mirror list x_train_lr for the low-resolution pairs by sequentially resizing each image in x_train and placing it at the same index location in x_train_lr. Finally, we normalize the pixel data in both sets of images.

In the post-upsampling case, the LR images are left as 16×16 and not resized back to 32×32, as was in the case of pre-upsampling; whereby the lower resolution was injected by the loss of pixel information through static interpolation when resizing back to 32×32.

```
from tensorflow.keras.datasets import cifar10
import numpy as np
import cv2

(x_train, y_train), (x_test, y_test) = cifar10.load_data()
```

Downloads into memory the CIFAR-10 dataset as the high-resolution images

```
x_train_lr = []
for image in x_train:
    x_train_lr.append(cv2.resize(image, (16, 16),
                      interpolation=cv2.INTER_CUBIC))
x_train_lr = np.asarray(x_train_lr)

x_train = (x_train / 255.0).astype(np.float32)
x_train_lr = (x_train_lr / 255.0).astype(np.float32)
```

Makes a low-resolution pairing of the training images

Normalizes the pixel data for training

The following is a code implementation of a post-upsampling SR model that gets good HR reconstruction quality on small images like CIFAR-10. We've coded this implementation specifically for CIFAR-10. To train it, we treat the original CIFAR-10 32 × 32 images (x_train) as the HR images, and the mirrored pairing images (x_train_lr) as the LR images. For training, the LR images are the input, and the paired HR images are the corresponding label.

This example gets fairly good reconstruction results on CIFAR-10 in just 20 epochs with a 90% reconstruction accuracy. In this example, the stem() and learner() components do the low-resolution feature extraction, and progressively expand the feature map dimensionality from 16, 32, and then 64 feature maps. The output from the last convolution of 64 feature maps is the high-dimensional representation. The decoder() consists of a deconvolution to learn the mapping from the low-resolution representation to a high-resolution for reconstruction:

```
from tensorflow.keras import Input, Model
from tensorflow.keras.layers import Conv2D, BatchNormalization
from tensorflow.keras.layers import ReLU, Conv2DTranspose, Activation
from tensorflow.keras.optimizers import Adam

def stem(inputs):
    x = Conv2D(16, (3, 3), padding='same')(inputs)
    x = BatchNormalization()(x)
    x = ReLU()(x)
    return x

def learner(x):
    x = Conv2D(32, (3, 3), padding='same')(x)
    x = BatchNormalization()(x)
    x = ReLU()(x)
    x = Conv2D(64, (3, 3), padding='same')(x)
    x = BatchNormalization()(x)
    x = ReLU()(x)
    return x

def decoder(x):
    x = Conv2DTranspose(3, (3, 3), strides=2, padding='same')(x)
    x = BatchNormalization()(x)
    x = Activation('sigmoid')(x)
    return x

inputs = Input((16, 16, 3))
```

The low-resolution feature extraction

The high-dimensional representation

The low- to high-resolution reconstruction

```
x = stem(inputs)
x = learner(x)
outputs = decoder(x)

model = Model(inputs, outputs)
model.compile(loss='binary_crossentropy', optimizer=Adam(lr=0.001),
              metrics=['accuracy'])
model.fit(x_train_lr, x_train, epochs=25, batch_size=32, verbose=1,
          validation_split=0.1)
```

Let's go back to those same peacock images we looked at earlier. In figure 9.10, the first two images are the low- and high-resolution pair used in training, and the third is the super-resolution reconstruction of the same peacock image after the model was training. As in the previous pre-upsampling SR model, the post-upsampling SR model produced a reconstructed SR image with fewer artifacts than the low-resolution image.

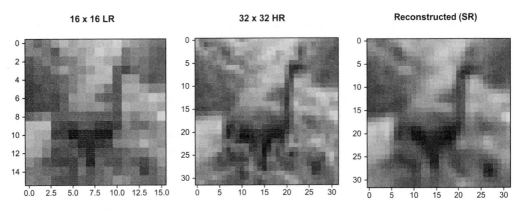

Figure 9.10 Comparison of LR, HR pairing, and reconstructed SR image for post-upsampling SR

A complete code rendition using the Idiomatic procedure reuse design pattern for SRCNN is available on GitHub (http://mng.bz/w0a2).

9.6 Pretext tasks

As we have discussed, autoencoders can be trained without labels to learn feature extraction of essential features, which we can repurpose beyond the examples given so far: compression and denoising.

What do we mean by *essential features*? For imaging, we want our models to learn the essential features of the data, and not the data itself. This enables the models to not only generalize to unseen data in the same distribution, but also be better able to correctly predict when a shift occurs in the input distribution after it is deployed.

For example, let's say we have a model trained to recognize airplanes, and the images used in training consisted of a wide variety of scenes, including on the tarmac, taxied to the terminal, and in the air, but none of them in a hanger. If, after deploying the model, it now sees planes in a hanger, we have a change in the input distribution; this is referred to as *data drift*. And when an image of a plane appears in a hanger, we get a lower accuracy.

In this example case, we might try to improve the model by retraining it with additional images that contain planes in the background. Great, now it works when deployed. But let's say the new model sees planes with other backgrounds it was not trained on, like planes on water (seaplanes), planes on sand in a plane boneyard, planes partially assembled in a factory. Well, in the real world there is always something you don't anticipate!

And that is why it is important to learn the essential features in a dataset and not the data. For autoencoders to work, they have to learn how the pixels are correlated— that is, representational learning. The more correlated, the more likely the relationship will show up in the latent space representation, and the less correlated, the more likely it will not.

We won't go into detail here on pretraining with pretext tasks, but we will briefly touch on it in the context of an autoencoder. For our purposes, we want to use an autoencoder approach to train the stem convolutional group to learn to extract the essential coarse-level features, before training the model on the dataset. Here are the steps:

1 Do warmup (supervised) training on the target model for numerical stabilization (subsequently discussed in chapter 14).
2 Construct an autoencoder consisting of the stem group from the model as the encoder and inverted stem group as the decoder.
3 Transfer the numerically stabilized weights from the target model to the encoder in the autoencoder.
4 Train (unsupervised) the autoencoder on the pretext task (for example, compression, denoising).
5 Transfer the pretext task's trained weights from the encoder of the autoencoder to the target model.
6 Train (supervised) the target model.

Figure 9.11 depicts these steps.

Let's cover one more part of this form of pretext task. It may occur to you that the output from a stem convolutional group will be larger than the input. While we do either a static or feature pooling on the channels, we increase the number of overall channels. For example, we might use pooling to reduce the channel size to 25% or even just 6%, but we increase the number of channels from three (RGB) to something like 64.

Thus, the latent space is now larger than the input and much more prone to overfitting. For this particular purpose, we build a sparse autoencoder to offset the potential to overfit.

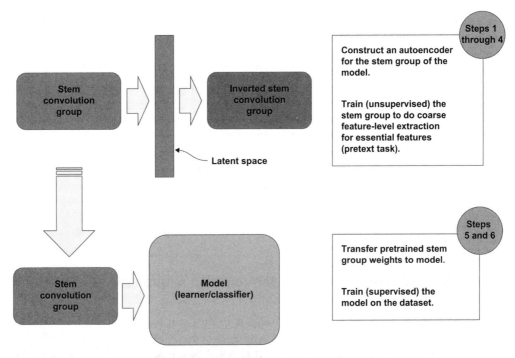

Figure 9.11 Pretraining a stem group using an autoencoder to improve generalization to unseen data when the model is fully trained with labeled data

The following is an example implementation. While we have not discussed the layer `UpSampling2D`, it is the inverse of a strided `MaxPooling2D`. Instead of using a static algorithm to decrease the height and width by one-half, it uses a static algorithm to increase the height and width by 2:

```python
from tensorflow.keras import Input, Model
from tensorflow.keras.layers import Conv2D, Conv2DTranspose
from tensorflow.keras.layers import MaxPooling2D, UpSampling2D
from tensorflow.keras.regularizers import l1

def stem(inputs):
    x = Conv2D(64, (5, 5), strides=(2, 2), padding='same',
               activity_regularizer=l1(1e-4))(inputs)
    x = MaxPooling2D((2, 2), strides=(2, 2))(x)
    return x

def inverted_stem(inputs):
    x = UpSampling2D((2, 2))(inputs)
    x = Conv2DTranspose(3, (5, 5), strides=(2, 2), padding='same')(x)
    return x

inputs = Input((128, 128, 3))
_encoder = stem(inputs)
_decoder = inverted_stem(_encoder)
model = Model(inputs, _decoder)
```

A 5 × 5 filter for coarse feature extraction with feature pooling

Uses max pooling to reduce feature maps to 6% of image size

Inverts the max pooling

Inverts the feature pooling and reconstructs the image

The following is the output from the `summary()` method for this autoencoder. Note that the input size equals the output size:

```
Layer (type)                 Output Shape              Param #
=================================================================
input_4 (InputLayer)         [(None, 128, 128, 3)]     0

conv2d_2 (Conv2D)            (None, 64, 64, 64)        4864

max_pooling2d_1 (MaxPooling2 (None, 32, 32, 64)        0

up_sampling2d (UpSampling2D) (None, 64, 64, 64)        0

conv2d_transpose (Conv2DTran (None, 128, 128, 3)       4803
=================================================================
Total params: 9,667
Trainable params: 9,667
Non-trainable params: 0
```

9.7   *Beyond computer vision: sequence to sequence*

Let's take a short look at a basic natural-language processing model architecture called *sequence-to-sequence* (Seq2Seq). This type of model incorporates both natural-language understanding (NLU)—understanding the text, and natural-language generation (NLG)—generating new text. For NLG, a Seq2Seq model could do things like language translation, summarization, and question and answering. For example, chatbots are Seq2Seq models that do question and answering.

At the end of chapter 5, we introduced NLU model architecture and saw how the component design was comparable to computer vision. We also looked at the attention mechanism, which is comparable to the identity link in a residual network. What we didn't cover is the transformer model architecture, which introduced the attention mechanism in 2017. This innovation converted NLU from a time-series-based solution, using an RNN, to a spatial problem. In an RNN, the model could look only at chunks of the text input at a time and preserve the ordering. Additionally, with each chunk, the model had to retain memory of the important features. This added complexity to the model design in that you needed cycles in the graph to implement retaining previously seen features. With the transformer and attention mechanism, the model looks at the text in a single shot.

Figure 9.12 shows the transformer model architecture, which implements a Seq2Seq model.

As you can see, the learner component consists of both an encoder for NLU and a decoder for NLG. You train the model by using text pairs, sentences, paragraphs, and the like. For example, if you are training a Q&A chatbot, the input would be the questions, and the labels are the answers. For summarization, the input would be the text and the label the summarization.

In the transformer model, the encoder sequentially learns a dimensionality reduction of the context of the input, comparable to representational learning by the

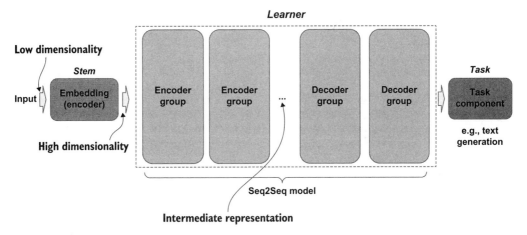

Figure 9.12 **Transformer architecture consists of both an encoder for NLU and decoder for NLG**

encoder in a computer vision autoencoder. The output from the encoder is referred to as the *intermediate representation*, comparable to the latent space in a computer vision autoencoder.

The decoder sequentially learns a dimensionality expansion of the intermediate representation into a transformed context, comparable to the transformational learning by a decoder in a computer vision autoencoder.

The output from the decoder is passed to the task component, which learns the text generation. The text generation task is comparable to the reconstruction task in a computer vision autoencoder.

Summary

- An autoencoder learns an optimal mapping of an input into a low-dimensional representation, and then learns a mapping back to high-dimensional representation, such that a transformation reconstruction of the image can be done.
- Examples of transformation functions that an autoencoder can learn include the identity function (compression), denoising an image, and constructing a higher resolution of the image.
- In a CNN autoencoder, pooling is done with a strided convolution, and unpooling is done with a strided deconvolution.
- Using an autoencoder in unsupervised learning can train a model to learn essential features of the dataset distribution without labels.
- Using an encoder as a pre-stem with an unsupervised learning pretext task can assist in subsequent supervised learning to learn essential features to better generalize.
- The Seq2Seq model pattern for NLU uses an encoder and decoder comparable to an autoencoder.

Part 3

Working with pipelines

In this third part, you learn to design and build production pipelines for model training, deployment, and serving. We start by introducing you to how hyperparameter tuning works under the surface and then show you both a do-it-yourself (DIY) method and automatic hyperparameter tuning using KerasTuner. In both cases, effective hyperparameter tuning requires good judgement in choosing the search space, so we discuss these best practices.

Next, we turn to transfer learning. In transfer learning, you reuse the weights from another trained model and fine-tune a new model with less data and less training time. We cover several variations of transfer learning, one for when the domain of the new dataset is very similar to the trained model (for example, vegetables versus fruits), and another when the domain is very different. Finally, we cover domain transfer techniques for initializing models when doing full training.

In the remaining chapters, we dive deep into the entire production-level pipeline. We start with the concepts behind data distributions and how they affect the ability of a deployed model to generalize to input in the real world that was unseen during training. You will learn techniques to improve training the model for generalization. Next, we go deep into the components, design, and configuration of a data pipeline, covering data warehousing, the ETL process, and model feeding. You'll learn to code these pipelines in a variety of ways, using TF.Keras, `tf.data`, TFRecords, and TensorFlow Extended (TFX).

Finally, we pull it all together and show how a pipeline extends into training, then deployment, and then serving. You'll see hardware resource details for deployment, like sandboxing, load balancing, and autoscaling. In serving, you learn to serve from the cloud by using prebuilt and custom containers, and from the edge, and get familiar with the details of doing production rollouts and A/B testing.

Hyperparameter tuning

10

This chapter covers

- Initializing the weights in a model prior to warm-up training
- Doing hyperparameter search manually and automatically
- Constructing a learning rate scheduler for training a model
- Regularizing a model during training

Hyperparameter tuning is the process of finding the optimal settings of the training hyperparameters, so that we *minimize the training time* and *maximize the test accuracy*. Usually, these two objectives can't be fully optimized. If we minimize the training time, we likely will not achieve the best accuracy. Likewise, if we maximize the test accuracy, we likely will need longer to train.

Tuning is finding the combination of hyperparameter settings that meet your targets for the objectives. For example, if your target is the highest possible accuracy, you may not concern yourself with minimizing the training time. In another situation, if you need only good (but not the best) accuracy, and you are continuously retraining, you may want to find settings that get this good accuracy while minimizing the training time.

Generally, an objective has no specific set of settings. More likely, within the search space various sets of settings will achieve your objective. You need to find only one of those sets—and that's what tuning is.

Now, what are the hyperparameters that we are tuning? We'll go into these in detail in this chapter, but basically they are the parameters that guide the training of the model to maximize achieving the objective. The parameters we will tune in this chapter, for instance, are batch size, learning rate, and learning rate schedulers.

In this chapter, we will look at several commonly used hyperparameter search (tuning) techniques. Figure 10.1 depicts the overall hyperparameter process in a conventional production environment. Don't worry about the details yet; we will cover them step-by-step.

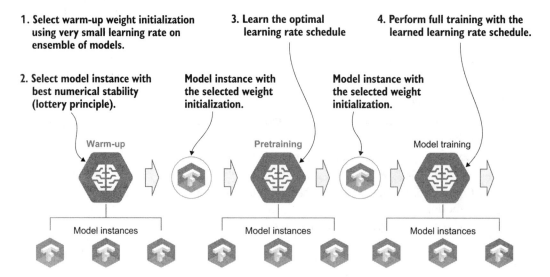

Figure 10.1 Hyperparameter process in a conventional production training environment

I'll briefly walk through this diagram to orient you to the process we'll be following in the rest of this chapter. The first step is to select the best initialization of the weights for a model, and we'll spend some time understanding why this choice can significantly affect the outcome when training. We'll start with predetermined distributions based on research and progress to an alternative way of selecting a draw from the distribution: the lottery ticket principle.

Next, with the weights initialized, we move to the warm-up pretraining. This process numerically stabilizes the weights, which will increase the likelihood of a more optimal outcome, both in training time and model accuracy.

Once the weights are numerically stable, we will look at techniques to search and tune the hyperparameters.

After we have good initialized and numerical stable weights and hyperparameters tuned, we move to the actual training, starting with techniques to further increase the likelihood of a more optimal outcome. One of those techniques, which we'll use here, is varying the learning rate in the later parts of training. This can significantly improve the chances of converging on a global or near-optimal optimum. In other words, these techniques increase the likelihood of producing more-accurate models at a lower overall economic cost.

We will wrap up the chapter by covering common practices of regularization techniques that are implemented in training during weight updates. Regularization helps reduce memorization (overfitting) while also increasing generalization to examples the model will see when deployed in production. We will go over the two most commonly used techniques in production: weight decay (also referred to as *kernel regularization* or *layer regularization*) and label smoothing.

10.1 *Weight initialization*

When we first start training a model from scratch, we need to give the weights an initial value. This process is called *initialization*. For simplicity, we could start by setting all the weights to the same value—say, 0 or 1. That won't work, however, because the way that gradient descent works in backward propagation means each weight would have identical updates.

That neural network would be symmetrical and equivalent to just a single node. A single node can make only a single binary decision, and can solve only a problem with linear separation, like a logical AND or OR. A logical XOR problem cannot be solved with a single node, since it requires a nonlinear separation. The failure of the early perceptron model to solve the XOR problem is attributed to the reduced funding and research in artificial intelligence, from 1984 to 2012, which is referred to as the *AI winter*.

So, we need to set the weights in the model to a random distribution of values. Ideally, the distribution should be a small range (between –1 and 1) and be centered at 0. Several ranges for random distributions have been used over the last several years for initializing weights. Why should the weights be within a small distribution range? Well, if our range is large, the larger initialized weights will dominate the updating of the model over the smaller weights, leading to sparsity, less accuracy, and possibly lack of converging.

10.1.1 *Weight distributions*

Let's start by clarifying the difference between weight initialization and weight distribution. *Weight initialization* is the initial set of values for the weights, the starting point, before training the model. *Weight distribution* is the source from which we select those initial weights.

Three weight distributions have proved to be the most popular with researchers. *Uniform distribution* is uniformly distributed across a range. This is no longer used. *Xavier*, or *Glorot, distribution*, which improved upon uniform distribution, is a random, normal distribution centered at zero. It has a standard deviation set to the following formula, where *fan_in* is the number of inputs to the layer:

sqrt(1 / *fan_in*)

This was a popular method in early SOTA models, and was best suited when activations were a tanh (hyperbolic tangent). It is now seldom used.

Finally, we have the *He-normal distribution*, which improved upon Xavier distribution. These days, almost all weight initialization is done with the He-normal distribution; it is the current mainstream distribution and is best suited for ReLU activations. This random distribution is a normal distribution centered at zero and with a standard deviation set to the following formula, where *fan_in* is the number of inputs to the layer:

sqrt(2 / *fan_in*)

Now let's see how to implement this. In TF.Keras, by default, weights are initialized to an Xavier distribution (referred to as `glorot_uniform`). To initialize the weights to a He-normal distribution, you must explicitly set the keyword parameter `kernel_initializer` to `he_normal`. Here's how that looks:

```
x = Conv2D(16, (3, 3), strides=1, padding='same', activation='relu',
          kernel_initializer='he_normal')(inputs)

outputs = Dense(10, activation='softmax',
               kernel_initializer='he_normal')(x)
```

Initializes the weights to a He-normal distribution

10.1.2 *Lottery hypothesis*

Once researchers had established a consensus on a distribution to draw weights from for initializing a neural network, the next question was, what was the best method to draw from the distribution? We will start by discussing the lottery hypothesis, which kicked off a sequence of rapid advances in drawing from a distribution, which then led to the concept of numerical stability (covered in section 10.1.3).

The *lottery hypothesis* for weight initialization was proposed in 2019. The hypothesis makes two presumptions:

- No two draws from a random distribution are equal. Some draws from the random distribution for weight initialization produce better results than others.
- Large models have high accuracy because they are really a collection of small models. Each has a different draw from the random distribution, and one of the draws is the winning ticket.

Subsequent attempts to identify and extract the submodel with the winning ticket into a compact model from a trained large model never panned out. As a result, the method as it was proposed in "The Lottery Ticket Hypothesis" by Jonathan Frankle and Michael Carbin (https://arxiv.org/abs/1803.03635) is not used today, but subsequent research led to other variations. In this subsection, we explore one of the variations that is commonly used.

The question, though, about the "winning ticket" has not yet been resolved. Another camp of ML practitioners uses the methodology of pretraining multiple instances of the model, each with a separate draw. Typically, when using this approach, we run a small number of epochs with a very small learning rate (for example, 0.0001). For each epoch, the number of steps is substantially fewer than the size of the training data. By doing so, we can pretrain a large number of instances in a short period of time. Once completed, the model instance with the best objective metric, such as training loss, is selected. The assumption is that this draw is a better winning ticket than the others.

Figure 10.2 illustrates pretraining model instances by using the lottery hypothesis method. Multiple copies of the reference model architecture to train are instantiated, each with a different draw from a random distribution. Each instance is then pretrained with the same tiny learning rate for a small number of epochs/reduced steps. If the compute resources are available, the pretraining is distributed. Once completed, the training loss of each pretrained model is inspected. The instance with the lowest training loss is the instance with the best draw—the winning ticket.

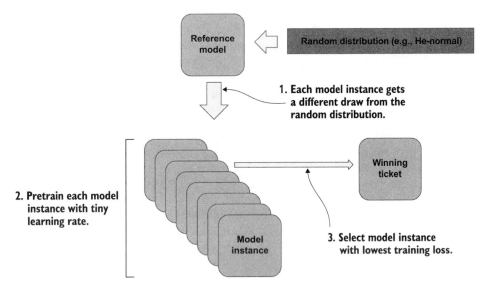

Figure 10.2 Pretraining with the lottery hypothesis method

We can implement this process with the following code. The major steps, shown in this sample, are as follows:

1 Create 10 instances of the model, each with a separate draw for weight initialization. We do this to emulate the principle that no two draws are the same. The choice of 10 is just arbitrary for this example. The larger the number of instances, each with a separate draw, the more likely one of those draws is the winning ticket.
2 Train each instance for a small number of epochs and steps.
3 Select the model instance (best) with the lowest training loss.

Here is the code:

```
def make_model():
    ''' make an instance of the model '''
    bottom = ResNet50(include_top=False, weights=None,
                      input_shape=(32, 32, 3))
    model = Sequential()
    model.add(bottom)
    model.add(Flatten())
    model.add(Dense(10, activation='softmax'))
    model.compile(loss='sparse_categorical_crossentropy',
                  optimizer=Adam(0.0001),
                  metrics=['acc'])
    return model

lottery = []                         ⟵————————┐ Creates 10 model instances, each with
for _ in range(10):                             a separate draw for initialization
    lottery.append(make_model())

from tensorflow.keras.datasets import cifar10
from tensorflow.keras.preprocessing.image import ImageDataGenerator
import numpy as np
(x_train, y_train), (x_test, y_test) = cifar10.load_data()
x_train = (x_train / 255.0).astype(np.float32)

best = (None, 99999)        ⟵———————┐ Does pretraining and selects the
datagen = ImageDataGenerator()       instance with the lowest training loss
for model in lottery:

    result = model.fit(datagen.flow(x_train, y_train, batch_size=32),
                       epochs=3,
                       steps_per_epoch=100)
    print(result.history['loss'][2])
    loss = result.history['loss'][2]
    if loss < best[1]:
        best = (model, loss)
```

Next, we look at another approach to weight initialization, using warm-up for numeric stabilization of the weights.

10.1.3 *Warm-up (numerical stability)*

The *numerical stability method*, which takes a different approach from the lottery hypothesis for weight initialization, is currently the prevailing technique for initializing the weights before full training. In the lottery hypothesis, a large model is viewed as a collection of submodels, and one submodel has the winning ticket. In the numerical stability method, a large model is divided into a higher (bottom) and lower (top) layers.

While we previously discussed *bottom* versus *top*, that terminology still may seem backward to some readers—it sure did to me. In a neural network, the input layer is the bottom, and the output layer is the top. Input is fed from the bottom of the model, and the predictions are outputted from the top.

The presumption is that the lower (top) layers provide numerical stability to the higher (bottom) layers during training. Or specifically, the lower layers provide the numerical stability for the higher layers to *learn* the winning ticket (initialization draw). Figure 10.3 depicts this process.

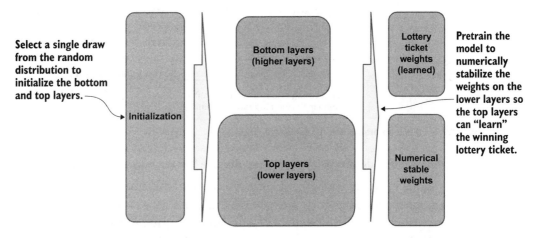

Figure 10.3 Pretraining for numerical stability of lower layers, so higher layers learn the winning lottery ticket initialization

This method is typically implemented as a warm-up training cycle before full training of the model. For warm-up training, we start with a very tiny learning rate to avoid causing large swings in weights and to get the weights to shift toward the winning ticket. Typical initial values for the warm-up learning rate are in range of 1e-5 to 1e-4.

We train the model for a small number of epochs, typically four or five, and gradually step up the learning rate after each epoch to the initial learning rate selected for training.

Figure 10.4 illustrates the warm-up training method, depicted previously as steps 1, 2, and 3 in figure 10.1. Unlike the lottery hypothesis, we start with a single instance of the reference model to train. Starting at a very low learning rate, where weights are adjusted by minute amounts, the model is trained with full epochs. Each time the learning rate is progressively proportional to the initial learning rate for full training. Upon reaching the final epoch, the weights in the model instance are deemed to be numerically stable.

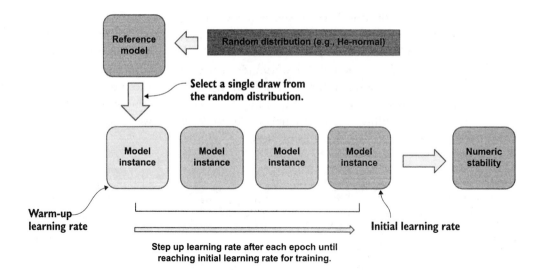

Step up learning rate after each epoch until
reaching initial learning rate for training.

Figure 10.4   Warm-up pretraining for numerical stability

In the following code sample, you can see the five key steps implemented:

1   Instantiate a single weight-initialized instance of the model.
2   Define the learning rate scheduler `warmup_scheduler()` to step up the learning
    rate after each epoch. Section 10.3 describes learning rate schedulers in detail.
3   Add the warm-up scheduler as a callback for the `fit()` method.
4   Train for a small number of epochs (for example, four).

```
def make_model(w_lr):
    ''' make an instance of the model '''
    bottom = ResNet50(include_top=False, weights=None,
                      input_shape=(32, 32, 3))
    model = Sequential()
    model.add(bottom)
    model.add(Flatten())
    model.add(Dense(10, activation='softmax'))
    model.compile(loss='sparse_categorical_crossentropy',
                  optimizer=Adam(w_lr),
                metrics=['acc'])
    return model

w_lr = 0.0001    ◁─── Sets warm-up learning rate and learning rate step
i_lr = 0.001
w_epochs = 4
w_step   = (i_lr - w_lr) / w_epochs

model = make_model(w_lr)    ◁───┐  Creates the model and sets the initial
                                │  learning rate to the warm-up rate
def warmup_scheduler(epoch, lr):
    """ learning rate scheduler for warmup training
        epoch : current epoch iteration
```

```
      lr     : current learning rate
  """
  if epoch == 0:
      return lr
  return lr + w_step
```
Incrementally increases from warm-up rate to initial learning rate for full training

Creates the callback to the learning rate scheduler

```
from tensorflow.keras.callbacks import LearningRateScheduler
lrate = LearningRateScheduler(warmup_scheduler, verbose=1)

from tensorflow.keras.datasets import cifar10
from tensorflow.keras.preprocessing.image import ImageDataGenerator
import numpy as np
(x_train, y_train), (x_test, y_test) = cifar10.load_data()
x_train = (x_train / 255.0).astype(np.float32)

result = model.fit(x_train, y_train, batch_size=32, epochs=4,
                   validation_split=0.1,
                   verbose=1, callbacks=[lrate])
```

Now that we've covered the pretraining, let's take a look at the fundamentals behind hyperparameter search. Then we'll put everything you've learned here into practice and do a full training of a model.

10.2 Hyperparameter search fundamentals

Once your model's weight initialization has numeric stability (whether by lottery or warm-up), we do *hyperparameter search*, also referred to as *hyperparameter tuning* or *hyperparameter optimization*.

Remember, the goal of hyperparameter search is to find the (near) optimal hyperparameter setting to maximize training of your model for your objective—which might be, for instance, speed of training or evaluation accuracy. And, as we've also discussed, we distinguish between parameters for model configuration, known as *metaparameters*, and those for training, known as *hyperparameters*. In this section, we focus only on tuning hyperparameters.

Typically, when training a preconfigured model, the only hyperparameters we attempt to tune are as follows:

- Learning rate
- Batch size
- Learning rate scheduler
- Regularization

NOTE   Do not perform a hyperparameter search on a model whose weights have not been numerically stabilized. Without numerical stabilization of the weights, the practitioner may inadvertently discard combinations with poor performance, which may otherwise be a good combination.

Let's start with a visual. Figure 10.5 depicts the search space. The black area represents combinations of hyperparameters that produce optimal results. Multiple areas of optimal combinations may exist in the search space; in this case, we have three black dots. Typically, within the vicinity of each optimal area is a larger area of near-optimal results, represented as gray. The vast majority of the search space, represented by white space, produces nonoptimal (and non-near) results.

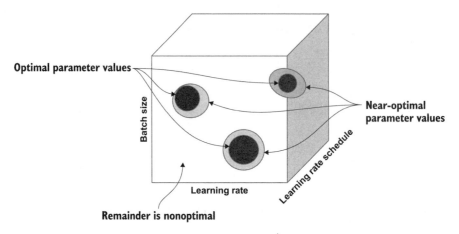

Figure 10.5   Hyperparameter search space

As you can see by the preponderance of white space to black space, if you were to pick a random handful of hyperparameter combinations, it's unlikely that you would find an optimal or near-optimal result. So, you need a strategy. A good strategy is one that has a high likelihood of landing in a near-optimal area(s); being within the near-optimal area narrows the search space to find the optimal area within the vicinity.

10.2.1 *Manual method for hyperparameter search*

Let's start by walking through a manual method, before we get into an automated search. I have a lot of experience training computer vision models and have a strong intuition when it comes to selecting hyperparameters. I am able to use this learned intuition to do a manually guided search. I generally follow these initial four steps:

1 Coarse-tune the initial learning rate.
2 Tune the batch rate.
3 Fine-tune the initial learning rate.
4 Tune the learning rate scheduler.

COARSE-TUNE INITIAL LEARNING RATE

I start by using a fixed batch size and fixed learning rate. If it is a small dataset, typically 50,000 examples or fewer, I use a batch size of 32; otherwise, I use 256. I pick a center point for the learning rate—typically, 0.001. I then run experiments at the center point (for example, 0.001) and one magnitude greater (for example, 0.01) and less (0.0001). I look at the validation loss and accuracy between the three runs and decide which direction leads to better convergence.

If I have a run with the lowest validation loss and highest validation accuracy, I will go with that one. Sometimes a lower validation loss on one run doesn't lead to a higher accuracy. In those cases, I follow more of a gut feeling, but tend to lean toward making the decision on the lowest validation loss.

I then pick a new center point halfway between the existing and the better convergence point. For example, if the center and convergent points are 0.001 and 0.01, I pick 0.005 as the center and use one magnitude greater (0.05) and lesser (0.0005), and repeat the experiment. I repeat this divide-and-conquer strategy until the center point gives me the best convergence, which becomes the coarse-tuned initial learning rate. There is a high likelihood I am in a near-optimal area (gray).

TUNE THE BATCH RATE

Next, I tune the batch size. In general, using 32 for small and 256 for large datasets represents the lowest levels. So I am going to try higher ones. I use a 2× factor. For example, if my batch size is 32, I try 64 with the coarse learning rate. If the convergence improves, I would then try 128, and so forth. When it does not improve, I select the previous good value.

FINE-TUNE THE INITIAL LEARNING RATE

At this point, there is a high likelihood that I have gotten closer to an optimal area (black). The larger the batch size, the less variance we will have on the loss per batch. As a result, we typically can raise the learning rate if we have increased the batch size.

Given the larger batch size, I repeat the tuning experiments for the learning rate, using the coarse learning rate as the initial center point.

LEARNING RATE SCHEDULE

At this point, I start a full training run with early stopping when the validation accuracy stops improving. I generally first try cosine annealing on the learning rate (discussed subsequently). If that makes a significant improvement, I generally stop there. Otherwise, I look back at the initial full run and find the epoch where validation accuracy plateaued or diverged. I then set a learning rate scheduler to drop the learning rate by one magnitude at one epoch before that point.

This generally gives me a really good starting point, and I can now focus on other pretraining steps like augmentation and label smoothing (discussed in section 10.4).

10.2.2 *Grid search*

Grid search is the oldest form of hyperparameter search. It means that you search every possible combination in a narrow search space; it's an innate human approach for a new problem to gain insight. This is practical only with a few parameters and values. For example, if we have three learning rate values and two batch sizes, the number of combinations would be 3 × 2 or 6, which is practical. Let's just slightly increase that to five learning rate values and three batch sizes. That's now 5 × 3 or 15. Wow, look how fast the combinations grow!

Since the (near) optimal area is much smaller in comparison to the entire search, we are unlikely to find a good combination early.

This approach is not used anymore because of its computational overhead. The following is an example implementation of a grid search. I present it here so you can make a comparison to random search in the next subsection.

In this example, we do a grid search on two hyperparameters: learning rate (lr) and batch size (bs). For both, we specify a set of values to try, such as [0.1, 0.01] for the learning rate. We then use two nested loop iterators to generate all combinations of the set of values for learning rate and batch size. For each combination, we get a copy of the pretrained instance of the model (get_model()) and train it for a few epochs. A running tally of the best validation score and corresponding hyperparameter combination is kept (best). When done, the tuple best contains the hyperparameter settings that resulted in the lowest validation loss.

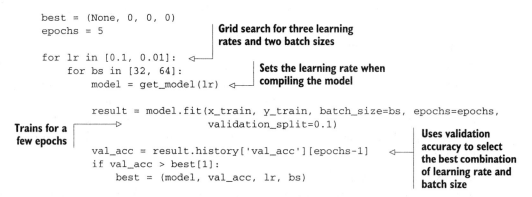

```
best = (None, 0, 0, 0)
epochs = 5                          Grid search for three learning
                                    rates and two batch sizes
for lr in [0.1, 0.01]:   ◄────────┘
    for bs in [32, 64]:             Sets the learning rate when
        model = get_model(lr)  ◄───┘ compiling the model

            result = model.fit(x_train, y_train, batch_size=bs, epochs=epochs,
                               validation_split=0.1)
Trains for a  ┌──────►
few epochs    │                                                    Uses validation
              │    val_acc = result.history['val_acc'][epochs-1]  ◄── accuracy to select
              │    if val_acc > best[1]:                             the best combination
              │        best = (model, val_acc, lr, bs)              of learning rate and
                                                                    batch size
```

10.2.3 *Random search*

Let's turn to a random search method, which is less computationally expensive than the grid search for finding good hyperparameters. Your first question might be, how could a random search be computationally less expensive than a grid search (it's just random)?

To answer this question, let's revisit our earlier depiction of the hyperparameter search space. We know that only a small portion of it has an optimal combination, so we have a very low probability of finding one randomly. But we also know that substantially larger areas are near-optimal, so we have a substantially higher probability of landing in one of those using a random search.

Once the search finds a near-optimal combination, we know there is a good likelihood that an optimal combination exists in the vicinity. At this point, we narrow the random search to an area surrounding the near-optimal combination. If a new combination improves the result, we may further narrow the random search around the vicinity of the new combination.

To summarize these steps:

1 Set the boundaries for the search space.
2 Do a random search within the entire search space.
3 Once a near-optimal combination is found, narrow the search space to the vicinity of the new combination.
4 Continuously repeat until a combination meets your objective criteria.
   - If a new combination improves the result, further narrow the search space around the new combination.
   - If, after a predefined number of trials, the result does not improve, return to searching the entire search space (step 2).

Figure 10.6 illustrates the first three steps.

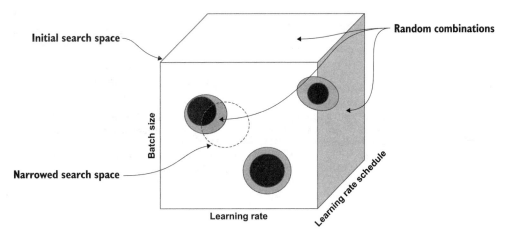

Figure 10.6 **Hyperparameter random search**

Here is an example implementation of the first three steps. In this code, we do the following:

1 Run five `trials` on the full search space. Because this example has just a small number of combinations, generally five trials is sufficient.
2 Select a random combination of the learning rate (`lr`) and batch size (`bs`).
3 Do a short training run on a pretrained instance of the model.
4 Maintain a running tally of the best validation accuracy and hyperparameter combination (`best`).
5 Select the best validation accuracy from the five trials as the near-optimal.
6 Set a narrow search space around the near-optimal hyperparameters ($2X$ and $1/2X$).
7 Run five more trials within the narrow search space.

```
from random import randint

learning_rates = [0.1, 0.01, 0.001, 0.0001]    If we did grid search, we would
batch_sizes = [ 32, 128, 512]                   have 4 × 3 = 12 combinations.

trials = 5
epochs = 3

best = (None, 0, 0, 0)            Step 1: First round of trials,
                                  finds the best near-optimal
                                  combination
for _ in range(trials):
    lr = learning_rates[randint(0, 3)]
    bs = batch_sizes[randint(0, 2)]            Step 2: Selects random combinations
    model = get_model(lr)
    result = model.fit(x_train, y_train, epochs=epochs, batch_size=bs,
                       validation_split=0.1, verbose=0)

    val_acc = result.history['val_acc'][epochs-1]
    if val_acc > best[1]:                  Steps 4 and 5: Maintains
        best = (model, val_acc, lr, bs)    tally of current best result

learning_rates = [ best[2] / 2, best[2] * 2]    Step 6: Narrows the search space to
batch_sizes = [best[3] // 2, int(best[3] * 2)]  within the vicinity of the best near-
for _ in range(trials):                          optimal
    lr = learning_rates[randint(0, 1)]
    bs = batch_sizes[randint(0, 1)]       Step 7: Runs another set of trials
    model = get_model(lr)                 around narrowed search space
    result = model.fit(x_train, y_train, epochs=epochs, batch_size=bs,
                       validation_split=0.1, verbose=0)

    val_acc = result.history['val_acc'][epochs-1]
    if val_acc > best[1]:
        best = (model, val_acc, lr, bs)
```

Step 3: Does short training run for trial

I ran this code without numerical stabilization, using the CIFAR-10 dataset. After the first five trials on the full search space, the best validation accuracy was 0.352. After narrowing the search space, the best validation accuracy leaped to 0.487, with learning rate = 0.0002 and batch size = 64.

I then repeated the process, but this time I first did numerical stabilization on the model before doing hyperparameter search. I updated the get_model() method to fetch a copy of the saved numerical stabilized model. After the first five trials on the full search space, the best validation accuracy was 0.569. After narrowing the search space, the best validation accuracy leaped to 0.576, with learning rate = 0.1 and batch size = 512. Wow, that is amazingly better. And we haven't yet tuned for learning rate scheduling, regularization, augmentation, and label smoothing!

Next, we will discuss how to use the automated hyperparameter search tool Keras-Tuner, which is an add-on module to TF.Keras. You might ask, why learn a manual method when we can just use an automated method? Even with an automated method, you need to guide the search space. Using manual methods helps you gain expertise in guiding the search space. For me, and researchers, developing manual methods gives us insight into future improvements to automated searches. Finally, you may find that the out-of-the-box automated method is not well suited for your proprietary dataset and model, and you can improve it with your unique learned approach.

10.2.4 KerasTuner

KerasTuner is an add-on module to TF.Keras for doing automated hyperparameter tuning. It has two methods: random search and hyperband search. For brevity, this section covers the random search method. An understanding of this method will give you insight to the overall approach for searching hyperparameters in what otherwise is a sparse space, when few good combinations exist within the larger search space.

> **NOTE** I refer you to the online documentation (https://keras-team.github .io/keras-tuner/) for hyperband, a bandit algorithm approach for improving times for random search. You can find more information in "Hyberband" by Lisha Li et al. (https://arxiv.org/abs/1603.06560).

Like all automated tools, KerasTuner has pros and cons. Being automated and fairly straightforward to use is obviously good. For me, the lack of the ability to tune the batch size is a big con, as you end up having to tune the batch size manually.

Here is the `pip` command for installing KerasTuner:

```
pip install -U keras-tuner
```

To use KerasTuner, we start by creating an instance of the tuner. In the following example, we instantiate an instance of the `RandomSearch` class. This instantiation takes three required parameters:

1 Hyperparameter tunable (hp) model
2 The objective measurement (for example, validation accuracy)
3 The maximum number of training trials (experiments)

```
from kerastuner.tuners import RandomSearch

tuner = RandomSearch(hp_model,            ◄─── Gets the hyperparameter tunable model
                     objective='val_acc',  ◄───
                     max_trials=3)              Training metric to compare (improve on)
```
The number of training trials ──▷ `max_trials=3`

In this example, I set the number of trials low (3) for demonstration purposes. At most, three random combinations will be tried. Depending on the size of your search space, you will generally use a larger number. This is a tradeoff. The more trials, the more of the search space is explored, but the more computational expense (time) required.

Next, we create the function that instantiates a hyperparameter-tunable model. The function takes one parameter, denoted by `hp`. This is a hyperparameter control variable passed in by KerasTuner.

In our example, we will tune just the learning rate. We start with getting an instance of a numerically stabilized version of our model, as I previously recommended. We then set the learning rate for the instance with the `optimizer` parameter in the `compile()` method. In our example, we will specify four choices of the learning rate by using the hyperparameter tuner (hp) control method `hp.Choice()`. This tells the tuner the set of values for a parameter to search. In this case, we set the choices to [1e-1, 1e-2, 1e-3, 1e-4]:

```
def hp_model(hp):
    ''' hp is passed in by the tuner '''
    model = tf.keras.models.load_model('numeric')

    model.compile(loss='sparse_categorical_crossentropy', metrics=['acc'],
                optimizer=Adam(hp.Choice('learning_rate',
                                values=[1e-1, 1e-2, 1e-3, 1e-4])))
    return model
```

Loads the saved (on disk) model

Recompiles the model to reset the learning rate

Makes the learning rate a tunable parameter

Next, we are ready to perform the hyperparameter tuning. We initiate the search with the `search()` method of tuner. The method takes the same parameters as the Keras model `fit()` method. Note, the batch size is explicitly specified in `search()` and thus is not automatically tunable. In our example, our training data is the CIFAR-10 training data:

```
tuner.search(x_train, y_train, batch_size=32, validation_data=(x_test, y_test))
```

And now the results! First, use the `results_summary()` method to view a summary of the trials:

```
tuner.results_summary()
```

Here is the output, which shows 0.1 was the best learning rate:

```
Results summary
|-Results in ./untitled_project
|-Showing 10 best trials
|-Objective(name='val_acc', direction='max')
Trial summary
|-Trial ID: 0963640822565bfc03280657d5350d26
|-Score: 0.4927000105381012
|-Best step: 0
Hyperparameters:
|-learning_rate: 0.0001
Trial summary
|-Trial ID: 9c6ed7a1276c55a921eaf1d3f528d64d
|-Score: 0.28610000014305115
|-Best step: 0
Hyperparameters:
|-learning_rate: 0.01
```

```
Trial summary
|-Trial ID: d269858c936c2b6a2941e66f880304c7
|-Score: 0.10599999874830246
|-Best step: 0
Hyperparameters:
|-learning_rate: 0.1     ◁———— The selected best learning rate
```

You then use the `get_best_models()` method to get the corresponding model. This method returns a list of the best models in descending order based on the parameter `num_models`. In this case, we want just the best one, so we set it to 1.

```
models = tuner.get_best_models(num_models=1)
model = models[0]
```

Finally, your results and models are stored in a folder, which can be specified by the parameter `project_name` when instantiating the tuner. When not specified, the folder name defaults to `untitled_project`. To clean up after your trials, you would delete this folder.

10.3 *Learning rate scheduler*

So far in our examples, we have kept the learning rate constant throughout training. You can get good results with a constant learning rate, but it is not as effective as adjusting the learning rate during training.

Typically, you progress from a larger learning rate to a lower learning rate during training. Initially, you want to start with as large a learning rate as possible, without causing numerical instability. The larger learning rate allows the optimizer to explore different paths (local optima) to convergence and make some initial large gains in minimizing the loss to speed up training.

But once we are making good progress toward a good local optimum, if we keep using the high learning rate, we may start oscillating back and forth without converging or inadvertently jump out of the good local optimum and start converging in a less good local optimum.

So as we get closer to convergence, we start to lower the learning rate to make smaller and smaller steps, so as to not oscillate and find the best path in the local optimum to converge on.

So what is meant by the term *learning rate scheduler*? It means that we will have a method that monitors the training process, and based on a certain condition makes a change to the learning rate to find and converge within the best or near local optimum. In this section, we will cover several common methods: including time decay, ramp, constant step, and cosine annealing. We will start with describing the time decay method, which is the method built into the TF.Keras set of optimizers for progressively lowering the learning rate during training.

10.3.1 *Keras decay parameter*

The TF.Keras optimizers support progressively lowering the learning rate with the decay parameter. The optimizers use the time-decay method. The mathematical formula for time decay is as follows, where lr is the learning rate, k is the decay and t is the number of iterations (for example, epochs):

$$lr = lr0 \;/\; (1 + kt)$$

In TF.Keras, the time decay is implemented as follows:

$$lr = lr \times (1.0 \;/\; (1.0 + \text{decay} \times \text{iterations}))$$

Here is an example of setting a time decay for the learning rate when specifying the optimizer in the `compile()` method:

```
model.compile(optimizer=SGD(lr=0.1, decay=1e-3))
```

Table 10.1 shows the progression in learning rate for 10 epochs with the preceding settings; typical decay values are between 1e-3 and 1e-6.

Table 10.1 Decay progression of learning rate over epochs

Iteration (epoch)	Learning rate
1	0.0999
2	0.0997
3	0.0994
4	0.0990
5	0.0985
6	0.0979
7	0.0972
8	0.0964
9	0.0955
10	0.0945

10.3.2 *Keras learning rate scheduler*

If using time decay does not produce optimal results, you can implement your own custom method for progressively lowering the learning rate, using the `LearningRate-Scheduler` callback. It's not uncommon in a production environment for the ML team over time to experiment and find custom tweaks that make the training more time efficient and result in better outcomes on the objective, such as accuracy on classification when deployed into production.

The following code is an example implementation whose steps are outlined here:

1 Define a function for our learning rate scheduler callback.
2 During training (via the `fit()` method), the parameters passed to the callback are the current epoch count (epoch) and learning rate (`lr`).
3 For the first epoch, return the current (initial) learning value.
4 Otherwise, implement a progressively lowering of the learning rate.
5 Instantiate a callback for the learning rate scheduler.
6 Pass in the callback to the `fit()` method.

```
from tensorflow.keras.callbacks import LearningRateScheduler

def lr_scheduler(epoch, lr):
    ''' Set the learning rate at the beginning of epoch
        epoch: The epoch count (first epoch is zero)
        lr:  The current learning rate
    '''
    if epoch == 0:
        return lr

    return n_lr

model.compile(loss='categorical_crossentropy', optimizer=Adam(lr=0.01))

lr_callback = LearningRateScheduler(lr_scheduler)

model.fit(x_train, y_train, epochs=epochs, batch_size=batch_size,
          callbacks=[lr_callback])
```

Step 3: For the first (0) epoch, starts with the initial learning rate

Step 1: Sets the initial learning rate

Step 4: Adds your implementation for progressively lowering the learning rate

Step 5: Creates the callback for the learning rate scheduler

Steps 2 and 6: Enables the learning rate scheduler for training

10.3.3 Ramp

So, you've done the pretraining step for numerical stability and the hyperparameter tuning for batch size and initial learning rate. Now you're ready to tackle implementing your algorithm for the learning rate scheduler. Often you can do that with a ramp algorithm, which resets the learning rate at a specified number of epochs. Typically, at this point I will do an extended training run. I usually start with 50 epochs and set an early stop condition on the valuation loss (with a `patience` of 2). Regardless of the dataset, I tend to see one of two things:

- Steady and consistent reduction in validation loss through the last (50) epochs.
- Before the last epoch, a plateauing occurs in the validation loss and the early stop has kicked in.

If I see a steady reduction in the validation loss, I will continue to repeat for an additional 50 epochs, until I have an early stop.

Once I have an early stop, I look at what epoch it occurred at. Let's say it was on epoch 40. I will then subtract a few epochs, typically 5 (in this case, resulting in 35). I then hardwire my learning rate scheduler to do a one-magnitude drop in learning rate at the epoch. Nearly 100% of the time, my training improves to a lower validation loss and higher validation accuracy. Figure 10.7 shows a ramped-down learning rate.

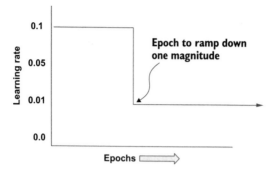

Figure 10.7   Ramped-down learning rate

The following is an example implementation of a ramp learning rate scheduler:

```
epoch_ramp = 35      ⬅——— Sets the epoch for ramping down a magnitude

def lr_scheduler(epoch, lr):
    if epoch == epoch_ramp:        │ Lowers the learning rate by a magnitude
        return lr / 10.0           │ when it is at the ramp epoch
    return lr
```

This is typically not my last step, but instead I use it to get an idea of what the loss landscape likely looks like for this dataset. From that, I plan my full training learning rate scheduler. At this level, it would be too challenging to explain a loss landscape. I will instead cover a variety of learning rate scheduler strategies you can try.

10.3.4 Constant step

In the constant step method, we want to go from the initial learning rate to zero on the last epoch in even increments. The method is straightforward. You take the initial learning rate and divide it by the number of epochs. Figure 10.8 illustrates the method.

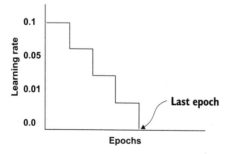

Figure 10.8   Constant step learning rate

This is an example implementation of the step method for a learning rate scheduler:

The number of epochs for training

The initial learning rate determined by hyperparameter tuning

```
epochs = 200
lr = 0.001
step = lr / epochs
```

The size of the step decay after each epoch

```
def lr_scheduler(epochs, lr):
    ''' step learning rate '''
    return lr - step
```

10.3.5 *Cosine annealing*

The *cosine annealing method* has been popular among researchers and appears frequently in research papers about ablation studies. It is also known as a *cyclic learning rate*. The concept here is, instead of progressively lowering the learning rate across training, to do it in cycles.

More simply, we start with the initial learning rate and progressively lower to a lower learning rate, and then we progressively raise it again. We continuously repeat this cycle, but each time the rate that the cycle starts at (high) and ends at (low) is lower—so we are still progressing lower across the cycles.

So what's the advantage? It provides the opportunity to periodically explore other local optima (jump out) and to escape saddle points. For the local optima, it's like doing a beam search. The training will likely jump out of a current local optimum and start diving into another. While at first nothing indicates that the new local optimum is better, eventually it will. Here's why. As the training progresses, we will dive deeper into better optima than less good ones. With the declining upper learning rate, it becomes less and less likely we would jump out of a good local optimum. Another way to think of this cyclic behavior is as exploration versus exploitation: on the high end of the cycle, the training is exploring new paths, and on the low end, it is exploiting good paths. As we progress in training, we move to less and less exploration and to more and more exploitation.

Another advantage is that after we are diving deep with the lower end of the learning rate cycle, we may get stuck on a saddle point. Let's use the following diagram to aid in understanding what a saddle point is.

If our features (independent variables) have a linear relationship to the labels (dependent variables), once we discover the slope of change, we will dive to the global optimum, regardless of the learning rate (as depicted in the first curve).

On the other hand, if the relationship is polynomial, we will see something more like a convex curve, with the global optimum as the lowest point of the curve. In principle, as long as we continuously reduce the learning rate, we will descend to the lowest point, avoiding bouncing back and forth between the sides of the curve (as depicted in the second curve).

But the power of deep learning is with features that have a nonlinear (and non-polynomial) relationship to the labels (as depicted in the third curve). In this case, think of the loss space consisting of valleys, peaks, and saddle points, and one valley is the global optima. Our goal is, of course, to find that valley, hence the advantage of exploring multiple local optima (valleys).

A saddle point is a portion of the loss space in a valley that has a plateau; it levels off before continuing down. If our learning rate is very low, we will bounce around the plateau endlessly. So, while we want that tiny learning rate as we near the end of the training, we want it to occasionally go up to push us off saddle points on the way down to the lowest point.

Figure 10.9 contrasts the loss surface between linear/polynomial to a nonlinear relationship, which shows peaks, valleys, and plateaus—which can become a saddle point.

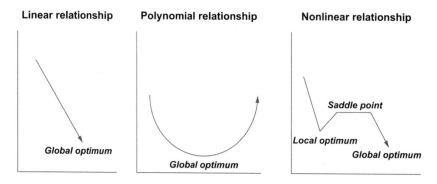

Figure 10.9   Gradient descent and slope of rate of change

When using cosine decay in conjunction with early stopping, we must rethink the objective (validation accuracy) for stopping. If we are training with a noncyclic decay, we would likely use a very small threshold of difference between epochs before stopping. But with cyclic behavior, we are likely to see sudden spikes in difference (increased validation loss) when exploring (the high end of cycle). Thus, we need to use a wider gap for the early stop. The alternative is to use a custom early stop that progressively decreases the difference in conjunction with the high end of the cycle decreasing.

The following is an example implementation of a learning rate scheduler using cosine decay. The function is a bit complex. We are using the cosine function np.cos() to generate a sine wave from 0 to 1. For example, cosine(π) is –1 and cosine(2π) is 1, so the calculation of the value to pass to np.cos() is a multiple of π. So that the value is positive, a 1 is added to the calculation, and the result will now be in the range of 0 to 2. This value is then reduced by one-half (0.5 times), so the result will now be in the range of 0 to 1. The decay is then adjusted by alpha, which sets a lower bound on the minimum learning rate.

```
def cosine_decay(epoch, lr, alpha=0.0):
        """ Cosine Decay
    """
```

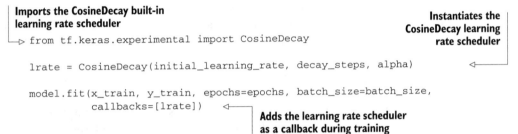

Adjusts value by alpha — Calculates cosine value between 0 and 2 and reduces by one-half

```
cosine_decay = 0.5 * (1 + np.cos(np.pi * (e_steps * epoch) / t_steps))
decayed = (1 - alpha) * cosine_decay + alpha
return lr * decayed
```
Returns the decayed learning rate

```
def lr_scheduler(epochs, lr):
    ''' cosine annealing learning rate '''
    return cosine_decay(epochs, lr)
```
Connects learning rate scheduler callback to cosine decay function

In TF 2.x, cosine decay was added as a built-in learning rate scheduler:

Imports the CosineDecay built-in learning rate scheduler

Instantiates the CosineDecay learning rate scheduler

```
from tf.keras.experimental import CosineDecay

lrate = CosineDecay(initial_learning_rate, decay_steps, alpha)

model.fit(x_train, y_train, epochs=epochs, batch_size=batch_size,
          callbacks=[lrate])
```
Adds the learning rate scheduler as a callback during training

10.4 *Regularization*

The next important hyperparameter is *regularization*. This refers to methods of adding noise to the training such that the model doesn't memorize the training data. The longer we can delay memorization, the better the opportunity to gain higher accuracy in the model when predicting on data not trained on—such as the test (holdout) data.

Let's restate this more simply. We want the model to learn the essential features (generalization) and not the data (memorization).

A note on dropout for regularization: nobody does that anymore; it's arcane.

10.4.1 *Weight regularization*

The most widely used form of regularization currently is *weight regularization*, also referred to as *weight decay*. Weight regularization is applied on a per layer basis. Its purpose is to add noise to the update of the weights during backward propagation that is relative to the size of the weights. This noise is commonly referred to as a *penalty*, and layers with larger weights have a larger penalty than layers with smaller weights.

Without diving deep into gradient descent and backward propagation, it is sufficient to say that the loss calculation is part of the computation for updating the weights at each layer. For example, in a regressor model, we typically use a mean square error for the loss between the predicted values ($\hat{y}$) and the actual (ground truth – y) values, which can be denoted as follows:

loss = MSE$(\hat{y}, y)$

To add noise per layer, we want to add a tiny bit as a penalty in proportion to the size of the weights:

loss = MSE$(\hat{y}, y)$ + *penalty*

penalty = *decay* × $R(w)$

Here, *decay* is the weight decay, which is a value $\ll 1$. And $R(w)$ is a regularizer function applied to the weights w for that layer. TF.Keras supports the following regularizer functions:

- *L1*—Sum of the absolute weights, also known as *Lasso regularization*
- *L2*—Sum of the squared weights, also known as *Ridge regularization*
- *L1L2*—Sum of the absolute and the squared weights, also referred to as *Elastic Net regularization*

Ablation studies cited in modern SOTA research papers use L2 weight regularization around the value ranges of 0.0005 to 0.001. From my own experience, I found values above 0.001 to be too aggressive in weight regularization, and the training does not converge.

In TF.Keras, the keyword parameter `kernel_regularizer` is used to set weight regularization per layer. If you use it, you should specify it on all layers that have learned parameters (for example, `Conv2D`, `Dense`). Here is an example implementation of specifying an L2 weight decay regularization for a convolutional layer (`Conv2D`):

```
from tensorflow.keras.regularizers import L2

inputs = Input((128, 128, 3))
x = Conv2D(16, (3, 3), strides=(1, 1), kernel_regularizer=L2(0.001))(inputs)
```

10.4.2 *Label smoothing*

Label smoothing approaches regularization from a different direction. Up to now, we discussed techniques of adding noise to prevent memorization, so that models will generalize to examples within the same distribution that was not seen by the model during training.

What we find, though, is that even when we penalize these weight updates to prevent memorization, these models tend to be overconfident in their prediction (high probability value).

When a model is overconfident, the distance between the ground-truth label and non-ground-truth labels can vary greatly. When plotted, it would tend to appear more of a scatter plot than a cluster; it would be more desirable if the ground-truth labels clustered together, even if the confidence is lower. Figure 10.10 depicts an overconfident model using hard targets for labels.

Label smoothing aids in generalizing the model by making the predictions less confident, which results in the distances between ground truths and non-ground-truths to cluster together.

In label smoothing, we alter the one-hot-encoding labels (ground truths) from being absolute certainty (1 and 0) to something less than absolute certainty, denoted as α (alpha). For example, for the ground-truth label instead of setting the value to 1 (100%), we set it to something slightly less, like 0.9 (90%), and then change all the non-truths from 0 (0%) to the same amount we lowered the ground-truth label (for example, 10%).

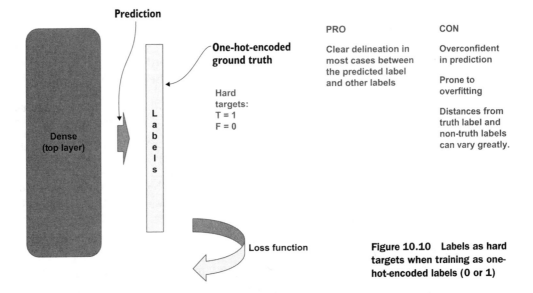

Figure 10.10 Labels as hard targets when training as one-hot-encoded labels (0 or 1)

Figure 10.11 illustrates label smoothing. In this depiction, the predictions from the outputting dense layer are compared to the ground-truth labels after label smoothing, referred to as *soft targets*. The loss is calculated from the soft targets instead of the hard targets, which has been shown in practice to make the distance between the ground

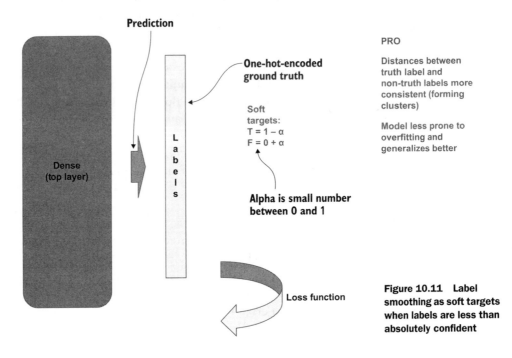

Figure 10.11 Label smoothing as soft targets when labels are less than absolutely confident

truth and non-ground truth more consistent. These distances then are more likely to form clusters, which aids in the model being more generalized.

In TF 2.x, label smoothing is built into the loss functions. To use, explicitly instantiate the corresponding loss function and set the keyword parameter `label_smoothing`. In practice, the α factor is kept small, with 0.1 being the most widely used value.

```
from tensorflow.keras.losses import CategoricalCrossentropy

model.compile(loss=CategoricalCrossentropy(label_smoothing=0.1),
              optimizer='adam', metrics=['acc'])
```

> **Sets the label smoothing when compiling the model**

Next, we will summarize everything we covered on hyperparameters and how they impact achieving the optimal outcome in training time and objective (for example, accuracy) during training.

10.5   *Beyond computer vision*

All deep learning model architectures, regardless of the data type or field, have tunable hyperparameters. And the strategies for tuning them are the same. Regardless of whether you are working with computer vision, natural-language understanding, or structured data, the big four hyperparameters exist in all deep learning fields: learning rate, learning rate decay, batch size, and regularization.

The hyperparameters for regularization can vary in type across model architectures and across different fields. Many times they do not. For example, weight decay can be applied to any layer with learnable weights, regardless of whether it is a computer vision, NLU, or structured data model.

Some model architectures, like deep neural networks and boosted trees, have some historically unique hyperparameters. For example, for DNNs, you may see the tuning of the number of layers and number of units per layer. For boosted trees, you may see tuning the number of trees and leaves. But, since the division into hyperparameters (for training the model) and metaparameters (for configuring the model architecture), these tunable parameters are now referred to as *metaparameters*. So, if you're tuning the number of layers and units in conjunction with the learning rate on a deep neural network, you are, in effect, doing macro-architecture search and hyperparameter tuning in parallel.

Summary

- Different weight distributions and draws affect convergence during training.
- The difference between searching for an optimal weight initialization (lottery principle) versus learning the optimal weight initialization (warm-up) is that the model learns the best initialization instead of empirically finding it.
- A manual approach to hyperparameter search is best used when the dataset is small, and has the drawback that you might overlook hyperparameter values that achieve a better outcome during training.

- Grid search is used in a small search space, and random search is substantially more efficient in a larger search space for hyperparameter tuning.
- Using KerasTuner for hyperparameter search allows you to automate the search, but has the disadvantage that you cannot hand-guide the search.
- Various algorithms are used for learning rate decay, such as time decay, constant step, ramp step, and cosine annealing.
- Setting up a learning rate scheduler involves defining a callback function, implementing the custom learning rate algorithm in the callback function, and adding the callback function to the `fit()` method.
- The conventional approaches for regularization are weight decay and label smoothing.

Transfer learning

11

This chapter covers

- Using prebuilt and pretrained models from TF.Keras and TensorFlow Hub
- Performing transfer learning between tasks in similar and distinct domains
- Initializing models with domain-specific weights for transfer learning
- Determining when to reuse high-dimensionality or low-dimensionality latent space

TensorFlow and TF.Keras support a wide availability of prebuilt and pretrained models. *Pretrained* models can be used as is, while *prebuilt* models can be trained from scratch. By replacing the task group, pretrained models can also be reconfigured to perform any number of tasks. The process of replacing or reconfiguring the task group with retraining is called *transfer learning*.

In essence, transfer learning means transferring the knowledge for solving one task to solving another task. The benefit of transfer learning versus training a model from scratch is that the new task can be trained faster and with less data. Think of it as a form of reuse: we are reusing the model with its learned weights.

You might ask, can I reuse the weights learned for one model architecture for another? No, the two models have to be the same architecture, such as ResNet50 to a ResNet50. Another common question: can I reuse the learned weights on *any* different task? You could, but the results will vary depending on the level of similarity between the domain of the pretrained model and the new dataset. So what we really mean by the learned weights are the learned essential features, the corresponding feature extraction, and latent space representation—the representational learning.

Let's look at a couple of examples in which transfer learning may or may not produce desirable results. Say we have a pretrained model for types and varieties of fruits and we have a new dataset for types and varieties of vegetables. It is highly likely that the learned representations for fruits are reusable for vegetables, and we just need to train the task group. But what if our new dataset consists of makes and models of trucks and vans. In this case, the dataset domains are so different from each other, it is very unlikely that the representations learned for fruits can be reused for trucks and vans. In the case of similar domains, the task we want our new model to do works on a domain that is similar to the data the original model is trained on.

Another approach for learned representations is to use a model trained on a massively diverse set of classes of images. Numerous AI companies provide this type of transfer learning service. Typically, their pretrained models are trained on the order of tens of thousands of image classes. The presumption here is that with such broad diversity, some portion of the learned representation is reusable on any arbitrary new dataset. The downside is that to cover such a broad diversity, the latent space must be very large—so you end up with a model that is very large (overparameterized) in the task group.

A third approach is to find a sweet spot between the two approaches, the parameter-efficient, narrow-domain-trained model and the massively trained model. Model architectures like ResNet50 and, more recently, EffcientNet-B7 are pretrained with an ImageNet dataset consisting of a diverse set of 1000 classes. DIY transfer learning projects often make use of these models. ResNet50, for example, has a reasonably efficient but large enough latent space, before the task component, for the purpose of transfer learning to a wide variety of image classification datasets; the latent space consists of 2048 4×4 feature maps.

Let's summarize these three approaches:

- Similar domain transfer:
  - Parameter-efficient, narrow-domain pretrained model
  - Retrains a new task component
- Distinct domain transfer:
  - Parameter-overcapacity, narrow-domain pretrained model
  - Retrains a new task component with fine-tuning of other components
- General transfer
  - Parameter-overcapacity, general-domain pretrained model
  - Retrains a new task component

A pretrained model can also be reused in transfer learning to learn a different type of task from the pretrained model. For example, let's say we have a pretrained model that classifies the architectural style from pictures of the front exterior of the house. And let's say now we want to learn to predict the selling price of the house. It's highly likely that the essential features, feature extraction, and latent space will transfer over to a different type of task, such as a regressor—a model that outputs a single real number (for example, the selling price of a house). This type of transfer learning to another task type is generally possible if the other task type could also be trained with the original dataset.

This chapter covers obtaining prebuilt and pretrained SOTA models from public resources: TF.Keras and TensorFlow Hub. Then I'll walk you through using these models out-of-the box. And finally, you'll learn various ways of using the pretrained models for transfer learning.

11.1 TF.Keras prebuilt models

The TF.Keras framework comes with prebuilt models that you can either use as is to train a new model, or modify and/or fine-tune for transfer learning. These are based on best-in-class models for image classification, award-winning models in competitions like ImageNet that are cited frequently in deep learning research papers.

Documentation on the prebuilt Keras models is found on the Keras website (https://keras.io/api/applications/). Table 11.1 lists the Keras prebuilt model architectures.

Table 11.1 Keras prebuilt models

Model type	SOTA model architecture
Sequential CNN	VGG16, VGG19
Residual CNN	ResNet, ResNet v2
Wide residual CNN	ResNeXt, Inception v3, InceptionResNet v2
Alternatively connected CNN	DenseNet, Xception, NASNet
Mobile CNN	MobileNet, MobileNet v2

The prebuilt Keras models are imported from the `keras.applications` module. The following are examples of the prebuilt SOTA models that can be imported. For example, if you wanted to use VGG16, simply replace the VGG19 with VGG16. Some of the model architectures can be selected with different numbers of layers, such as the VGG, ResNet, ResNeXt, and DenseNet.

```
from tensorflow.keras.applications import VGG19
from tensorflow.keras.applications import ResNet50
from tensorflow.keras.applications import InceptionV3
from tensorflow.keras.applications import InceptionResNetV2
```

```
from tensorflow.keras.applications import DenseNet121
from tensorflow.keras.applications import DenseNet169
from tensorflow.keras.applications import DenseNet201
from tensorflow.keras.applications import Xception
from tensorflow.keras.applications import NASNetLarge
from tensorflow.keras.applications import NASNetMobile
from tensorflow.keras.applications import MobileNet
```

11.1.1 Base model

By default, the TF.Keras prebuilt models are complete but untrained, meaning the weights and biases are randomly initialized. Each untrained prebuilt CNN model is configured for a specific input shape (see the documentation), and number of output classes. In most cases, the input shape is either (224, 224, 3) or (299, 299, 3). The models will also take input in channel-first format, as in (3, 224, 224) and (3, 299, 299). The number of output classes is typically 1000, meaning the models can identify 1000 common image labels. These prebuilt but untrained models won't be that useful to you as-is, since you would have to fully train them on a dataset with the same number of labels (1000). It's important to know what's in these prebuilt models, so you can reconfigure with either pretrained weights, new task components, or both. We will cover all three of these subsequent reconfigurations throughout this chapter.

Figure 11.1 depicts the architecture of a prebuilt CNN model. The architecture consists of the stem convolutional group preset for an input shape, one for more convolutional groups (learner), the bottleneck layer, and the classifier layer preset for 1000 classes.

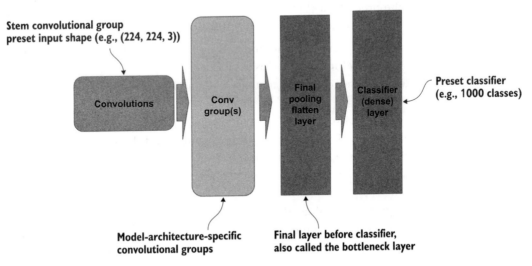

Figure 11.1 A prebuilt CNN model architecture with the layers of the task group in dark gray

The prebuilt models do not have an assigned loss function and optimizer. Prior to using them, we must issue the compile() method to assign the loss, optimizer, and performance measurements. In the following code example, we first import and then instantiate a ResNet50 prebuilt model, and then we compile the model:

**Gets a complete and untrained
prebuilt ResNet50 model**

```
from tensorflow.keras.applications import ResNet50

model = ResNet50()

model.compile(loss='categorical_crossentropy', optimizer='adam',
              metrics=['accuracy'])
```

**Compiles the model for
training as a classifier
for a dataset**

Using the prebuilt models in this manner is pretty limited, considering not only is the input size fixed, but so is the number of categories for the classifier, which is 1000. It's unlikely whatever you need to do will use the default configuration. Next we will explore ways to configure the prebuilt models to perform various tasks.

11.1.2 *Pretrained ImageNet models for prediction*

All of the prebuilt models come with weights and biases pretrained from the *ImageNet 2012* dataset, which contains 1.2 million images across 1000 classes. If your need is simply to predict whether an image is within the 1000 classes of the ImageNet dataset, you can use the pretrained prebuilt models as is. The mapping of label identifiers to class names can be found on GitHub (https://gist.github.com/yrevar/942d3a0 ac09ec9e5eb3a). Examples of classes include things like bald eagle, toilet paper, strawberry, and balloon.

Let's use the prebuilt ResNet model, pretrained with ImageNet weights, to classify (or predict) an image of an elephant. Here's the process, step by step:

1 The `preprocess_input()` method will preprocess the image according to the method used by the prebuilt ResNet model.
2 The `decode_predictions()` method will map label identifiers back to the class name.
3 The prebuilt ResNet model is instantiated with ImageNet weights.
4 An image of an elephant is read in by OpenCV and then resized to (224, 224) to fit the input shape of the model.
5 The image is then preprocessed using the model's `preprocessed_input()` method.
6 The image is then reshaped into a batch.
7 The image is then classified by the model by using the `predict()` method.
8 The top three predicted labels are then mapped to their class names by using `decode_predictions()` and printed. In this example, we might see African Elephant as the top prediction.

Figure 11.2 depicts a TF.Keras pretrained model with its accompanying preprocessing input and post-processing output functions.

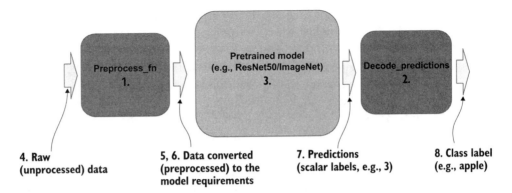

4. Raw (unprocessed) data

5, 6. Data converted (preprocessed) to the model requirements

7. Predictions (scalar labels, e.g., 3)

8. Class label (e.g., apple)

Figure 11.2 TF.Keras pretrained model with accompanying model-specific functions for preprocessing the input and post-processing the output

Now let's see how to code this process:

Gets a ResNet50 model, pretrained on ImageNet

```
from tensorflow.keras.applications import ResNet50
from tensorflow.keras.applications.resnet import preprocess_input,
                                                 decode_predictions

model = ResNet50(weights='imagenet')

image = cv2.imread('elephant.jpg', cv2.IMREAD_COLOR)

image = cv2.resize(image, (224, 224), cv2.INTER_LINEAR)

image = preprocess_input(image)

image = image.reshape((-1, 224, 224, 3))

predictions = model.predict(image)

print(decode_predictions(predictions, top=3))
```

Reads the image to predict into memory as a NumPy array

Resizes the image to fit the input shape of the pretrained model

Preprocesses the image using the same image processing used by the pretrained model

Reshapes from single image shape (224, 224, 3) to a batch of one image (1, 224, 224, 3) for the predict() method

Displays the class name based on the predicted label using the decode function for the pretrained model

Calls the predict() method to classify the image

11.1.3 New classifier

The final classifier layer in all the prebuilt models can be removed and replaced with a new classifier—as well as another task, such as a regressor. The new classifier can then be used to train the prebuilt model for a new dataset and set of classes. For example, if you had a dataset of 20 classes of noodle dishes, you would simply remove the existing classifier layer, replace it with a new 20-node classifier layer, compile the model, and train it with the noodle dishes dataset.

In all the prebuilt models, the classifier layer is referred to as the *top layer*. For TF.Keras prebuilt models, the input shape defaults to (224, 224, 3), and the number of classes in the output layer is 1000. When instantiating an instance of a TF.Keras prebuilt model, you would set the parameter `include_top` to `False` to get a model instance without the classifier layer. Additionally, when `include_top=False`, we can specify a different input shape of the model with the parameter `input_shape`.

Let's now describe this process and its uses in the context of our 20-noodle dish classifier. Let's say you own a noodle restaurant, and the cooking staff continuously places various freshly cooked noodle dishes on an ordering counter. A customer can pick any dish and, for simplicity's sake, let's say that all noodle dishes have the same price. The cashier simply needs to count the number of noodle dishes. But you still have some kinks to work out. Sometimes your cooking staff prepares too many of one or more dishes, and they go cold and have to be tossed out, so you have lost revenue. Other times, your cooking staff prepares too few of one or more dishes, and customers go to another restaurant because their dish was not available—a case of loss opportunity.

To solve both problems, you plan to place one camera at the checkout and another camera on the cooking area where the cold noodle dishes are tossed out. You want the cameras to classify both the noodle dishes purchased and those tossed out in real time, and display that information to the cooking staff so they can better estimate which dishes to prepare.

Let's start implementing your plan. First, since you're an existing noodle restaurant, you hire someone to take pictures of the dishes that are placed on the ordering counter. When a picture is taken, the chef shouts the name of the dish, which is recorded with the picture. Let's say at the end of a business day, your volume is 500 noodle dishes. And let's say you have a fairly even distribution of dishes, which would give you an average of 25 pictures per noodle dish. That might seem like a small number per class, but since they are your dishes and the backgrounds are always the same, it's probably enough. Now you just need to label the pictures from the audio recordings.

Now you're ready for training. You get a prebuilt model from TF.Keras and specify `include_top=False` to drop the 1000-class classifier dense layer—which you will subsequently replace with a 20-node dense layer. You want your model to predict fast because you move a lot of noodle dishes, so you want to reduce the number of parameters without a negative effect on the model's accuracy. Instead of predicting from the ImageNet size of (224, 224, 3), you specify `input_shape=(100, 100, 3)` to change the input vector for the model to size (100, 100, 3).

We could also drop the final flattening/pooling layer (the bottleneck layer) in the prebuilt model, to replace with your own by setting the parameter `pooling=None`.

Figure 11.3 depicts a reconfigurable prebuilt CNN model architecture. It consists of a stem convolutional group whose input size is configurable, one or more convolutional groups (learner), and optionally a configurable bottleneck layer.

As for the input shape, the documentation for the prebuilt models has a limitation on the minimum input shape size. For most models, this is (32, 32, 3). I generally don't advise using the prebuilt models in this manner, because for most of these architectures, the final feature maps before the global average pooling layer (bottleneck layer) will be 1×1 (single-pixel) feature maps—essentially losing all spatial relationships. However,

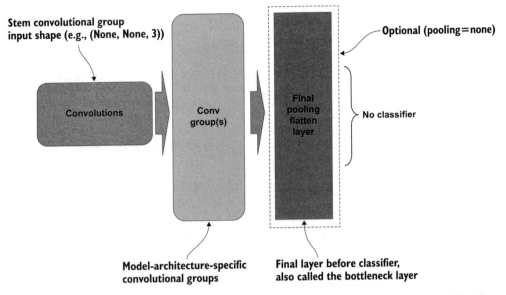

Figure 11.3 In this reconfigurable prebuilt model architecture without the classifier layer, retaining the pooling layers is optional.

researchers have found that when used with CIFAR-10 and CIFAR-100, which are (32, 32, 3) images, they are able to find good hyperparameter settings before advancing to competition-grade (such as ImageNet) image datasets (224, 224, 3).

In the following code, we instantiate a prebuilt ResNet50 model and replace it with a new classifier for our 20-noodle dish example:

1 We remove the existing 1000-node classifier with the parameter `include_top=False`.

2 We set the input shape to (100, 100, 3) with the parameter `input_shape` for our smaller input size.

3 We decide to retain the final pooling/flattening layer (bottleneck layer) as a global average pooling layer with the parameter pooling.

4 We add back a replacement dense layer with 20 nodes, corresponding to the number of noodle dishes, and a softmax activation function as the top layer.
   – The last (output) layer in the prebuilt ResNet50 model is `model.output`. This corresponds to the bottleneck layer, since we dropped the default classifier.
   – We bind the prebuilt ResNet50 `model.output` as the input to our replacement dense layer.

5 We build the model. The input is the input to the ResNet model, which is `models.input`.

6 Finally, we compile the model for training, and set the loss function to `categorical_crossentropy` and the optimizer to `adam`, as best practices for an image-classification model.

```
from tensorflow.keras.applications import ResNet50
from tensorflow.keras.layers import Dense

model = ResNet50(include_top=False, input_shape=(100, 100, 3), pooling='avg')
outputs = Dense(20, activation='softmax')(model.output)
model = Model(model.input, outputs)

model.compile(loss='categorical_crossentropy', optimizer='adam',
              metrics=['accuracy'])
```

Gets a prebuilt model for input shape (100,100,3) and without the final classifier

Adds a classifier for 20 classes

Compiles the model for training

For most of the TF.Keras prebuilt models, the bottleneck layer is a global average pooling layer. This layer acts as both a final pooling layer for the feature maps and a flatten operation that converts the feature maps to a 1D vector. In some cases, we might want to replace this layer with our own custom final pooling/flatten layer. In this case, we either specify the parameter `pooling=None` or don't specify it, which is the default setting. So why might we do this?

To answer this question, let's go back to our noodle dishes. Let's assume when you trained the model, you got 92% accuracy and want to do better. First, you decide to add in image augmentation. Well, we probably won't bother with horizontal flip, since the noodle dish will never be seen upside down! Likewise, vertical flip probably won't help since the bowl of noodles is fairly uniform (no mirror). We can skip rotation, since the bowl of noodles is fairly uniform, and we skip scaling since the position of the camera to the dishes is fixed. Hmm, so you ask, what's left?

How about shifting the location of the bowl, since bowls will shift around both at the checkout and toss-out counters? You do this and get 94% accuracy. But you want even more accuracy. On a hunch, we speculate that perhaps there isn't enough retained in the feature information, when each final feature map is reduced to a single pixel for flattening into a 1D vector by the default pooling of `GlobalAveragePooling2D`. You look at your model summary and see the size of the final feature maps is 4 × 4. So you decide to drop the default pooling, and replace it with `MaxPooling2D` with stride of 2, so each feature map will be reduced to 2 × 2, 4 pixels versus a single pixel, and then do a flattening into a 1D vector.

In this code example, we replace the bottleneck layer with a max pooling (`outputs = MaxPooling2D(model.ouputs)`) and flattening (`outputs = Flatten(outputs)`), for our 20-noodle dish classifier:

```
from tensorflow.keras.applications import ResNet50
from tensorflow.keras.layers import Dense, Flatten
from tensorflow.keras import Model

model = ResNet50(include_top=False, input_shape=(100, 100, 3), pooling=None)

outputs = MaxPooling2D(model.output)
outputs = Flatten()(ouputs)
```

Gets a prebuilt model for input shape (100,100,3) and without the classifier group

Pools and flattens the feature maps into a 1D vector

```
outputs = Dense(20, activation='softmax')(outputs)        ◁──┐  Adds a classifier
                                                             │  for 20 classes
model = Model(model.input, outputs)
model.compile(loss='categorical_crossentropy', optimizer='adam',
              metrics=['accuracy'])
```

In this section, we covered both prebuilt and pretrained models from TF.Keras. To summarize, a prebuilt model is an existing model, generally based on a SOTA architecture, whose input shape and task group are reconfigurable, and the weights are not trained. A prebuilt model is typically used for training a model from scratch, and has the advantage of reuse and can be reconfigured to suit your dataset and task. The drawback is that the architecture might not be tuned to your dataset/task, so you end up with a model that is less efficient in size as well as less accurate.

A pretrained model is essentially the same, except the weights have been pretrained with another dataset, such as from the ImageNet dataset. Pretrained models are used for either out-of-the-box predicting or transfer learning, and have the advantage of representational learning reuse to train new datasets/tasks faster and with less data. The drawback is that the pretrained representational learning may not be well suited for the domain of your dataset/task.

In the next section, we cover the same concepts using prebuilt models from the TensorFlow Hub repository.

11.2 TF Hub prebuilt models

TensorFlow Hub, or *TF Hub*, is an open source public repository of both prebuilt and pretrained models, and vastly more extensive than TF.Keras. TF.Keras prebuilt/pretrained models are good for learning and practicing transfer learning, but are too limited in offerings for production purposes. TF Hub consists of a substantially greater number of prebuilt SOTA architectures, an extensive category of tasks, pretrained weights specific to domains, and public submissions beyond the models provided directly by the TensorFlow organization.

This section covers the prebuilt models for image classification. TF Hub provides two versions of each model, which are described as follows:

- Modules to do image classification with the particular classes that the module has been trained for. This process is the same as for the pretrained models.
- Modules to extract image feature vectors (bottleneck values) for use in custom image classifiers. These classifiers are the same as the new classifier we described for TF.Keras.

We will be working with two prebuilt models, one that does out-of-the-box classification, and one that does transfer learning. We will download these from the TensorFlow Hub open source repository of prebuilt models, which is located www.tensorflow.org/hub.

To use TF Hub, you will need to first install the `tensorflow_hub` Python module:

```
pip install tensorflow_hub
```

In your Python script, you access the TF Hub by importing the `tensorflow_hub` module:

```
import tensorflow_hub as hub
```

You are now set up to download our two models.

11.2.1 Using TF Hub pretrained models

TF Hub is also very versatile, when compared to TF.Keras, for the model format types that you can load:

- *TF2.x SavedModel*—Use as a local, REST, or microservice on cloud, desktop/laptop, or workstation.
- *TF Lite*—Use as an application service on a mobile or memory-constrained IoT device.
- *TF.js*—Use within a client-side browser application.
- *Coral*—Optimized to use as an application service on a Coral Edge/IoT device.

We will cover only TF 2.x SavedFormat models in this section. To load a model, you will do the following:

1. Get the URL to the image classifier model in the TF Hub repository.
2. Retrieve the model data from the repository specified by the URL with `hub.KerasLayer()`.
3. Construct a TF.Keras SavedModel from the model data by using the TF.Keras sequential API.
4. Specify the input shape to (224, 224, 3), which matches the input shape the pre-trained model was trained on for the ImageNet database.

Location of model data for
ResNet50 v2 in TF Hub repository

```
model_url = "https://tfhub.dev/google/imagenet/resnet_v2_50/classification/4"

model = tf.keras.Sequential([hub.KerasLayer(model_url,
                             input_shape=(224,224,3))])
```

Retrieves model data and
constructs a SavedModel
format model

When you do a `model.summary()`, the output will appear as follows:

```
Layer (type)                   Output Shape              Param #
=================================================================
keras_layer_7 (KerasLayer)     (None, 1001)              25615849
=================================================================
Total params: 25,615,849
Trainable params: 0
Non-trainable params: 25,615,849
```

Now you can use the model to do predictions, which is known as *inference*. Figure 11.4 depicts the following steps to use a TF Hub ImageNet pretrained model for prediction:

1 Get the label (class names) information for ImageNet so we can convert the predicted label (numeric index) to the class name.
2 Preprocess the images to predict the following:
   – Resize the image input to match the input of the model: (224, 224, 3).
   – Normalize the image data: divide by 255.
3 Invoke predict() for the images.
4 Use np.argmax() to return the label index of the highest probability.
5 Convert the predicted label index to the corresponding class name.

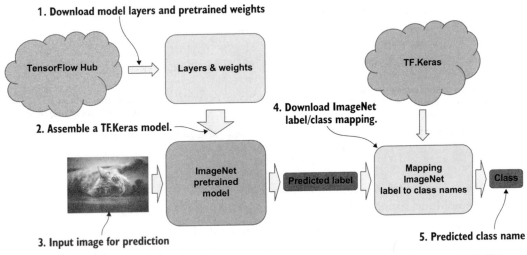

Figure 11.4 Using an ImageNet pretrained model from TF Hub to predict a label, and then using ImageNet mapping to show predicted class name

Here is an example implementation of these five steps.

> Gets the conversion from ImageNet label index to class names

```
path = tf.keras.utils.get_file('ImageNetLabels.txt',
'https://storage.googleapis.com/download.tensorflow.org/data/
ImageNetLabels.txt')
imagenet_labels = np.array(open(path).read().splitlines())
```

```
import cv2
import numpy as np
data = cv2.imread('apple.png')
data = cv2.resize(data, (224, 224))
data = (data / 255.0).astype(np.float32)
```
> Preprocesses an image for prediction

```
p = model.predict(np.asarray([data]))
y = np.argmax(p)
```
> Makes prediction with the model

```
print(imagenet_labels[y])
```
⟵ **Converts predicted label index to class name**

11.2.2 New classifier

For building new classifiers for pretrained models, we load the corresponding model URL denoted as the *feature vector* version of the model. This version loads the pretrained model without the model top, or classifier. This allows you to add your own top, or task group. The output from the model is the output layer. We can also specify a new input shape that is different from the default input shape of the TF Hub model.

The following is an example implementation of loading a feature vector version of a pretrained ResNet50 v2 model, where we will add our own task component for training a CIFAR-10 model. Since our input size for CIFAR-10 is different from TF Hub's version for ResNet50 v2, which is (224, 224, 3), we will also optionally specify the input shape:

1 Get the URL to the image classifier model in the TF Hub repository.
2 Use hub.KerasLayer() to retrieve the model data from the repository specified by the URL.
3 Specify a new input shape of (32, 32, 3) for the CIFAR-10 dataset.

Location of the feature vector version model data for ResNet50 v2 in the TF Hub repository

Retrieves model data as a TF.Keras layer and sets the input shape

```
f_url = "https://tfhub.dev/google/imagenet/resnet_v2_50/feature_vector/4"

f_layer = hub.KerasLayer(f_url, input_shape=(32,32,3))
```

Here is an example implementation of constructing a new classifier for CIFAR-10 in SavedModel format:

1 Create a SavedModel using the sequential API.
  - Specify the feature vector version of the pretrained ResNet v2 as the model bottom.
  - Specify a dense layer of 10 nodes (one per CIFAR-10 class) as the model top.
2 Compile the model.

```
model = tf.keras.Sequential([
                    f_layer,
                    Dense(10, activation='softmax')
                    ])
model.compile(loss='sparse_categorical_crossentropy', optimizer='adam',
          metrics=['acc'])
```

When you do a model.summary(), the output will appear as follows:

Layer (type)	Output Shape	Param #
keras_layer_4 (KerasLayer)	(None, 2048)	23561152
dense_2 (Dense)	(None, 10)	20490

```
Total params: 23,581,642
Trainable params: 20,490
Non-trainable params: 23,561,152
```

So far, we've covered using pretrained models for doing out-of-the-box prediction and using reconfigurable prebuilt models for more convenient training of new models. Next, we will cover how to use and reconfigure pretrained models for more efficient training and using less data for new tasks.

11.3 *Transfer learning between domains*

In transfer learning, we use pretrained models for one task and retrain the classifier and/or fine-tune layers for a new task. This process is similar to what we just did with building the new classifier onto a prebuilt model, but otherwise fully trained the model from scratch.

Transfer learning has two general approaches:

- *Similar tasks*—The pretrained dataset and new dataset are from similar domains (such as fruits to vegetables).
- *Distinct tasks*—The pretrained dataset and new dataset are from dissimilar domains (such as fruits and trucks/vans).

11.3.1 *Similar tasks*

As discussed earlier in this chapter, when deciding on the approach, we look at the similarity of the source (pretrained) domain of images and the destination (new) domain. The more similar, the more of the existing bottom layers we can reuse without retraining. For example, if we had a model trained on fruits, it's likely that all of the bottom layers of the pretrained model can be reused without retraining for building a new model to recognize vegetables.

We are assuming that the coarse and detailed features learned at the bottom layers will be the same for the new classifier, and can be reused as is, prior to entering the topmost layer(s) for classification. Let's consider reasons we could speculate that fruits and vegetables are from very similar domains. Both are natural food. While fruits generally grow above ground and vegetables below ground, they have similar physical characteristics in shape and texture, and adornments such as stems and leaves.

When the source and destination domains have this high level of similarity, we generally can replace the existing topmost classifier layer with a new classifier layer, freeze the lower layers, and train only the classifier layer. Since we don't need to learn the weights/biases for the other layers, we can generally train a model for the new domain with substantially less data and fewer epochs.

While having more data is always better, transfer learning between similar source and destination domains provides the ability to train with substantially smaller datasets. The two best practices for the minimum size of the dataset are as follows:

- Each class (label) is 10% as big as in the source dataset.
- Each class (label) has at least 100 images.

In contrast to the method shown for the *new classifier*, we modify the code to freeze all the layers preceding the topmost classifier layer prior to training. Freezing prevents the weights/biases of these layer(s) from being updated (retrained) during training of the classifier (topmost) layer. In TF.Keras, each layer has the property `trainable`, which defaults to `True`.

Figure 11.5 depicts the retraining on the classifier layer of a pretrained model; here are the steps:

1. Use a prebuilt model with pretrained weights/biases (ImageNet 2012),
2. Drop the existing classifier from the prebuilt model (topmost layer).
3. Freeze the remaining layers.
4. Add a new classifier layer.
5. Train the model through transfer learning.

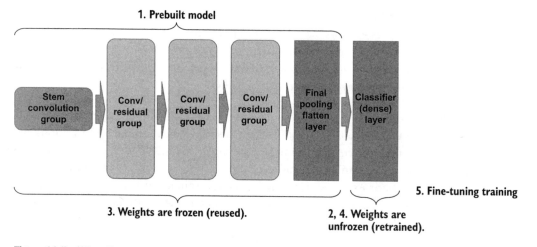

Figure 11.5 When the source and destination domains are similar, only the classifier weights are retrained, while the remaining model bottom weights are frozen.

Here is an example implementation:

```
from tensorflow.keras.applications import ResNet50
from tensorflow.keras.layers import Dense
from tensorflow.keras import Model

model = ResNet50(include_top=False, pooling='avg', weights='imagenet')

for layer in model.layers:
    layer.trainable = False

output = Dense(20, activation='softmax')(model.output)

model = Model(model.input, output)
model.compile(loss='categorical_crossentropy', optimizer='adam',
              metrics=['accuracy'])
```

Gets a pretrained model without the classifier and retains the global average pooling layer

Freezes the weights of the remaining layer

Adds a classifier for 20 classes

Compiles the model for training

Note that in this code example, we retained the original input shape (224, 224, 3). In practice, if we change the input shape, the preexisting trained weights/biases won't match the resolution of the feature extraction they were trained on. In this case, it's better to handle this as a distinct task case.

11.3.2 Distinct tasks

When the source and destination domain of the image datasets are dissimilar, such as our example of fruits and trucks/vans, we start with the same steps as in the previous similar task approach, but then follow up with fine-tuning the bottom layers. The steps, depicted in figure 11.6, generally are as follows:

1. Add a new classifier layer and freeze the remaining bottom layers.
2. Train the new classifier layer for the target number of epochs.
3. Repeat for fine-tuning:
   - Unfreeze the next bottom-most convolutional group (moving in the direction of top to bottom).
   - Train for a few epochs to fine-tune.
4. After the convolutional groups are fine-tuned:
   - Unfreeze the convolutional stem group.
   - Train for a few epochs to fine-tune.

In Figure 11.6, you can see the training cycles of steps 2 through 4: the classifier is retrained in cycle 1, the convolutional groups are fine-tuned in sequential order in cycles 2 through 4, and the stem is fine-tuned in cycle 5. Note that this is different from when the source and destination domains are similar and we fine-tune only the classifier.

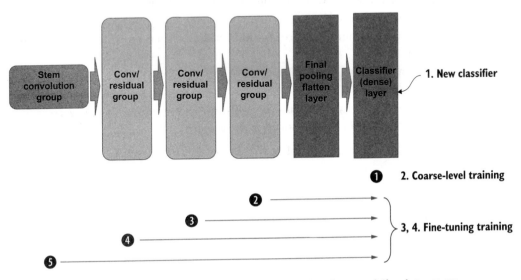

Figure 11.6 In this distinct source-to-destination transfer learning, the convolutional groups are progressively fine-tuned.

The following is an example implementation that demonstrates a coarse training for the new classifier level (cycle 1), followed by fine-tuning of each convolutional group (cycles 2 through 4), and finally the stem convolutional group (cycle 5). The steps are as follows:

1 The layers in the model bottom are frozen (`layer.trainable = False`).
2 A classifier layer for 20 classes is added as the model top.
3 The classifier layer is trained with 50 epochs:

```
from tensorflow.keras.applications import ResNet50
from tensorflow.keras.layers import Dense
from tensorflow.keras import Model

model = ResNet50(include_top=False, pooling='avg', weights='imagenet')

for layer in model.layers:        ◁── Freezes the weights of
    layer.trainable = False          all the pretrained layers

                                                              Adds a new
output = Dense(20, activation='softmax')(model.output)  ◁── untrained classifier

model = Model(model.input, output)
model.compile(loss='categorical_crossentropy', optimizer='adam',
              metrics=['accuracy'])              ◁──
                                        Compiles the model for training
model.fit(x_data, y_data, batch_size=32, epochs=50, validation_split=0.2)
Coarse level trains the new classifier
```

After the classifier is trained, the model is fine-tuned (cycles 2 through 4):

1 Traverse the layers from bottom to top, identifying the stem convolution and the end of each ResNet group, which is detected by an `Add()` layer.
2 For each convolutional group, build a list of each convolutional layer in the group.
3 Build a list of the groups in reverse order (`groups.insert(0, conv2d)`): top to bottom.
4 Traverse the convolutional groups from top to bottom and progressively train the groups, and predecessors, for five epochs.

The following is an example implementation of these four steps.

```
stem = None
groups = []
conv2d = []

first_conv2d = True
for layer in model.layers:
```

```
        if type(layer) == layers.convolutional.Conv2D:
          if first_conv2d == True:
              stem = layer
              first_conv2d = False
          else:
              conv2d.append(layer)
        elif type(layer) == layers.merge.Add:
              groups.insert(0, conv2d)
              conv2d = []

    for i in range(1, len(groups)):
        for layer in groups[i]:
            layer.trainable = True

    model.compile(loss='categorical_crossentropy', optimizer='adam',
                  metrics=['accuracy'])

    model.fit(x_data, y_data, batch_size=32, epochs=5)
```

In ResNet50, the first Conv2D is the stem convolutional layer.

Keeps list of convolutional layers per convolutional group

Maintains list in reverse order (topmost conv group is top of list)

Each convolutional group in residual networks ends with an Add() layer.

Unfreezes a convolutional group at a time (from top to bottom)

Fine-tunes (trains) that layer

Finally, the stem convolutional, and hence the whole model, is trained for an additional five epochs (cycle 5). Here is an example implementation of this last step:

```
stem.trainable = True
model.compile(loss='categorical_crossentropy', optimizer='adam',
              metrics=['accuracy'])
model.fit(x_data, y_data, batch_size=32, epochs=5, validation_split=0.2)
```

Unfreezes the stem convolutional

Does a final fine-tuning

In this example, when unfreezing layers for fine-tuning, the model must be recompiled prior to issuing the next training session.

11.3.3 Domain-specific weights

In the previous examples for transfer learning, we initialized the frozen layers of the model with weights learned from the ImageNet 2012 dataset. But let's say you want to use pretrained weights from a specific domain other than ImageNet 2012, as in our example of fruits.

For instance, if you're building a domain transfer model for plants, you may want images of trees, shrubs, flowers, weeds, leaves, branches, fruits, vegetables, and seeds. But we don't need every possible plant type—just enough to learn essential features and feature extraction that can be generalized to more specific and comprehensive plant domains. You might also consider the background you want to generalize to. For example, the destination domain might be houseplants, and so you have home interior backgrounds, or it might be produce, so you want a shelf background. You should have a certain number of these backgrounds in the source domain, so the source model has learned to filter them out from the latent space.

In the next code example, we first train a ResNet50 prebuilt architecture for a specific domain; in this case, fruit produce. We then use the pretrained, domain-specific weights and initialization to train another ResNet50 model in a similar domain, such as vegetables.

Figure 11.7 depicts transferring domain-specific weights and fine-tuning a retraining from fruits to a similar domain, vegetables, as follows:

1   Instantiate an uninitialized ResNet50 model without the classifier and pooling layer, which we designate as the base model.
2   Save the base model architecture for later reuse in transfer learning (`produce-model`).
3   Add a classifier (`Flatten` and `Dense` layers) and train for a specific (source) domain (for example, produce).
4   Save the weights for the trained model (`produce-weights`).
5   Load the base model architecture (`model-produce`), which does not contain the classifier layer.
6   Initialize the base model architecture with the pretrained weights for the source domain (`model-produce`).
7   Add a classifier for the new similar domain.
8   Train the model/classifier for the new similar domain.

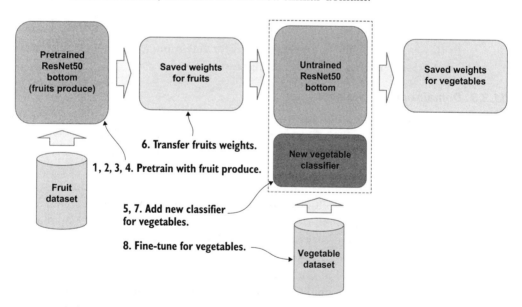

Figure 11.7   Transfer learning between a pretrained model of a domain similar to a source domain

Here is an example implementation for transferring the domain-specific weights for fruit for transfer learning to the similar domain of vegetables:

```
from tensorflow.keras.applications import ResNet50
from tensorflow.keras import Model
from tensorflow.keras.layers import Dense, Flatten
from tensorflow.keras.models import load_model

model = ResNet50(include_top=False, pooling=None, input_shape=(100, 100, 3))

model.save('produce-model')    <──── Saves the base model

output = Flatten(name='bottleneck')(model.output)    │ Adds the classifier
output = Dense(20, activation='softmax')(output)      │


model.save_weights('produce-weights')    <──── Saves the trained model weights

model = load_model('produce-model')      │ Trains the model
model.load_weights('produce-weights')    │

output = Flatten(name='bottleneck')(model.output)    │ Reuses the base model
output = Dense(20, activation='softmax')(output)      │ and trained weights

model = Model(model.input, output)    <──┐ Adds a classifier
model.compile(loss='categorical_crossentropy', optimizer='adam',
              metrics=['accuracy'])
```
Compiles and trains the new model for new dataset

11.3.4 Domain transfer weight initialization

Another form of transfer learning is the transfer of domain-specific weights to use as weight initialization in a model we will otherwise fully retrain. In this case, we are trying to improve on using an initializer based on a random weight distribution algorithm (for example, He-normal for ReLU activation functions) versus using the lottery hypothesis or numerical stabilization. Let's look again at our produce example and assume we have fully trained a model for a dataset instance, such as fruits. Instead of transferring weights from a fully trained instance of the model, we use an earlier checkpoint where we have established numerical stability. We will reuse this earlier checkpoint as the initializer for full retraining of a domain-similar dataset, such as vegetables.

Transferring domain-specific weights is a one-shot weight initialization approach. The presumption is to generate a set of weight initializations that is generalized enough that model training will lead to the best local (or global) optimum. Ideally, during initial training, the weights of the model will do the following:

- Point in the general right direction for convergence
- Be overgeneralized to prevent diving into an arbitrary local optimum
- Be used as the initialization weights for a single (one-shot initialization) training session that will converge on the best local optimum

Figure 11.8 depicts domain transfer for weight initialization.

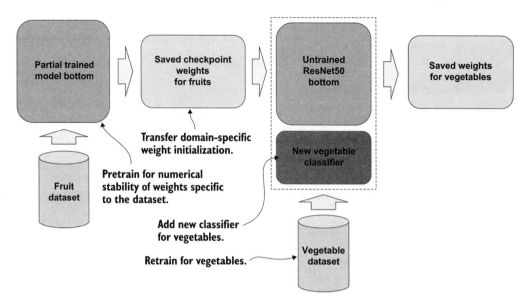

Figure 11.8   Using earlier checkpoints from a similar domain as the weight initialization for full retraining of new mode

The pretraining steps for this form of weight initialization are as follows:

1   Instantiate a ResNet50 model, with a random weight distribution (for example, Xavier or He-normal).
2   Use a high level of regularization (l2(0.001) to prevent fitting to the data and small learning rate.
3   Run a few epochs (not shown).
4   Save the weights with the model method save_weights().

```
from tensorflow.keras.regularizers import l2

model = ResNet50(include_top=False, pooling='avg', input_shape=(100, 100, 3))

model.save('base_model')

output = layers.Dropout(0.75)(model.output)
output = layers.Dense(20, activation='softmax',
                      kernel_regularizer=l2(0.001))(output)
model   = Model(model.input, output)

model.save_weights('weights-init')
```

Instantiates base model with default weight initialization (He-normal)

Saves the model

Saves the model and weights after pretraining

Adds a dropout layer and classifier to the base ResNet model and uses an aggressive level of regularization

In the next code example, we then start a full training session using the saved pre-trained weights. First we load the uninitialized base model (base_model), which does not include the topmost layer. Then we load into the model the saved pretrained weights (weights-init). Next, we add a new topmost layer that is a dense layer with 20 nodes for 20 classes. We build the new model, compile, and then start the full training.

```
model = load_model('base_model')    ◁─┐ Reloads the
                                         base model        Initializes the weights
                                                           using domain transfer
model.load_weights('weights-init')               ◁────────┘ weight initialization

output = Dense(20, activation='softmax')(model.output)  ◁──┐ Adds classifier
                                                             without dropout
model = Model(model.input, output)
model.compile(loss='categorical_crossentropy', optimizer='adam',
              metrics=['accuracy'])
```
Compiles and trains the new model

11.3.5 Negative transfer

In some cases, we will find that transfer learning results in lower accuracy than training from scratch: when using a pretrained model to train a new model, the overall accuracy during training is less than what it would be if the model was not pretrained. This is referred to as *negative transfer*.

In this case, the source and destination domains are so distinct that the learned weights for the source domain cannot be reused on the destination domain. Additionally, when the weights are reused, the model will not converge, and quite possibly will diverge. In general, we can usually spot negative transfer within five to ten epochs.

11.4 Beyond computer vision

The methods for transfer learning discussed in this chapter for computer vision are applicable to NLU models. Except for some terminology, the process is the same. Removing the top is sometimes referred to as *removing the head* on NLU models.

In both cases, you're removing all or a portion of the task component and replacing it with a new task. What you are relying on is like the latent space in computer vision; the intermediate representation has the essential context (features) for learning a new task. Methods for similar tasks and distinct tasks are the same for computer vision and NLU.

The same is *not* true for structured data, however. Actually, transfer learning is not possible with pretrained models across domains (datasets). You can learn a different type of task (for instance, regression versus classification) on the same dataset, but you can't reuse the learned weights across different datasets that have different features. There is no concept—at least not yet—of a latent space that has essential features that are reusable across datasets with different fields (columns).

Summary

- Prebuilt and pretrained models from TF.Keras and TF Hub model repositories can be used for either reuse as-is for prediction or for transfer learning a new classifier.

- The classifier group of a pretrained model can be replaced, either generalized or with a similar domain, and retrained for a new domain with less training time and smaller size dataset.

- In transfer learning, if the new domain is similar to the previous trained domain, you freeze all the layers except the new task layer and do fine-tuned training.

- In transfer learning, if the new domain is dissimilar to the previous trained domain, you sequentially freeze and unfreeze layers as you retrain, starting from the bottom of the model and moving toward the top.

- In domain transfer weights, you use the weights of the trained model as the initial weights and fully train a new model.

Data distributions

This chapter covers

- Applying statistical principles of distributions in machine learning
- Understanding the differences between curated and uncurated datasets
- Using population, sampling, and subpopulation distributions
- Applying distribution concepts when training a model

As a data scientist and educator, I get a lot of questions from software engineers on how to improve the accuracy of a model. The five basic answers I give out to increase the accuracy of a model are as follows:

- Increase training time.
- Increase the depth (or width) of the model.
- Add regularization.
- Expand the dataset with data augmentation.
- Increase hyperparameter tuning.

These are the five most likely places to address, and often working on one or another will improve model accuracy. But it's important to understand that the limitations to accuracy ultimately lie in *the dataset used to train the model*. That's what we are going to look at here: the nuances of datasets, and how and why they affect accuracy. And by *nuances*, I mean the distribution patterns of the data.

In this chapter, we do a deep dive into the three types of data distributions: population, sampling, and subpopulation. In particular, we will look at how these distributions affect the ability of the model to accurately generalize to data in the real world. The model's accuracy, you'll see, often differs from the predictions generated by the training or evaluation dataset, a difference referred to as *serving skew and data drift*.

In the second half of the chapter, we walk through a hands-on example of applying different data distributions to the same model during training, and see the differing outcomes, during inference, on real-world serving skew and data drift.

To understand distributions and how they affect outcomes and accuracy, we need to go back to basic statistics, which you likely studied in high school or college. The term *model* was not created by AI, or by machine learning, or by any other newer development in computer technology. The term originates from statistics. As a software engineer, you're used to coding an algorithm that generally has a many-to-one relationship between the input and output. We typically refer to this as the inputs having a *linear relationship* to the output—or in other words, the output is *deterministic*.

In statistics, the output is not deterministic, but a probability distribution. Let's consider a coin toss. You cannot write an algorithm that will output the correct result of heads or tails on any single coin toss, because it is not deterministic. But you can *model* the probability distribution over a single, ten, or thousands of coin tosses.

12.1 *Distribution types*

The field of statistics deals with algorithms that are not deterministic, but whose outcome is a probability distribution. As in our coin toss example, if I toss a coin two times, the outcome is not deterministic. Instead, there is a 50% probability that one toss is heads and one is tails, and a 25% probability for both tosses being heads and both tosses being tails, respectively. These algorithms are called *models*, and they model a behavior that makes an output (or outcome) of a prediction over a probability distribution. That sure sounds like statistics, right?

In this section, we examine three of the distributions most often used in ML modeling: population, sampling, and subpopulation distributions. Our goal here is to see how each distribution affects the training of a deep learning model, especially its accuracy.

The advent of deep learning using neural networks to develop models is from the field of artificial intelligence. In recent years, the two separate fields of statistical modeling and deep learning have fused together, and we now categorize both under machine learning. But whether you are doing what I refer to as classical machine learning (statistics) or deep learning with neural networks, the limitation in what you can model or learn comes down to the dataset.

To look at these three distributions, we will use the MNIST dataset (https://keras.io/datasets/). This dataset is small enough that we can use it to demonstrate each of these concepts, as well as leave you with code samples that you can reproduce and use, to see with your own eyes why (and how) the data is the limitation.

12.1.1 Population distribution

When you make a model and it turns out to not generalize as you expected "in the wild" (in production), one of the reasons is usually that you did not understand the population distribution of what you are modeling.

Let's say you were building a model to predict the shoe size of an adult male in the United States based on physical characteristics (height, hair color, and so forth). The population distribution of this model would be *all* adult males in the United States. Let me emphasize *all*. When we say a *population distribution*, it has every single example in the population—the whole population. With a population distribution, we would know the complete distribution of shoe sizes and the corresponding features (height, hair color, and so forth).

The problem, of course, is that you won't have data for all adult males in the United States. Instead, you will have a subset of data: we take batches of the data at random (which we call a *random sample*) to determine a distribution within the batch that you hope comes close to matching the distribution of the overall population.

Figure 12.1 depicts random sampling within a population distribution. The outer circle, labeled *Population*, represents all examples in the population, such as in our example for shoe size of all adult males in the United States. The inner circle, labeled *Random Sample*, represents a randomly chosen subset of examples, such as a random chosen number of adult males in the United States. For the population distribution, we know things like the exact size (number of adult males), the mean (average shoe size), and standard deviation (percentage of different sizes). These are referred to in

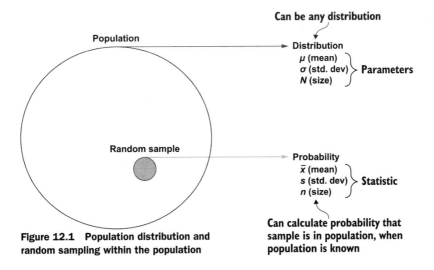

Figure 12.1 Population distribution and random sampling within the population

statistics as the *parameters* of the population, which is a deterministic distribution. Assuming we don't have the population distribution, we want to use the random sample to estimate the parameters—which is called the *statistic*. The larger and more random the sample, the more likely our estimate will be closer to the parameters.

12.1.2 *Sampling distribution*

The goal with a sampling distribution is to have enough random samples of the population so that, collectively, the distributions within these samples can be used to predict the distribution within the population as a whole, and thus we can generalize a model to a population. The keyword here is *predict*, meaning we are determining a probabilistic distribution from the samples versus a deterministic distribution from the population.

Let's take our shoe size example. If we had just one example, we probably could not adequately model the parameters of the distribution. But if we had a thousand examples, perhaps we could substantially increase our ability to model the parameters. But wait, what if those thousand were not really random—say they were collected from purchases at a professional athletic shoe store. Those examples would likely be biased to certain characteristics (features) of the nonrandom examples. So the examples in the sampling distribution need to be randomly selected.

Figure 12.2 depicts a sampling distribution of a population. A *sampling distribution* consists of a collection of examples that have been randomly selected and are gener-

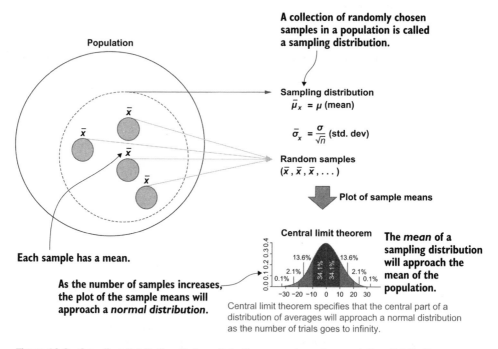

Figure 12.2   Sampling distribution that predicts the parameters of a population distribution

ally the same size. For example, we might have hired different survey companies to collect our shoe size data, with each using its own selection criteria. Each company collects the data on a hundred random examples, based on its selection criteria.

We can presume that each of these separate random samples is a weak predictor of the parameters of the population. Instead, we treat them as an ensemble. For example, if we take the average of each random sample mean, given enough random samples of enough size, we can more strongly predict the mean of the population.

In general, the dataset you use to train a model is a sampling distribution, and the larger the sample size and the more random the examples, the more likely your model will generalize to the parameters of the population.

12.1.3 *Subpopulation distribution*

You need to understand that regardless of how large and comprehensive your dataset is, it is likely a sampling distribution of a subpopulation and not the population. A *subpopulation* is a subset of a population that is defined by a set of characteristics and that would not have the same probability distribution as the population. As in our earlier adult male shoe example, let's assume our samples are all from a chain of stores that specialize in selling sports shoes to professional athletes. With sufficient samples, we can develop a sampling distribution that is representative and therefore predictive of the subpopulation of professional athletes, but it is unlikely to be representative of the entire population.

This is not the same as a bias, as long as our intent is to model that subpopulation and not the population at large. A *bias* occurs when we draw from batches of random samples but, no matter how many we draw from, the corresponding sampling distribution will not be representative of the population we are modeling—because we drew the random samples from a subpopulation. Figure 12.3 shows a subpopulation distribution.

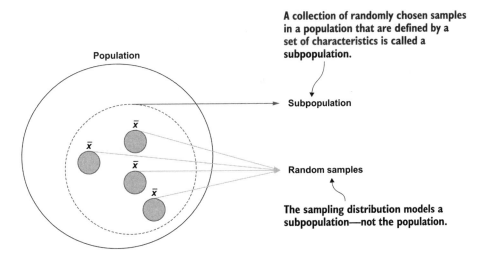

Figure 12.3 **Subpopulation distribution**

12.2 *Out of distribution*

Let's assume you've trained a model and deployed it on a dataset, but it does not generalize to what it really sees in production as well as your evaluation data. This model is possibly seeing a different distribution of examples than what the model was trained on. We refer to this as being *out of distribution*, also referred to as *serving skew*. In other words, your model was trained on a subpopulation distribution that is different from what the deployed model sees.

In this section, we will use the MNIST dataset to demonstrate how to detect out-of-distribution populations when the model is deployed. Then we'll explore approaches to improve the model to generalize to an out-of-distribution population. We first discussed the MNIST dataset in chapter 2. We will start with a brief refresher on the dataset.

12.2.1 *The MNIST curated dataset*

MNIST is a dataset of 70,000 images of handwritten digits that is proportionally balanced across each digit. It's super easy to train a model to get near 100% accuracy on the dataset (hence it's the "hello, world" example of machine learning). But almost all "in the wild" applications of the trained model will fail—because the distribution of images in MNIST is a subpopulation.

MNIST is a *curated* dataset. The data curator selected samples for inclusion whose characteristics meet a certain definition. In other words, a curated dataset is sufficiently representative of a subpopulation that it can model the parameters of that subpopulation, but otherwise may not be representative of the entire population (for example, all digits).

In the case of MNIST, each sample is a 28-×-28-pixel image, with the drawing of the digit centered in the middle. The digit is white, and the background is gray, and a padding of at least 4 pixels is around the digit. Figure 12.4 shows the layout of a MNIST image. This instance of the digit 7 is just an arbitrary random selection from the dataset, which is used for example purposes only.

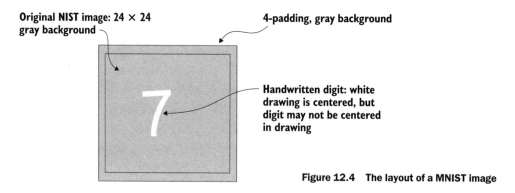

Original NIST image: 24 × 24 gray background

4-padding, gray background

Handwritten digit: white drawing is centered, but digit may not be centered in drawing

Figure 12.4   The layout of a MNIST image

12.2.2 *Setting up the environment*

Let's first do what I call *housekeeping*. The following is a code snippet we will use throughout our examples. It includes importing the TF.Keras API for designing and training models, various Python libraries we will use, and, finally, the loading of the MNIST dataset that is prebuilt into the TF.Keras API:

```
from tensorflow.keras import Sequential
from tensorflow.keras.layers import Flatten, Dense, Activation, ReLU,
from tensorflow.keras.layers import MaxPooling2D, Conv2D, Dropout

import numpy as np
import random
import cv2

from tensorflow.keras.datasets import mnist

(x_train, y_train), (x_test, y_test) = mnist.load_data()
```
Gets the built-in dataset for MNIST

The dataset from Keras is in a generic format, so we need to do some initial data preparation to use it for training either a DNN or a CNN. This preparation includes the following:

- The pixel data (x_train and x_test) contains the original INT8 values (0 to 255). We will normalize the pixel data to be from 0 to 1 as a FLOAT32.
- The image data matrices are of shape *Height × Width* ($H \times W$). Keras expects tensors in the shape of *Height × Width × Channel*. These are grayscale images, so we will reshape the train and test data to ($H \times W \times 1$).

We are also going to set aside a copy of the test and training data before it's been prepared (which we discuss in section 12.2.3).

```
x_test_copy  = x_test
x_train_copy = x_train
```
Sets aside a copy of the original training and test data

```
x_train = (x_train / 255.0).astype(np.float32)
x_test  = (x_test  / 255.0).astype(np.float32)
```
Normalizes the pixel data and casts to 32-bit float

```
x_train = x_train.reshape(-1, 28, 28, 1)
x_test  = x_test.reshape(-1, 28, 28, 1)
```
Reshapes into H × W × 1 for TF.Keras model API

```
print("x_train", x_train.shape, "x_test", x_test.shape)

print("y_train", y_train.shape, "y_test", y_test.shape)
```

12.2.3 *The challenge ("in the wild")*

In addition to randomly choosing test data (known as the *holdout set*) from this curated dataset, we will also create two more test datasets as examples of what the trained model may see in the wild. These two additional datasets, known as the *inverted set* and the *sifted set*, will contain examples that are not represented by the training data. In other words, the original MNIST dataset is one subpopulation of the population of digits, and our two new datasets are different subpopulations of digits. The inverted and sifted sets have a different distribution than the MNIST dataset, and so we refer to them as being *out of distribution* relative to the MNIST dataset.

We will use these two additional test datasets to demonstrate how the model will fail, and to find ways we might modify the training and dataset to overcome this, and the limitations. What constitutes each set?

- *Inverted set*—The pixel data is inverted such that the images are now gray digits on a white background.
- *Shifted set*—The images are shifted 4 pixels to the right, and thus are not centered anymore. Since there is at least a padding of 4 pixels, none of the digits will be clipped.

Figure 12.5 is an example of a single test image from the original test data, the inverted test data, and the shifted test data.

Original	Inverted	Shifted

Figure 12.5   The original and in the wild out-of-distribution examples

In this code, we make our two additional test datasets from the copy of the original test dataset:

```
x_test_invert = np.invert(x_test_copy)                          The "in the wild"
x_test_invert = (x_test_invert / 255.0).astype(np.float32)      inverted data

x_test_shift = np.roll(x_test_copy, 4)                          The "in the wild"
x_test_shift = (x_test_shift / 255.0).astype(np.float32)        shifted data

x_test_invert = x_test_invert.reshape(-1, 28, 28, 1)
x_test_shift  = x_test_shift.reshape(-1, 28, 28, 1)
```

12.2.4 *Training as a DNN*

We will start by training a model based on the as-is MNIST subpopulation, compare the accuracy to the holdout set that is from the same subpopulation, and finally test and compare them against the out-of-distribution data.

MNIST is so easy we can build a classifier with 97%+ accuracy with a DNN. The next code example is a function for constructing simple DNNs, consisting of the following:

- The parameter nodes is a list specifying the number of nodes per layer.
- The input to the DNN are images in the shape $28 \times 28 \times 1$
- The input is flattened into a 1D vector of length 784.
- There is an optional dropout (for regularization) after each layer.
- The last dense layer of 10 nodes with a softmax activation function is the classifier.

Figure 12.6 illustrates the configurable DNN architecture for this example.

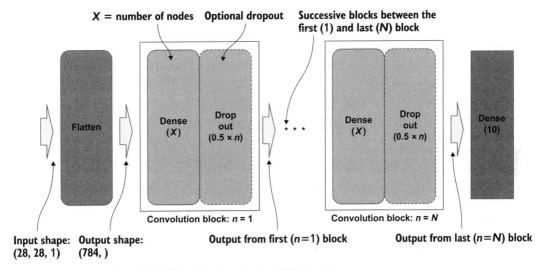

Figure 12.6 The configurable DNN architecture for the MNIST model

```
def DNN(nodes, dropout=False):                     ◁──────┐ Function for constructing
  model = Sequential()                                    │ simple DNNs
  model.add(Flatten(input_shape=(28, 28, 1)))
  for n_nodes in nodes:
    model.add(Dense(n_nodes))
    model.add(ReLU())
    if dropout:
      model.add(Dropout(0.5))
      dropout /= 2.0
  model.add(Dense(10))
  model.add(Activation('softmax'))

  model.compile(optimizer='adam', loss='sparse_categorical_crossentropy',
                metrics=['accuracy'])   ◁───────┐ Compiles the DNN for
  model.summary()                               │ a multiclass classifier
  return model
```

For our first test, we will train the dataset on a single layer (excluding the output layer) of 512 nodes. Figure 12.7 depicts the corresponding architecture.

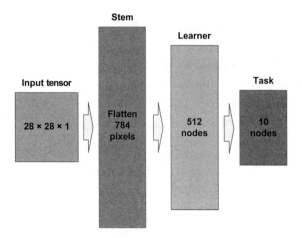

Figure 12.7   The single-layer, 512-node DNN for our first MNIST model to train

Here is the code for building, training, and evaluating the model for our first test:

```
model = DNN([512])
model.fit(x_train, y_train, epochs=10, batch_size=32, shuffle=True,
          verbose=2)                              ◁──────── Trains the model on MNIST
score = model.evaluate(x_test, y_test, verbose=1)
print("test", score)
Evaluates the trained model
```

The output from the `summary()` method will look like this:

```
Layer (type)                    Output Shape              Param #
=================================================================
flatten_1 (Flatten)             (None, 784)               0

dense_1 (Dense)                 (None, 512)               401920

re_lu_1 (ReLU)                  (None, 512)               0

dense_2 (Dense)                 (None, 10)                5130

activation_1 (Activation)       (None, 10)                0
=================================================================
Total params: 407,050
```

The number of trainable parameters is a measurement of the complexity of our model, which is 408,000 parameters. We train it for a total of 10 epochs (we feed the entire training data through the model 10 times). The following is the output from the training. The training accuracy quickly reaches 99%+, and our accuracy on the test (holdout) data is nearly 98%.

```
Epoch 1/10
2019-02-08 12:14:59.065963: I
    tensorflow/core/platform/cpu_feature_guard.cc:141] Your CPU supports
    instructions that this TensorFlow binary was not compiled to use: AVX2
    AVX512F FMA
 - 5s - loss: 0.2007 - acc: 0.9409
Epoch 2/10
 - 5s - loss: 0.0897 - acc: 0.9743
Epoch 3/10
 - 5s - loss: 0.0651 - acc: 0.9817
Epoch 4/10
 - 5s - loss: 0.0517 - acc: 0.9853
Epoch 5/10
 - 5s - loss: 0.0419 - acc: 0.9887
Epoch 6/10
 - 5s - loss: 0.0341 - acc: 0.9913
Epoch 7/10
 - 5s - loss: 0.0273 - acc: 0.9928
Epoch 8/10
 - 5s - loss: 0.0236 - acc: 0.9939
Epoch 9/10
 - 5s - loss: 0.0188 - acc: 0.9953
Epoch 10/10
 - 5s - loss: 0.0163 - acc: 0.9961
10000/10000 [==============================] - 0s 21us/step

test [0.11250439590732676, 0.9791]
```

So far, it looks good. Let's now try the model on the inverted and shifted test datasets:

```
score = model.evaluate(x_test_invert, y_test, verbose=1)
print("inverted", score)
score = model.evaluate(x_test_shift, y_test, verbose=1)
print("shifted", score)
```
Evaluates the model on the out-of-distribution inverted dataset

Evaluates the model on the out-of-distribution shifted dataset

The following is the output. Our accuracy on the inverted dataset is only 2%, and on the shifted dataset, it does better but only 41%:

```
inverted [15.660332287597656, 0.0206]
shifted [7.46930496673584, 0.4107]
```

What happened? For the inverted dataset, it looks like our model learned the gray background and the whiteness of the digit as part of the digit recognition. Thus, when we inverted the data, the model totally failed to classify it.

For the shifted dataset, a dense layer does not preserve spatial relationships between the pixels. Each pixel is a unique feature. Thus, even the shift of a few pixels was enough to dramatically drop the accuracy.

So to improve the accuracy, we might try to increase the number of nodes in the input layer—the more nodes, the better learning. Let's repeat the same test with 1024 nodes. Figure 12.8 depicts the corresponding architecture.

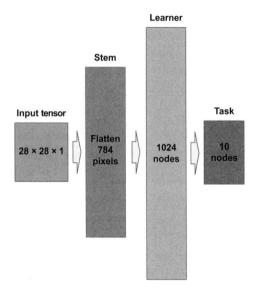

Figure 12.8   The wider, single-layer, 1024-node DNN for our second MNIST model to train

Here is the code for building, training, and evaluating the model for our second test:

The number of nodes is doubled (widened).

```
model = DNN([1024])
model.fit(x_train, y_train, epochs=10, batch_size=32, shuffle=True,
verbose=2)
score = model.evaluate(x_test, y_test, verbose=1)
print("test", score)
```

The output from `model.summary()` is as follows:

Layer (type)	Output Shape	Param #
flatten_2 (Flatten)	(None, 784)	0
dense_3 (Dense)	(None, 1024)	803840
re_lu_2 (ReLU)	(None, 1024)	0
dense_4 (Dense)	(None, 10)	10250
activation_2 (Activation)	(None, 10)	0

```
Total params: 814,090
Trainable params: 814,090
```

You can see that by doubling the number of nodes on the input layer, we double the computational complexity (the number of trainable parameters). Let's see if this improves the accuracy on our alternate test data.

Nope, we see a marginal increase on the inverted dataset to about 5%, but it's so low that's probably just noise, and the accuracy on the shifted dataset is about the same at 40%. So increasing the number of nodes in the input layer (widening) did not aid in either filtering out (not learning) the background and whiteness of the digits or learning the spatial relationships:

```
inverted [15.157325344848633, 0.0489]
shifted [7.736222146606445, 0.4038]
```

Another approach we might try is to increase the number of layers (deepening). This time, let's make the DNN with two 512-node layers. Figure 12.9 depicts our model architecture.

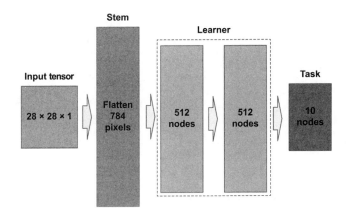

Figure 12.9 The deeper two-layer DNN (512 + 512 nodes) for our third MNIST model to train

Here is the code for building, training, and evaluating the model for our third test:

```
model = DNN([512, 512])          ⟵────── Increases the number of layers (deepen)
model.fit(x_train, y_train, epochs=10, batch_size=32, shuffle=True,
verbose=2)
score = model.evaluate(x_test, y_test, verbose=1)
print("test", score)
```

The ending output from `model.summary()`:

```
Total params: 669,706
Trainable params: 669,706
```

Let's see if this improves the accuracy on our alternate test data:

```
inverted [14.464950880432129, 0.1025]
shifted [8.786513813018798, 0.3887]
```

We see another slight increase in the shifted dataset to 10%. But did it really improve? We have 10 classes (digits). If we made random guesses, we would be right 10% of the time. This is still purely a random outcome—nothing learned here. Looks like adding layers did not aid in learning the spatial relationships either.

Another approach would be to add some regularization to prevent overfitting the model to the training data and be more generalized. We will use the same two-layer DNN of 512 nodes per layer, and add a 50% dropout after the first layer and 25% dropout after the second layer. It used to be a common practice to use a higher dropout at the first layer, which is learning coarse features, and to use a smaller dropout at subsequent layers, which are learning finer features. Figure 12.10 shows the model architecture.

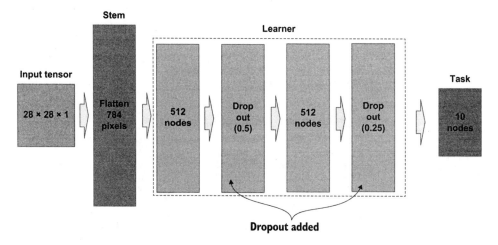

Figure 12.10   The DNN with dropout added to improve generalizing

Here is the code for building, training, and evaluating the model for our fourth test:

```
                                        Adds dropout for regularization
model = DNN([512, 512], True)    ⟵
model.fit(x_train, y_train, epochs=10, batch_size=32, shuffle=True,
          verbose=2)
score = model.evaluate(x_test, y_test, verbose=1)
print("test", score)
```

Let's see if this improves the accuracy on our alternate test data:

```
inverted [15.862942279052735, 0.0144]
shifted [8.341207506561279, 0.3965]
```

Nope, no improvement. Thus, widening a layer, deepening layers, and regularization did not help in training the model to recognize the digits in the out-of-distribution test datasets. Perhaps the issue is that a DNN is just not the right type of model architecture to generalize to an out-of-distribution model. Next, we will try a CNN and see what happens.

12.2.5 Training as a CNN

OK, now let's test the accuracy of the three datasets in a convolutional neural network. With convolutional layers, we should at least learn the spatial relationships. Perhaps the convolutional layers will filter out the background as well as the whiteness of the digits.

The following code constructs our CNNs as follows:

- The parameter `filters` is a list specifying the number of filters per convolution.
- The inputs to the CNN are images in the shape $28 \times 28 \times 1$.
- A max pooling reduces the feature map sizes by 75% after each convolution.
- A dropout (regularization) of 25% occurs after each convolution/max pooling layer.
- The last dense layer of 10 nodes with a softmax activation function is the classifier.

```
def CNN(filters):              ◁──┐  Function for constructing
  model = Sequential()            │  simple CNNs
  first = True
  for n_filters in filters:
    if first:
      model.add(Conv2D(n_filters, (3, 3), strides=1, input_shape=(28, 28, 1)))
    else:
      model.add(Conv2D(n_filters, (3, 3), strides=1))
    model.add(ReLU())
    model.add(MaxPooling2D((2, 2), strides=2))
    model.add(Dropout(0.25))
  model.add(Flatten())
  model.add(Dense(10))
  model.add(Activation('softmax'))

  model.compile(optimizer='adam', loss='sparse_categorical_crossentropy',
                metrics=['accuracy'])   ◁──┐  Compiles the CNN for
  model.summary()                          │  a multiclass classifier
  return model
```

Let's start with a CNN with a single convolutional layer of 16 filters. Figure 12.11 illustrates the model architecture.

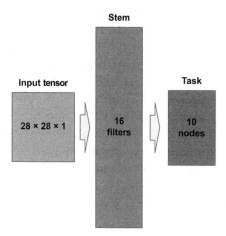

Figure 12.11   The single-layer CNN for our MNIST training

Here is the code for building, training, and evaluating the model for our first test with a CNN:

```
model = CNN([16])                          Constructs the CNN with 16 filters
model.fit(x_train, y_train, epochs=10, batch_size=32, shuffle=True,
          verbose=2)
score = model.evaluate(x_test, y_test, verbose=1)
print("test", score)
```

The output from `model.summary()` is as follows:

```
Layer (type)                 Output Shape              Param #
=================================================================
conv2d_1 (Conv2D)            (None, 26, 26, 16)        160

re_lu_1 (ReLU)               (None, 26, 26, 16)        0

max_pooling2d_1 (MaxPooling2 (None, 13, 13, 16)        0

dropout_1 (Dropout)          (None, 13, 13, 16)        0

flatten_1 (Flatten)          (None, 2704)              0

dense_1 (Dense)              (None, 10)                27050

activation_1 (Activation)    (None, 10)                0
=================================================================
Total params: 27,210
Trainable params: 27,210
```

Here is the result from our training of the CNN:

```
test [0.05741905354047194, 0.9809]
```

You can see we can get comparable accuracy (98%) on the test data with a CNN with a lot fewer trainable parameters (27,000 versus more than 400,000).

Let's see if this improves the accuracy on our alternate test data:

```
inverted [2.1893138484954835, 0.5302]
shifted [2.231996842956543, 0.5682]
```

Yes, it made a measurable difference. We went from a previous high of 10% accuracy on the inverted dataset to 50% accuracy. Thus, it does seem the convolutional layers help filter out (not learn) the background or whiteness of the digits.

But it's still far too low in accuracy. For the shifted dataset, we increased to 57%. That's still below our target, but we can also see that now the convolutional layers are learning the spatial relationships. So, what did we learn here? Well, if you have the wrong model architecture, it does not matter how deeper or wider you make the model, or how much regularization you add; the model will not generalize to out-of-distribution test data. We also learned that a CNN not only better generalizes, but is also a lot more efficient in parameters, and in our first test, we did it with only a stem and no learner component.

If one convolutional layer improved things, let's see how much better we can do with two convolutional layers. We will use two layers: the first with 16 filters and the second with 32 filters. It's a common practice to double the number of filters as you get successively deeper into a CNN. Figure 12.12 depicts our model architecture.

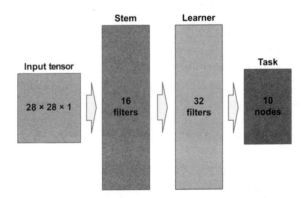

Figure 12.12 **The deeper two-layer CNN for our MNIST training**

Here is the code for building, training, and evaluating the model for our second test with a CNN:

```
                                    Constructs a two-layer CNN
model = CNN([16, 32])        ⟵
model.fit(x_train, y_train, epochs=10, batch_size=32, shuffle=True,
verbose=2)
score = model.evaluate(x_test, y_test, verbose=1)
print("test", score)
```

Here is the result from our training of the CNN:

```
test [0.03628469691830687, 0.9882]
```

Again, we get comparable accuracy, with slight improvement to ~99% on the test data. Let's see whether adding convolutional layers will improve the accuracy on our alternate test data:

```
inverted [1.2761547603607177, 0.6332]
shifted [0.6951200264453888, 0.7679]
```

We do see some incremental improvement. Our inverted dataset went up to 63%. So it's learning to better filter out the background and whiteness of the digits, but it's still not there. Our shifted dataset test jumped to 76%. So you can see how convolutional layers are learning the spatial relationships in the digits versus the position in the image (compared to a DNN).

12.2.6 *Image augmentation*

Finally, let's use image augmentation to try to improve on generalizing to the out-of-distribution alternate test data. Recall that *image augmentation* is a process of generating new samples from existing samples by making small modifications. These modifications would not change what the image would be classified as, and the image would be still recognized by the human eye as being of that class.

Figure 12.13 depicts an example of image augmentation, in which an image of a cat was randomly rotated and then cropped and resized back to the original shape. The picture is still recognizable by the human eye as a cat.

In addition to adding more samples to the training set, certain types of augmentation can aid in generalizing the model to accurately classify images outside the test (holdout) dataset that it would've otherwise failed on.

As we saw on our CNN, we still had insufficient accuracy on shifted images; thus our model has not fully learned the spatial relationships of the digits separate from

Original   **Random rotation, then cropped and resized**

Figure 12.13   Image augmentation pipeline to generate examples with randomly selected translations

the location and background in the image. We could add more filters and convolutional layers in an attempt to increase the accuracy on shifted images. This would make the model more computationally complex and longer to train, and have a larger memory print and longer latency when deployed to do predictions (inference).

Alternately, we are going to improve the model by using image augmentation to randomly shift the image left or right up to 20%. Since our images are 28 pixels wide, 20% would mean that the image gets shifted a maximum of 6 pixels in either direction. We have a minimum of a 4-pixel boundary, so there will be little to no clipping of the digits.

We will use the `ImageDataGenerator` class in TF.Keras to do the image augmentation. In the following code example, we do the following:

- Create the same CNN model as before.
- Instantiate an `ImageDataGenerator` generator object whose parameter `width_shift_range=0.2` will augment the dataset during training by randomly shifting images +/− 20%.
- Invoke the `fit_generator()` method to train the model using our image augmentation generator with our existing training data.
- Specify the number of `steps_per_epoch` in the generator as the number of training samples divided by the batch size; otherwise, the generator would loop indefinitely on the first epoch:

```
                                      Instantiates generator for randomly
                                         shifting images +/− 20%
from tensorflow.keras.preprocessing.image import ImageDataGenerator

model = CNN([16, 32])
datagen = ImageDataGenerator(width_shift_range=0.2)        ◄────────────
model.fit_generator(datagen.flow(x_train, y_train, batch_size=32),
                steps_per_epoch= 60000 // 32 , epochs=10)  ◄──── Trains the
score = model.evaluate(x_test, y_test, verbose=1)                model using
print("test", score)                                             the image
                                                                 augmentation
```

The following is the result from our training of the CNN:

```
test [0.046405045648082156, 0.986]
```

Let's see if this improves the accuracy on the out-of-distribution test data:

```
inverted [4.463096208190918, 0.2338]
shifted [0.06386796866590157, 0.9796]
```

Wow, our accuracy on the shifted data is now nearly 98%. So we were able to train the model to learn the spatial relationships of digits when they shifted in the image without increasing the complexity of the model. But we did not see any improvement yet on the inverted data.

Let's now tackle training the model to filter out the background and whiteness of the digits to improve the model's ability to generalize to the out-of-distribution inverted test data. In the following code, we take 10% of the training data (x_train_copy[0:6000]) and invert it as we did with the test data. Why 10% instead of the whole training data? When we want to train a model to filter out something, we generally can do it with as little as 10% of the distribution of the entire training data.

Next we combine the original training data with the additional inverted training data by appending the two training sets together—both x_train (the data) and y_train (the labels—for a total of 66,000 images (versus 60,000) in our training set:

```
x_train_invert = np.invert(x_train_copy[0:6000])          Selects 10% of the
x_train_invert = (x_train_invert / 255.0).astype(np.float32)   (copy of) training
x_train_invert = x_train_invert.reshape(-1, 28, 28, 1)    data and inverts it

y_train_invert = x_train[0:6000]      ◄──┤ Selects the same 10% of
                                          the corresponding labels    Combines the two
                                                                      training datasets into
x_combine = np.append(x_train, x_train_invert, axis=0)              a single training set
y_combine = np.append(y_train, y_train_invert, axis=0)

model = CNN([16, 32])
datagen = ImageDataGenerator(width_shift_range=0.2)
datagen.fit(x_train_combine)
model.fit_generator( datagen.flow(x_combine, y_combine, batch_size=32),
                     steps_per_epoch= 66000 // 32 , epochs=10) ◄──┐ Trains the
score = model.evaluate(x_test, y_test, verbose=1)                   model with
print("test", score)                                                the combined
                                                                    training
                                                                    dataset
```

Here is the result from our training of the CNN:

```
test [0.04763028650498018, 0.9847]
```

Let's see if this improves the accuracy on our alternate test data:

```
inverted [0.13941174189522862, 0.9589]
shifted [0.06449916120804847, 0.979]
```

Wow, our test accuracy on the inverted images is nearly 96%.

12.2.7 *Final test*

As a final test, I randomly selected "in the wild" images of a handwritten single digit from a Google image search. These included images that were colored, drawn with a felt-tip pen, painted with a paintbrush, and drawn in crayon by a young child. After I did my testing, I got only 40% accuracy with the CNN we just trained in this chapter.

Why only 40%, and how would we diagnose the cause? The question should be what subpopulation distribution did the model learn? Did the model learn to generalize the contours of the digits independent of the contrast to the background, or did it simply learn that digits are either white or black? What would happen if we tested with a black digit on a gray background (instead of white)?

The training and test data from MNIST are digits drawn with a pen or pencil, so the lines are thin. Some of my "in the wild" images were thicker, made by a felt-tip pen, paintbrush, or crayon. Did the model learn to generalize the thickness of the lines? What about texture? The crayon- and paint-drawn digits had uneven texture; were these differences in texture learned as edges in the convolutional layers?

As a final example, say you developed a model for use in a factory to detect defects in parts. The camera is in a fixed position with its perspective over a gray conveyor belt that has ridges running down it. All works well until one day the owner replaces the conveyor belt with a smooth yellow belt to add some color to the factory, and now the defect detection model fails. What happened? Well, because the gray conveyor belt was in all the training images, it would've become part of the learned features in the latent space, before entering the task learner (the classifier). This is similar to the classic case of dogs versus wolves, in which all the wolf pictures were taken in the winter. In this classic case, when the trained model was given a picture of a dog with snow in the background (out of distribution), the model predicted *wolf.* The model simply learned in that case that *snow* means *wolf.*

Summary

- A sampling distribution models the parameters of a population distribution.
- A subpopulation distribution models a bias, which is a subportion, of the population distribution.
- If you trained on a subpopulation distribution, and your model does not generalize in production on the examples it sees, the production data is likely out of distribution from the subpopulation you trained. This is also referred to as serving skew.
- Adding deeper or wider layers and/or more regularization generally will not help generalizing to an out-of-distribution population.
- Generating training samples from image augmentation can aid in generalizing to an out-of-distribution population in some cases.
- When image augmentation is insufficient to generalize, you will need to add training examples from the out-of-distribution subpopulation.

Data pipeline 13

This chapter covers

- Understanding the common types of data formats and storage for training datasets
- Using TensorFlow TFRecord format and tf.data for dataset representations and transformations
- Constructing a data pipeline for feeding a model during training
- Preprocessing using TF.Keras preprocessing layers, layer subclassing, and TFX components
- Using data augmentation to train models for translational, scale, and viewport invariance

You've built your model, using composable models as needed. You've trained and retrained it, and tested and retested. Now you're ready to launch it. In these last two chapters, you'll learn how to launch a model. More specifically, you'll migrate a model from the preparation and exploratory phases to a production environment, using the TensorFlow 2.x ecosystem in conjunction with TensorFlow Extended (TFX).

In a production environment, operations such as training and deploying are executed as pipelines. *Pipelines* have the advantage of being configurable, reusable, version-controlled, and retain history. Because of how extensive a production pipeline is, we need two chapters to cover it. This chapter focuses on the data pipeline components, which make up the frontend of a production pipeline. The next chapter covers the training and deployment components.

Let's start with a diagram, so you can see the process from start to finish. Figure 13.1 shows an overall view of the basic end-to-end (e2e) production pipeline.

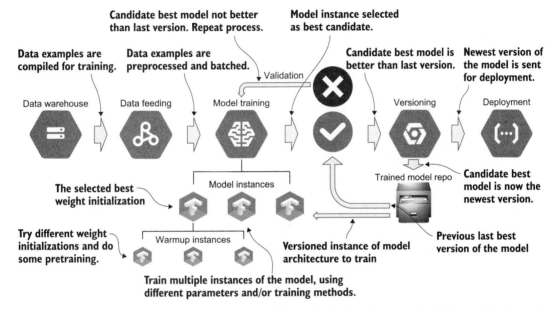

Figure 13.1 The basic e2e production pipeline starts with a data pipeline, then moves to training and deployment pipelines.

The modern basic machine learning e2e pipeline starts with data warehousing, which is the repository of the training data for all the production models. The number of models an enterprise-size company is training varies. But here are some examples from my experience in 2019. The time between retraining (a new version) of a production model has reduced from a monthly to a weekly cycle, and in some cases is a daily cycle. Google (my employer) retrains over 4000 models a day. Data warehousing at this scale is an enormous undertaking.

From the data warehouse, we need to efficiently feed data for model training and provide the data just in time and without input/output (I/O) bottlenecks. The upstream process that compiles and assembles batches for training must do it fast enough in real time so as not to stall the GPU/CPU training hardware.

At an enterprise scale, the data warehouse is generally distributed across a large or vast number of compute instances, whether on premises, in the cloud, or hybrid, making it more challenging to efficiently feed data during training.

Now comes the model training. But we are not training a single instance of a model. We train multiple instances in parallel to find the best version, and we do this in multiple stages, from data collection, preparation, augmentation, and pretraining to hyperparameter search for full training.

If we roll the clock back a few years, this pipeline process started with domain experts making educated guesses and automating them. Today these stages are becoming self-learning. We have advanced from automation (with experts setting the rules) to automatic learning, where the machine is continuously learning to self-improve from the expert human guidance. And that is why multiple instances of models get trained: to automatically learn which model instance will become the best trained model.

Then we have version control. We need a means of evaluating the new trained instance with past versions to answer the question of whether the new instance is better than the last. If so, version it; otherwise, repeat the process. And for new versions, deploy the model into production use.

In this chapter, we cover moving data from storage, preprocessing the data, and batching it to feed to the model instances during training. In the next chapter, we cover training, retraining, and continuous training, candidate model validation, versioning, deployment, and testing after deployment.

13.1 Data formats and storage

We will start by looking at the various formats for storing image data for machine learning. Historically, image data was stored in one of the following:

- Compressed image format (for example, JPG)
- Uncompressed raw-image format (for example, BMP)
- A high-dimensional format (for example, HDF5 or DICOM)

With TensorFlow 2.x, we store image data in TFRecord format. Let's look more closely at each of these four formats.

13.1.1 Compressed and raw-image formats

When deep learning first became popular for computer vision, we were generally training straight from the raw image data, after that image data was decompressed. There were two basic ways of preparing this image data: drawing the training batches from disk in JPG, PNG, or other compressed format; and drawing batches from compressed images in RAM.

DRAWING BATCHES FROM DISK

In the first approach, as we build batches for training, we read the batches of images from disk in a compressed format, like JPG or PNG. We then decompress them in memory, resize, and do the image preprocessing, like normalizing the pixel data.

Figure 13.2 depicts this process. In this example, a subset of the JPG images, specified by the batch size, are read into memory, and then decompressed and finally resized to the input shape of the model to train.

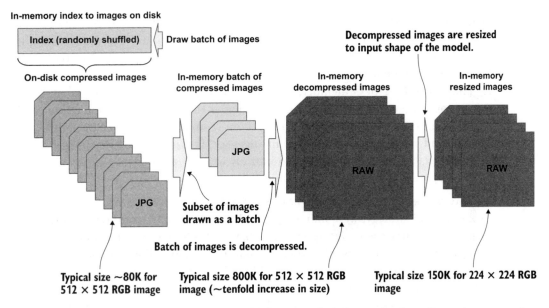

Figure 13.2 Drawing compressed images from a disk is easy to do, but expensive to continuously reprocess for training.

Let's look at some pros and cons of this method. First, it is very easy to do. Here are the steps:

1. Create an index to all the paths of the images on disk and corresponding labels (for example, CSV index file).
2. Read the index into memory and randomly shuffle the index.
3. Draw a batch of images and corresponding labels into memory by using the shuffled index file.
4. Decompress the images.
5. Resize the decompressed images to the input shape of the model to train.

The big con is that when training a model, you have to repeat the preceding steps for each epoch. The step that can be problematic is drawing data from the disk. This step may become I/O bound and is specifically dependent on the type of disk storage and the location of the data. Ideally, we want the data stored in as fast of a read-access disk operation as possible, and as close (by limiting network bandwidth) to the compute device doing the training.

To compare this tradeoff between on-disk and in-memory, let's assume you are using a SOTA model with an ImageNet input shape of (224, 224, 3). This size is typical for general image classification, while for image object detection or segmentation, a large size like (512, 512, 3) is used.

An image of shape (224, 224, 3) requires 150,000 bytes of memory ($224 \times 224 \times 3 = 150,000$). In order to hold 50,000 training images continuously in memory in the ImageNet input shape, you will need 8 GB ($50,000 \times 150,000$) of RAM—above what you need for the operating system, background applications, and model training. Now let's say you have 100,000 training images. Then you would need 16 GB of RAM. If you had a million images, you would need 160 GB of RAM.

That would be a lot of memory, and having all the images in uncompressed format in memory is generally practical for only smaller datasets. For academic and other tutorial purposes, training datasets are generally small enough to have the decompressed and resized images entirely in memory. But in production environments, where the dataset is too large to hold entirely in memory, we need to use a strategy that incorporates drawing images from the disk.

DRAWING BATCHES FROM COMPRESSED IMAGES IN RAM

In this second strategy, we eliminate the disk I/O but still decompress and resize in memory each time the image appears in a batch. By eliminating disk I/O, we prevent being I/O bound, which would otherwise slow the training. For example, if the training consists of 100 epochs, each image will be decompressed and resized 100 times— but all the compressed images stay in memory.

The average JPEG compression is about 10:1. The size of the compressed image will be dependent on the image source. For example, if the images are from a 3.5-megapixel mobile phone (3.5 million pixels), the compressed image will be around 350,000 bytes. If our images are web-optimized for browser loading, the uncompressed image is more typically in the 150,000 to 200,000 byte range.

Assuming you have 100,000 training images that are web-optimized, 2 GB of RAM would be enough (100K × 15K = 1.5 GB). If you have a million training images, 16 GB of RAM would be enough (1M × 15K = 15 GB).

Figure 13.3 illustrates this second approach, outlined here:

1 Read all the compressed images and corresponding labels into memory as a list.
2 Create an index to all the list indices of the images in memory and corresponding labels.
3 Randomly shuffle the index.
4 Draw a batch of images and corresponding labels from memory by using the shuffled index file.
5 Decompress the images.
6 Resize the decompressed images.

In-memory index to in-memory images

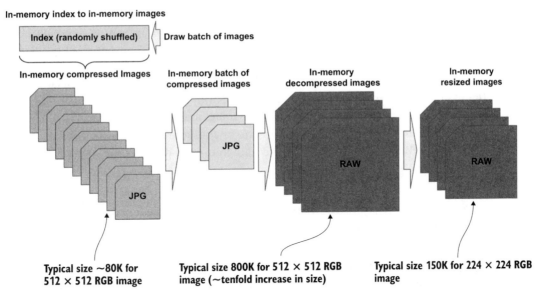

Figure 13.3 Drawing compressed images from RAM eliminates the disk I/O, thus speeding up the process.

This approach tends to be a reasonable tradeoff for mid-size datasets. Let's assume we have 200,000 images that are web-optimized in size. We need only 4 GB of memory to hold all the compressed images in memory without repeatedly reading from disk. Even with a large batch size (say, 1024 web-optimized images), we would need only an additional 150 MB of memory to hold the decompressed images—averaging 150,000 bytes per image.

Here's my general practice:

1 If the decompressed size of my training data is less than or equal to my RAM, I train with decompressed images in memory. This is the fastest option.

2 If the compressed size of my training data is less than or equal to my RAM, I train with compressed images in memory. This is the next-fastest option.

3 Otherwise, I train with the images drawn from the disk or use a hybrid approach, which I discuss next.

HYBRID APPROACH

Next, let's consider a hybrid approach of feeding the training images from disk and from memory. Why would we do this? We want to find a sweet spot in the tradeoff between available memory space and otherwise being I/O bound by continuously rereading images from the disk.

To do this, we'll revisit the concept of a sampling distribution from chapter 12, which approximates the distribution of a population. Imagine you have 16 GB of memory to hold data, and the preprocessed dataset after resizing is 64 GB. In a hybrid feeding, we take a large segment of the preprocessed data at a time (8 GB in our example) that has been *stratified* (examples match the training data class distribution). We then repeatedly feed the same segment to the neural network as epochs. But each time, we do image augmentation such that each epoch is a unique sampling distribution of the entire preprocessed image dataset.

I recommend this approach on extremely large datasets, like a million images. With 16 GB of memory, you can hold very large subdistributions of your dataset, and be able to get convergence at comparable training batches as compared to repeatedly reading from disk, while reducing your training time or compute instance requirements.

Here are the steps for doing a hybrid in-memory/on-disk feeding. You can also see the process depicted in figure 13.4:

1 Create a stratified index to the preprocessed image data on disk.
2 Partition the stratified index into partitions based on the available memory to hold a segment in memory.
3 For each segment, repeat for a specified number of epochs:
    – Randomly shuffle the segment per epoch.
    – Randomly apply image augmentation to create a unique sampling distribution per epoch.
    – Feed the mini-batches to the neural network.

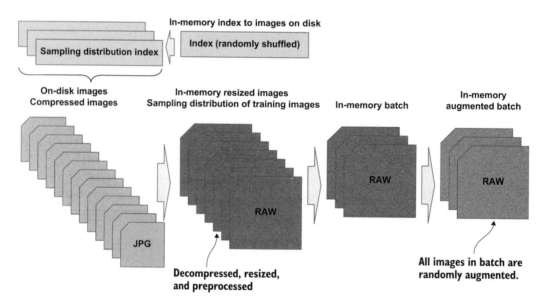

Figure 13.4   Hybrid drawing images from disk as sampling distributions of the training data

13.1.2 HDF5 format

Hierarchical Data Format 5 (HDF5) has been a long-standing common format for storing high-dimensionality data, such as high-resolution satellite imagery. So you may be asking, what is *high dimensionality*? We associate this term with data that is very dense in information for a single dimension, and/or has many dimensions (which we refer to as *multidimensional data*). As in the previous discussions on TFRecords, these formats themselves do not substantially reduce the amount of disk space for storage. Instead, their purpose is for rapid read access to reduce I/O overhead.

HDF5 is an efficient format for storing and accessing large amounts of multidimensional data, such as images. The specification can be found at the HDF5 for Python website (www.h5py.org/). The format supports dataset and group objects, as well as attributes (metadata) per object.

The benefits of using HDF5 for storing image training data include the following:

- Has broad scientific use, as in satellite imagery used by NASA (see http://mng.bz/qevJ)
- Optimized for high-speed data-slice access
- Is NumPy-compatible with NumPy syntax that allows accessing from disk as if in memory
- Has hierarchical access for multidimensional representations, properties, and classification

The HDF5 package for Python can be installed as follows:

```
pip install h5py
```

Let's start by creating a dataset with the most basic HDF5 representation consisting of raw (decompressed) image data and corresponding integer label data. In this representation, we create two dataset objects, one for the image data and the other for the corresponding labels:

```
dataset['images'] : [...]
dataset['labels'] : [...]
```

The following code is an example implementation. The training data and labels are in NumPy format. We open an HDF5 file for write access, and create two datasets, one for the images and one for the labels:

Stores the training images as
the dataset named "images"
```
from tensorflow.keras.datasets import cifar10
(x_train, y_train), (x_test, y_test) = cifar10.load_data()

with h5py.File('myfile.h5', 'w') as hf:          ⟵——— Opens HDF5 file for write access
    hf.create_dataset("images", data=x_train)
    hf.create_dataset("labels", data=y_train)    ⟵┐ Stores the training labels as
                                                   ┘ the dataset named "labels"
```

Now, when we want to read back the images and labels, we first open the HDF5 for read access. Then we create an iterator for the dataset's images and labels. The HDF5 file handle is a dictionary object, and we refer to our named datasets via the dataset name as the key.

Next, we reopen the HDF5 file for read access and then create an HDF5 iterator for the dataset's images and labels, using the keys images and labels. Here, x_train and y_train are aliases for the HDF5 iterators. The data is not actually in memory yet:

Creates HDF5 iterator for the images dataset
```
hf = h5py.File('myfile.h5', 'r')  ⟵──── Opens HDF5 file for read access
x_train = hf['images']
y_train = hf['labels']       ⟵──┤ Creates HDF5 iterator
                                 │ for the labels dataset
```

Since the HDF5 iterators use NumPy syntax, we can directly access the data by using NumPy array slicing, which fetches the data from disk into an in-memory NumPy array. In the following code, we are getting a single batch by using array slicing of the images (x_batch) and corresponding labels (y_batch):

The first 100 images are now in memory as a NumPy array.
```
x_batch = x_train[0:100]
y_batch = y_train[0:100]   ⟵──┤ The first 100 labels are now
                              │ in memory as a NumPy array.
```

Next, we iterate through the entire dataset, as batches, and feed each batch to the model for training. Let's assume that there are 50,000 images (for example, in the CIFAR-10 dataset) stored in our HDF5 dataset.

We iterate through the HDF5 dataset with a batch size of 50. Each time, we reference the next sequential array slice. The iterator will then draw 50 images each time from disk and load them into x_batch as an in-memory NumPy array. We do the same for the corresponding labels, which are loaded into y_batch as a NumPy array. We then pass the batch of images and corresponding labels to the TF.Keras method train_on_batch(), which does a single batch update on the model:

```
examples = 50000
batch_size = 50
batches = examples / batch_size
for batch in range(batches):
    x_batch = x_train[batch*batch_size:(batch+1)*batch_size]
    y_batch = y_train[batch*batch_size:(batch+1)*batch_size]
    model.train_on_batch(x_batch, y_batch)   ⟵──┐
```

Draws the next batch from HDF5 file as an in-memory NumPy slice

Updates the model for the batch

HDF5 GROUPS

Next, we will look at an alternate storage representation using groups for storing a dataset in HDF5 format. This alternative method has more efficient storage, eliminates storing labels, and can store hierarchical datasets. In this representation, we will create a separate group for each class (label) and corresponding dataset.

The following example depicts this representation. We have two classes, cats and dogs, and create a group for each. Within both groups, we create one dataset for the corresponding images. Note that we don't need to store an array of labels anymore, since they are implied by the group name:

```
Group['cats']
    Dataset['images']: [...]
Group['dogs']
    Dataset['images']: [...]
```

The following code is an example implementation, where x_cats and x_dogs are the corresponding in-memory NumPy arrays for the cat and dog images:

Creates a group for the dog class and corresponding dataset within the group for storing the dog images

Creates a group for the cat class and corresponding dataset within the group for storing the cat images

```
with h5py.File('myfile.h5', 'w') as hf:
    cats = hf.create_group('cats')
    cats.create_dataset('images', data=x_cats)
    dogs = hf.create_group('dogs')
    dogs.create_dataset('images', data=x_dogs)
```

Then we read a batch from our group version of cats and dogs. In this example, we open HDF5 group handles to the cats and dogs groups. The HDF5 group handles are then referenced using dictionary syntax. For example, to get an iterator to the cats images, we reference it as cats['images']. Next we draw 25 images from the cats dataset and 25 images from the dogs dataset, using NumPy array slicing, into memory as x_batch. As a last step, we generate the corresponding integer labels in y_batch. We assign 0 to cats and 1 to dogs:

Opens HDF5 group handles for the cats and dogs groups

Draws a batch from the cats and dogs datasets within the corresponding groups

```
hf = h5py.File('myfile.h5', 'r')
cats = hf['cats']
dogs = hf['dogs']
x_batch = np.concatenate([cats['images'][0:25], dogs['images'][0:25]])
y_batch = np.concatenate([np.full((25), 0), np.full((25), 1)])
```

Creates the corresponding labels

The format supports hierarchical storage of groups, when images are multilabeled hierarchically. If the images are hierarchically labeled, each group is further partitioned into a hierarchy of subgroups, as depicted next. Additionally, we use the Group attribute to explicitly assign a unique integer value to the corresponding label:

```
Group['cats']
        Attribute: {label: 0}
        Group['persian']:
                Attribute: {label: 100}
                Dataset['images']: [...]
        Group['siamese']:
                Attribute: {label: 101}
                Dataset['images']: [...]
Group['dogs']
```

```
Attribute: {label: 1}
Group['poodles']:
        Attribute: {label: 200}
        Dataset['images']: [...]
Group['beagle']:
        Attribute: {label: 201}
        Dataset['images']: [...]
```

To implement this hierarchical storage, we create top-level groups and subgroups. In this example, we create a top-level group for cats. Then, using the HDF5 group handle for cats, we create subgroups for each breed, such as persian and siamese. Then for each breed subgroup, we create a dataset for the corresponding images. Additionally, we use the attrs property to explicitly assign a unique label value:

Creates top-level group for cats and assigns label 0 as an attribute

```
with h5py.File('myfile.h5', 'w') as hf:
    cats = hf.create_group('cats')
    cats.attrs['label'] = 0

    breed = cats.create_group('persian')
    breed.attrs['label'] = 100
    breed.create_dataset('images', data=x_cats['persian'])
    breed = cats.create_group('siamese')
    breed.attrs['label'] = 101
    breed.create_dataset('images', data=x_cats['siamese'])
```

Creates a second-level subgroup under cats for the breed persian, assigns label, and adds images for persian cats

Creates a second-level subgroup under cats for the breed siamese, assigns label, and adds images for siamese cats

In summary, the HDF5 group feature is an easy and efficient storage method for accessing hierarchical labeled data, particularly for multilabel datasets, where the labels also have a hierarchical relationship. Another common multilabel hierarchical example is produce. At the top of the hierarchy, you have two classes: fruit and vegetable. Below each of these two classes are type (for example, apple, banana, orange), and below type, you have variety (for example, granny smith, gala, golden delicious).

13.1.3 DICOM format

While the HDF5 format is widely used in satellite imagery, the *Digital Imaging and Communications in Medicine* (DICOM) format is used in medical imaging. In fact, DICOM is the ISO 12052 international standard for storing and accessing medical imaging data, such as CT scans and X-rays, as well as patient information. This format, which predates HDF5, is specialized for and broadly used throughout medical research and healthcare systems with an abundance of public de-identified health imaging datasets. If you are working with medical imaging data, you will need to be familiar with this format.

Here I'll introduce some basic guidelines for using the format, along with a demonstration sample. But if you are, or plan to be, specializing in medical imaging, I recommend the DICOM specification and training tutorials located at the DICOM website (www.dicomstandard.org/).

The DICOM package for Python can be installed as follows:

```
pip install pydicom
```

Generally, DICOM datasets are extremely large, in hundreds of gigabytes. This is because the format is solely used for medical imaging, and generally consists of extremely high-resolution images for segmentation, and may additionally consist of layers of 3D slices per image.

Pydicom, a Python open source package for medical images in DICOM format, provides a small dataset for demonstration purposes. We will use this dataset for our coding examples. Let's start by importing the Pydicom package and getting the test dataset CT_small.dcm:

```
import pydicom
from pydicom.data import import get_testdata_files

dcm_file = get_testdata_files('CT_small.dcm')[0]
```

This Pydicom method returns a list of filenames for the demonstration datasets.

In DICOM, the labeled data also contains tabular data, such as patient information. The image, label, and tabular data can be used to train a *multimodal model* (a model that has two or more input layers), and each input layer has a different data type (for example, image or numerical).

Let's see how the images and labels are read from a DICOM file format. We'll read in our demonstration dataset, which mimics a real-world example of a patient's medical imaging data, and start by getting some basic information about the dataset. Each dataset contains a large volume of patient information, which can be accessed as a dictionary. This example shows just a few of the fields, most of which have been de-identified. The study date indicates when the image was taken, and the modality is the type of imaging (in this case, CT scan):

```
dataset = pydicom.dcmread(dcm_file)
for key in ['PatientID', 'PatientName', 'PatientAge', 'PatientBirthDate',
            'PatientSex', 'PatientWeight', 'StudyDate', 'Modality']:
    print(key, dataset[key])
```

```
PatientID (0010, 0020) Patient ID                          LO: '1CT1'
PatientName (0010, 0010) Patient's Name                      PN:
    'CompressedSamples^CT1'
PatientAge (0010, 1010) Patient's Age                       AS: '000Y'
PatientBirthDate (0010, 0030) Patient's Birth Date          DA: ''
PatientSex (0010, 0040) Patient's Sex                       CS: 'O'
PatientWeight (0010, 1030) Patient's Weight                 DS: "0.0"
StudyDate (0008, 0020) Study Date                           DA: '20040119'
Modality (0008, 0060) Modality                              CS: 'CT'
```

Finally, we will extract the image data and display it as shown here and in figure 13.5:

```
rows = int(dataset.Rows)
cols = int(dataset.Columns)
print("Image size.......: {rows:d} x {cols:d}, {size:d} bytes".format(
        rows=rows, cols=cols, size=len(dataset.PixelData)))


plt.imshow(dataset.pixel_array, cmap=plt.cm.bone)
plt.show()
```

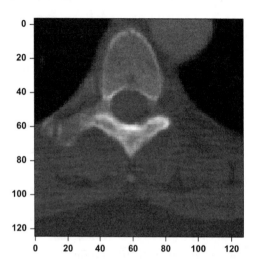

Figure 13.5   An image extracted from a DICOM file

Further details on accessing and parsing DICOM images can be found in the standard as well as the tutorials for Pydicom (https://pydicom.github.io/).

13.1.4 *TFRecord format*

TFRecord is the TensorFlow standard for storing and accessing datasets for training with TensorFlow. This binary format was originally designed for efficient serialization of structured data using Google's protocol buffer definitions, but was further developed by the TensorFlow team for efficient serialization of unstructured data, such as images, video, and text. In addition to being the TensorFlow organization's recommended format for training data, the format has been seamlessly integrated across the TF ecosystem, including in `tf.data` and TFX.

Here, again, we'll just get a taste for how the format can be used for images for training CNNs. For the fine details and information on the standard, check out the tutorials (www.tensorflow.org/tutorials/load_data/tfrecord).

Figure 13.6 is a pictorial overview of using TFRecords for a training dataset as a hierarchy of tf.data representations. The three steps are as follows:

1 At the top level is `tf.data.Dataset`. This is the in-memory representation of the training dataset.

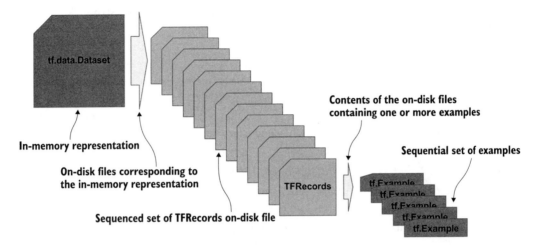

Figure 13.6 Hierarchical relationships of `tf.data`, TFRecords, and `tf.Example`

2 The next level is a sequence of one or more TFRecords. These are the on-disk storage of the dataset.

3 At the bottom level are `tf.Example` records; each contains a single data example.

Let's now describe this relationship from the bottom up. We will convert every data example in the training data to a `tf.Example` object. For example, if we have 50,000 training images, we have 50,000 `tf.Example` records. Next we serialize these records so they will have fast read access on disk as TFRecord files. These files are designed for sequential access, not random access, to minimize read access, since they will be written once but read many times.

For large amounts of data, the records are generally partitioned into multiple TFRecord files to further minimize read-access times specific to the storage device. While the size of each serialized `tf.Example` entry, the number of examples, the storage device type, and distribution will best determine the partitioning size; the TensorFlow team recommends 100 to 200 MB each as a general rule of thumb.

TF.EXAMPLE: FEATURES

The format for `tf.Example` has similarities to both a Python dictionary and JSON objects. An example (for instance, an image) and corresponding metadata (for example, the label) are encapsulated within a `tf.Example` class object. This object consists of a list of one or more `tf.train.Feature` entries. Each feature entry can be one of these data types:

- `tf.train.ByteList`
- `tf.train.FloatList`
- `tf.train.Int64List`

The tf.train.ByteList type is used for sequences of bytes or a string. An example of bytes would be the encoded or raw bytes of an image, and an example of a string would be a text string for an NLP model or the class name for a label.

A tf.train.FloatList type is used for 32-bit (single-precision) or 64-bit (double-precision) floating-point numbers. A continuous real value for a column in a structured dataset is an example.

A tf.train.Int64List type is used for both 32-bit and 64-bit signed and unsigned integers, and Booleans. For an integer, this type is used for a categorical value for a column in a structured dataset, or a scalar value for a label, for example.

Several common practices are used to encode image data into tf.Example format:

- A feature entry for encoding the image data
- A feature entry for the image shape (for reconstruction)
- A feature entry for the corresponding label

The following is a generic example of defining tf.train.Example for encoding an image; /entries here/ is a placeholder for the dictionary entries for the image data and corresponding metadata, which we will discuss subsequently. Note that Tensor-Flow refers to the format as tf.Example, and the data type as tf.train.Example. This can be initially confusing.

```
example = tf.train.Example(features = { /entries here/ })
```

TF.EXAMPLE: COMPRESSED IMAGE

In the next example, we create a tf.train.Example object for an image that has not been decoded (it is in the compressed on-disk format). The benefit with this approach is that we use the least amount of disk space when stored as part of a TFRecord. The drawback is that each time we read a TFRecord from disk while feeding the neural network during training, the image data must be uncompressed; this is a tradeoff of time versus space.

In the following code example, we define a function for converting an on-disk image file (parameter path) and corresponding label (parameter label) as follows:

- The on-disk image is first read in and uncompressed into a raw bitmap using the OpenCV method cv2.imread() to obtain the shape of the image (rows, columns, channels).
- The on-disk image is read in a second time using tf.io.gfile.GFile() in its original compressed format. Note, the tf.io.gfile.GFile() is equivalent to a file open(), but if the image is stored in a GCS bucket, the method is optimized for I/O read/write performance.
- A tf.train.Example() instance is instantiated with three dictionary entries for the features object:
  - image—A BytesList for the uncompressed (original on-disk data) image data

- label—An Int64List for the label value
- shape—An Int64List for the tuple (rows, height, channels) shape of the image

In our example, if we assume that the size of the on-disk image is 24,000 bytes, then the size of the tf.train.Example entry in a TFRecord file will be about 25,000 bytes.

```
import tensorflow as tf
import numpy as np
import sys
import cv2

def TFExampleImage(path, label):
        ''' The original compressed version of the image '''

        image = cv2.imread(path)
        shape = image.shape

        with tf.io.gfile.GFile(path, 'rb') as f:
            disk_image = f.read()

        return tf.train.Example(features = tf.train.Features(feature = {
        'image': tf.train.Feature(bytes_list = tf.train.BytesList(value =
                            [disk_image])),
        'label': tf.train.Feature(int64_list = tf.train.Int64List(value =
                            [label])),
        'shape': tf.train.Feature(int64_list = tf.train.Int64List(value =
                            [shape[0], shape[1], shape[2]]))
        }))

example = TFExampleImage('example.jpg', 0)
print(example.ByteSize())
```

Uses OpenCV to obtain the shape of the image

Uses TensorFlow to read in the compressed image from a GCS bucket

Creates a feature entry for the compressed image byte data

Creates a feature entry for the corresponding label

Creates a feature entry for the corresponding shape as H × W × C

TF.EXAMPLE: UNCOMPRESSED IMAGE

In the next code example, we create a tf.train.Example entry for storing the uncompressed version of the image in a TFRecord. This has the benefit of reading the image from disk only once, and it does not need to be uncompressed each time the entry is read from a TFRecord on disk during training.

The drawback is that the size of the entry will be substantially larger than the on-disk version of the image. In the preceding example, assuming a 95% JPEG compression, the size of the entry in a TFRecord would be 500,000 bytes. Note, in the BytesList encoding of the image data, the np.uint8 data format is retained.

```
def TFExampleImageUncompressed(path, label):
        ''' The uncompressed version of the image '''

        image = cv2.imread(path)
        shape = image.shape

        return tf.train.Example(features = tf.train.Features(feature = {
        'image': tf.train.Feature(bytes_list = tf.train.BytesList(value =
                            [image.tostring()])),
```

Uses OpenCV to read in the uncompressed image

Creates a feature entry for the uncompressed image byte data

```
                  'label': tf.train.Feature(int64_list = tf.train.Int64List(value =
                                      [label])),
                  'shape': tf.train.Feature(int64_list = tf.train.Int64List(value =
                                      [shape[0], shape[1], shape[2]]))
              }))

example = TFExampleImageUncompressed('example.jpg', 0)
print(example.ByteSize())
```

Creates a feature entry for the corresponding label (margin left, top)

Creates a feature entry for the corresponding shape as H × W × C (margin right)

TF.EXAMPLE: MACHINE LEARNING READY

In our final code example, we first normalize the pixel data (by dividing by 255) and store the normalized image data. The advantage to this method is that we do not need to normalize the pixel data each time the entry is read from a TFRecord on disk during training. The drawback is that now the pixel data is stored as np.float32, which is four times bigger than the corresponding np.uint8. Assuming the same image example, the size of the TFRecord will now be 2 million bytes.

Uses OpenCV to read in the uncompressed image and normalize the pixel data (margin right)

```
def TFExampleImageNormalized(path, label):
    ''' The normalized version of the image '''

    image = (cv2.imread(path) / 255.0).astype(np.float32)
    shape = image.shape

    return tf.train.Example(features = tf.train.Features(feature = {
        'image': tf.train.Feature(bytes_list = tf.train.BytesList(value =
                             [image.tostring()])),
        'label': tf.train.Feature(int64_list = tf.train.Int64List(value =
                             [label])),
        'shape': tf.train.Feature(int64_list = tf.train.Int64List(value =
                             [shape[0], shape[1], shape[2]]))
    }))

example = TFExampleImageNormalized('example.jpg', 0)
print(example.ByteSize())
```

Creates a feature entry for the uncompressed image byte data (margin left)

Creates a feature entry for the corresponding label (margin left)

Creates a feature entry for the corresponding shape as H × W × C (margin right)

TFRECORD: WRITING A RECORD

Now that we have constructed a tf.train.Example entry in memory, the next step is to write it to a TFRecord file on disk. We will do this for the purpose of later feeding training data from the disk when training a model.

To maximize the efficiency of writing to and reading back from on-disk storage, the records are serialized to a string format for storing in Google's protocol buffer format. In the following code, tf.io.TFRecordWriter is a function that will write a serialized record to a file in this format. It is also a common convention when writing a TFRecord to disk to use the suffix .tfrecord in the filename.

Creates a TFRecord file writer object

Writes a single serialized tf.train.Example entry to the file

```
with tf.io.TFRecordWriter('example.tfrecord') as writer:
    writer.write(example.SerializeToString())
```

An on-disk TFRecord file may contain multiple tf.train.Example entries. The following code writes multiple serialized tf.train.Example entries to a TFRecord file:

Creates a TFRecord file writer object

Writes each tf.train .Example entry sequentially to TFRecord file

```
with tf.io.TFRecordWriter('example.tfrecord') as writer:
    for example in examples:
        writer.write(example.SerializeToString())
```

TFRecord: Reading a record

The next code example demonstrates how to read each tf.train.Example entry from a TFRecord file in sequential order. We assume that the file example.tfrecord contains multiple serialized tf.train.Example entries.

The tf.compat.v1.io.record_interator() creates an iterator object that when used in a for statement will read into memory each serialized tf.train.Example in sequential order. The method ParseFromString() is used to deserialize the data into an in-memory tf.train.Example format.

Creates an iterator for iterating through tf.train.Example entries in sequential order

Iterates through each entry and converts serialized string to tf.train.Example

```
iterator = tf.compat.v1.io.tf_record_iterator('example.tfrecord')
for entry in iterator:
    example = tf.train.Example()
    example.ParseFromString(entry)
```

Alternatively, we can read and iterate through a set of tf.train.Example entries from a TFRecord file by using the tf.data.TFRecordDataset class. In the next code example, we do the following:

- Instantiate a tf.data.TFRecordDataset object as an iterator for the on-disk records
- Define the dictionary feature_description to specify how to deserialize the serialized tf.train.Example entries
- Define the helper function _parse_function() for taking a serialized tf.train .Example (proto) and deserializing it using the dictionary feature_description
- Use the map() method to iteratively deserialize each tf.train.Example entry

Creates an iterator for the on-disk dataset

Creates a dictionary description for deserializing a tf.train.Example

Function for sequential parsing of tf.train.Example

Parses each entry in the dataset using map()

```
dataset = tf.data.TFRecordDataset('example.tfrecord')

feature_description = {
    'image': tf.io.FixedLenFeature([], tf.string),
    'label': tf.io.FixedLenFeature([], tf.int64),
    'shape': tf.io.FixedLenFeature([3], tf.int64),
}

def _parse_function(proto):
    ''' parse the next serialized tf.train.Example using the feature
    description '''
    return tf.io.parse_single_example(proto, feature_description)

parsed_dataset = dataset.map(_parse_function)
```

If we print `parsed_dataset`, the output should be as follows:

```
<MapDataset shapes: {image: (), shape: (), label: ()},
types: {image: tf.string, shape: tf.int64, label: tf.int64}>
```

13.2 Data feeding

In the previous section, we discussed how data is structured and stored for training, both in memory and on disk. This section covers ingesting the data into a pipeline with `tf.data`, which is a TensorFlow module for constructing a dataset pipeline. It can construct pipelines from a variety of sources, such as NumPy and TensorFlow tensors in memory and TFRecords from on disk.

A dataset pipeline is created as a generator with the class `tf.data.Dataset`. Thus, `tf.data` refers to the Python module, while `tf.data.Dataset` refers to the dataset pipeline. The data pipeline is used for both preprocessing and feeding data for training a model.

First we'll cover constructing a data pipeline from in-memory NumPy data and then subsequently cover constructing one from on-disk TFRecords.

13.2.1 NumPy

To create an in-memory dataset generator from NumPy data, we use the `tf.data` `.Dataset` method `from_tensor_slices()`. The method takes as a parameter the training data, which is specified as a tuple: `(images, labels)`.

In the following code, we create a `tf.data.Dataset` from the CIFAR-10 NumPy data, which we specify as the parameter value `(x_train, y_train)`:

```
from tensorflow.data import Dataset
from tensorflow.keras.datasets import cifar10
(x_train, y_train), (x_test, y_test) = cifar10.load_data()

dataset = Dataset.from_tensor_slices((x_train, y_train))
```
Creates a dataset generator for in-memory NumPy training data

Note that the `dataset` is a generator; thus it is not subscriptable. You cannot do a `dataset[0]` and expect to get the first element. That will throw an exception.

Next, we will iterate through the dataset. But we want to do this in batches, as we do when feeding data by using the `fit()` method in TF.Keras and we specify a batch size. In the next code example, we use the method `batch()` to set the batch size for the dataset to 128. Note that `batch` is not a property. It does not change the state of the existing dataset, but creates a new generator. That's why we assign `dataset .batch(128)` back to the original `dataset` variable. TensorFlow refers to these types of dataset methods as *dataset transformations*.

Next, we iterate through the dataset and for each batch `(x_batch, y_batch)` we print the shape. For each batch, this will output (128, 32, 32, 3) for the image data and (128, 1) for the corresponding labels:

```
                                          │ Transforms the dataset to
                                          │ iterate in batches of 128
dataset = dataset.batch(128)    ◁─────┘
for x_batch, y_batch in dataset:            │ Iterates through the
    print(x_batch.shape, y_batch.shape)     │ dataset in batches of 128
```

If we repeat the same `for` loop iteration a second time, we would get no output. Why? What happened? By default, dataset generators iterate only once through a dataset. To continuously repeat, as if we have multiple epochs, we use the `repeat()` method as another dataset transformation. Since we want every epoch to see a different random ordering of the batches, we use the `shuffle()` method as another dataset transformation. This sequence of dataset transformations is demonstrated here:

```
dataset = dataset.shuffle(1024)
dataset = dataset.repeat()
dataset = dataset.batch(128)
```

The dataset transformation methods are also chainable. It's common to see them chained together. This single line is identical to the preceding three-line sequence:

```
dataset = dataset.shuffle(1024).repeat().batch(128)
```

The order that the transformations are applied is important. If we use `repeat()` first and then the `shuffle()` transformation, then on the first epoch, the batches would not be randomized.

Also note that we specify a value to the `shuffle()` transformation. This value indicates the number of examples to pull from the dataset into memory and shuffle at a time. For example, if we have enough memory to hold the entire dataset in memory, we set this value to the total number of examples in the training data (for example, 50000 for CIFAR-10). That will shuffle the entire dataset at once—a complete shuffle. If we don't, we need to calculate how much memory we can spare and divide by the size of each in-memory example. Let's say we have 2 GB to spare, and each in-memory example is 200,000 bytes. In this case, we would set the size to 10,000 (2 GB / 200K).

In the next code example, we train a simple ConvNet with CIFAR-10 data using `tf.data.Dataset` as the data pipeline. The `fit()` method is compatible with `tf.data.Dataset` generators. Instead of passing the raw image data and corresponding labels, we pass the dataset generator, specified by the variable `dataset`.

Because it is a generator, the `fit()` method does not know how many batches will be in an epoch. So we need to additionally specify the `steps_per_epoch` and set it to the number of batches in the training data. In our case, we calculated this as the number of examples in the training data divided by the batch size (`50000 // 128`):

```
from tensorflow.keras import Sequential
from tensorflow.keras.layers import Conv2D, ReLU, Activation,
from tensorflow.keras.layers import BatchNormalization, Dense, Flatten
```

```
model = Sequential()
model.add(Conv2D(16, (3,3), strides=1, padding='same', input_shape=(32, 32,
    3)))
model.add(BatchNormalization())
model.add(ReLU())
model.add(Conv2D(32, (3,3), strides=1, padding='same'))
model.add(BatchNormalization())
model.add(ReLU())
model.add(Flatten())
model.add(Dense(10, activation='softmax'))
model.compile(loss='sparse_categorical_crossentropy', optimizer='adam',
            metrics=['acc'])

batches = 50000 // 128
model.fit(dataset, steps_per_epoch=batches, epochs=5, verbose=1)
```

Trains with the fit() method
using the dataset generator

Calculates the number of
batches in the dataset

In this section, we covered constructing a data pipeline from an in-memory source of data, such as in a NumPy or TensorFlow tensor format. Next, we will cover constructing a data pipeline from an on-disk source of data using TFRecords.

13.2.2 *TFRecord*

To create an on-disk dataset generator from TFRecord files, we use the `tf.data` method `TFRecordDataset()`. The method takes as a parameter the path to a single TFRecord file or a list of paths to multiple TFRecord files. As covered in the previous section, each TFRecord file may contain one or more training examples, such as images, and for I/O performance purposes, the training data may span multiple TFRecord files.

This code creates a dataset generator for a single TFRecord file:

```
dataset = tf.data.TFRecordDataset('example.tfrecord')
```

This code example creates a dataset generator for multiple TFRecord files, when the dataset spans multiple TFRecord files:

```
dataset = tf.data.TFRecordDataset(['example1.tfrecord', 'example2.tfrecord'])
```

Next, we have to tell the dataset generator how to parse each serialized entry in the TFRecord file. We use the `map()` method, which allows us to define a function for parsing a TFRecord-specific example, which will be applied (mapped) to each example, each time the example is read from the disk.

In the following example, we first define the `feature_description` to describe how to parse the TFRecord-specific entries. Using the earlier example, we assume the layout of our entry is a byte-encoded image key/value, an integer label key/value, and a three-element integer shape key/value. We then use the method `tf.io.parse_single_example()` to parse the serialized example in the TFRecord file based on the feature description:

```
feature_description = {
    'image': tf.io.FixedLenFeature([], tf.string),
    'label': tf.io.FixedLenFeature([], tf.int64),
    'shape': tf.io.FixedLenFeature([3], tf.int64),
}
```
Creates a dictionary description for deserializing a tf.train.Example

```
def _parse_function(proto):
```
Function for sequential parsing of tf.train.Example
```
    ''' parse the next serialized tf.train.Example using the feature
      description '''
    return tf.io.parse_single_example(proto, feature_description)

dataset = dataset.map(_parse_function)
```
Parses each entry in the dataset using map()

Let's now do a few more dataset transformations and then take a peek at what we have when we iterate through the on-disk TFRecord. In this code example, we apply the transformation to shuffle and set the batch size to 2. We then iterate through the dataset in batches of two examples, and display the corresponding `label` and `shape` keys/values:

```
dataset = dataset.shuffle(4).batch(2)
```
Creates an iterator for the on-disk database
```
for entry in dataset:
    print(entry['label'], entry['shape'])
```
Iterates through the on-disk TFRecord in batches of two examples

The following output shows that each batch consists of two examples, the labels in the first batch are 0 and 1, and the labels in the second batch are 1 and 0, and all images are of the size (512, 512, 3):

```
tf.Tensor([0 1], shape=(2,), dtype=int64) tf.Tensor(
[[512 512    3]
 [512 512    3]], shape=(2, 3), dtype=int64)
tf.Tensor([1 0], shape=(2,), dtype=int64) tf.Tensor(
[[512 512    3]
 [512 512    3]], shape=(2, 3), dtype=int64)
```

TFRECORD: COMPRESSED IMAGE

So far, we haven't addressed the format in which the serialized image data is encoded. Generally, the image is encoded in either a compressed format (such as JPEG) or uncompressed format (raw). In the next code example, we add an additional step in `_parse_function()` to decode the image data from a compressed format (JPEG) to an uncompressed format using `tf.io.decode_jpg()`. Thus, as each example is read from disk and deserialized, now the image data is decoded:

```
dataset = tf.data.TFRecordDataset(['example.tfrecord'])

feature_description = {
    'image': tf.io.FixedLenFeature([], tf.string),
    'label': tf.io.FixedLenFeature([], tf.int64),
    'shape': tf.io.FixedLenFeature([3], tf.int64),
}
```

```
def _parse_function(proto):
    ''' parse the next serialized tf.train.Example
        using the feature description
    '''
    example = tf.io.parse_single_example(proto, feature_description)
    example['image'] = tf.io.decode_jpg(example['image'])   <──┐   Decodes the
    return example                                               compressed
                                                                 JPEG image
dataset = dataset.map(_parse_function)
```

TFRECORD: UNCOMPRESSED IMAGE

In the next code example, the encoded image data is in an uncompressed format in the TFRecord file. Thus, we do not need to uncompress it, but we still need to decode the encoded bytelist into the raw bitmap format by using `tf.io.decode_raw()`.

The raw decoded data at this point is a 1D array, so we need to reshape it back into its original shape. After we get the raw decoded data, we get the original shape from the key/value `shape` and then reshape the raw image data by using `tf.reshape()`:

```
dataset = tf.data.TFRecordDataset(['tfrec/example.tfrecord'])

feature_description = {
    'image': tf.io.FixedLenFeature([], tf.string),
    'label': tf.io.FixedLenFeature([], tf.int64),
    'shape': tf.io.FixedLenFeature([3], tf.int64),
}                                                    Decodes the image data as
                                                     uncompressed raw format
def _parse_function(proto):
    ''' parse the next serialized tf.train.Example using the
        feature description
    '''
    example = tf.io.parse_single_example(proto, feature_description)
    example['image'] = tf.io.decode_raw(example['image'], tf.uint8)  <──┘
    shape = example['shape']
    example['image'] = tf.reshape(example['image'], shape)   <──┐   Reshapes the
    return example                                                decoded image back
                                                                 to original shape
dataset = dataset.map(_parse_function)
```

Gets the original image shape (annotation pointing to `shape = example['shape']`)

13.3 *Data preprocessing*

So far, we've covered data formats, storage, and reading training data from memory or disk, along with some data preprocessing. In this section, we will go into more detail on preprocessing. First, we will look at how preprocessing can be moved out of the upstream data pipeline and moved into the pre-stem model component, and then we will look at how to set up a preprocessing pipeline using TFX.

13.3.1 *Preprocessing with a pre-stem*

You should recall that one of the recommendations when TensorFlow 2.0 was released was to move preprocessing into the graph. We could take two approaches. First, we could hardwire it into the graph. Second, we could make the preprocessing independent of the model but be plug-and-play such that the preprocessing occurs on the graph and can be interchangeable. The benefits to this plug-and-play pre-stem approach are as follows:

- Reusable and interchangeable component in a training and deployment pipeline
- Runs on the graph instead of upstream on a CPU, eliminating potentially being I/O bound when feeding a model for training

Figure 13.7 depicts using plug-and-play pre-stems for preprocessing. This depiction shows a collection of plug-and-play pre-stem components to choose from when training or deploying the model. The requirement for attaching a pre-stem is that its output shape must match the input shape of the model.

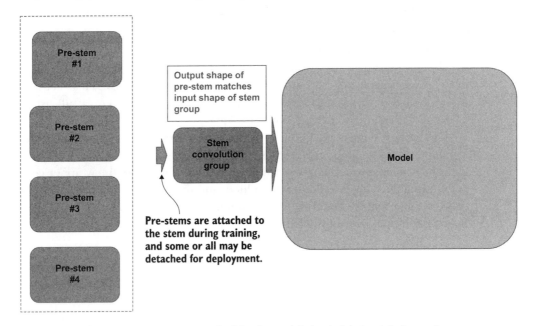

Figure 13.7 Plug-and-play pre-stems can be interchanged during training and deployment.

Pre-stems have two requirements to be plug-and-play with existing models, trained and untrained:

- The output from the pre-stem must match the input from the model. For example, if the model takes as input (224, 224, 3)—such as a stock ResNet50—then the output of the pre-stem must also be (224, 224, 3).
- The input shape for the pre-stem must match the input source, whether for training or prediction. For example, the input source may be a different size than what the model was trained on, and the pre-stem has been trained to learn the optimal method to resize the images.

Plug-and-play pre-stems generally fall into two types:

- Stays with the model after deployment for prediction. For example, the pre-stem handles resizing and normalization of the input source, when the prediction request consists of raw bytes from an uncompressed image.
- Used only during training, and not used after deployment. For example, the pre-stem does random image augmentation for learning translational and scale invariance during training, eliminating the need to configure the data pipeline to do image augmentation.

We will cover two methods of constructing a pre-stem for moving data preprocessing into the graph. The first method adds layers to TF.Keras 2.x for this purpose, and the second uses subclassing to create your own custom preprocessing layers.

TF.KERAS PREPROCESSING LAYERS

To further aid and encourage moving preprocessing into the graph, TF.Keras 2.2 and subsequent versions introduced new layers for preprocessing. This eliminated the need to use subclassing to build common preprocessing steps. This section covers three of these layers: `Rescaling`, `Resizing`, and `CenterCrop`. For a full list, see the TF.Keras documentation (http://mng.bz/7jqe).

Figure 13.8 depicts attaching a plug-and-play pre-stem to an existing model by using a wrapper technique. Here, a second model instance is created, which we refer to as the *wrapper model*. Using the sequential API, for example, the wrapper consists of two components: first the pre-stem is added, and then the existing model is added. To connect the existing model to the pre-stem, the output shape of the pre-stem must match the input shape of the existing model.

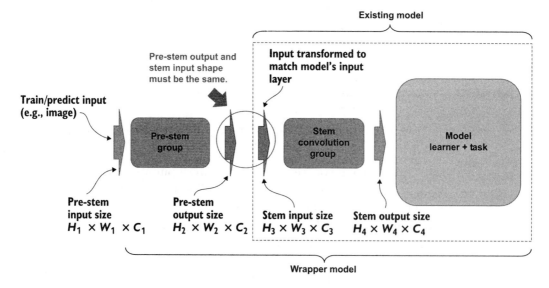

Figure 13.8   A wrapper model attaches a pre-stem to an existing model.

The next code example implements a plug-and-play pre-stem that we add to an existing model prior to training. First, we create an untrained ConvNet with two convolutional (Conv2D) layers of 16 and 32 filters, respectively. We then flatten (Flatten) the feature maps into a 1D vector, without dimensionality reduction, as the bottleneck layer and then the final Dense layer for classification. We will use this ConvNet model as the model we want to train and deploy.

Next, we instantiate another empty model, which we will call the wrapper model. The wrapper will consist of two parts: the pre-stem, and the untrained ConvNet model. For the pre-stem, we add the preprocessing layer Rescaling to normalize the integer pixel data between floating-point values 0 and 1. Since the pre-stem will be the input layer in the wrapper model, we add the parameter (input_shape=(32, 32, 3)) to specify the input shape. Since Rescaling does not change the size of the input, the output from the pre-stem matches that of the input to the model.

Finally, we train the wrapper model and use the wrapper model for prediction. Thus, for both training and prediction, the normalizing of the integer pixel data is now part of the wrapper model, executed on the graph, instead of upstream on the CPU.

```
from tensorflow.keras import Sequential
from tensorflow.keras.layers import Conv2D, ReLU, Activation,
from tensorflow.keras.layers import BatchNormalization, Dense, Flatten
from tensorflow.keras.layers.experimental.preprocessing import Rescaling
```
Imports the preprocessing layer for Rescaling

```
model = Sequential()
```
Constructs a simple ConvNet
```
model.add(Conv2D(16, (3,3), strides=1, padding='same', input_shape=(32, 32, 3)))
model.add(BatchNormalization())
model.add(ReLU())
model.add(Conv2D(32, (3,3), strides=1, padding='same'))
model.add(BatchNormalization())
model.add(ReLU())
model.add(Flatten())
model.add(Dense(10, activation='softmax'))

wrapper = Sequential()
wrapper.add(Rescaling(scale=1.0/255, input_shape=(32, 32, 3)))
```
Constructs a pre-stem with Rescaling

```
wrapper.add(model)
wrapper.compile(loss='sparse_categorical_crossentropy', optimizer='adam',
              metrics=['acc'])
```
Adds the pre-stem to the ConvNet

```
from tensorflow.keras.datasets import cifar10
(x_train, y_train), (x_test, y_test) = cifar10.load_data()
wrapper.fit(x_train, y_train, epochs=5, batch_size=32, verbose=1)
wrapper.evaluate(x_test, y_test)
```
Trains and tests the ConvNet with the pre-stem

A plug-and-play pre-stem can have more than one preprocessing layer, as shown in figure 13.9, such as a resizing of the image input followed by a rescaling of the pixel data.

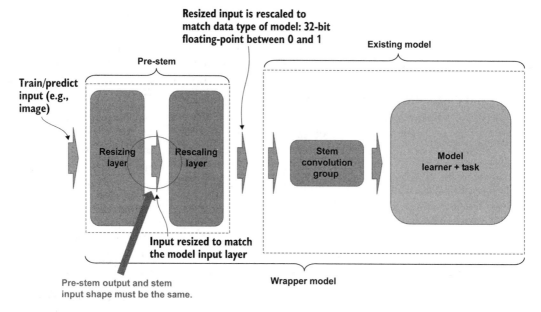

Figure 13.9   A pre-stem with two preprocessing layers

In this depiction, since rescaling does not change the output shape, the output shape from the preceding resizing layer must match the input shape of the stem group.

The following code implements a plug-and-play pre-stem that performs two functions: resizes the input and normalizes the pixel data. We start by creating the same ConvNet as in the previous example. Next, we create the wrapper model with two preprocessing layers: one to do the image resizing (Resizing) and one to do the normalization (Rescaling). In this example, the input to the ConvNet is of shape (28, 28, 3). We use a pre-stem to resize an input from (32, 32, 3) to (28, 28, 3) to match the ConvNet and normalize the pixel data:

```
from tensorflow.keras import Sequential
from tensorflow.keras.layers import Conv2D, ReLU, BatchNormalization,
from tensorflow.keras.layers import Dense, Flatten
from tensorflow.keras.layers.experimental.preprocessing import Rescaling
from tensorflow.keras.layers.experimental.preprocessing import Resizing

from tensorflow.keras.datasets import cifar10
(x_train, y_train), (x_test, y_test) = cifar10.load_data()

model = Sequential()
model.add(Conv2D(16, (3,3), strides=1, padding='same', input_shape=(28, 28, 3)))
model.add(BatchNormalization())
model.add(ReLU())
model.add(Conv2D(32, (3,3), strides=1, padding='same'))
model.add(BatchNormalization())
model.add(ReLU())
```

```
model.add(Flatten())
model.add(Dense(10, activation='softmax'))

wrapper = Sequential()          ⟵——————| Creates the wrapper model
wrapper.add(Resizing(height=28, width=28, input_shape=(32, 32, 3)))
wrapper.add(Rescaling(scale=1.0/255))
wrapper.add(model)
wrapper.compile(loss='sparse_categorical_crossentropy', optimizer='adam',
metrics=['acc'])

wrapper.fit(x_train, y_train, epochs=5, batch_size=32, verbose=1)
wrapper.evaluate(x_test, y_test)
```

Adds the pre-stem to the wrapper model

Adds the ConvNet to the model and trains it

Now that we have trained the model, we can remove the pre-stem and use the model for inference. In the next example, we assume that the image test data is already sized (28, 28, 3) to match our ConvNet, and we normalize the pixel data upstream from the model. We know that the first two layers of the wrapper model are the pre-stem, which means our underlying trained model starts at the third layer; hence will we set the model to wrapper.layers[2]. Now we can do inference with the underlying model without the pre-stem:

```
x_test = (x_test / 255.0).astype(np.float32)    ⟵——| Data preprocessing occurs
model = wrapper.layers[2]       ⟵——————               upstream on the CPU
model.evaluate(x_test, y_test)
```

Gets the underlying model w/o the pre-stem

Does an evaluation (prediction) with the underlying model

CHAINING PRE-STEMS

Figure 13.10 depicts chaining together pre-stems; one pre-stem will stay with the model deployment, and the other will be removed when the model is deployed. Here,

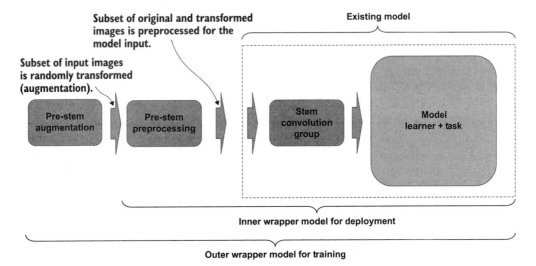

Figure 13.10 Pre-stems chained together—the inner pre-stem stays with the model after deployment, and the outer pre-stem is removed.

we create two wrapper models: an inner and outer wrapper. The inner wrapper contains a preprocessing pre-stem that will stay with the model when deployed, and the outer wrapper contains an image augmentation pre-stem that will be removed from the model when deployed. For training, we train the outer wrapper model, and for deployment, we deploy the inner wrapper model.

In our final example, we will chain two pre-stems together. The first pre-stem is used for training and then removed for inference, and the second one stays with the model. In the first (inner) pre-stem, we do normalization of the integer pixel data (Rescaling). In the second (outer) pre-stem, we do center cropping (CenterCrop) of the input images for training. We also set the input size to the second pre-stem to be any height and width: (None, None, 3). As a result, we can feed images of different sizes to the second pre-stem during training, and it will center-crop them to (32, 32, 3), which is then passed as the input to the first pre-stem, which does the normalization.

Finally, when trained, we remove the second (outer) pre-stem and do inference without the center cropping:

```
from tensorflow.keras import Sequential
from tensorflow.keras.layers import Conv2D, ReLU, BatchNormalization,
from tensorflow.keras.layers import Dense, Flatten
from tensorflow.keras.layers.experimental.preprocessing import Rescaling,
from tensorflow.keras.layers.experimental.preprocessing import CenterCrop

from tensorflow.keras.datasets import cifar10
(x_train, y_train), (x_test, y_test) = cifar10.load_data()
model = Sequential()                          ⟵——| Constructs the ConvNet model
model.add(Conv2D(16, (3,3), strides=1, padding='same', input_shape=(32, 32, 3)))
model.add(BatchNormalization())
model.add(ReLU())
model.add(Conv2D(32, (3,3), strides=1, padding='same'))
model.add(BatchNormalization())
model.add(ReLU())
model.add(Flatten())
model.add(Dense(10, activation='softmax'))
model.compile(loss='sparse_categorical_crossentropy',
              optimizer='adam', metrics=['acc'])

wrapper1 = Sequential()
wrapper1.add(Rescaling(scale=1.0/255, input_shape=(32, 32, 3)))
wrapper1.add(model)
wrapper1.compile(loss='sparse_categorical_crossentropy',
              optimizer='adam', metrics=['acc'])

wrapper2 = Sequential()
wrapper2.add(CenterCrop(height=32, width=32, input_shape=(None, None, 3)))
wrapper2.add(wrapper1)
wrapper2.compile(loss='sparse_categorical_crossentropy',
              optimizer='adam', metrics=['acc'])

wrapper2.fit(x_train, y_train, epochs=5, batch_size=32, verbose=1)

wrapper2.layers[1].evaluate(x_test, y_test)
```

Annotations:
- **Attaches the first pre-stem for normalizing the image data during training and inference**
- **Attaches the second pre-stem for center-cropping the image data during training**
- **Does inference with only the first pre-stem**
- **Trains the model with the first and second pre-stem**

TF.KERAS SUBCLASSING LAYERS

Alternatively to using TF.Keras built-in preprocessing layers, we can create our own custom preprocessing layers by using layer subclassing. This is useful when you need a custom preprocessing step that is not prebuilt into TF.Keras preprocessing layers.

All the predefined layers in TF.Keras are subclassed from the `TF.Keras.Layer` class. To create your own custom layer, you need to do the following:

1 Create a class that subclasses (inherits) the `TF.Keras.Layer` class.
2 Override the initializer `__init__()`, `build()`, and `call()` methods.

Let's now build our own version of the preprocessing layer `Rescaling` by using subclassing. In the next example code implementation, we define the class `Rescaling`, which inherits from `TF.Keras.Layer`. Next, we override the initializer `__init__()`. In the underlying `Layer` class, the initializer takes two parameters:

- `input_shape`—When used as the first layer in the model, the input shape of the model input
- `name`—The user-definable name for this layer instance

We pass these two parameters down to the underlying `Layer` initializer via the `super()` call.

Any remaining parameters to `__init_()` are layer-specific (custom) parameters. For `Rescaling`, we add the parameter `scale` and save its value in the class object.

Next, we override the `build()` method. This method is called when we `compile()` the model or bind one layer to another using the functional API. The underlying method takes the parameter `input_shape`, which specifies the input shape to the layer. The underlying parameter `self.kernel` sets the shape of the kernel for the layer; the kernel shape specifies the number of parameters. If we did have learnable parameters, we would set the kernel shape and how to initialize it. Since `Rescaling` has no learnable parameters, we set it to `None`.

Finally, we override the `call()` method. This method is invoked when the graph is executing for training or inference. The underlying method takes as a parameter `inputs`, which is the input tensor to the layer, and the method returns the output tensor. In our case, we will multiply each pixel value in the input tensor by the `scale` factor set when the layer was initialized, and output the rescaled tensor.

We add the decorator `@tf.function` to tell TensorFlow AutoGraph (www.tensorflow.org/api_docs/python/tf/autograph) to convert the Python code in this method to graph operations in the model. AutoGraph, a tool introduced with TensorFlow 2.0, is a precompiler that can convert a variety of Python operations into static graph operations. This allows Python code that can be converted into static graph operations to be moved from executing upstream on the CPU to execution in the graph. While many Python constructs are supported for conversion, the conversion is limited to graph operations on non-eager tensors.

```
import tensorflow as tf
from tensorflow.keras import Sequential
from tensorflow.keras.layers import Conv2D, ReLU, Activation,
from tensorflow.keras.layers import BatchNormalization, Dense, Flatten
from tensorflow.keras.layers import Layer

class Rescaling(Layer):
    """ Custom Layer for Preprocessing Input """
    def __init__(self, scale, input_shape=None, name=None):
        """ Constructor """
        super(Rescaling, self).__init__(input_shape=input_shape, name=name)
        self.scale = scale

    def build(self, input_shape):
        """ Handler for building the layer """
        self.kernel = None

    @tf.function
    def call(self, inputs):
        """ Handler for layer object is callable """
        inputs = inputs * self.scale
        return inputs
```

Defines a custom layer using Layer subclassing

Overrides the initializer and adds input parameter scale

Overrides the build() method

Saves the scaling factor in the layer object instance

Tells AutoGraph to convert method into graph operations that are put into the model

There are no learnable (trainable) parameters.

Overrides the call() method

Scales each pixel (element) in the input tensor

For detailed information on Layer and Model subclassing, see the variety of tutorials and notebook examples on subclassing from the TensorFlow team, such as "Making New Layers and Models via Subclassing" (http://mng.bz/my54).

13.3.2 *Preprocessing with TF Extended*

So far, we've discussed constructing data pipelines from low-level components. Here we see how to construct data pipelines using higher-level components, which encapsulate more of the steps, using TensorFlow Extended.

TensorFlow Extended (TFX) is an e2e production pipeline. This section covers the data pipeline portion of TFX, as depicted in figure 13.11.

At a high level, the ExampleGen component ingests data from a dataset source. The StatisticsGen component analyzes the examples from the dataset and produces statistics on the dataset distribution. The SchemaGen component, typically used for structured data, derives a data schema from the dataset statistics. For example, it may infer feature types, such as categorical or numeric, data types, ranges, and set data policies such as how to handle missing data. The ExampleValidator component monitors the training and serving data for anomalies, based on the data schema. These four components collectively compose the TFX Data Validation library.

The Transform component does data transformations, such as feature engineering, data preprocessing, and data augmentation. This component composes the TFX Transform library.

The TFX package is not part of the TensorFlow 2.x release, so you will need to install it separately, as follows:

```
pip install tfx
```

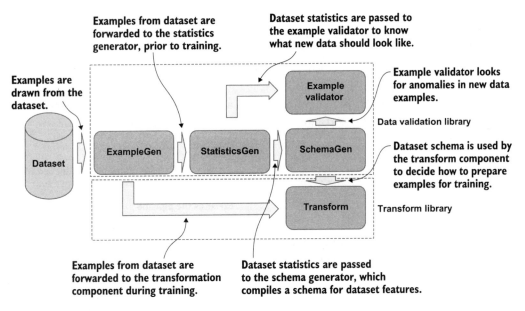

Examples from dataset are forwarded to the statistics generator, prior to training.

Dataset statistics are passed to the example validator to know what new data should look like.

Examples are drawn from the dataset.

Example validator looks for anomalies in new data examples.

Data validation library

Dataset schema is used by the transform component to decide how to prepare examples for training.

Transform library

Examples from dataset are forwarded to the transformation component during training.

Dataset statistics are passed to the schema generator, which compiles a schema for dataset features.

Figure 13.11   TFX data pipeline

The remainder of this subsection covers each of these components at a high level only. For detailed references and tutorials, see the TensorFlow documentation for TFX (www.tensorflow.org/tfx).

Next, let's create a code snippet for importing modules and classes we will use in all the subsequent code examples:

Imports ExampleGen component instance for TFRecords

Imports util for reading datasets from external sources

Imports remaining TFX data pipeline components

```
from tfx.utils.dsl_utils import external_input
from tfx.components import ImportExampleGen
from tfx.components import StatisticsGen, SchemaGen, ExampleValidator
from tfx.components import Transform
from tfx.orchestration.experimental.interactive.interactive_context import
InteractiveContext
```

Imports TFX pipeline orchestration

We will use the TFX pipeline orchestration module in the subsequent code examples for an interactive demonstration. These code sequences set up a pipeline, but nothing happens until orchestration, when the pipeline is executed.

```
context = InteractiveContext()
```
Instantiates the interactive pipeline orchestration

EXAMPLEGEN

The ExampleGen component is the entry point into the TFX data pipeline. Its purpose is to draw batches of examples from a dataset. It supports a wide variety of dataset formats, including CSV files, TFRecords, and Google BigQuery. The output from ExampleGen are tf.Example records.

The next code example instantiates the ExampleGen component for a dataset on disk in TFRecord format (for example, images). It consists of two steps.

Let's start with the second step. We instantiate the ExampleGen component as subclass ImportExampleGen, where the initializer takes as a parameter the input source for the examples (input=examples).

Now let's back up a step and define a connector to the input source. Since the input source is TFRecords, we use the TFX utilities method external_input() to map a connector between the TFRecords on disk and our instance of ImportExampleGen:

```
examples = external_input('tfrec')              Instantiates an ExampleGen where
example_gen = ImportExampleGen(input=examples)   TFRecords are the input source
context.run(example_gen)    ◄───────
                                      Executes the pipeline
```

STATISTICSGEN

The StatisticsGen component generates dataset statistics from an input source of examples. These examples can be either training/evaluation data or serving data (the latter is not covered here). In the next code example, we generate dataset statistics for the training/evaluation data. We instantiate an instance of StatisticsGen(), and pass to the initializer the source of the examples. Here, the source for the examples is the output from our example_gen instance in the previous code example. The output is specified via the ExampleGen property outputs, which is a dictionary, for the key/value pair examples:

```
statistics_gen = StatisticsGen(                 Instantiates a StatisticsGen
    examples=example_gen.outputs['examples'])  ◄  with the input from the
context.run(statistics_gen)        ◄─────────   output of ExampleGen
statistics_gen.outputs['statistics']._artifacts[0]   Executes the pipeline
```
Displays interactive output of the statistics

The output from the last line of code will look something like the following. The uri property is a local directory that stores the statistics. The split_names property indicates two sets of statistics, one for training and one for evaluation:

```
Artifact of type 'ExampleStatistics' (uri: /tmp/tfx-interactive-2020-05-
    28T19_02_20.322858-8g1v59q7/StatisticsGen/statistics/2) at
    0x7f9c7a1414d0
```

.type	<class 'tfx.types.standard_artifacts.ExampleStatistics'>
.uri	/tmp/tfx-interactive-2020-05-28T19_02_20.322858-8g1v59q7/StatisticsGen/statistics/2
.span	0
.split_names	["train", "eval"]

SchemaGen

The `SchemaGen` component generates a schema from the dataset statistics. In the next code example, we generate a schema from the dataset statistics for the training/evaluation data. We instantiate an instance of `SchemaGen()`, and pass to the initializer the source of the dataset statistics. In our example, the source for the statistics is the output from our `statistics_gen` instance in the previous code example. The output is specified via the `StatisticsGen` property `outputs`, which is a dictionary, for the key/value pair `statistics`:

```
schema_gen = SchemaGen(                                    ⟵ Instantiates a SchemaGen
    statistics=statistics_gen.outputs['statistics'])         with the input from the
context.run(schema_gen)                                       output of ExampleGen
schema_gen.outputs['schema']._artifacts[0]   ⟵  Displays interactive
                                                 output of the schema
```

The output from the last line of code will look something like the following. The `uri` property is a local directory that stores the schema. The filename for the schema will be schema.pbtxt.

Artifact of type **'Schema'** (uri: /tmp/tfx-interactive-2020-05-28T19_02_20
➥ .322858-8g1v59q7/SchemaGen/schema/4) at 0x7f9c500d1790

.type	<class 'tfx.types.standard_artifacts.Schema'>
.uri	/tmp/tfx-interactive-2020-05-28T19_02_20.322858-8g1v59q7/SchemaGen/schema/4

For our example, the contents of schema.pbtxt will look like this:

```
feature {
  name: "image"
  value_count {
    min: 1
    max: 1
  }
  type: BYTES
  presence {
    min_fraction: 1.0
    min_count: 1
  }
}
feature {
  name: "label"
  value_count {
    min: 0
    max: 1
  }
  type: INT
  presence {
    min_fraction: 1.0
    min_count: 1
```

```
    }
  }
feature {
  name: "shape"
  value_count {
    min: 3
    max: 3
  }
  type: INT
  presence {
    min_fraction: 1.0
    min_count: 1
  }
}
```

EXAMPLE VALIDATOR

The ExampleValidator component identifies anomalies in a dataset using both the dataset statistics and schema as inputs. In the next code example, we identify anomalies from the dataset statistics and schema for the training/evaluation data. We instantiate an instance of ExampleValidator(), and pass to the initializer the source of the dataset statistics and the schema. In our example, the sources for the statistics and schema are the output from our statistics_gen instance and schema_gen instances, respectively, in the previous code examples.

```
example_validator = ExampleValidator(
    statistics=statistics_gen.outputs['statistics'],   ◁── Instantiates an ExampleValidator
    schema=schema_gen.outputs['schema'])               ◁──┘
context.run(example_validator)                                  Displays interactive
example_validator.outputs['anomalies']._artifacts[0]  ◁──┘     output of the anomalies
```

The output from the last line of code will look something like the following. The uri property is a local directory that stores information on anomalies, if any would be stored.

Artifact of type **'ExampleAnomalies'** (uri:) at 0x7f9c780cbdd0

.type	<class 'tfx.types.standard_artifacts.ExampleAnomalies'>
.uri	
.span	0

TRANSFORM

The Transform components perform the dataset transformations as examples are drawn into batches during training or inference. Dataset transformations are typically feature engineering for structured data, and data preprocessing.

In the following code example, we transform batches of examples from the dataset. We instantiate an instance of Transform(). The initializer takes three parameters:

the input source for the `examples` to transform, the data `schema`, and a custom Python script to do the transformation (for example, `my_preprocessing_fn.py`). We won't cover how to write custom Python scripts for transformation; for more details, review the TensorFlow tutorial on TFX components (http://mng.bz/5Wqa).

```
transform = Transform(
    examples=example_gen.outputs['examples'],
    schema=schema_gen.outputs['schema'],
    module_file='my_preprocessing_fn.py')
context.run(transform)
```

The next section covers how to incorporate image augmentation into an existing data pipeline, such as one constructed using `tf.data` and/or using pre-stems.

13.4 Data augmentation

Image (data) augmentation has had a variety of purposes over the years. At first, it was seen as a means of extending (adding) to an existing dataset more images to train on by doing some random transformations on the existing images. Subsequently, researchers learned that certain types of augmentation can extend a model's detection capabilities, such as for invariance and occlusion.

This section shows how to add image augmentation into your existing data pipeline. We will start with the basic concepts behind image augmentation and how it helps the model generalize to examples it was not trained on. Then we'll turn to methods to integrate into a `tf.data` pipeline. Finally, we'll see how to integrate it using preprocessing layers in a pre-stem that is attached to your model during training, and then detached for inference.

This section focuses on the common augmentation techniques and implementation for extending your model's detection capabilities for invariance. Next, we will describe what invariance is and why it is important.

13.4.1 Invariance

Today, we don't view the purpose of image augmentation as simply to add more examples to the training set. Instead, it's a means to train the model to be translational, scale, and viewport invariant by having a specific purpose to generate additional images from existing images.

OK, so what does all that mean? It means we want to recognize objects in an image (or in a video frame) regardless of the location in the image (translational), the size of the object (scale), and viewing perspective (viewport). Image augmentation enables us to train our models to be invariant without needing additional real-world human-labeled data.

Image augmentation works by randomly transforming the images in the training data for different translations, scales, and viewports. In research papers, it is a common practice to perform the following four image augmentation types:

- Random center crop
- Random flip
- Random rotation
- Random shift

Let's look at these four types in detail.

RANDOM CENTER CROP

In a *crop*, we take a portion of the image. Typically, a crop is rectangular. A center crop is square and is centered in the original image (figure 13.12). The size of the crop randomly varies, so in some instances it's a small portion of the image, and in others, a large portion. The cropped image is then resized to the input size for the model.

This transformation contributes to training the model for scale invariance, in that we are randomly enlarging the size of the object(s) in the image. You may be wondering whether these random crops may cut out all or too much of the objects of interest, resulting in an image that's not useful. Generally, this is not the case for the following reasons:

- Foreground objects (objects of interest) tend to appear at or near the center of pictures.
- We set a minimum size for the crop, preventing a crop being so small it contains no usable data.
- Having the edges of an object cut out contributes to training the model for occlusion, in which other objects obscure a portion of the object of interest.

Figure 13.12   Random center crop

RANDOM FLIP

In a *flip*, we flip the image on the horizontal or vertical axis. If we flip on the vertical axis, we have a mirrored image. If we flip on the horizontal axis, we have an upside-down image. This transformation contributes to training the model for viewport invariance.

You may think that in some cases, a mirror or upside-down image makes no sense in a real-world application. For example, you might say a mirror image of a stop sign makes no sense, or an upside-down truck. Maybe it does. Perhaps the stop sign is being viewed in a rear-view mirror? Perhaps your car has flipped over, and the truck is really upside down from your viewport.

Another thing that random flips contribute to is learning essential features of the objects, separated from the background—regardless of the actual viewport when the model is deployed for real-world predictions.

RANDOM ROTATION

In a *rotation,* we rotate the image along the center point. We could rotate up to 360 degrees, but since the common practice for random transformations is to chain them, a range of +/– 30 degrees is sufficient when combined with random flips. This transformation contributes to training the model for viewport invariance.

Figure 13.13 is an example of two chained random transformations. The first is a random rotation, followed by a random center crop.

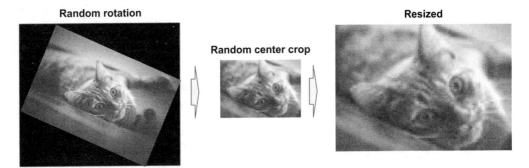

Figure 13.13   Chain of random transformations

RANDOM SHIFT

In a *random shift,* we shift the image vertically or horizontally. If we shift horizontally, we are dropping pixels from either the left or right side and replacing them with the same number of black pixels (no signal) on the opposite side. If we shift vertically, we are dropping pixels from either the top or bottom and replacing them with the same number of black pixels (no signal) on the opposite side. A general rule of thumb is to limit the shift to no more than +/–20% of the image width/height to prevent cutting out too much of the object of interest. This transformation contributes to training the model for translational invariance.

A vast number of other transformation techniques exist for invariance beyond the four covered here.

13.4.2   Augmentation with tf.data

Image transformations can be added to a `tf.data.Dataset` pipeline by using the `map()` method. In this case, we code the transformation as a Python function, which takes the image as input and outputs the transformed image. We then specify the function as the parameter to the `map()` method, which will apply the function to each element in a batch.

In the next example, we define a function `flip()` that will perform a random flip translation on each image in a dataset, each time the image is drawn into a batch. In the example, we create the `tf.data.Dataset` from a NumPy tuple of the image training data and corresponding labels, as `(x_train, y_train)`. We then apply the `flip()` function to the dataset, as `dataset.map(flip)`. Since each image in the batch will be a tuple of the image and label, we need two parameters for the transformation function: `(image, label)`. Likewise, we need to return the corresponding tuple, but with the input image replaced with the transformed image: `(transform, label)`:

```
import tensorflow as tf
from tensorflow.keras.datasets import cifar10
(x_train, y_train), (x_test, y_test) = cifar10.load_data()

def flip(image, label):
    transform = tf.image.random_flip_left_right(image)
    transform = tf.image.random_flip_up_down(transform)

    return transform, label
dataset = tf.data.Dataset.from_tensor_slices((x_train, y_train))
dataset = dataset.map(flip)
```

Function that performs an image transformation, which takes as input the image and corresponding label — `def flip(image, label):`

Randomly flips the input image

Returns the transformed image and corresponding label — `return transform, label`

Applies the flip transformation function to each image/label pair — `dataset = dataset.map(flip)`

Next, we'll chain multiple transformations for a `tf.data.Dataset`. In the following code example, we add a second transformation function to do a random crop. Note that the `tf.image.random_crop()` method is not a center crop. Unlike a center crop, which has a random size and is always centered, this TensorFlow method sets a fixed size, specified by `shape`, but the crop location in the image is random. We then chain our two transformations to first do a random flip, followed by a random crop: `dataset.map(flip).map(crop)`.

Function that performs an image transformation and takes as input the image and corresponding label

```
def crop(image, label):
    shape = (int(image.shape[0] * 0.8), int(image.shape[1] * 0.8),
                image.shape[2])
    transform = tf.image.random_crop(image, shape)
    return transform, label
dataset = tf.data.Dataset.from_tensor_slices((x_train, y_train))
dataset = dataset.map(flip).map(crop)
```

Selects a crop size based on 80% of the original image size

Randomly crops the input image

Applies a chain of transformations

13.4.3 *Pre-stem*

The `TF.Keras.layers.experimental.preprocessing` module provides several preprocessing layers that provide the means to perform image augmentation as a pre-stem component in the model. Thus, these operations would occur on the GPU (or equivalent) instead of upstream on the CPU. Since the pre-stem is plug-and-play, after training is completed, this pre-stem component can be detached prior to deploying the model into production.

In TensorFlow 2.2, the preprocessing layers that support translational, scale, and viewport invariance are as follows:

- `CenterCrop`
- `RandomCrop`
- `RandomRotation`
- `RandomTranslation`
- `RandomFlip`

In the following example, we combine two preprocessing layers for invariance as a plug-and-play pre-stem: `RandomFlip()` and `RandomTranslation()`. We create an empty `wrapper` model, add the plug-and-play pre-stem, and then add the `model`. For deployment, we detach the plug-and-play pre-stem, as demonstrated earlier in the chapter.

```
                                              Adds invariance pre-stem
wrapper = Sequential()  ◁────── Creates wrapper model
wrapper.add(RandomFlip())
wrapper.add(RandomTranslation(fill_mode='constant', height_factor=0.2,
                              width_factor=0.2))

wrapper.add(model)  ◁────── Adds the underlying model
```

Summary

- The basic components of a data pipeline are data storage, data retrieval, data preprocessing, and data feeding.
- For best I/O performance, use in-memory data feeding during training if the entire dataset can fit into memory; otherwise, use on-disk data feeding.
- There are additional space and time performance tradeoffs depending on whether the data is stored compressed or uncompressed on disk. You may be able to balance the tradeoffs using a hybrid approach based on subpopulation sampling distributions.
- If you work with satellite data, you will need to know the HDF5 format. If you work with medical imaging data, you will need to know DICOM.
- A primary purpose of image augmentation is to train a model for translational, scale, and viewport invariance so it can generalize better to examples not seen during training.
- A data pipeline can be constructed upstream from the model by using `tf.data` or TFX.
- A data pipeline can be constructed downstream in the model by using TF.Keras preprocessing layers of subclassing.
- A pre-stem can be designed as a preprocessing plug-and-play component and stay attached during training and serving.
- A pre-stem can be designed as an augmentation plug-and-play and attached during training and detached during inference.

Training and
deployment pipeline

In the previous chapter, we went through the data pipeline portion of an end-to-end production ML pipeline. Here, in the final chapter of the book, we will cover the final portion of the end-to-end pipeline: training, deployment, and serving.

To remind you with a visual, figure 14.1 shows the whole pipeline, borrowed from chapter 13. I've circled the part of the system we'll address in this chapter.

You may ask, what exactly is a pipeline and why do we use one, whether for ML production or any programmatic production operation that is managed by

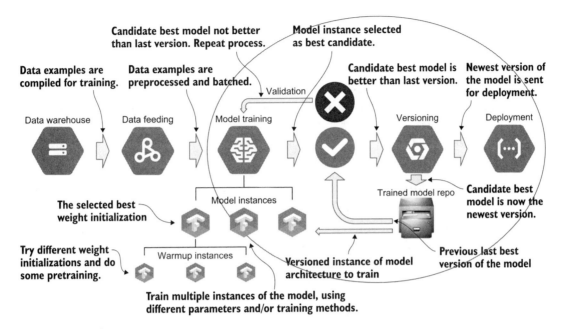

Figure 14.1 Production e2e pipeline with this chapter's emphasis on training and deployment

orchestration? You typically use pipelines when the job, such as training or other operations handled by orchestration, has multiple steps that occur in sequential order: do step A, do step B, and so on.

Putting these steps into an ML production pipeline provides multiple benefits. First, the pipeline is reusable for subsequent training and deployment jobs. Second, the pipeline can be containerized and, as such, run as an asynchronous batch job. Third, pipelines can be distributed across multiple compute instances, where different tasks within the pipeline are executed on different compute instances, or portions of the same task are executed in parallel on different compute instances. Finally, all the tasks associated with the execution of the pipeline can be tracked and the status/outcome preserved as history.

This chapter starts with the procedures for feeding models for training in a production environment, including both sequential and distributed systems, and example implementations using tf.data and TensorFlow Extended (TFX). We then learn how to schedule training and provision compute resources. We will start by covering reusable pipelines, how metadata is used for integrating pipelines into a production environment, along with history and versioning for tracking and auditing.

Next we'll see how models are evaluated for release into a production environment. These days, we do not simply compare the metrics from the test (holdout) data against the test metrics of the previous version of the model. Instead, we identify different subpopulations and distributions that are seen in the production environment and construct additional evaluation data, which are commonly referred to as *evaluation slices*.

Then the model is evaluated in a simulated production environment, commonly called a *sandbox*, to see how well it performs for response times and scaling. I include example TFX implementations for evaluating a candidate model in a sandbox environment.

Then we'll move to the process of deploying models into production and serving predictions for both on-demand and batch. You'll find methods for scaling and load balancing for current traffic demand. You'll also see how serving platforms are provisioned. Lastly, we discuss how models are further evaluated against a previous version after they are deployed to production using A/B testing methods, and subsequent retraining from insights gained during production using continuous evaluation methods.

14.1   Model feeding

Figure 14.2 is a conceptual overview of the model-feeding process within a training pipeline. On the frontend is the data pipeline, which performs the tasks for extracting and preparing the training data (step 1 in the figure). Because today we work with very large amounts of data in a production environment, we will assume that the data is being drawn from disk on demand. As such, the model feeder acts as a generator and does the following:

- Makes requests to the data pipeline for examples (step 2)
- Receives those examples from the data pipeline (step 3)
- Assembles the received examples into a batch format for training (step 4)

The model feeder hands off each batch to the training method, which sequentially forward-feeds each batch (step 5) to the model, calculates the loss at the end of the forward feed (step 6), and updates the weights by backward propagation (step 7).

Positioned between the data pipeline and the train function, the model feeder can potentially be an I/O bottleneck in the training process, and thus it is important to consider the implementation so the feeder can generate batches as fast as the training method can consume them. For example, if the model feeder is running as a single

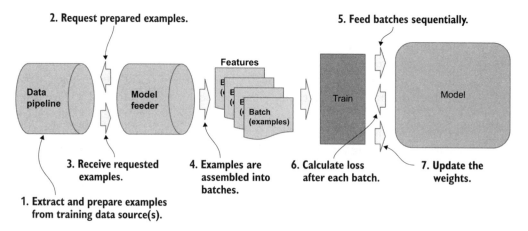

Figure 14.2   Interaction of model-feeding process between the data pipeline and the train method

CPU thread, and the data pipeline is a multi-CPU or GPU and the training process is a multi-GPU, it would likely result in the feeder unable to either process examples as fast as they are received, or to generate batches as fast as the training GPUs can consume them.

Given its relationship to the train method, the model feeder must have the next batch ready in memory at or before the train method has consumed the current batch. A model feeder in production is typically a multithreaded process operating on more than one CPU core. There are two ways to feed training examples to models during training: sequentially and distributed.

MODEL FEEDER FOR SEQUENTIAL TRAINING

Figure 14.3 shows a sequential model feeder. We start with an area of shared memory and then go through four steps, as follows:

- An area of shared memory reserved for the model feeder for holding two or more batches in memory (step 1).
- A first in, first out (FIFO) queue gets implemented in the shared memory (step 1).
- A first asynchronous process posts ready batches into the queue (steps 2 and 3).
- A second asynchronous process pulls the next batch out of the queue, when requested by the train method (steps 3 and 4).

Generally, a sequential approach is the most cost-efficient for compute resources, and is used when the time period to complete the training is within your time-to-train requirements. The benefits are straightforward: there is no compute overhead, as in a distributed system, and the CPU/GPUs can be run at full capacity.

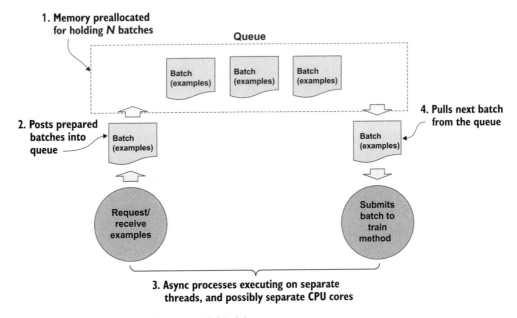

Figure 14.3   A model feeder for sequential training

MODEL FEEDER FOR DISTRIBUTED TRAINING

In distributed training, such as on multiple GPUs, the impact of an I/O bottleneck at the model feeder can become more severe. As you can see in figure 14.4, it differs from the single instance, nondistributed sequential approach, in that multiple asynchronous submit processes are pulling batches from the queue, to feed the training of multiple instances of the model in parallel.

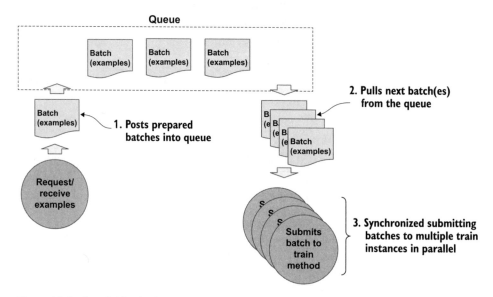

Figure 14.4   A model feeder for distributed training

While a distributed approach will introduce some compute inefficiencies, it is used when your time frame doesn't allow for a sequential approach to complete the training. Usually, the time requirement is based on a business requirement, and not meeting the business requirement has a higher cost than the compute inefficiencies.

In distributed training, the first asynchronous process must submit multiple batches into the queue (step 1) at a speed equal to or greater than the other plural asynchronous processes are pulling batches (step 2). Each of the distributed training nodes has an asynchronous process for pulling batches from the queue. Finally, a third asynchronous process coordinates pulling batches from the queue and waiting for completion (step 3). In this form of distributed training, there is a second asynchronous process for each distributed training node (step 2), where a node can be

- Separate compute instances networked together
- Separate hardware accelerators (such as a GPU) on the same compute instance
- Separate threads on a multicore compute instance (such as a CPU)

You might ask, how does the model get trained when each instance will see only a subset of the batches? Good question. In this distributed method, we use batch smoothing of the weights.

Think of it this way: each model instance learns from a subsampling distribution of the training data, and we need a way to merge the learned weights from each subsampling distribution. Each node, upon completion of a batch, will send its weight updates to the other nodes. When the recipient nodes receive the weight updates, it will average them with the weight updates from its own batch—hence the batch smoothing of weights.

There are two common network approaches to sending the weights. One is to broadcast the weights on the subnet that all the nodes are connected to. The other is to use a ring network, where each node sends its weight updates to the next connected node.

This form of distributed training has two consequences, whether broadcast or ring. First, there is all the network activity. Second, you don't know when the message with the weight updates will show up. It's totally uncoordinated and ad hoc. As a result, the batch smoothing of the weights has inherent inefficiencies and will result in more epochs needed to train the model versus the sequential approach.

MODEL FEEDER WITH A PARAMETER SERVER

Another version of distributed training uses a parameter server. The parameter server typically runs on another node, which is usually a CPU. As an example, in Google's TPU pods, each group of four TPUs has a CPU-based parameter server. Its purpose is to overcome the inefficiencies of the asynchronous updating for batch smoothing of the weights.

In this form of distributed training, the batch smoothing of weight updates happens synchronously. The parameter server, depicted in figure 14.5, dispatches different batches to each of the training nodes, and then waits for each to finish consuming its corresponding batch (step 1), and send the loss calculation back to the parameter server (step 2). Upon receiving the loss calculation from each training node, the parameter server averages the loss and updates the weights on a master copy maintained by the parameter server, and then sends the updated weights to each training node (step 3). The parameter server then signals the model feeder to dispatch the next set of parallel batches (step 4).

The advantage of this synchronous method is that it does not require as many epochs to be trained as the aforementioned asynchronous method. But the drawback is that each training node must wait on the parameter server to signal receiving the next batch, and thus the training nodes may run below GPU, or other compute, capacity.

There are a couple of more things to point out. For each round, each distributed training node receives a different batch from another. Because there could be significant variance in the loss across the training nodes, and overhead waiting on the parameter to update the weights, distributed training generally uses larger batch sizes.

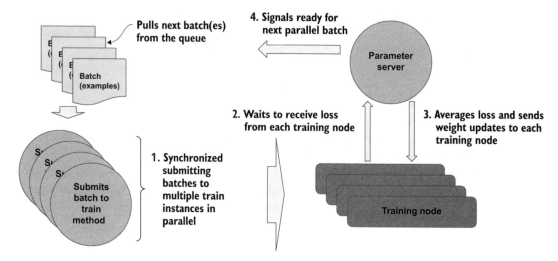

Figure 14.5 **Parameter server in distributed training**

The larger batches smooth out or reduce variance across the parallel batches as well as reducing I/O bottlenecks during the training process.

14.1.1 *Model feeding with tf.data.Dataset*

In chapter 13, we saw how `tf.data.Dataset` can be used to construct a data pipeline. It can be used as the mechanism for model feeding. In essence, an instance of `tf.data.Dataset` is a generator. It can be integrated into both sequential and distributed training. However, in a distributor feeder, the instance does not act as a parameter server, because that function is performed by the underlying distribution system.

Some of the primary benefits of a `tf.data.Dataset` are setting of the batch size, shuffling the data for randomized batches, and prefetching the next batches in parallel to feeding a current batch.

The following code is an example of using `tf.data.Dataset` for feeding a model during training, using a dummy model—a `Sequential` model with a single layer (`Flatten`) with no parameters to train. For demonstration, we use the CIFAR-10 data from TF.Keras built-in datasets.

Since the CIFAR-10 data in this example will already be in memory, when loaded by `cifar.load_data()`, we will create a generator that will feed batches from the in-memory source. The first step is to create the generator for our in-memory dataset. We do this using `from_tensor_slices()`, which takes as a parameter a tuple of the in-memory training examples and corresponding labels (`x_train, y_train`). Note, this method does not make a copy of the training data. Instead, it builds an index to the source of the training data and uses the index to shuffle, iterate, and fetch examples:

```
from tensorflow.keras.datasets import cifar10
import numpy as np
from tensorflow.keras import Sequential
```

```
from tensorflow.keras.layers import Flatten

(x_train, y_train), (x_test, y_test) = cifar10.load_data()
x_train = (x_train / 255.0).astype(np.float32)
x_test  = (x_test  / 255.0).astype(np.float32)

model = Sequential([ Flatten(input_shape=(32, 32, 3))] )
model.compile(loss='sparse_categorical_crossentropy', optimizer='adam')

dataset = tf.data.Dataset.from_tensor_slices((x_train, y_train))
dataset = dataset.batch(32).shuffle(1000).repeat().prefetch(2)

model.fit(dataset, epochs=10, steps_per_epoch=len(x_train//32))
```

Creates a tf.data.Dataset as a generator for model feeding of CIFAR-10 training data

Sets model feeding attributes

Uses the generator as the model feeder when training

Now that we have a generator in the preceding code example, we will add some attributes to complete it as a model feeder:

- We set the batch size to 32 (batch(32)).
- We set randomly shuffling 1000 examples at a time in memory (shuffle(1000)).
- We reiterate through the entire training data repeatedly (repeat()). Without repeat(), the generator would make only a single pass through the training data.
- In parallel to feeding a batch, prefetch up to two batches in the feeder queue (prefetch(2)).

Next, we can pass the generator as the training input source to the fit(dataset, epochs=10, steps_per_epoch=len(x_train//32)) command for training. This command will treat the generator as an iterator, and for each interaction the generator will perform the model-feeding task.

Because we are using a generator for model feeding and repeat() will cause the generator to iterate forever, the fit() method does not know when it has consumed the entire training data for an epoch. So we need to tell the fit() method how many batches constitute an epoch, which we set with the keyword parameter steps_per_epoch.

DYNAMICALLY UPDATING THE BATCH SIZE

In chapter 10, we discussed how the batch size is inversely related to the learning rate. During training, this inverse relationship means that conventional model-feeding techniques will increase the batch in proportion to decreases in the learning rate. While TF.Keras has a built-in method for dynamically updating the learning rate with the LearningRateScheduler callback, it presently does not have the same capability for the batch size. Instead, I will show you the DIY version of updating the batch size dynamically during training while lowering the learning rate.

I'll explain the DIY process as I describe the code that implements it. In this case, we add an outer training loop to dynamically update the batch size. Recall, in the fit() method, the batch size is specified as a parameter. So, to update the batch size, we will partition up the epochs and call `fit()` multiple times. Inside the loop, we train the model for a specified number of epochs. As for the loop, each time we iterate through it, we will update the learning rate and batch size, and set the number of epochs to train for in the loop. In the `for` loop, we use a list of tuples, and each tuple will specify the learning rate (`lr`), batch size (`bs`), and number of epochs (`epochs`); for example, `(0.01, 32, 10)`.

Resetting the number of `epochs` in the loop is straightforward since we can specify it as a parameter to the `fit()` method. For the learning rate, we reset it by (re)compiling the model and reset the learning rate when we specify the optimizer parameter—`Adam(lr=lr)`. It's OK to recompile a model in the middle of training, as it does not affect the model's weights. In other words, recompiling does not undo previous training.

Resetting the batch size for a `tf.data.Dataset` is not is not as straightforward, since once it's set, you cannot reset it. Instead, we will have to create a new generator for the training data in each loop iteration, where we will specify the current batch size with the method `batch()`.

```
from tensorflow.keras.datasets import cifar10
import numpy as np
from tensorflow.keras import Sequential
from tensorflow.keras.layers import Flatten, Dense, Conv2D, MaxPooling2D
from tensorflow.keras.optimizers import Adam

(x_train, y_train), (x_test, y_test) = cifar10.load_data()
x_train = (x_train / 255.0).astype(np.float32)
x_test  = (x_test  / 255.0).astype(np.float32)

model = Sequential([ Conv2D(16, (3, 3), activation='relu',
                        input_shape=(32, 32, 3)),
                    Conv2D(32, (3, 3), strides=(2, 2), activation='relu'),
                    MaxPooling2D((2, 2), strides=2),
                    Flatten(),
                    Dense(10, activation='softmax')
                    ])

for lr, bs, epochs in [ (0.01, 32, 10), (0.005, 64, 10), (0.0025, 128, 10) ]:
    print("hyperparams: lr", lr, "bs", bs, "epochs", epochs)
    dataset = tf.data.Dataset.from_tensor_slices((x_train, y_train))
    dataset = dataset.shuffle(1000).repeat().batch(bs).prefetch(2)

    model.compile(loss='sparse_categorical_crossentropy',
                optimizer=Adam(lr=lr),
                metrics=['acc'])
    model.fit(dataset, epochs=epochs, steps_per_epoch=200, verbose=1)
```

Creates a new generator to reset the batch size

Outer loop for dynamic resetting of hyperparams during training

Recompiles the model to reset the learning rate

Trains the model with the reset number of epochs

Let's take a look at the abbreviated output from running our DIY version of dynamically resetting hyperparameters while training. You can see in the first iteration of the outer loop, the training accuracy is 51% on the 10th epoch. On the second iteration, where the learning rate is halved and the batch size is doubled, the training accuracy is 58% on the 10th epoch, and on the third iteration it reaches 61%. As you can observe from the output, we were able to maintain a consistent reduction in the loss and increase in accuracy over the three iterations, as we narrow down into the loss space.

```
hyperparams: lr 0.01 bs 32 epochs 10
Epoch 1/10
200/200 [==============================] - 1s 3ms/step - loss: 1.9392 - acc: 0.2973
Epoch 2/10
200/200 [==============================] - 1s 3ms/step - loss: 1.6730 - acc: 0.4130
...
Epoch 10/10
200/200 [==============================] - 1s 3ms/step - loss: 1.3809 - acc: 0.5170


hyperparams: lr 0.005 bs 64 epochs 10
Epoch 1/10
200/200 [==============================] - 1s 3ms/step - loss: 1.2248 - acc: 0.5704
Epoch 2/10
200/200 [==============================] - 1s 3ms/step - loss: 1.2740 - acc: 0.5510
...
Epoch 10/10
200/200 [==============================] - 1s 3ms/step - loss: 1.1876 - acc: 0.5853

hyperparams: lr 0.0025 bs 128 epochs 10
Epoch 1/10
200/200 [==============================] - 1s 4ms/step - loss: 1.1186 - acc: 0.6063
Epoch 2/10
200/200 [==============================] - 1s 3ms/step - loss: 1.1434 - acc: 0.5997
...
Epoch 10/10
200/200 [==============================] - 1s 3ms/step - loss: 1.1156 - acc: 0.6129
```

14.1.2 *Distributed feeding with tf.Strategy*

The TensorFlow module `tf.distribute.Strategy` provides a convenient and encapsulated interface, with everything done for you, for distributed training across multiple GPUs on the same compute instance, or across multiple TPUs. It implements a synchronous parameter server as described earlier in the chapter. This TensorFlow module is optimized for distributed training of TensorFlow models, as well as for distributed training on parallel Google TPUs.

When training on a single compute instance with multiple GPUs, you use `tf`
`.distribute.MirrorStrategy`, and when training on TPUs, you use `tf.distribute`
`.TPUStrategy`. We won't cover distributed training across machines in this chapter, other than noting you would use `tf.distribute.experimental.ParameterServerStrategy`, which implements an asynchronous parameter server across a network. The setup for distributed training across multiple machines is somewhat complex, and would need a chapter in its own right. I recommend using this approach, as well as studying TensorFlow

documentation, if you're building TensorFlow models and meeting your business objectives requires substantial or massive parallelism during training.

Here's our approach for setting up a distributed training run on a single machine, with multiple CPUs or GPUs:

1 Instantiate a distribution strategy.
2 Within the scope of the distribution strategy
   – Create the model.
   – Compile the model.
3 Train the model.

These steps may seem counterintuitive, in that we set up the distribution strategy when we build and compile the model, instead of when we train it. It's a requirement in TensorFlow that the construction of the model needs to be aware that it will be trained using a distributed training strategy. As of this writing, the TensorFlow team has recently released a newer experimental version for which the distribution strategy can be set independent of compiling the model.

And the following is the code for implementing the preceding three steps, and two substeps, described here:

1 We define the function `create_model()` to create an instance of the model to train.
2 We instantiate the distribution strategy: `strategy = tf.distribute.Mirror-Strategy()`.
3 We set the distribution context: `with strategy.scope()`.
4 Within the distribution context, we create an instance of the model: `model = create_model()`. Then we compile it: `model.compile()`.
5 Finally, we train the model.

```
def create_model():        ◁————————  Function for creating an
    model = Sequential([ Conv2D(16, (3, 3), activation='relu',    instance of the model
                            input_shape=(32, 32, 3)),
                         Conv2D(32, (3, 3), strides=(2, 2),
                            activation='relu'),
                         MaxPooling2D((2, 2), strides=2),
                         Flatten(),
                         Dense(10, activation='softmax')
                       ])
    return model

  strategy = tf.distribute.MirroredStrategy()

  with strategy.scope():  bbbb
      model = create_model()
      model.compile(loss='sparse_categorical_crossentropy', optimizer='adam')

  model.fit(dataset, epochs=10, steps_per_epoch=200)    ◁———— Trains the model
```

Instantiates the distribution strategy

Within the scope of the distribution strategy, creates and compiles the model

You may ask, can I use a model that has already been built? The answer is no; you must build the model within the scope of the distribution strategy. For example, the following code will cause an error indicating the model was not built within the scope of the distribution strategy:

```
                              Model is not built within the
                              scope of the distribution strategy
model = create_model()    <──┘
with strategy.scope():
    model.compile(loss='sparse_categorical_crossentropy', optimizer='adam')
```

Again, you might ask: I already have a prebuilt or pretrained model that was not built for a distribution strategy; can I still do distributed training? The answer here is yes. If you have an existing TF.Keras model saved to disk, when you load it back into memory using load_model(), it implicitly builds the model. The following is an example implementation of setting a distribution strategy from a pretrained model:

```
                                               Model is implicitly rebuilt
                                               when loaded from disk
with strategy.scope():
    model = tf.keras.models.load_model('my_model')  <──┘
    model.compile(loss='sparse_categorical_crossentropy', optimizer='adam')
```

Likewise, when a prebuilt model is loaded from a model repository, there is an implicit load and correspondingly an implicit build. The following code sequence is an example of loading a model from the tf.keras.applications built-in model repository, where the model is implicitly rebuilt:

```
                                              Model is implicitly rebuilt when
                                              loaded from a repository
with strategy.scope():
    model = tf.keras.applications.ResNet50()  <──┘
    model.compile(loss='sparse_categorical_crossentropy', optimizer='adam')
```

By default, the mirrored strategy will use all the GPUs on the compute instance. You can get the number of GPU or CPU cores that will be used with the property num_replicas_in_sync. You can also explicitly set which GPUs, or cores, to use. In the following code example, we set the distribution strategy to use two GPUs:

```
strategy = tf.distribute.MirroredStrategy(['/gpu:0', '/gpu:1'])
print("GPUs:", strategy.num_replicas_in_sync)
```

The preceding code example generates the following output:

```
INFO:tensorflow:Using MirroredStrategy with devices
    ('/job:localhost/replica:0/task:0/device:GPU:0',
     '/job:localhost/replica:0/task:0/device:GPU:1')
GPUs: 2
```

14.1.3 *Model feeding with TFX*

Chapter 13 covered the data pipeline portion of a TFX end-to-end production pipeline. This section covers the corresponding TFX model-feeding aspect of the training pipeline components, as an alternative implementation. Figure 14.6 depicts the training

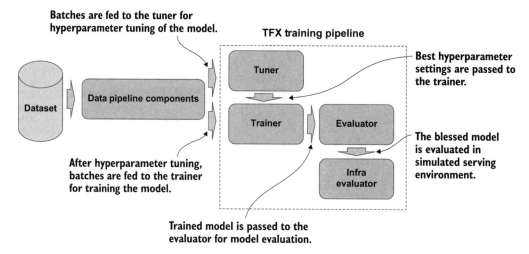

Figure 14.6   TFX components that make up a training pipeline consist of the tuner, trainer, evaluator, and infra-evaluator components.

pipeline components and their relationships to the data pipeline. The training pipeline consists of these components:

- *Trainer*—Trains the model
- *Tuner*—Tunes the hyperparameters (for example, the learning rate)
- *Evaluator*—Evaluates the model's objective(s), such as accuracy, and compares the results against a baseline (for example, a previous version)
- *Infra evaluator*—Tests the model in a sandbox serving environment, before deployment

ORCHESTRATION

Let's review the benefits of TFX and pipelines in general. If we execute each step in training/deploying a model individually, we refer to this as a *task-aware architecture*. Each component is aware of itself, but not aware of connecting components or of the history of a previous execution.

TFX implements *orchestration*. In orchestration, a management interface oversees the execution of each component, remembers the execution of past components, and maintains history. As previously covered in chapter 13, the output of each component is artifacts; these are the results and history of the execution. In orchestration, these artifacts, or references to them, are stored as metadata. For TFX, the metadata is stored in a relational format, and thus can be stored and accessed via a SQL database.

Let's dive a little deeper into the benefits of orchestration, and then we will cover how within TFX model feeding works. With orchestration, which is depicted in figure 14.7, we can do the following:

- Schedule execution of a component after another component(s) is completed. For example, we can schedule the execution of data transformations after completion of generating a feature schema from training data.
- Schedule execution of components in parallel when the execution of the components is not dependent on one another. For example, we can schedule in parallel hyperparameter tuning and training after completion of the data transformations.
- Reuse the artifacts from a previous execution of a component (cache) if nothing has changed. For example, if the training data has not changed, the cached artifacts (that is, the transform graph) from the transformation component can be reused without re-execution.
- Provision different instances of compute engines for each component. For example, the data pipeline components may be provisioned on a CPU compute instance, and the training component on a GPU compute instance.
- If a task supports distribution, such as tuning and training, the task can be distributed across multiple compute instances.
- Compare artifacts of a component to previous artifacts from previous executions of the component. For example, the evaluator component can compare the model's objective (for example, accuracy), to previously trained versions of the model.
- Debug and audit execution of the pipeline by being able to move forward and backward through the generated artifacts.

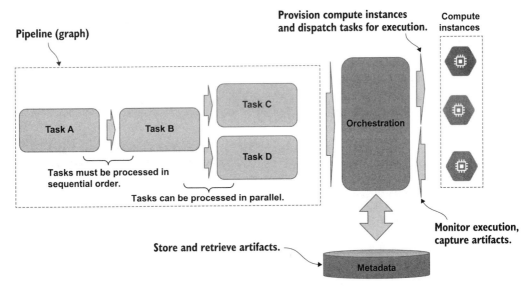

Figure 14.7 Orchestration ingests a pipeline represented as a graph, and provisions instances and dispatches tasks.

400 CHAPTER 14 *Training and deployment pipeline*

TRAINER COMPONENT

The `Trainer` component supports training TensorFlow estimators, TF.Keras models, and other custom training loops. Since TensorFlow 2.x recommends phasing out estimators, we will focus only on configuring a trainer component for TF.Keras models, and feeding it data. The trainer component takes the following minimum parameters:

- `module_file`—This is the Python script for custom training the model. It must contain a `run_fn()` function as the entry point for training.
- `examples`—The examples to train the model, which come from the output of the `ExampleGen` component, `example_gen.outputs['examples']`.
- `schema`—The dataset schema, which comes from the output of the `SchemaGen` component, `schema_gen['schema']`.
- `custom_executor_spec`—The executor for a custom training, which will invoke the `run_fn()` function in `module_file`.

```
from tfx.components import Trainer
from tfx.components.base import executor_spec        Imports for
from tfx.components.trainer import GenericExecutor   custom training

trainer = Trainer(                    The custom training Python script
    module_file=module_file,
    examples=example_gen.outputs['examples'],      The training data source for feeding
    schema=schema_gen.outputs['schema'],           the model during training
    custom_executor_spec=executor_spec.ExecutorClassSpec(GenericExecutor)
)                                                                    The custom executor
                                                                     for custom training
The schema inferred from the dataset
```

If the training data is to be preprocessed by the `Transform` component, we need to set the following two parameters:

- `transformed_examples`—Set to the output of the `Transform` component, `transform.outputs['transformed_examples']`.
- `transform_graph`—The static transformation graph produced by the `Transform` component, `transform.outputs['transformed_graph']`.

```
trainer = Trainer(                       Training data is fed from the Transform
    module_file=module_file,             component into the static transform graph.
    transformed_examples=transform.outputs['transformed_examples'],
    transform_graph=transform.outputs['transform_graph'],
    schema=schema_gen.outputs['schema'],
    custom_executor_spec=executor_spec.ExecutorClassSpec(GenericExecutor)
)
```

Generally, we want to pass other hyperparameters into the training module. These can be passed as additional parameters `train_args` and `eval_args` to the `Trainer` component. These parameters are set as a list of key/value pairs converted to Google's protobuf format. The following code passes the number of steps for training and evaluation:

```
from tfx.proto import trainer_pb2
trainer = Trainer(
    module_file=module_file,
    transformed_examples=transform.outputs['transformed_examples'],
    transform_graph=transform.outputs['transform_graph'],
    schema=schema_gen.outputs['schema'],
    custom_executor_spec=executor_spec.ExecutorClassSpec(GenericExecutor),
    train_args=trainer_pb2.TrainArgs(num_steps=10000),
    eval_args=trainer_pb2.EvalArgs(num_steps=5000)
)
```

Imports for the TFX protobuf format for passing hyperparameters

Hyperparameters passed into the Trainer component as protobuf messages

Let's look now at the basic requirements for the `run_fn()` function in the custom Python script. The arguments to `run_fn()` are constructed from the parameters passed into the `Trainer` component, and are accessed as properties. In the following example implementation, we do the following:

- Extract the total number of steps for training: `training_args.train_steps`.
- Extract the number of steps for validation after each epoch: `training_args.eval_steps`.
- Gets the TFRecord file paths for the training and eval data: `training_args.train_files`. Note that `ExampleGen` is not feeding in-memory `tf.Examples`, but on-disk TFRecords containing the `tf.Examples`.
- Get the transform graph, `training_args.transform_output`, and construct a transform execution function, `tft.TFTransformOutput()`.
- Call the internal function `_input_fn()` to create the dataset iterators for training and validation datasets.
- Build, or load, a TF.Keras model with the internal function `_build_model()`.
- Train the model with the `fit()` method.
- Get the serving directory to store the trained model, `training_args.output`, which is optionally specified as the parameter `output` to the `Trainer` component.
- Save the trained model to the specified serving output location, `model.save(serving_dir)`.

```
from tfx.components.trainer.executor import TrainerFnArgs
import tensorflow_transform as tft

BATCH_SIZE = 64
STEPS_PER_EPOCH = 250

def run_fn(training_args: TrainerFnArgs):
    train_steps = training_args.train_steps
    eval_steps  = training_args.eval_steps

    train_files = training_args.train_files
    eval_files  = training_args.eval_files
```

Hyperparameters set as constants

Training/validation steps passed as parameters to the Trainer component

Training/validation data passed as parameters to the Trainer component

**Builds or
loads the
model to
train**

```
    tf_transform_output = tft.TFTransformOutput(training_args.transform_output)
    train_dataset = _input_fn(train_files, tf_transform_output, BATCH_SIZE)
    eval_dataset  = _input_fn(eval_files, tf_transform_output, BATCH_SIZE)
 ⌐▷ model = _build_model()
```

**Creates the dataset iterators for
training and validation data**

**Calculates
the number
of epochs**

```
 ⌐▷ epochs = train_steps // STEPS_PER_EPOCH

    model.fit(train_dataset, epochs=epochs, validation_data=eval_dataset,
              validation_steps=eval_steps)    ◁── | Trains the model
```

```
    serving_dir = training_args.output      | Saves the model in SavedModel format
    model.save(serving_dir)                 | to the specified serving directory
```

There are a lot of fine details and various directions we could go when constructing the custom Python training script. For more details and directions, we recommend reviewing TFX's guide for the `Trainer` component (www.tensorflow.org/tfx/guide/trainer).

TUNER COMPONENT

The `Tuner` component is an optional task in the training pipeline. You can either hardwire the hyperparameters for training in the custom Python training script, or use the tuner to find the best values for hyperparameters.

The parameters to the `Tuner` are very similar to the `Trainer`. That is, the `Tuner` will do short training runs to find the best hyperparameters. But unlike the `Trainer`, which returns a trained model, the `Tuner`'s outputs are the tuned hyperparameter values. Two of the parameters that typically differ are the `train_args` and `eval_args`. Since these will be shorter training runs, the number of steps for the tuner is typically 20% or less than that of the full training.

The other requirement is that the custom Python training script, module_file, contains the function entry point `tuner_fn()`. The typical practice is to have a single Python training script that has both the `run_fn()` and `tuner_fn()` functions.

```
tuner = Tuner(
    module_file=module_file,
    transformed_examples=transform.outputs['transformed_examples'],
    transform_graph=transform.outputs['transform_graph'],
    schema=schema_gen.outputs['schema'],
    train_args=trainer_pb2.TrainArgs(num_steps=2000),   | The number of steps for shorter
    eval_args=trainer_pb2.EvalArgs(num_steps=1000)      | training runs when tuning
)
```

Next, we will look at an example implementation of `tuner_fn()`. We will use Keras-Tuner to do hyperparameter tuning, but you can use any tuner compatible with your model framework. We previously covered using KerasTuner in chapter 10. It is a separate package from TensorFlow, so you need to install it as follows:

```
pip install keras-tuner
```

Like the `Trainer` component, the parameters and default values to the `Tuner` component are passed in to `tuner_fn()` as properties of the parameter `tuner_args`. Note that the function starts the same as `run_fn()`, but differs when we get to the training step. Instead of calling the `fit()` method and saving the trained model, we do this:

1 Instantiate a KerasTuner:
   - We use `build_model()` as our hyperparameter model argument.
   - Call an internal function `_get_hyperparameters()` to specify the hyperparameter search space.
   - The maximum number of trials is set to 6.
   - Set the objective for selecting the best values for the hyperparameters. In this case, it is validation accuracy.
2 Pass the tuner and remaining parameters for training to an instance of `TunerFnResult()`, which will execute the tuner.
3 Return the results from the tuning trials.

```python
import kerastuner

def tuner_fn(tuner_args: FnArgs) -> TunerFnResult:   ◁─┐ The entry point function for
    train_steps = tuner_args.train_steps               │ hyperparameter tuning
    eval_steps  = tuner_args.eval_steps

    train_files = tuner_args.train_files
    eval_files  = tuner_args.eval_files

    tf_transform_output = tft.TFTransformOutput(tuner_args.transform_output)
    train_dataset = _input_fn(train_files, tf_transform_output, BATCH_SIZE)
    eval_dataset  = _input_fn(eval_files, tf_transform_output, BATCH_SIZE)

    tuner = kerastuner.RandomSearch(_build_model(),   ◁─┤ Instantiates KerasTuner
                  max_trails=6,                            for RandomSearch
                  hyperparameters=_get_hyperparameters(),  ◁─┐
                  objective='val_accuracy'                    Retrieves the
                  )                                           hyperparameter
                                                              search space
    result = TunerFnResult(tuner=tuner,
                  fit_kwargs={
                      'x': train_dataset,
                      'validation_data': eval_dataset,
                      'steps_per_epoch': train_steps,
                      'validation_steps': eval_steps
                  })
    return result
```

Instantiates and executes the tuning trials with the specified tuner instance

Training parameters for the short training runs during tuning

Now let's see how the `Tuner` and `Trainer` components are chained together to form an executable pipeline. In the example implementation that follows, we make a single modification to the instantiation to the `Trainer` component by adding the optional parameter `hyperparameters` and connecting the input to the output of the `Tuner` component. Now when we execute the `Trainer` instance with `context.run()`, the orchestrator will see the dependency on the `Tuner` and will schedule its execution prior to the full training by the `Trainer` component:

```
tuner = Tuner(
    module_file=module_file,
    transformed_examples=transform.outputs['transformed_examples'],
    transform_graph=transform.outputs['transform_graph'],
    schema=schema_gen.outputs['schema'],
    train_args=trainer_pb2.TrainArgs(num_steps=2000),
    eval_args=trainer_pb2.EvalArgs(num_steps=1000)
)
trainer = Trainer(
    module_file=module_file,
    transformed_examples=transform.outputs['transformed_examples'],
    transform_graph=transform.outputs['transform_graph'],
    schema=schema_gen.outputs['schema'],
    custom_executor_spec=executor_spec.ExecutorClassSpec(GenericExecutor),
    hyperparameters=tuner.outputs['best_hyperparameters'],    �たー− Gets the tuned
    train_args=trainer_pb2.TrainArgs(num_steps=10000),             hyperparameters
    eval_args=trainer_pb2.EvalArgs(num_steps=5000)                 from the Tuner
)                                                                  component

context.run(trainer)    ⬅────  Executes the Tuner/Trainer pipeline
```

As with the trainer, the Python hyperparameter tuning script can be customized. See TFX's guide for the `Tuner` component (www.tensorflow.org/tfx/guide/tuner).

14.2   *Training schedulers*

In research or development environments, training pipelines are typically manually initiated; each task in the pipeline is manually initiated, such that each task can be observed and debugged if necessary. On the production side, they are automated; the automation makes executing the pipelines more efficient and less labor intensive and more scalable. In this section, we'll see how scheduling works in a production environment, as large numbers of training jobs can be queued for training and/or models are continuously retrained.

The needs of a production environment differ from research and development, as follows:

- The amount of compute and network I/O may vary substantially within a production environment, where a vast number of models may be continuously retrained in parallel.
- Training jobs may have different priorities, in that they must be completed within a delivery schedule for deployment.
- Training jobs may have on-demand requirements, such as special hardware that may be provisioned on a per-use basis, such as cloud instances.
- Length of training jobs may vary because of restarts and hyperparameter tuning.

Figure 14.8 depicts a job scheduler for end-to-end production pipelines that is typical for a massively scaled production environment with the aforementioned needs. We use a conceptual view that job scheduling within a production environment isn't yet adequately supported by open source ML frameworks, but are supported at varying degrees by paid ML services, such as cloud providers.

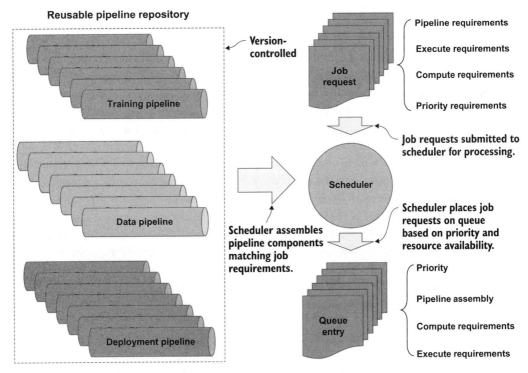

Figure 14.8 Job scheduling of pipelines in a massively scaled production environment

Let's dive into some of the assumptions for a production environment, as depicted in figure 14.8, typical in an enterprise environment:

- There are no custom jobs. Although there may have been custom jobs during development of a model, once a model enters into production, it is trained and deployed with predefined pipelines that are version-controlled.
- Pipelines have defined dependencies. For example, a training pipeline for an image-input model would have a dependency that can be combined only with data pipelines that are specific for image data.
- Pipelines may have configurable attributes. For example, the source input and output shape for a data pipeline is configurable.
- If an upgrade is made to a pipeline, it becomes the next version. The previous version and execution history is retained.

- A job request specifies the pipeline requirements. These may be specified either referencing specific pipelines and versions, or by attributes, whereby the scheduler determines the best matching pipelines. The requirements may also specify configurable attributes, such as the output shape from a data pipeline.

- A job request specifies the execution requirements. For example, if it is using an AutoML-like service, it might specify a maximum training budget in compute time. In another example, it may specify early stop conditions, or conditions for warm-starting or restarting a training job.

- A job request specifies the compute requirements. For example, if distributed training, it may specify the number and type of compute instances. The requirements generally include operating system and software requirements.

- A job request specifies the priority requirements. Typically, this is either on-demand or batch. On-demand jobs are generally dispatched when compute resources are available for provisioning. Batch requests are typically deferred until a certain condition is met. For example, it may specify a time window for execution, or wait for when the compute instances are most economical.

- An on-demand job may optionally set a priority condition. If not, typically it is dispatched in a FIFO manner. Jobs that specify a priority may change their position in the FIFO dispatch queue. For example, a job with estimated time length of X and completed by time Y may get moved up in a queue to satisfy the requirement.

- Once a job is dispatched from a queue, its pipeline assembly, execution, and compute requirements are handed off to the orchestrator.

14.2.1 Pipeline versioning

In a production environment, a pipeline is version-controlled. In addition to version control, each version of the pipeline will have metadata for tracking purposes. That metadata might include the following:

- When the pipeline was created and last updated
- The last time the pipeline was used and with what job
- Virtual machine (VM) dependencies
- Average execution time
- Failure rate

Figure 14.9 depicts a repository of data pipelines and corresponding reusable components, under version control. In this example, we have two repositories of reusable components:

- *On-disk image iterators*—Components for constructing a dataset iterator specific to the format that the dataset is stored in
- *In-memory transformations*—Components for data preprocessing and transformations for invariance

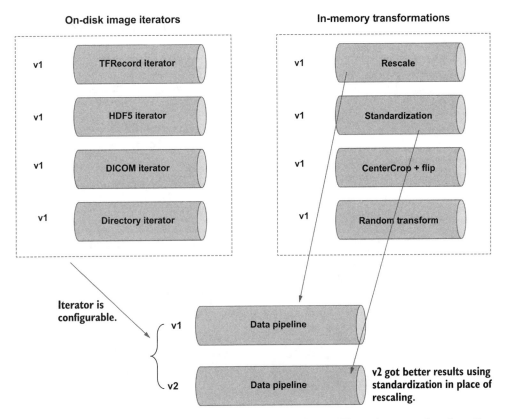

Figure 14.9   Different versions of the same data pipeline that use a different in-memory transformation reusable component

In this example, we show a single data pipeline with two versions; v2 is configured to use standardization in place of rescaling in v1. Additionally, the history for v2 has better training results than the history for v1. The data pipeline consists of an on-disk image iterator and an in-memory transformation reusable component, as well as code specific to the pipeline. Version v1 uses rescaling for normalizing the data. Let's say that later we find that standardization gives a better result, such as validation accuracy, for the data pipeline when training on an image dataset. So we replace the rescaling with standardization, which creates a new version v2 of the pipeline.

Let's now look at a versioning system that is less obvious (figure 14.10). We will continue with our existing example with the data pipeline, but this time the on-disk image iterator for TFRecords has been updated to v2, and v2 has a 5% performance improvement over v1.

Since this is a configurable attribute of the data pipeline, why would we update the version number of the corresponding data pipeline, which itself has not changed? If we want to reproduce or otherwise audit a training job that used the pipeline, we need

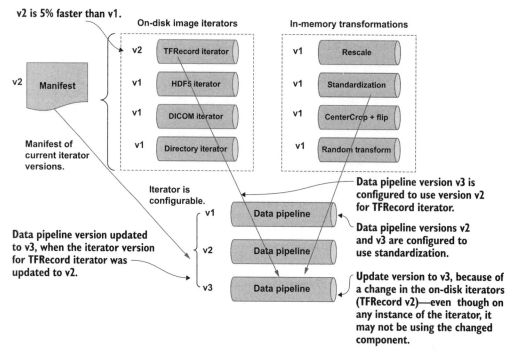

Figure 14.10   Using a version manifest for identifying the versions of available reusable components for a specific version of a pipeline

to know the version number of the reusable component at the time the job was done. In our example, we do this as follows:

- Have a manifest for the reusable components and corresponding version numbers.
- Update the data pipeline to include the updated manifest.
- Update the version number on the data pipeline.

14.2.2 *Metadata*

Let's now cover storing metadata with the pipeline and other resources, such as a dataset, and how it affects the assembly, execution, and scheduling of a training job. So what is metadata, and how is it different from artifacts and history? *History* is about retaining information about the *execution* of a pipeline, while *metadata* is about retaining information about the *state* of the pipeline. *Artifacts* are a combination of the history and metadata.

Referring to our example data pipeline, let's assume we are using version v3, but we use it with a new dataset resource. At the time, the only statistic we have on the dataset resource is the number of examples in the dataset. What we don't know is the mean and standard deviation of the examples. As a result, when the v3 data pipeline is assembled with the new dataset, the underlying pipeline management would query the state of the dataset for the mean and standard deviation. Since they are unknown, the pipeline management would add a component prior to the standardization component to calculate the values needed for the standardization component. The top half of figure 14.11 depicts the construction of the pipeline when the state of mean and standard deviation is unknown.

Now, let's say we run this pipeline again without any changes to the dataset. Do we recalculate the mean and standard deviation? No, when the pipeline management queries the dataset and finds the values are known, it will instead add a component to use the cached values. The bottom half of figure 14.11 depicts the construction of the pipeline when the state of the mean and standard deviation is unknown.

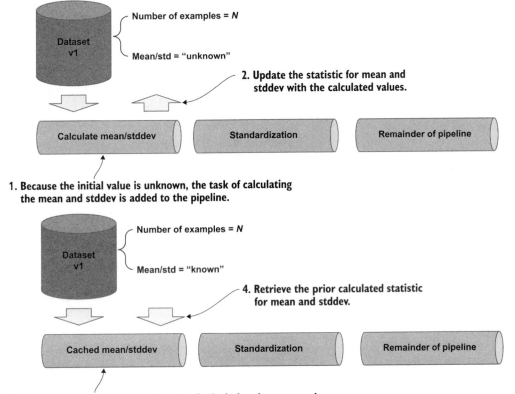

Figure 14.11 The pipeline management choosing to calculate the mean/stddev or use cache value based on the state information from the dataset

Now, let's update the dataset by adding some new examples, and we will call this version of the dataset v2. Since the examples have been updated, this invalidates the previous mean and standard deviation calculation, so the update reverts this statistic back to "unknown."

Since the statistic reverted to unknown, the next time v3 of the data pipeline is used with the updated v2 of the dataset, the pipeline management will again add the component to calculate the mean and standard deviation. Figure 14.12 depicts this reconstruction of the data pipeline.

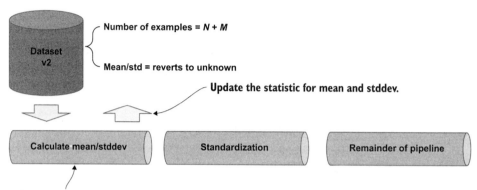

Figure 14.12 Pipeline management adds recalculating the mean and standard deviation to the pipeline after new examples are added to the dataset.

14.2.3 History

History refers to the outcome of the execution of an instance of the pipeline. For example, consider a training pipeline that performs hyperparameter search before full training of the model. The hyperparameter search space and the selected values from the search become part of the pipeline execution history.

Figure 14.13 depicts the execution of an instance of a pipeline, which consists of the following:

- The version of the pipeline components, v1
- The training data and corresponding state, the statistics

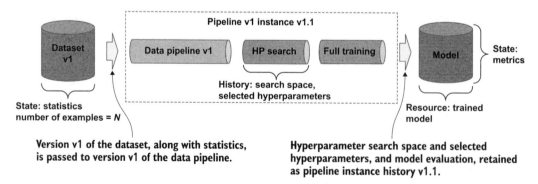

Figure 14.13 An execution history of a pipeline instance where the artifacts are the state, history, and resource

- The trained model resource and corresponding state, the metrics
- The version of the execution instance, v1.1, and corresponding history, the hyperparameters

Now, how would we incorporate history into subsequent execution instances of the same pipeline? Figure 14.14 depicts the same pipeline configuration as in figure 14.13, but with a new version of the dataset, v2. The v2 dataset differs from v1 by the inclusion of a small number of new examples; this number of new examples is substantially less than the total number of examples.

During the assembly of the pipeline instance, the pipeline management can use the history from the previous execution instance. In our example, the number of new examples is sufficiently low that the pipeline management reuses the selected hyperparameter values from the previous execution history, eliminating the overhead of reperforming hyperparameter search.

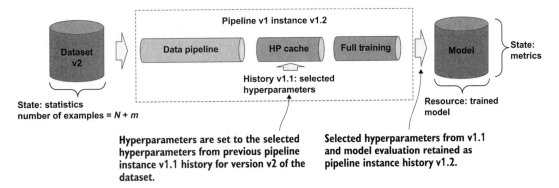

Figure 14.14 The pipeline management reusing selected hyperparameters from previous execution history when the number of new examples is substantially small

Figure 14.15 depicts an alternative approach for pipeline management in our example. In this alternative, the pipeline management continues to configure the task of performing hyperparameter search in the second execution instance, but differs as follows:

- Assumes that the new hyperparameter values for the second execution instance will be in the vicinity of the selected values from the first execution
- Narrows the search space to a small epsilon around the selected parameters from the first execution instance history

So far, we have covered the data and training portion of an e2e production pipeline and scheduling. The next section covers how models are evaluated prior to deployment to a production environment.

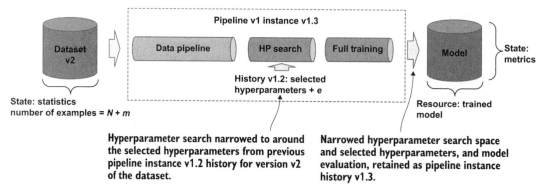

Hyperparameter search narrowed to around the selected hyperparameters from previous pipeline instance v1.2 history for version v2 of the dataset.

Narrowed hyperparameter search space and selected hyperparameters, and model evaluation, retained as pipeline instance history v1.3.

Figure 14.15   The pipeline management narrows the hyperparameter search space to be within the vicinity of previous execution history when the number of new examples is substantially small.

14.3   *Model evaluations*

In a production environment, the purpose of a model evaluation is to determine its performance relative to a baseline prior to being deployed to production. If it is the first time the model is to be deployed, the baseline is specified by the production team, generally referred to as *ML operations*. Otherwise, the baseline is the currently deployed production model, commonly referred to as the *blessed model*. The model to evaluate against the baseline is called the *candidate model*.

14.3.1   *Candidate vs. blessed model*

Previously, we covered model evaluations in the context of experimenting and development, in which the evaluation is based on objective metrics of a test (holdout) dataset. In production, however, evaluation is based on an expanded set of factors, such as resource consumption, scaling, and sample sets seen by the blessed model in production (these are not part of the test dataset).

   For example, let's assume we want to evaluate the next candidate version of a production model. We want to do an apples-to-apples comparison. To do this, we will evaluate both the blessed and the candidate models against the same test data, making sure that the test data has the same sampling distribution as the dataset used for training. We also want to test both models with the same subset of production requests; those requests should have the same sampling distribution that the blessed model actually saw during production. For the candidate model to replace the blessed model and become the next version to deploy, the metrics values (for example, accuracy for classification) must be better on both the test and production sample. In figure 14.16, you can see how we'd set up this test.

   So, you might ask, why don't we just evaluate the candidate model against the same test data as the blessed model? Well, the reality is that once a model is deployed, the distribution in the examples that it makes predictions on is likely not the same as it was trained on. We also want to evaluate the model against what it will likely see after

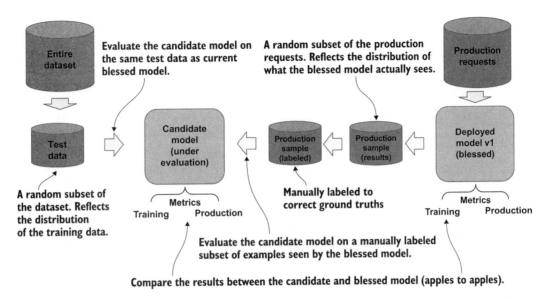

Figure 14.16 Evaluation of a candidate model includes data distributions from both training and production data.

it's deployed. Next we'll cover two types of changes in distribution from training and production: serving skew and data drift.

SERVING SKEW

Let's now dive deeper into why we evaluate the candidate model against production data. In chapter 12, we discussed how your training is probably a sampling distribution of a subpopulation, not a population. Let's first assume that the prediction requests to the deployed model are of the same subpopulation. For example, let's assume the model is trained to recognize 10 types of fruits, and that all the prediction requests for the deployed model were of the same 10 types of fruit—the same subpopulation.

But now let's say we don't have the same sampling distribution. The frequency per class seen by the production model is different from the training data. For example, let's say the training data is perfectly balanced with 10% examples for each type of the 10 fruits, and that the overall classification accuracy was 97% on the test data. But for one of the 10 classes (say, peaches), the accuracy was 75%. Now let's say 40% of the prediction requests made to the deployed blessed model are peaches. In this case, the subpopulation stayed the same, but the sampling distribution changed between the training data and production requests. This is known as *serving skew*.

So how do we do this? First, we must configure a system that captures a random selection of predictions and corresponding results. Let's say you want to collect 5% of all the predictions. You could create a uniform random distribution of integers between 1 and 20, and for each prediction draw a value from the distribution. If the drawn value is 1, you save the prediction and corresponding result. After a sampling period, you then manually inspect the saved predictions/results and determine the correct ground truth per prediction. You then compare the manually labeled ground truths to the predicted results to determine the metric on the deployed production model.

Then you evaluate the candidate model with the manually labeled version of the same production sample.

DATA DRIFT

Now let's say that the production sampling distribution is not from the same subpopulation of the training data, but a different subpopulation. Let's continue with our example of 10 types of fruits, and assume the training consists of freshly picked and ripe fruit. But our model is deployed on farm tractors in fruit orchards, where fruit can be at various stages of ripeness: green, ripe, rotten. The green and rotten versions of the fruit are a different subpopulation from the training data. In this case, the sampling distributions stayed the same, but the subpopulations changed between the training data and production requests. This is known as *data drift.*

In this case, we want to separate out and partition the production sample into one partition that is of the same subpopulation as the training data (for example, ripe) and one that is of the different subpopulation as the training data (for example, green and rotten). We would then do a separate evaluation for each partition of the production sample.

Collectively, the test, serving skew, and data drift samples are each referred to as an *evaluation slice*, which is depicted in figure 14.17. An organization may have a custom definition of evaluation slices that is specific to their production, whereas this collection of test, serving skew, and data drift is the general rule of thumb.

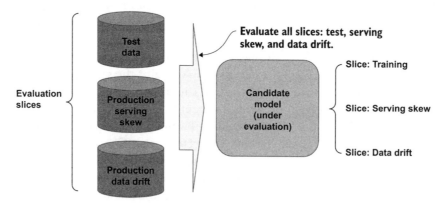

Figure 14.17   Evaluation slices in production consisting of samples from the training data, serving skew, and data drift of the production requests

SCALING

Let's now say that our candidate model is at least equal to or better on at least one metric for all the evaluation slices from the blessed model. Can we now version the candidate and deploy it as a replacement for the blessed model? Not yet. We don't yet know how the candidate model will computationally perform in comparison to the blessed model. Perhaps the candidate model takes more memory, or perhaps the candidate model has longer latency.

Before we make the final determination, we should deploy the model to a sandboxed environment that replicates the compute environment of the deployed blessed model. We also want to make sure that, for the evaluation period, the prediction requests in the production environment are duplicated in real time, and sent to both the production and the sandbox environments. Our goal for the sandbox model is to collect the utilization metric, such as compute and memory resources consumed, and latency time for prediction results. You can see this sandbox set up in figure 14.18.

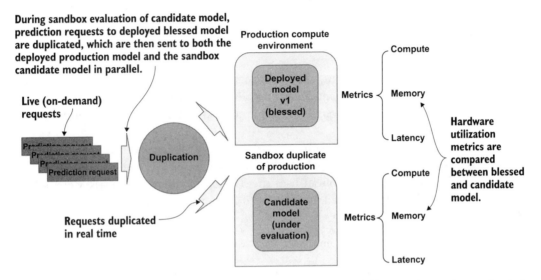

Figure 14.18 The last step before deployment is to run the candidate model in a sandbox environment, using the same prediction requests that the blessed model uses.

You might ask why we need to test the candidate model in a sandbox environment. We want to know that the new model continues to meet the business requirements in serving performance. Perhaps the candidate model has a substantial increase in matrix multiply operations so that the latency time to return a prediction is longer and does not meet the business requirements. Perhaps the memory footprint increased such that the model starts memory-to-page caching under high serving loads.

Let's now consider some scenarios. First, you might say that even if the memory footprint or the compute scaling is larger, or the latency is longer, we can simply add more compute and/or memory resources. But there are many reasons you may not be able to just add more resources. If the model is deployed in a constrained environment, such as a mobile device, for example, you don't have the ability to change the memory or compute device. Or perhaps the environment has fantastic resources, but can't be further modified, such as a spacecraft that has been launched into space. Or maybe the model is used by a school district that has a fixed allocated budget for the compute costs.

Regardless of the reason, a final scaling evaluation must be performed to determine the resources it uses. For constrained environments, such as mobile phones or IoT devices, you want to find out if the candidate model will continue to meet the operating requirements of the deployed model. And if your environment is not constrained, such as auto-scaled cloud compute instances, you need to know whether the new model meets the cost requirements for the ROI.

14.3.2 *TFX evaluation*

Now let's see how to use TFX to evaluate the current trained model, so we can decide whether it will become the next blessed model. Essentially, we use the `Evaluator` and `InfraValidator` components.

EVALUATOR

The `Evaluator` component, which is executed after the completion of the `Trainer` component, evaluates the model against a baseline. We feed the `Evaluator` an evaluation dataset from the `ExampleGen` component, as well as the trained model from the `Trainer` component.

We also feed it the previous blessed model, if one exists. If there is no previous blessed model, comparing against a baseline of a blessed model is skipped.

The `Evaluator` component uses the TensorFlow Model Analysis Metrics library, which needs to be imported in addition to TFX, as shown here:

```
from tfx.components import Evaluator, ResolverNode
import tensorflow_model_analysis as tfma
```

The next code example demonstrates the minimum requirements for constructing an `Evaluator` component into a TFX pipeline, with these parameters:

- `examples`—The output from `ExampleGen`, which generates batches of examples for evaluation
- `model`—The output from `Trainer` of the trained model to evaluate

```
evaluator = Evaluator(examples=example_gen.output['examples'],   Minimal requirements
                      model=trainer.output['model'],             for parameters
                      baseline_model=None,
       No baseline           eval_config=None     ◁———— Default dataset slice to evaluate against
       model to
       compare to           )
```

In the preceding example, the parameter `eval_config` is set to `None`. In this case, the `Evaluator` will use the entire dataset for evaluation and the metrics specified when the model was trained, such as the accuracy for a classification model.

The parameter `eval_config` when specified takes an instance of the `tfma.Eval-Config`, which takes three parameters:

- model_specs—A specification of the model input and output. By default, assumes the input is the default serving signature.
- metrics_specs—A specification of one or more metrics to use for evaluation. If not specified, the metrics specified when the model was trained are used.
- slicing_specs—A specification of one or more slices from the dataset to use for evaluation. If not specified, the entire dataset is used.

```
eval_config = tfma.EvalConfig(model_specs=[],
                              metrics_specs=[],
                              slicing_specs=[]
                              )
```

The parameters for EvalConfig vary widely, and I recommend reading TensorFlow TFX tutorials for the Evaluator component (www.tensorflow.org/tfx/guide/evaluator) for a deeper understanding than the scope I will cover here.

If there is a previously blessed model to compare against, the baseline_model parameter is set to an instance of the TFX component ResolverNode.

The following code example is the minimum specification for ResolverNode, where the parameters are as follows:

- instance_name—This is the name to assign to the next blessed model, which is stored as metadata.
- resolver_class—This is the instance type of a resolver object to use. In this case, we specify the instance type for blessing the latest model.
- model—This specifies the model type to bless. In this case, Channel (type=Model) can be either a TensorFlow estimator or TF.Keras model.
- model_blessing—This specifies how to store the blessed model in the metadata.

```
from tfx.dsl.experimental.lastest_blessed_model_resolver import
    LatestBlessedModelResolver
from tfx.types import Channel
from tfx.types.standard_artifacts import Model, ModelBlessing

baseline_model = ResolverNode(instance_name='blessed_model',
                              resolver_class=LatestBlessedModelResolver,
                              model=Channel(type=Model),
                              model_blessing=Channel(type=ModelBlessing)
                              )
```

In the preceding code example, if this is the first time the ResolverNode() instance is called for the model, then the current model becomes the blessed model and is stored in metadata as a blessed model with the instance name blessed_model.

Otherwise, the current model is evaluated against the previous blessed model, which is identified as blessed_model and retrieved from the metadata store accordingly. In this case, both models are evaluated against the same evaluation slices, and their corresponding metrics are compared. If the new model improves on the metrics, it becomes the next version of the `blessed_model` instance.

INFRAVALIDATOR

Next in the pipeline is the `InfraValidator` component. *Infra* refers to *infrastructure.* This component is called only if the current trained model becomes the new blessed model. The purpose of this component is to determine whether the model can be loaded and queried in a sandbox environment that mimics the production environment. It is up to the user to define the sandbox environment. In other words, it is up to the user to decide how close the sandboxed environment is to the production environment, and therefore how accurate the *InfraValidator* test is.

The next code example shows the minimum parameter requirements for the `InfraValidator`:

- `model`—The trained model (in this example, the currently trained model from the `Trainer` component)
- `serving_spec`—The specification for the sandbox environment

```
from tfx.components import Evaluator, ResolverNode          The trained model to deploy
                                                            to the sandbox environment

infra_validator = InfraValidator(model=trainer.outputs['model'],      ◁───┘
                                 serving_spec=serving_spec
                                 )
```
The specification for the sandbox environment

The serving specification consists of two parts:

- The type of serving binary. As of TFX version 0.22, only TensorFlow Serving is supported.
- The type of serving platform, which can be either
  - Kubernetes
  - Local Docker container

This example shows the minimum requirements for specifying a serving specification using TensorFlow Serving and a Kubernetes cluster:

```
from tfx.proto.infra_validator_pb2 import ServingSpec

serving_spec =
    ServingSpec(tensorflow_serving=TensorflowServing(tags=['latest']),
                kubernetes=KubernetesConfig()
                )
```

TFX documentation on the ServingSpec is currently sparse and will redirect you to read the protobuf definition (http://mng.bz/6NqA) in the GitHub repository for more information.

14.4 Serving predictions

Now that we have the new blessed model, we will look at how a model is deployed into production for serving predictions. A production model is generally deployed for either on-demand (live) or batch prediction.

How is a batch prediction different from on-demand (live) prediction from a deployed model? There is one key difference, but otherwise they are essentially the same as far as outcome:

- *On-demand (live)*—Does an on-demand prediction for the entire set of instances (one or more data items) and returns the results in real time
- *Batch prediction service*—Does a queued (batch) prediction for the entire set of instances in the background and stores the results in a cloud storage bucket when ready

14.4.1 On-demand (live) serving

For on-demand prediction, such as an online request via an interactive website, the model is deployed to one or more compute instances, and receives prediction requests as HTTP requests. A prediction request can consist of one or more individual predictions; each prediction is typically referred to as an *instance*. You can have single-instance requests, where the user wants to classify just one image, or multi-instance requests, where the model will return predictions for multiple images.

Let's say the model receives single-instance requests: the user submits an image and wants to get back a prediction, like a classification or an image caption. These are live, on-demand requests coming over the internet. They may come from a web application running in a user's web browser, for example, or a backend application on the server obtaining predictions as a microservice.

Figure 14.19 shows this process. In this depiction, the model is contained in a serving binary, which consists of a web server, serving function, and the blessed model. The web server receives the prediction request as an HTTP request packet, extracts the request content, and passes the content to the serving function. The serving function then preprocesses the content into a format and shape expected by the blessed model's input layer, which is then inputted to the blessed model. The blessed model returns the prediction to the serving function, which performs any post-processing for final delivery, which is then passed back to the web server, which returns the post-processed predictions as an HTTP response packet.

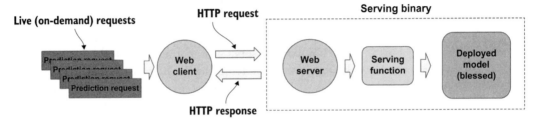

Figure 14.19   A production model on a serving binary receiving on-demand prediction requests over the internet

As you can see in figure 14.19, on the client side, one or more prediction requests are passed to a web client. The web client will then create either a single or multi-instance prediction HTTP request packet. The prediction requests are encoded, generally as base64, for safe transmission over the internet, and placed into the content section of the HTTP request packet.

The web server receives the HTTP request, decodes the content section, and passes the single or multiple prediction requests to the serving function.

Let's now take a deeper look into the purpose and construction of a serving function. Typically, on the client side, the content (such as images, videos, text, and structured data) are sent in raw format to the serving binary without any preprocessing. The web server, upon receiving the request, extracts the content from the request packet and passes it to the serving function. The content may or may not be decoded, such as base64 decoding, prior to passing the serving function.

Let's assume that the content is a single-instance request consisting of a compressed image, such as in JPG or PNG format. Assume the input layer to the model is uncompressed image bytes in the format of a multidimensional array, such as a Tensor-Flow tensor or NumPy array. At a minimum, the serving function has to perform any preprocessing that is not part of the model (for example, the pre-stem). Assuming the model has no pre-stem, the serving function will need to do the following:

- Determine the compressed format of the image data, such as from the MIME type
- Decompress the image into raw bytes
- Reshape the raw bytes into height × width × channel (for example, RGB)
- Resize the image to match the input shape of the model
- Rescale the pixel data for normalization or standardization

Next is an example implementation of a serving function for an image classification model, where the preprocessing of the image data happens upstream from the model, without a pre-stem. In this example, the method `serving_fn()` is registered with the web server in the serving binary by assigning the method as the signature `serving_default` for the model. We added to the serving function the decorator `@tf.function`, which instructs the AutoGraph compiler to convert the Python code to a static graph, which can then be run on the GPU along with the model. In this example, it is assumed the web server passes the extracted content from the prediction request (in this case, the JPG compressed bytes) as a TensorFlow string. The call to `tf.saved_model.save()` saves the serving function to the same storage location as the model, which is specified by the parameter `export_path`.

Let's now look into the body of this serving function. In the following code example, we assume the web server in the serving binary extracts the content from the HTTP request packet, decodes the base64 encoding, and passes the content (compressed JPG image bytes) as a TensorFlow string data type, `tf.string`. The serving function then performs the following:

- Calls a preprocessing function `preprocess_fn()` to decode the JPG image into raw bytes and resize and rescale to match the input layer of the underlying model, as a multidimensional TensorFlow array.
- Passes the multidimensional TensorFlow array to the underlying model, `m_call()`.
- Returns the prediction `prob` from the underlying model back to the web server.
- The web server in the serving binary packages the prediction result into the HTTP response packet back to the web client.

Definition of the serving function that receives the content of the prediction request via the serving binary's web server

The method that converts the content to match the input layer of the underlying model

```
@tf.function(input_signature=[tf.TensorSpec([None], tf.string)])
def serving_fn(bytes_inputs):
    images = preprocess_fn(bytes_inputs)        ◄
    prob = m_call(**images)       ◄
    return prob
```

The preprocessed data is passed to the underlying model for prediction.

```
tf.saved_model.save(model, export_path, signatures={
    'serving_default': serving_fn,
})
```

Saves the serving function as a static graph with the underlying model

The prediction result is returned to the serving binary's web server to return as the HTTP response.

The following is an example implementation of the preprocessing step of the serving function. In this example, the function `preprocess_fn()` takes as input the base64-decoded TensorFlow string from the web server and does the following:

- Calls the TensorFlow static graph operation `tf.io.decode_jpeg()` to decompress the input into a decompressed image as a multidimensional TensorFlow array.
- Calls the TensorFlow static graph operation `tf.image.convert_image_dtype()` to both convert the integer pixel values to 32-bit float values and rescale the values to the range 0 to 1 (normalization).
- Calls the TensorFlow static graph operation `tf.image.resize()` to resize the image to fit the input shape of the model. In this example, that would be (192, 192, 3), where the value 3 is the number of channels.
- Passes the preprocessed image data to the underlying model's input layer, designated by the layer's signature `numpy_inputs`.

Decodes the TensorFlow string as encoded JPG into TensorFlow multidimensional decompressed image raw bytes

Converts and rescales the pixels to 32-bit floating-point values

```
def _preprocess(bytes_input):
    decoded = tf.io.decode_jpeg(bytes_input, channels=3)
    decoded = tf.image.convert_image_dtype(decoded, tf.float32)   ◄
    resized = tf.image.resize(decoded, size=(192, 192))    ◄
    return resized
```

Resizes the image to the input shape of the underlying model

```
@tf.function(input_signature=[tf.TensorSpec([None], tf.string)])
def preprocess_fn(bytes_inputs):
    with tf.device("cpu:0"):
        decoded_images = tf.map_fn(_preprocess, bytes_inputs,
        dtype=tf.float32)
    return {"numpy_inputs": decoded_images}
```

Preprocesses each image in the request

Passes the preprocessed images to the input layer of the underlying model

The following is an example implementation of the call to the underlying model, described here:

- The parameter `model` is the compiled TF.Keras model, in which the method `call()` is the model's method for forward-feeding a prediction.
- The method `get_concrete_function()` constructs a wrapper around the underlying model for execution. The wrapper provides the interface from switching execution as a static graph in the serving function to a dynamic graph in the underlying model.

```
m_call = tf.function(model.call).get_concrete_function([tf.TensorSpec(shape=
        [None, 192, 192, 3], dtype=tf.float32, name="numpy_inputs")])
```

14.4.2 Batch prediction

Batch prediction differs from deploying a model for on-demand prediction. In on-demand prediction, you create a serving binary and serving platform for deploying the model to; we call this the *endpoint*. Then you deploy the model to that endpoint. Finally, users make on-demand (live) prediction requests to the endpoint.

In contrast, batch prediction starts with creating a batch job for predictions. The job service then provisions resources for the batch-prediction request, and the results get returned to the caller. Then the job service unprovisions the resources for the request.

Batch prediction is generally used when there is no need for an immediate response, so the response can be deferred; the number of predictions to process is massive (in the millions); and allocation of compute resources is needed only for processing the batch.

As an example, consider a financial institution that at the end of each banking day has a million transactions, and it has a model for forecasting out over the next 10 days the amount of deposits and cash on hand. Since forecasting is time-series, it doesn't make sense and would be inefficient to send one transaction at a time on a live prediction service. Instead, at the end of the banking day, the transaction data is extracted (for example, from a SQL database) and submitted as a single batch job. The compute resources for the serving binary and platform are then provisioned, the job is processed, and serving binary and platform are deprovisioned (the resources are deallocated).

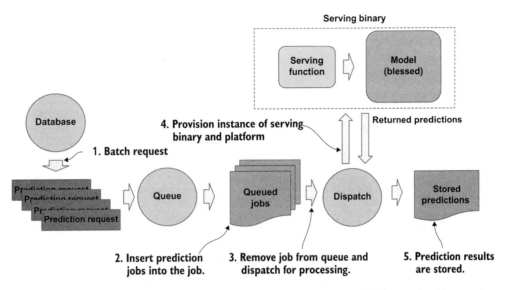

Figure 14.20 A queue and dispatcher coordinate the provision and deprovisioning serving binary and platform on a per job basis.

Figure 14.20 shows a batch prediction service. This process has five major steps:

1 The accumulated data is extracted and packaged into a batch request, such as from a SQL database.
2 The batch request is queued, and the queue manager determines compute resource requirements and priority.
3 The batch job, when ready, gets de-queued to the dispatcher.
4 The dispatcher provisions the serving binary and platform, then submits the batch job.
5 Upon completion of the batch job, the results are stored, and the dispatcher deprovisions the allocated compute resources.

Next, we will cover how models are deployed in TFX for both on-demand and batch prediction.

14.4.3 *TFX pipeline components for deployment*

In TFX, the deployment pipeline consists of the components `Pusher` and `Bulk Inference`, as well as a serving binary and platform. The serving platform can be cloud-based, local-based, edge devices, or browser-based. For cloud-based models, the recommended serving platform is TensorFlow Serving.

Figure 14.21 depicts the components for the TFX deployment pipeline. The `Pusher` component deploys models for either on-demand prediction or batch prediction. The component `Bulk Inference` handles batch predictions.

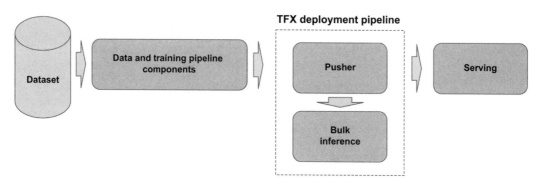

Figure 14.21   A TFX deployment pipeline can deploy a model for on-demand serving and/or bulk prediction.

PUSHER

The following is an example implementation that shows the minimal requirements for instantiating the Pusher component for deploying a model to a serving binary:

- model—The trained model to deploy to a serving binary and platform (in this case, the currently trained model instance from the Trainer component)
- push_destination—The directory location within a serving binary to install the model

```
from tfx.components import Pusher                    The trained
from tfx.proto import pusher_pb2                      model to deploy          The destination
                                                                               of a serving
                                                                               binary to deploy
pusher = Pusher(model=trainer.outputs['model'],      ◁────────┘               the model to
                push_destination=pusher_pb2.PushDestination(  ◁──┘

filesystem=pusher_pb2.PushDestination.FileSystem(
                                                      A directory location within the
                base_directory=serving_model_dir  ◁──┘  serving binary to install the model
                                                      )
            )
```

In a production environment, we typically incorporate into the deployment pipeline, deploying the model only if it is the new blessed model. The following is an example implementation of the minimal parameters where the model is deployed only if it is the new blessed model:

- model—The currently trained model from the Trainer component
- model_blessing—The currently blessed model from the Evaluator component

In this example, the model is deployed only if both the model and blessed model are the same model instance:

```
pusher = Pusher(model=trainer.outputs['model'],      ◁────────┘  The currently trained model
              ┌─▷  model_blessing=evaluator.outputs['blessing'],
The currently blessed       push_destination=pusher_pb2.PushDestination(
model instance  │
```

```
        filesystem=pusher_pb2.PushDestination.FileSystem(

        base_directory=serving_model_dir
                                                        )
                                                      )
    )
```

Next, we will cover doing bulk prediction in TFX.

BULK INFERRER

The `BulkInferrer` component performs the batch prediction service, which the TFX documentation refers to *as bulk inference.* The following code is an example implementation of the minimal parameters for performing batch prediction with the currently trained model:

- `examples`—The examples to do predictions for. In this case, they come from an instance of the `ExampleGen` component.
- `model`—The model to use for the batch prediction (in this case, the currently trained model).
- `inference_result`—Where to store the batch prediction results.

```
from tfx.components import BulkInferrer                    The examples to do
                                                           batch prediction for

bulk_inferrer = BulkInferrer(examples=examples_gen.outputs['examples'],  ◁─
                         ┌─▷    model=trainer.outputs['model'],
    The model used for          inference_result=location  ◁──┐
    the batch prediction │           )               The location for storing
                                                      the prediction results
```

The following is an example implementation of the minimal parameters for performing batch prediction with the currently trained model only if it is the blessed model, which is specified by the parameter `model_blessing`. In this example, the batch prediction is performed only if the currently trained model and the blessed model instance are the same.

```
from tfx.components import BulkInferrer

bulk_inferrer = BulkInferrer(examples=examples_gen.outputs['examples'],
                             model=trainer.outputs['model'],
                             model_blessing=evaluator.outputs['blessing'],
                       ┌─▷    inference_result=location
    The current blessed │           )
    model instance      │
```

14.4.4 A/B testing

We've now completed two tests of our newly trained model to see whether it is ready to become the next production version, the blessed model. We've done a direct comparison of model metrics between the two models, using predetermined evaluation data. And we've tested the candidate model in the sandbox-simulated production environment.

Yet without actually deploying the candidate, we are still not sure that it is the better model. We need to evaluate the candidate's performance in the *live production environment*. To do this, we feed the candidate a subset of the live predictions, and measure the outcome per prediction between the candidate and the current production model. Then we analyze the measured data, or metrics, to see whether the candidate model is actually a better model.

This is *A/B testing* in an ML production environment. Figure 14.22 demonstrates the process. As you can see, both the models are deployed to the same live production environment, with the prediction traffic split between the current blessed (A) and the candidate blessed (B). Each model sees a randomly chosen selection of predictions, which is based on a percentage.

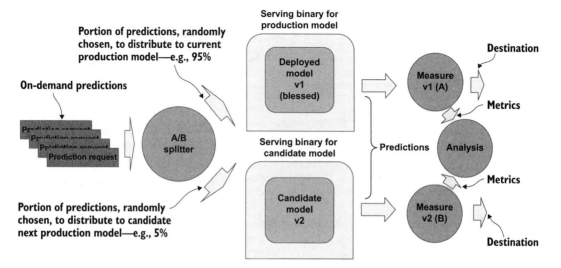

Figure 14.22   A/B testing of current and candidate model in live production environment, where the candidate model gets a small percentage of the live predictions

We don't want to have a bad result in production if the candidate model is less good than the current model. So, we generally keep the percentage of traffic as small as possible, but enough to measure the difference between the two. A typical split is 5% for the candidate model and 95% for the production model.

The next question is, what do you measure? You've already measured and compared the model's objective metrics, so there's not much value in repeating that, especially if the evaluation slices include both serving skew and data drift. What you want to measure here is how good the outcome is for a business objective.

For example, assume your model is an image classification model deployed to a manufacturing assembly line that looks for defects. For each model, you have two bins: one for good parts, and one for defects. After a specified period of time, your QA personnel manually inspect a sampling distribution from the bins of both the production model and the candidate model, and then compare the two. In particular, they want to answer two questions:

- Does the candidate model detect an equal or greater number of defects than the production model detects? These are the true positives.
- Does the candidate detect an equal or lesser number of non-defects? These are false positives.

As in this example, you have to determine the business objective: increasing true positives, decreasing false positives, or both.

Let's consider one more example. Let's say we are working on a language model on an e-commerce site, which does tasks such as image captioning, has a chatbot for questions on transactions, and language translation for chatbot responses to users. In this case, the metric we measure might be the total number of completed transactions or the average revenue from each transaction. In other words, does the candidate model reach a larger audience and/or make more revenue?

14.4.5 Load balancing

Once a model is deployed to an on-demand production environment, the volume of prediction requests over time could vary substantially. Ideally, the model would meet demand at the highest peak level within a latency constraint, and also minimize the compute costs.

We could meet the first requirement simply by increasing the compute resources or number of GPUs, if the model is monolithic, meaning it is deployed as a single model instance. But this would undermine the second requirement, to minimize the compute costs.

Like other contemporary cloud applications, when request traffic varies substantially, we use autoscaling and load balancing for distributed processing of the requests. Let's see how autoscaling works for ML.

The terms *autoscaling* and *load balancing* may seem to be used interchangeably. But they are really two separate processes that work in conjunction. In *autoscaling*, the process is provisioning (adding) and deprovisioning (deleting) compute instances, in response to the overall current prediction request load. In *load balancing*, the process is determining how to distribute the current prediction request load across existing provisioned compute instances, and determining when to instruct the autoscaling process to provision or deprovision compute instances.

Figure 14.23 depicts a load-balancing scenario for an ML production environment. Essentially, a load-balancing compute node receives the prediction requests, then reroutes them to a serving binary, which receives the prediction responses and routes them back to the client caller.

Let's go deeper into figure 14.23. The load balancer monitors traffic loads, such as the frequency of prediction requests per unit of time, the inbound and outbound volume of network traffic, and the latency time in returning a response to a prediction request.

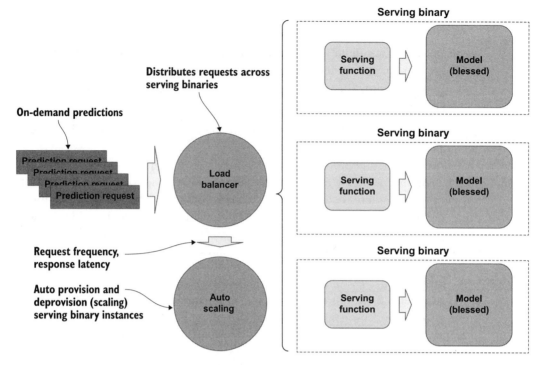

Figure 14.23   A load balancer distributes requests across serving binaries that are dynamically provisioned and deprovisioned by an autoscaling node.

This monitored data is fed in real time to an autoscaling node. The autoscaling node is configured by the MLOps personnel to meet a performance criteria. If the performance is below a prespecified threshold and length of time, the autoscaler will dynamically provision one or more new duplicated instances of the serving binary. Likewise, if the performance is above a prespecified threshold and length of time, the autoscaler will dynamically deprovision one or more existing duplicated instances of the serving binary.

As the autoscaler adds serving binaries, it registers the serving binaries with the load balancer. Likewise, as it removes serving binaries, it unregisters the serving binaries with the load balancer. This tells the load balancer which serving binaries are active that the load balancer can distribute the prediction results.

Typically, the load balancer is configured with a health monitor to monitor the health of each serving binary. If the serving binary is determined to be unhealthy, the health monitor instructs the autoscaling node to deprovision the serving binary and provision a new serving binary as a replacement.

14.4.6 *Continuous evaluation*

Continuous evaluation (CE) is an ML production extension of the software development process continuous integration (CI) and continuous deployment (CD). This extension is commonly denoted as CI/CD/CE. *Continuous evaluation* means that we monitor the prediction requests and responses that the model receives after being deployed to production, and perform evaluations on the prediction responses. This is similar to what is done in evaluating the model with the existing test, serving skew, and data drift slices. This is done to detect a deterioration in the model performance due to changes in the prediction requests over time seen in production.

The typical process for continuous evaluation is as follows:

- A preconfigured percent (for example, 2%) of prediction requests and responses will be saved for manual evaluation.
- The prediction requests and responses that are saved are randomly chosen.
- At some periodic basis, the saved prediction requests and response are manually reviewed and evaluated against the model's objective metrics.
- If the evaluation determines that the model is performing below the model's pre-deployment evaluation of the objective metrics, the manual evaluators identify underperforming examples that are a result of serving skew, data drift, and any unanticipated situation. These are anomalies.
- The identified examples are manually labeled and added to the training dataset, and a portion is set aside as corresponding evaluation slices.
- The model is either incrementally retrained or fully retrained.

Figure 14.24 depicts a CI/CD/CE approach of integrating continuous evaluation from a deployed production model into the model development process.

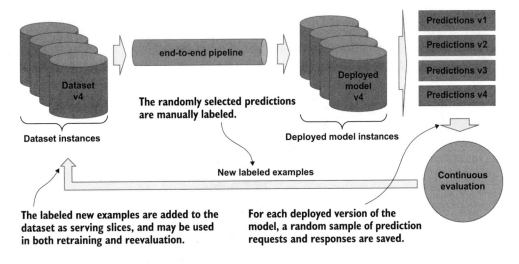

Figure 14.24 A production-deployed model is continuously evaluated to identify underperforming examples, which are then added to the dataset for retraining the model.

14.5 *Evolution in production pipeline design*

Let's wrap up the book with a brief discussion on how the concepts and necessity of a pipeline evolved when machine learning went from research to full-scale production. You may find the part on model amalgamation particularly interesting in that it is one of the next forefronts in deep learning.

How did the evolution in machine learning approaches affect how we actually do machine learning? The development of deep learning models evolved from experimentation in the lab to deployment and serving in a full-scale production environment.

14.5.1 *Machine learning as a pipeline*

You've likely seen this before. A successful ML engineer will need to decompose a machine learning solution into the following steps:

1   Identify the type of model for the problem.
2   Design the model.
3   Prepare the data for the model.
4   Train the model.
5   Deploy the model.

ML engineer(s) organized these steps into a two-stage e2e pipeline. The first e2e pipeline consists of the first three steps, which is depicted in figure 14.25 as modeling, data engineering, and training. Once the ML engineer(s) is successful with this stage, it would be coupled with the deployment step to form a second e2e pipeline. Typically, the model was deployed into a container environment and accessed via a REST-based or microservice interface.

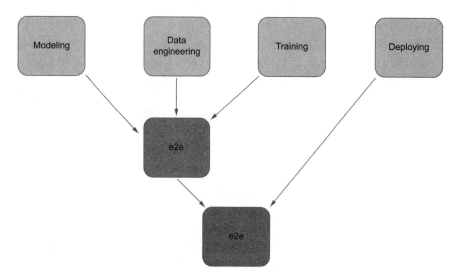

Figure 14.25   **2017 prevailing practice for end-to-end machine learning pipeline**

That was the prevailing practice in 2017. I refer to it as the *discovery phase*. What are the parts and how do they fit together?

14.5.2 Machine learning as a CI/CD production process

In 2018, businesses were formalizing the CI/CD production process, which I refer to as the *exploration phase*. Figure 14.26 is a slide I used in a Google presentation to business decision makers in late 2018 that captures where we were then. It wasn't just a technical process anymore, but included the integration of planning and quality assurance. The data engineering became more defined as extraction, analysis, transformation, management, and serving steps. Model designing and training included feature engineering, and the deployment expanded to include continuous learning.

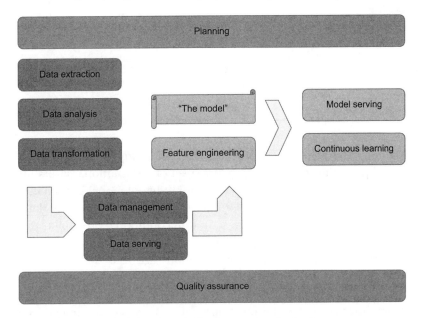

Figure 14.26 By 2018, Google and other large enterprise businesses were formalizing the production process to include the planning and quality assurance stages as well as the technical process.

14.5.3 Model amalgamation in production

Models today in production don't have a single output layer. Instead they have multiple output layers, from essential feature extraction (common layers), representational space, latent space (feature vectors, encodings), and probability distribution space (soft and hard labels). The models now are the whole application; there is no backend.

These models learn the optimal way to interface and data communication. The enterprise ML engineer of 2021 is now guiding the search space within the model amalgamation, a generalized example of which is depicted in figure 14.27.

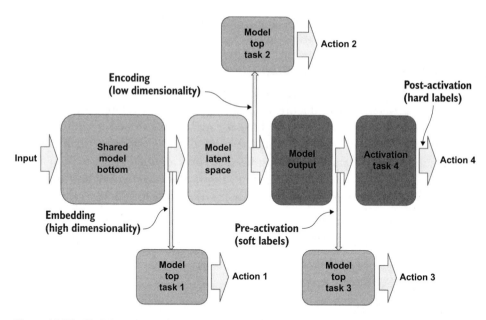

Figure 14.27   Model amalgamation—when the models become the entire application!

Let's break down this generalized example. On the left side is the input to the amalgamation. The input is processed by a common set of convolutional layers into what is called the *shared model bottom*. The output from the shared model bottom in this depiction has four learned output representations: 1) high-dimensional latent space, 2) low-dimensional latent space, 3) pre-activation conditional probability distribution, and 4) post-activation independent probability distribution.

Each of these learned output representations are reused by specialized downstream learned tasks that perform an action (for example, state transition change or transformation). Each task, represented in the figure as tasks 1, 2, 3, and 4, reuses the output representation that is the most optimal (size, speed, accuracy) for the task's goal. These individual tasks may then produce multiple learned output representations or combine learned representations from multiple tasks (dense embeddings) for reuse for further downstream tasks, as you saw in the sports broadcasting example in chapter 1.

Not only do serving pipelines enable these types of solutions, but the components within the pipelines can be version-controlled and reconfigured. This enables these components to be reusable, which is a fundamental principle in modern software engineering.

Summary

- The basic components of a training pipeline are model feeding, model evaluation, and training schedulers.

- The objective metrics of each instance of a model are saved as metadata. A model instance is blessed when its objective metrics are better than the current blessed model.
- Each blessed model is tracked and versioned in a model repository.
- When a model is fed for distributed training, the batch size is increased to smooth out variances among the different batches that are fed in parallel.
- In orchestration, a management interface oversees the execution of each component, remembers the execution of past components, and maintains history.
- Evaluation slices consist of examples of the same distribution as the training data, and from out-of-distribution examples seen in production. These include serving skew and data drift.
- The basic components of a deployment pipeline are deployment, serving, scaling, and continuous evaluation.
- A/B testing is used in live production environments to determine whether the candidate model is better than the current production model, such as not to disrupt production if something unexpected occurs.
- Continuous evaluation is used in live production environments to identify serving skews, data drift, and anomalies, from which new labeled data can be added to the dataset and the model further retrained.

index

RELATED MANNING TITLES

Deep Learning with Python, Second Edition
by François Chollet

ISBN 9781617296864
400 pages (estimated), $59.99
Fall 2021 (estimated)

Deep Learning with PyTorch
by Eli Stevens, Luca Antiga, and Thomas Viehmann
Foreword by Soumith Chintala

ISBN 9781617295263
520 pages, $49.99
July 2020

Grokking Deep Learning
by Andrew W. Trask

ISBN 9781617293702
336 pages, $49.99
January 2019

For ordering information go to www.manning.com